Timely Topics

An Advanced Reading, Grammar, & Vocabulary Book

Patrick J. Aquilina

American Language Program
Columbia University

Heinle & Heinle Publishers
A Division of Wadsworth, Inc.
Boston, Massachusetts 02116 USA

The publication of *Timely Topics* was directed by the members of the Heinle & Heinle ESL Publishing Team:

Erik Gundersen, Editorial Director
Susan Mraz, Marketing Manager
Kristin Thalheimer, Production Editor

Also participating in the publication of this program were:

Publisher: Stanley J. Galek
Editorial Production Manager: Elizabeth Holthaus
Associate Editor: Lynne Telson Barsky
Project Management: Hispanex
Manufacturing Coordinator: Mary Beth Lynch
Photo Coordinator: Martha Leibs-Heckly
Interior Design and Composition: Hispanex
Cover Illustrator: Rhonda Voo
Cover Designer: Bortman Design Group

Heinle & Heinle Publishers is a division of Wadsworth, Inc.

Manufactured in the United States of America.

Library of Congress Cataloging-in-Publication Data
Aquilina, Patrick.
    Timely topics / Patrick Aquilina.
        p. cm.
    ISBN 0-8384-4200-5
    1. English language—Textbooks for foreign speakers. 2. Readers.
    I. Title.
    PE1128.A59 1993
    428.2'4—dc20   92-41843
                                                            CIP

ISBN 0-8384-4200-5

10 9

To my parents,
who instilled in me a love of education,
and to my students
at the American Language Program,
who have helped keep this love alive.

CONTENTS

TO THE TEACHER

Overview

Timely Topics is a reading, vocabulary, and grammar book for advanced students of English as a Second or Foreign Language. It contains twelve chapters: ten are centered around themes while two review vocabulary and grammar items. Each chapter is composed of two or three authentic readings, with prereading activities, comprehension and discussion questions, vocabulary exercises, grammar explanations and exercises, class project activities, discussion and writing topics, and a list of key vocabulary practiced in each chapter. An answer key provides the answers to vocabulary and grammar exercises as well as to true-false comprehension questions.

The themes of the readings are current, but they are not likely to be dated any time in the near future. They are often discussed in the media and can serve as a window into the life, laws, problems, values, and ways of thinking of the people of the United States at the end of the 20th century. The topics are thought-provoking, sometimes controversial, and can lead to a great deal of discussion. Students are very likely to encounter these themes in newspapers or magazines outside of class. Having read about similar topics in or for the class, they are more likely to read a related article when they see it on their own. In addition, these readings give students information, and vocabulary, for discussions with Americans on topics that appear with great frequency in the American media. For students not studying in the United States, these articles can give them an idea of some of the current issues being discussed on a national level.

Organization of the Text

Prereading Activities. These chapter-opening activities include a set of questions that relate to the theme of the reading but may also include a number of other types of activities, such as vocabulary-predicting, survey-taking, or word analysis. These activities serve as a warm-up for the reading; they help get the students ready to read by introducing them to the general topic and ideas contained in the articles and by allowing them to enter the reading with some background knowledge, with curiosity, and with their own questions.

Students may be asked to look at and think about the pre-reading activities before class and then discuss them in class, or the questions may just be given as an in-class activity. You can have the class work together as a whole group discussing each question or completing each activity, or ask them to discuss the questions briefly in small groups, if possible in groups of mixed nationalities, before going over them together as a whole group. In this case, move from group to group, helping with content, vocabulary, and structure. Such small-group work often tends to help quieter students speak out and practice saying

in front of a few people what they can later express in front of the entire class. It can also act as a brainstorming device so that when the whole-group discussion is held, students will come to it with more to talk about. However, all small-group work should be closely monitored to ensure that the task is being followed. You can give time limits and assign "group captains" to take the responsibility to keep the group discussion on track and moving from question to question.

Vocabulary Practice. In this second section, a number of words are selected and presented in the context in which they appear in the reading. Have students guess the meaning of the word, using the context to help them, by choosing a definition or synonym from various possibilities. Urge students to try to get a general meaning of the word from the context before looking at the choices. If they go to the definitions or synonyms with a general idea in mind, picking the correct answer will be easier and the task itself will be a more valuable one. The words in context also serve as another form of prereading preparation. Students are both looking at new vocabulary that they will see in the reading and previewing the content of the reading. Here, too, students may work alone first, then compare their answers with a classmate, and finally check them with you and the entire class. Alternatively, have pairs or small groups work on the exercise, and then talk about it with the entire class. Each reading also contains a glossary. The purpose of the glossary is to help the students understand cultural allusions and slang and to reduce the number of new words they might feel they have to look up in a dictionary.

Readings. These selections, many of which are journalistic in form, may be assigned as homework or done in class, particularly in the case of some chapters which have very short first readings. Then the first reading will serve as an introduction to the topic and to the second reading. Alternatively, you could start a reading in class, for example, the first two or three paragraphs. Have the students discuss what they have read, try to predict what will come next, and then finish the reading at home. If you feel that there is not enough time for all of the students to do all of the readings, or if you feel that there is a need to do a chapter differently, just to break the routine, divide the readings up among the students. Have everyone do the first reading so that all of the students have a common base of knowledge about the topic. Then assign half of the students the second reading and the other half the third. Pairs or groups of four are responsible for telling each other about their readings, using the discussion and comprehension questions as a guide. They are also responsible for teaching their partners the vocabulary in their reading. Encourage students who have more time or interest to read the other selection on their own.

Comprehension and Discussion Questions. Have the students look over these questions before they begin reading so that they will have an idea about the information they should be looking for as they read. To test comprehension, True/False statements and information questions are given. Have students explain why a True/False statement is false and ask them to expand on a statement that is true. Urge students to explain their answers to the information questions in as much detail as possible, in their own words but with an attempt, when possible, to integrate the new vocabulary items. Many of the questions

require the reader to make inferences or to get the answer for one question from more than one place in the reading. Assign the students questions to do in class or assign them as homework. Ask them to work on them alone or in study groups.

In addition to information questions, every reading contains opinion questions or statements with which they can agree or disagree. These questions should be used to get the students to relate what they have read to their personal feelings and experiences. These items help students explore cross-cultural differences and think about how these issues would be viewed in the their countries. Most important of all, urge the students to express their interpretations of the readings or their personal views in complex utterances and not just in simple phrases. Expressing one's thoughts intelligently on complex issues in a foreign language is not an easy task, but it is one that should be practiced rigorously by students at this level of proficiency.

Post-Reading Vocabulary Practice. Vocabulary items that were given before the reading are practiced once again after the comprehension and discussion questions. Since the acquisition and use of different forms of words is an important but difficult task for students of English as a Second Language, a *Word Form* chart is given before the Vocabulary Practice. Urge students to use their knowledge of other words and their different forms and to make guesses. Through this exercise, they can see that although English contains many irregularities, many patterns of word formation do exist in the language. This is a particularly good exercise to do in pairs or small groups as very often one student will know a form, or will be a good guesser, and will be able to act as a peer informant or expert for the others. Of course, the students could simply just look at the word list at the end of the chapter, just as answers to the exercises could be found at the back of the book. They should be strongly discouraged from doing so and, instead, be encouraged to start testing their own hypotheses. (It should be noted here that since many verbs can become adjectives by using the participial form (-ing or -ed), these forms are not used in the Word Form chart unless they were used in the reading or unless the form is given a separate entry in the dictionary.)

Once the students have determined the correct forms of the words, have them try to use them in the postreading *Vocabulary Practice*. Students should use the context of the sentence to determine the correct word and the structure to determine the correct form. Seeing the words again will aid the students in remembering them and help to clear up any misunderstanding about meaning. Of course, choosing the definition of a word and then using it in a completion activity will not necessarily mean that the students have acquired it. Therefore, you should encourage them to use these new words in their discussions and their writing. You could give extra homework in which the students write their own sentences for each new word or for any that give them trouble. For example, you could ask them to write a summary of the reading using as many of the new words as possible. Or have them simply pick a context of their own choice for each word. You can also use the vocabulary practice exercises for discussion. Students should feel free to agree, disagree, or simply comment on the content of the sentences used to practice the new words and not just accept them as fact.

Vocabulary Building. In addition to the vocabulary practice exercises, many of the chapters contain *Vocabulary Building* activities. Through these activities, the students again learn to look at regularities in the language. This may be done by looking at prefixes, suffixes, or stems, deriving word-building rules, and brainstorming other words they know that may follow the same rules. Vocabulary building activities are particularly good for group work as the students can act as teachers for each other, and can all contribute to the group effort.

Focus on Form. These sections give the students a chance to look more closely at the structure of the language by using the general context of the chapter. The grammatical structures chosen for practice are those which often cause difficulty for students at this level of proficiency and which are suggested by the content. However, *Timely Topics* is not intended to be an extensive grammar book. The grammar explanations cover the main points of the structure, not every detail or exception. In some of the grammar explanations, the students are asked to participate and perhaps even to supply a form that they have not yet studied. Here again, they are being allowed to use their intuitive knowledge of English, not necessarily their conscious knowledge of the grammar, to hypothesize, and to teach each other. You can assign these grammar explanations as homework or read them in class. Or you may elect to begin this section by using the samples provided to ask questions which will elicit the structure. After the structure has been elicited, have students look at the explanation in the text.

Contextualized *Grammar Practice* follows the grammar explanation. You can start the exercises in class, assign them for homework, and then correct them together as a whole group in class to clear up any ambiguities. At times the content of the grammar practice itself can also be used for discussion. These exercises should not just be looked at as grammar exercises but also as content material.

Pair Work. Some of the chapters contain *Pair Work* exercises on grammatical forms that are typically used as conversational gambits. These exercises are not based on the context of the chapter; instead, the structures are presented and practiced as they are commonly used in normal conversation. By doing pair work, the students have the opportunity for more practice with the structure. Each student has the correct response of the other so immediate feedback can be given. You can extend this activity by having the students make up their own Question/Statement and Answer using the desired structures. If, for some reason, you feel that this particular class does not work well in pairs or in peer-correction activities, you can do this exercise by giving the question or statement yourself and having the students answer.

Class Project. Depending on the amount of time available for each chapter and for class discussion or student presentation, students can use the knowledge gained from the readings to take the topic one step farther through the suggestions offered in the *Class Project* section. If there is enough time, and if the focus of the course allows it, assign students, or ask them to pick, one of the projects in this section. This may involve doing research in the library, taking a poll outside of class, or conducting interviews or mock trials. Encourage students to give presentations in class, or assign a certain number of students to do a group

project for each chapter. In this way, each student would be asked to make a class presentation one to two times per semester or course. If time does not permit such extensive student presentation, this section may be omitted or used occasionally at your discretion.

Questions for Discussion and Composition. By the end of each chapter, the students will have read and discussed a great deal about the topic. They will have acquired knowledge about the subject from the readings and from the discussions. They will also have started to form their own opinions on various aspects of the theme of the chapter. The *Discussion and Writing* questions get them to focus their ideas on one aspect of the subject. These topics could be discussed first in small groups, and then with the whole class. Each group could discuss all of the questions, or students could form into groups according to which question they might like to write about. By explaining their ideas to the group, and then to the whole class, the students can clarify their thoughts, get more information from each other, and receive feedback concerning the validity, logic, persuasiveness, or interest of what they are trying to express. Finally, with all of the information they have gathered from the readings and discussions, they can begin to write on the topic of their choice.

Word List. Each chapter ends with a list of words that contains all of the new words presented in the chapter, except for those given in the glossary that goes with each reading. This list is simply to help the students review the new vocabulary by having it all in one place.

Review Chapters. The text includes two review chapters, one after each five chapters. These include examples of all of the grammatical structures practiced in each chapter and a selection of the words from the vocabulary practice exercises. The reviews may be done as homework, with the students correcting themselves from the Answer Key and then bringing any problem questions into class for general discussion, or they may be done in class and corrected together. The "Definition Game" is a way of testing the new vocabulary and having fun at the same time.

Concluding Thoughts

You might want to start with Chapter One, both to give the students some historical perspective on the United States and to get a general idea of how the book works, and end with Chapter Ten, because it deals with the future. In addition, it will be easier for the students to study certain grammatical structures before others, such as noun clauses before subjunctive noun clauses or conditionals before wishes. However, there is no definite need to follow the chapters of *Timely Topics* in sequence. Although some vocabulary items that are practiced in an earlier chapter appear again without practice in a later one, that should not be a problem for students at this level. Feel free to move from Chapter One to Chapter Ten in sequence or to pick and choose chapters according to theme or grammatical structure.

Since all of the topics in this book are truly timely, teachers, particularly those in classes in the United States, are urged to keep an eye and an ear open for current news items on the same general issues. Even pointing out a newspaper or magazine article on an issue previously discussed in class will often be enough to get the students to buy the journal, go to the library to look at it, or borrow your copy. Radio and/or television broadcasts on the topics, assuming an audio or video recorder is available for use in class and copyright laws are respected, could be used to add a listening component to the lesson and to give the students even more of a view into what is happening in the United States.

I hope you and your students enjoy working with and through *Timely Topics*. May it help them to acquire more fluency and more accuracy in English, a better understanding of the United States, its people, and its varied ways, and perhaps even a better understanding of their own cultures.

PJA

CREDITS

Engardio, Pete with Robert Neff. "Asia: A New Front in the War on Smoking." Reprinted from February 25, 1991 issue of *Business Week* by special permission, © 1991 by McGraw-Hill, Inc.

Chapter 7: Cartoon by Douglas Marlette, "Surrogate Mother's Day", originally seen in *Newsweek*, February 16, 1987. Reprinted by permission. Kantrowitz et. al. "Whose Baby Will It Be?" From *Newsweek*, August 27, 1990, © 1990, Newsweek, Inc. All rights reserved. Reprinted by permission. Goodman, Ellen. "A Custody Fight for an Egg," © 1989 The Boston Globe Newspaper Co./Washington Post Writers Group. Reprinted with permission. Nash, J. Madeleine. "All in the Family," August 19, 1991, © 1991 The Time Inc. Magazine Company. Reprinted by permission.

Chapter 8: Hopkins, Ellen. Excerpts from "Heavy Petting," December 10, 1984, © 1992 K-III Magazine Corporation. All rights reserved. Reprinted with permission of *New York Magazine*. Begley et. al. "Freud Should Have Tried Barking." From *Newsweek* September 1, 1986 © 1986, Newsweek, Inc. All rights reserved. Reprinted by permission. Nordheimer, Jon. "High-Tech Medicine at High-Rise Costs Is Keeping Pets Fit," September 17, 1990, © 1990 by The New York Times Company. Reprinted by permission.

Chapter 9: Patner, Andrew. "Shifting Suburbs," March 9, 1990. Reprinted by permission of *The Wall Street Journal*, © 1990 Dow Jones & Company, Inc. All Rights Reserved Worldwide. Gibbs, Nancy. "The Dreams of Youth," Fall 1990, © 1990 The Time Incorporated Magazine Company. Reprinted by permission. Poll "What Youth Think." Fall 1990, © 1990 Time Inc. Reprinted by permission.

Chapter 10: Cairncross, Frances. "The Warming Globe," September 2, 1989. © *The Economist Newspaper*, Reprinted with permission. Asimov, Isaac and Frederik Pohl. "How Hard Will It Be?" © 1991 from *Our Angry Earth* by Isaac Asimov and Frederik Pohl. Reprinted by permission of Tom Doherty and Associates, Inc., New York, N.Y. World rights permission given by Ian Ballantine, Rufus Publications, Inc.

Photo Credits

p. 1 Courtesy of the author; **p. 19** Mimi Forsyth, Monkmeyer Press; **p. 29** David R. Frazier Photolibrary; **p. 38** Elizabeth Crews, Stock Boston; **p. 57** Michael Dwyer, Stock Boston; **p. 75** Sidney, The Image Works; **p. 91** Joyce Dopkeen, NYT Pictures; **pp. 97, 185** Jerry Howard, Stock Boston; **p. 117** Brandy Anderson, Mothers Against Drunk Driving (MADD); **p. 131** Arlene Collins, Monkmeyer Press; **p. 159** Marta Lavandier; **p. 177** David H. Wells, The Image Works; **p. 193** Alexander Tsiaras, Stock Boston; **pp. 213, 243** Michael Weisbrot, Stock Boston; **pp. 222, 263** Elizabeth Crews, The Image Works; **p. 277** Lionel Delevigne, Stock Boston; **p. 299** Aaron Haupt, David R. Frazier Photolibrary

Reading 1: "We, the People"

Prereading Questions

1. What do you know about immigration to the United States? Who came first? Who came later? What major groups of people came? Why did they come?

2. Immigration to the United States in the 19th and 20th centuries has been a period of peaks and valleys or highs and lows. What factors, either in the immigrants' native countries or in the United States, might account for these changes in the number of people who immigrated to the United States?

3. Look at the graph of "Total U.S. Immigration from 1821 to 1980" on page 6. Why do you think that any of the events noted on the graph might have affected the rate of immigration?

4. Was there ever a time when a great number of people left your country to come to the United States? If so, when and why did it happen?

Vocabulary Practice

We can often guess the general meaning of a new word when we see it in context. We may not get the exact meaning, but the ideas and the words in the sentence or in the reading give us a clue to the meaning of the word. Look at the italicized words in the sentences below and use the context of the sentence to help you guess the meaning. Then, when you think you have some idea of the meaning, select the definition which best fits the word as it is used in the sentence.

Example: "The bosom of America is open to receive not only the *opulent* and respectable stranger, but the oppressed and persecuted of all nations." ("Opulent" and "respectable" are contrasted with "oppressed" and "persecuted." "Respectable" is a positive attribute; "oppressed" and "persecuted" have negative meanings. Therefore, we can assume that "opulent" is also positive.

What type of positive-sounding word might go with "respectable"? What kind of people are often considered respectable? "America will accept not only _____ and respectable strangers, but also the oppressed and the persecuted."

a. *poor*

b. *wealthy*

c. *pleasant*

The answer is b. wealthy. Poor *can show more of a similarity than a contrast with "the oppressed and persecuted." Although* pleasant *has a positive meaning, it does not offer a direct contrast and does not make sense within the context of the sentence.*

1. A (A.) *haven* since its very beginnings, America would (B.) *absorb* an astonishing number of people within its expanding borders.

    (A.) a. safe place
            b. paradise
            c. restricted place
    (B.) a. turn away
            b. take in
            c. restrict

2. Large, *sparsely* populated lands lay open elsewhere in those years—in Canada and Australia, Argentina and Brazil.

    a. heavily
    b. densely
    c. thinly

3. In Europe, political (A.) *turmoil* and socio-economic (B.) *upheavals* marked nations entering the industrial age.

    (A.) a. peace
            b. confusion
            c. stability
    (B.) a. increases
            b. improvements
            c. disturbances

4. A basic cause of change was the (A.) *unprecedented* population explosion that (B.) *stemmed from* better health conditions.

    (A.) a. usual
            b. not prepared for
            c. never seen before
    (B.) a. led to
            b. had its origin in
            c. harmed

5. 3,574,974 people are known to have left the United States—*roughly*, a third of the number that entered.

    a. harshly
    b. approximately
    c. exactly

6. Poles and Italians, in particular, were *apt* to come as temporary visitors, to earn enough money in America to establish themselves comfortably in the homeland.

    a. likely
    b. unlikely
    c. had an aptitude for

7. Sometimes the native-born child of immigrants would ignore the parents' *heritage*.

    a. cultural traditions
    b. ancestors
    c. heroes

8. The United States has accepted millions of people over the years, those who (A.) *sought* a better life, and those who (B.) *fled* oppression or natural disaster or (C.) *pernicious* combinations of both. ~flee~

   (A.) a. had
         b. tried to find
         c. left
   (B.) a. found
         b. ran away from
         c. found a flaw in
   (C.) a. fortunate
         b. unusual
         c. extremely dangerous

9. At times fear has emerged among citizens that these immigrants may (A.) *overwhelm* the civilization they find, take jobs from those already here, (B.) *diminish* the wealth of the land, or destroy the ideals on which the nation was founded.

   (A.) a. enjoy
         b. take over and change
         c. overdevelop
   (B.) a. steal
         b. use well
         c. lessen

We, the People

By LESLIE ALLEN   (from the book *Liberty: The Statue and the American Dream*)

The bosom[1] of America is open to receive not only the opulent and respectable stranger," declares a statement attributed to George Washington, "but the oppressed and persecuted of all nations and religions."

A haven since its very beginnings, America would, in the century and a half after the Founding Fathers[2], absorb an astonishing number of people within its expanding borders. Large, sparsely populated lands lay open elsewhere in those years—in Canada and Australia, Argentina and Brazil. But it was the United States that took in by far the greatest number of newcomers.

In Europe, political turmoil and socioeconomic upheavals marked nations entering the industrial age. A basic cause of change was the unprecedented population explosion that stemmed from better health conditions. Aliens continue to enter the U.S. today—many for similar reasons.

The graph below tracks[3] immigration in five-year intervals between 1820 and 1980. Its totals cannot be exact, because of variations in recordkeeping. Still, official sources show that by 1981 a total of 50 million had

---

1. Literally the breast, it is used here to mean the heart, protection; like a mother protecting a child   2. the men who wrote the United States Constitution

3. to follow

come into the area now encompassed by the U.S.

How many stayed? In technical terms, what is the net[4] total of immigration? No one is sure. The net total may well be the most significant figure of all; from it have come new citizens. But if the figures for those entering the U.S. are imperfect, the figures for those leaving are worse—for early decades, almost nonexistent. Experts estimate that only one migrant left for every eight who entered during the 19th century. Between 1908 and 1924, a period that does offer some documentation, 3,574,974 people are known to have left—roughly, a third of the number that entered. By the 1880s, cheap steamship fares had made it possible for workers to think of America as a place of short-term employment.

Poles and Italians, in particular, were apt to come as temporary visitors, to earn enough money in America to establish themselves comfortably in the homeland. In the years 1899 to 1924, nearly four million Italians entered the U.S., but more than two million departed. Some individuals undoubtedly traveled back and forth more than once. Moreover, Canadians and Mexicans had always moved freely across the borders.

Thus the sharp peaks and deep troughs on the graph indicate abrupt changes in gross immigration only. One-year intervals would give a more ragged profile—the all-time high of 1,285,349 in the fiscal year 1907 contributes to the spike for 1905-1909. In two other years of this period the tally topped 1,000,000. (That five-year peak of nearly 5,000,000, if it recorded net immigration, would shrink to about 3,300,000.)

Of events noted on the graph, two—the dedication of the Statue and the opening of Ellis Island[5]—mark a time frame. Others affected immigration to some degree. Sharp dips indicate the falling numbers associated with the world wars, the Great Depression, and the quota laws[6] of the 1920s. (In two brief intervals, 1918-19 and 1932-36, more people left the U. S. than entered it.) The rise in recorded immigration since 1965 is also apparent. It has helped to bring the ratio of the foreign-boom in the current population to about 6 percent.

"Providence has been pleased to give this one connected country to one united people," proclaimed the *Federalist Papers* in 1787, "a people descended from the same ancestors, speaking the same language, professing the same religion, attached to the same principles of government, very similar in their manners and customs." In succeeding years this society based on similarities would become a heterogenous mixture, and yet it would retain its underlying bond of principles, goals, ideas of freedom.

Sometimes the native-born child of immigrants would ignore the parents' heritage. Then sons and daughters of the next generation in America would grow up eager to hear stories of the old country, to revive a holiday custom, to trace their ancestry or revisit a place of origin. "What the son wishes to forget, the grandson wishes to remember," notes one historian. Thus the cultural strands of individual and family are woven into a single fabric that forms the living richness of the nation.

The United States has accepted millions of people over the years, those who sought a better life, and those who fled oppression or natural disaster or pernicious combinations of both. At times fear has emerged among the citizens that these immigrants may overwhelm the civilization they find, take jobs from those already here, diminish the wealth of the land, destroy the ideals on which the nation is founded.

Yet consistently the newcomers have accepted the discipline of citizenship. And, in

---

4. total, after all additions and subtractions have been made   5. the island in New York Harbor through which all new immigrants had to pass

6. laws which put a fixed limit on the number of people allowed to immigrate to the United States each year

one writer's summary, "the immigrant's grit[7] and courage, and even his anxieties, impart productive energy" to America. Artists, inventors, unskilled workers, musicians, scholars, and artisans—all have made their contribution.

"A willingness of the heart"—in this phrase the perceptive novelist Scott Fitzgerald defined America. Perhaps the willingness is that of those already here to give newcomers a place, to accept their ideas and cultural contributions. Perhaps it is the willingness, too, of those courageous ones who came to stay—who struggled to succeed, to enrich and, finally, to belong to their adopted land.

TOTAL U.S. IMMIGRATION FROM 1821 TO 1980

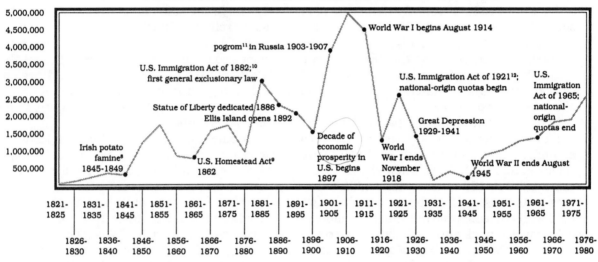

7. strong spirit 8. a period during which a disease killed many of the potato plants in Ireland, causing great hunger 9. an act giving a family a large piece of land free after it had been improved and lived on for five years

10. a law excluding Chinese from immigrating to the United States 11. an organized killing and persecution, often officially approved, of a minority group 12. a law establishing a system of quotas of immigrants from each country. This system favored Europeans.

Comprehension and Discussion

A. *Circle the correct answer. If the answer is false, tell why.*

1. Ironically, the improvement of health conditions in Europe indirectly led to many people immigrating to the United States.

   True   False

2. It was possible for workers to come to the United States to work temporarily in the 1880s because steamship tickets started to become cheaper in that decade.

    True   False

3. It is difficult, if not impossible, to know the exact number of immigrants to the United States because no one knows for sure how many people returned to their countries.

    True   False

4. In the early part of the 20th century, roughly half of the Italians who entered the United States stayed.

    True   False

5. Ellis Island opened in 1892 and caused the rate of immigration to decrease.

    True   False

6. From the beginning, the United States has been a heterogeneous country.

    True   False

B. *Answer the question as completely as possible.*

Explain the following sentence from the reading: "What the son wishes to forget, the grandson wishes to remember."

Word Forms

Working with a partner, complete the following chart with the different forms of the words. Use your knowledge of other words and their different forms to help you. Do not be afraid to guess. A dash means there is no form.

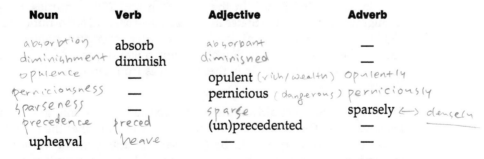

Noun	Verb	Adjective	Adverb
absorption	absorb	absorbant	—
diminishment	diminish	diminished	—
opulence	—	opulent (rich/wealth)	opulently
perniciousness	—	pernicious (dangerous)	perniciously
sparseness	—	sparse	sparsely ⟷ densely
precedence	preced	(un)precedented	—
upheaval	heave	—	—

Vocabulary Building

Many, but unfortunately not all, words in English follow certain word-building rules. For example, *-ant* or *-ent* can be used at times to make adjectives from nouns that end in *-ance*, *-ence*:

independence   independent
importance   important
patience   patient

The suffix *-ment* is often used to make a noun form from a verb form:

punish	punishment
induce	inducement
entertain	entertainment

The words below all follow word-building rules. What are these rules? What other words do you know that follow these rules?

Word	Rule	Other Words
opulent	*adj. -ent = noun -ence*	
sparse		
pernicious	ness	happyness
diminish	ment	

Vocabulary Practice

Match the italicized words in the sentences with the words in the list below. Then rewrite the sentences with the correct form or tense of the new word.

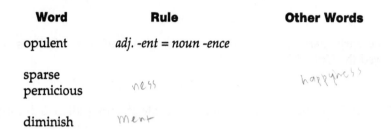

5	unprecedented	16	heritage	4	haven
14	pernicious	9	upheavals	8	absorb
7	sparsely	2	turmoil	13	overwhelm ed
1	flee	15	apt to	12	diminish ed
10	stem (from)	6	roughly	3	seek sought
11	opulent				

a.   For many years, people from all over the world (1.) *have run away from* political (2.) *confusion* in their countries and have (3.) *tried to find* a (4.) *safe place* in the United States. In the early 19th and 20th centuries, people immigrated to the United States in (5.) *never seen or heard before* numbers. In 1907 (6.) *approximately* a million and a quarter immigrants entered the country. Because the population of the United States was (7.) *not dense*, the country was able to (8.) *take in* these refugees from famine and social (9.) *disturbances.*

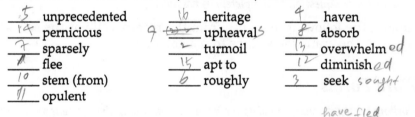

b.   The people who were already here often reacted to this immigration in a negative way. This reaction (10.) *had its origin in* fears that the (11.) *great wealth* of this country would be (12.) *lessened* and that the values and customs would be (13.) *completely taken over* by these new people with their different customs.

c.   When people leave a country because of an (14.) *extremely dangerous* series of events, and when they find safety in a new land, the children of these newcomers are (15.) *likely* not *to* care too much about their cultural (16.) *tradition that is passed down to them.*

Focus on Form: Simple Past, Present Perfect, and Past Perfect Tenses

Circle the correct verb tense for each of the following sentences.

1. By 1897, immigration (a.) fell (b.) have fallen (c.) had fallen by nearly 50 percent from its high in 1882.

2. In 1897, a decade of economic prosperity (a.) began (b.) has begun (c.) had begun in the United States.

3. Since 1897, millions and millions of people (a.) immigrated (b.) have immigrated (c.) had immigrated to the United States.

Focus on Form: Simple Past Tense

The simple past tense is used to show:

- an action or state of being that was completed at a definite time in the past.

  The 1965 law *abolished* the old system of national quotas and *replaced* it with one favoring family reunification. (The law was changed in 1965.)

- an action that took place over a period of time in the past but no longer does.

  The Chinese *were prohibited* from immigrating to the United States for many years. **(Passive)** (They are no longer prohibited from immigrating.)

- an action that happened repeatedly or habitually in the past.

  Both the Poles and the Italians, among others, *traveled* back and forth many times between the United States and their countries. (They no longer do.)

Grammar Practice

Look at the graph of "Total Immigration to the United States from 1821 to 1980" on page 6. Write at least five sentences using the simple past tense about the information in the graph or in the reading. Give at least one example for each of the uses of the simple past tense given above.

Reading 2: "The Hunt for New Americans"

Prereading Questions

1. Since 1965, preference has been given to immigrants who have family in the United States. The following article is about a new law which would change this preference. Who do you think the "new Americans" in the title of this article might be?

2. What are some of the possible reasons for or against an open immigration policy?

3. Imagine that you live in a country with great resources but a small population. The government has asked you to serve on a panel to formulate a policy on immigration. With other students acting as your co-members, outline the basis of this policy. What categories of immigrants will you allow in? What restrictions will there be? List the categories in order of importance and be prepared to explain your reasoning to the class. If there are differences of opinion in your group, try to come to a consensus.

The Hunt for New Americans

By STEPHEN V. ROBERTS with ANN E. ANDREWS
(from *U.S. News and World Report*)

America is about to redefine its immigration policies for the first time in 25 years, and the result will reshape the nation's work force for the next century. The tired and the poor[13] are fine, but the United States now needs the best and the brightest from other countries in order to compete in the cutthroat[14] world of global markets. Since 1965, almost all new immigrants have received visas based on family connections, but now the emphasis is shifting to talent and training. Under legislation now being drafted on Capitol Hill, hundreds of thousands of new places would open up for foreigners who can make special contributions to the economy and culture: businessmen from Hong Kong, machinists from Italy, musicians from the Soviet Union.

---

13. The inscription on the Statue of Liberty begins: "Give me your tired, your poor, / your huddled masses, yearning to breathe free, . . ."   14. without mercy; cruel

Pulling up the ladder. Throughout American history, fearful voices have warned against increased immigration, the "pulling up the ladder behind us" syndrome. This nativist[15] mind-set has long held two strong but contradictory beliefs—that immigrants are either shiftless[16] louts[17] who live off the dole,[18] or money-grubbing[19] rascals who undercut pay scales and steal American jobs. And those myths retain their power. In a recent *Los Angeles Times* poll, half of those surveyed said that immigrants take more from society than they contribute; only one quarter said that newcomers pay back what they receive. Representative Lamar Smith, a Texas Republican who has led the fight against looser immigration laws says, "America simply cannot accommodate[20] every person who wants to come here. Why shouldn't we be training and educating Americans first?"

But the antiforeigner impulse has been undermined[21] by several new studies that reach a different conclusion: Despite short-term dislocations in certain places, immigration is clearly good for the country. Both stereotypes—dole taker or job stealer—are seriously flawed. Julian Simon, professor of business administration at the University of Maryland, concludes that the average immigrant family, being youthful and strong, uses fewer public services than the average native family. After five years in the country, newcomers actually pay higher taxes than natives do, and their contributions exceed the cost of the services they use.

On the jobs side, the impact of immigrants is benign.[22] Economist George Borjas of the University of California at Santa Barbara studied job patterns and found that immigrants have a negligible[23] impact on unemployment rates. He adds that "the earnings of the typical native are barely affected by the entry of immigrants into the local labor market." Simon says the explanation is that new members of the work force "take jobs, but they also make jobs" through increased productivity and purchasing power. "The new businesses which they start up," he argues, "are at least as numerous as the jobs which immigrants fill." Another new study by the Hudson Institute says that immigrants "help to stimulate economic growth" and advocates a liberalized immigration policy.

An aging work force. Moreover, new immigrants just entering their prime working years will be sought to fill new jobs, increase the tax rolls and bolster[24] the Social Security trust fund. The American work force is growing more slowly than it did in the 70s, and its average age is increasing. "When the baby-boomers[25] go on Geritol,[26] where are we going to be?" asks Senator Alan Simpson, a Wyoming Republican.

An even bigger problem is that the United States faces a "skills gap" in the years ahead that can be filled only by immigrant labor. Employers are pleading with Congress for permission to import machinists and engineers, nurses and sushi[27] chefs. "Aren't there people here to do this work?" asks Democratic Representative Bruce Morrison of Connecticut. "Unfortunately, the answer is no." But immigrants provide more than special skills; the experts agree that they also

---

15. favoring interests of native inhabitants over immigrants   16. lazy; without ambition   17. stupid, clumsy person   18. money provided by the state for poor people   19. doing anything for, and thinking only of, money   20. provide for; have space for   21. weaken   22. gentle, kind and beneficial; not evil   23. a very small amount; not worth thinking about   24. support   25. a person born in about the ten to fifteen year period after the Second World War, when there was a "boom" in population growth   26. a commercial tonic or vitamin for older people (*geriatric*=of old people)   27. raw fish with rice, a Japanese specialty

contribute the kind of energy and sophistication the United States needs to compete in global markets. In the words of New York Representative Charles Schumer, a Democrat, "We have to understand the world and be part of it."

The newest immigration studies all support the argument that immigrants are "self-selected strivers,"[28] in Morrison's phrase, people who have the courage and the imagination to pull up their roots and start over in a new land. Their less motivated, less skillful countrymen either do not survive the journey, or never start.

Reinforced by these findings, Congress is preparing to increase the total number of legal immigrants. A bill passed by the Senate last year would raise the annual limit by more than 100,000, to at least 630,000. A companion measure drafted[29] by a House subcommittee headed by Morrison would permit at least 800,000, and perhaps as many as 1 million. (The totals do not include either illegal aliens or the approximately 125,000 refugees who are admitted for political reasons.)

More important, the bills would also change the way legal immigration totals are reached. The 1965 law abolished the old system of national quotas and replaced it with one favoring family reunification. This opened the way for a vast influx of Asian and Latin immigrants, and in subsequent years, those newcomers used up almost all available visas bringing in their close relatives from Korea and the Philippines, El Salvador and the Dominican Republic. Most Europeans, whose ancestors came to the United States 100 years ago, or Africans, whose relatives were brought as slaves, lacked the current family ties needed to get in. Only a few highly visible individuals with special talents were able to qualify. The current practice of focusing on families has brought many valuable, if lower-skilled, workers, from domestics and taxi drivers to grocers and babysitters. But there have not been enough physicists or physical therapists or tool-and-die makers.[30]

That is now about to change. The Senate bill would permit an extra 150,000 immigrants who lack family connections but possess other virtues—advanced degrees, money to invest, a specialty in rural medicine. The House bill is even more generous, providing up to 235,000 visas for skilled workers or entrepreneurs[31] and their families. Both bills would set aside slots[32] for countries like Ireland and Poland, which get few slots under current rules. Hong Kong, loaded with wealthy investors who fear the Chinese takeover in 1997, would also get special treatment.

Training the underclass. Debate over the new law underscores the fact that American workers are not trained for these jobs—that the educational and social system has left some people out. Julian Simon notes that 13 of 17 valedictorians in Boston high schools last spring were immigrants or children of immigrants. Those are the kids industry wants, not the ones who dropped out of high school. As a result, some blacks have joined the anti-immigration cause. One is Frank Morris, dean of graduate studies at Morgan State University in Baltimore, who told Congress, "Many immigrants compete directly with blacks in the same labor markets and occupations." And testifying before Congress in March, former Colorado Governor Richard Lamm said the problem of the nation's poor and unskilled would not disappear simply because "we import foreign workers instead of training and retraining our own."

---

28. one who struggles hard to get or acquire   29. to write a first version or plan   30. machinist who makes tools and forms for metal objects   31. one who organizes, operates, and takes the risk for a business   32. place; opening

Despite the controversy, however, more immigrants are on the way. And the new law may also bring another major change: a national worker identity card. The idea is aimed at preventing discrimination against foreign-looking job seekers, and that proposal could get attached to any revision for visa allotments.[33] Despite the opinion polls, the lawmakers and their constituents are beginning to learn from the new studies a lesson that each generation must understand for itself. Every wave of newcomers is reviled[34] when it arrives, and every one winds up[35] refreshing America's strength and spirit.

---

33. share; portion   34. speak strongly against; curse   35. end or finish

Comprehension and Discussion

A. *Circle the correct answer. If the answer is false, tell why.*

1. Under the new law, only highly trained or talented people will be allowed to immigrate to the United States.

   True   False

2. Studies have shown that new immigrants do not tend to be welfare recipients but that they do take a significant number of jobs away from longtime residents.

   True   False

3. Americans have a national identity card.

   True   False

B. *Answer the following questions as completely as possible.*

1. The article mentions the "pulling up the ladder behind us" syndrome but never explicitly states what that means. From the words themselves and from the rest of the article, what do you think this expression means?

2. The article gives a number of reasons, some based on fact and some not, for and against increased immigration. List as many reasons as possible and, when possible, try to show opposing views.

   <u>For</u>   <u>Against</u>

3. Briefly summarize the change in immigration laws, from national quotas to family reunification to skills and training. How did or would these changes in law make a change in the immigrants coming to the United States?

4. What does the need for a new immigration law say about American society?

5. Why have some blacks joined the anti-immigration cause?

C. *Agree or disagree. Explain your reasons for agreeing or disagreeing with the following statements.*

1. The problem of the nation's poor and unskilled would not disappear simply because "we import foreign workers instead of training and re-training our own."

2. Each wave of newcomers is reviled when it arrives, and every one winds up refreshing America's strength and spirit.

Focus on Form: Present Perfect and Present Perfect Continuous

have (has) (not) + Past Participle *(-ed)* (Active)
have (has) (not) + been + Past Participle (Passive)
have (has) (not) + been + Present Participle *(-ing)* (Continuous)

The present perfect tense is used to show or describe:

-   a situation or event that began in the past and continues up to the present (often used with *for, since, so far, up until now,* etc.). With this use of the present perfect, the continuous may be used to emphasize continuing action or lack of completion. (The continuous may not be used with "stative" verbs—verbs that express a state or condition, such as *know, like, understand,* etc.)

    Since 1965, almost all new immigrants *have received* visas based on family connections. (You could also say: "have been receiving.")

    BUT: So far, I *haven't understood* very much of what he has said. It's all babble to me. (NOT: "I haven't been under-standing...")

-   a situation that happened at an unspecific time in the past (often used with words such as *ever, never, always, already,* etc.).

    This antiforeigner impulse *has been undermined* by several new studies that reach a different conclusion. **(Passive)** (We do not know when exactly it was undermined.)

-   a situation that has been repeated in the past and probably will be repeated again.

    At times, fear *has emerged* among the citizens. (This has happened with every new wave of immigration and will probably continue to happen.)

> • a situation that was recently completed in the past and which we connect in our minds with the present (often used with *just*).
>
> The law *has* just *been changed*.
>
> Note: Some of the words used with the present perfect, such as *recently*, *for*, *always*, etc., can also be used with other tenses. Do not think that every time you see one of these words, a certain tense must be used. For example, *for* is often used with the present perfect: "My family has been in this country for about 90 years." However, *for* may be used with other tenses in the past: "He lived there for 10 years." This means that he used to live here. He doesn't live here any longer. These words are clues, but the tense depends on the meaning and the time.

Grammar Practice

Simple Past vs. Present Perfect. Complete the sentences with the correct verb tense of the words in parentheses. If it is possible to use the continuous, use it. Be careful of irregular verbs and the passive voice. Use time words, the context of the entire sentence, and what you learned about immigration in this chapter to help you decide which tense to use. You may know the exact dates or times of an action from the readings or the graph.

1. Throughout American history, fearful voices (warn) ___has warned___ against increased immigration.

2. In 1965 Congress (replace) ___replaced___ the immigration law favoring national quotas with one favoring family reunification. This change of law (open) ___opened___ the way for a great increase in the number of Asian and Latin American immigrants.

3. In the past, the majority of immigrants (come) ___came___ from Europe. However, in the past 25 years, the Caribbean, Latin America and Asia (replace) ___have replaced___ the nations of Europe as points of origin.

4. Many immigrants (criticize) ___have been criticized___ for not making stronger efforts to learn English. However, public funding for ESL programs (cut) _____ back sharply.

5. An unprecedented population explosion in Europe, causing many people to immigrate to the United States, (stem) ___stemed___ from better health conditions.

6. During the early part of the twentieth century, Poles and Italians (be) ___were___ apt to come to the United States as temporary workers.

7. In the decade of economic prosperity in the United States beginning in 1897, the rate of immigration (rise) ___rose___ sharply.

8. The new immigrants (have) ___have had___ a powerful and largely positive economic and social impact on the city.

9. Problems sometimes arise between different immigrant groups. A New York store owner who (accuse) _was accused_ of assaulting a woman in January 1990 went to trial and (acquit) _____ of the charges against him. However, the woman (file) _has filed_ a damage suit against him. Both are recent immigrants.

10. The immigration laws (change) _have change been changed_ many times, and each change (have) _____ enormous effects on the mixture of people coming here.

Focus on Form: *In contrast* vs. *On the contrary*

The expressions *in contrast* and *on the contrary* are frequently misused by students of English. They have very different uses.

In contrast:

- shows a contrast or difference, often surprising, between two people, events, states, conditions, etc.
- contrasts different subjects.
- does not show opposites.

> Early immigrants came to the New World for religious reasons. *In contrast*, later immigrants tended to come for economic reasons. ("Early immigrants" and "later immigrants" are different subjects. They are different, not opposite.)

On the contrary:

- contrasts some aspect of the same subject in the same time frame.
- is used to express the opposite of what has just been said or heard.
- is not used just to show a difference.

> New immigrants are not usually welfare recipients. *On the contrary*, being young and strong, they use fewer social services than the average native family. (In both sentences we are talking about the same subject—new immigrants. The ideas expressed about the subject are opposites—being a welfare recipient or not being one.)

On the contrary:

- may be used as the beginning of a response to what someone else has said.

> Q: Don't new immigrants usually go on welfare?
> A: *On the contrary*, they use fewer social services than the average native family.

Grammar Practice

A. *Look at the following pairs of sentences. Decide whether you need* in contrast *or* on the contrary *to connect them.*

1. In the past, many immigrants came to the United States with almost nothing in their pockets. _____, new immigrants often come with money to invest.

2. The Irish came for economic reasons. _____, the Jews came for religious or political reasons.

3. Congress is not considering cutting down immigration. _____, the new bill would provide up to 235,000 new visas per year.[36]

4. Opponents of open immigration policies feel that the problems of the poor and unskilled will not go away with the new immigration policy. _____, they feel that the new immigrants will be competing in the job market with many of the nation's poor.

5. Studies show that immigrants are not lazy. _____, they are "self-selected strivers."

6. The children of immigrants often tended to try to forget "the old country." _____, their children often try to rediscover their roots.

7. In the past, immigrants often changed or were forced to change their names to make them sound more "American" or Anglo. _____, immigrants today keep and are proud of the names from their homelands.

B. *Look at your answers to questions 2 and 3 in the* **Comprehension and Discussion** *section B (page 13) as well as any of the information in Readings 1 and 2. Write your own sentences using* in contrast *and* on the contrary.

Reading 3: "Newcomers Alter Society, Politics of the Big Apple"

Prereading Questions

1. What effects do you think immigrants could have on a city in the following areas? Explain these effects as completely as possible and give reasons for them.

   a. housing/neighborhoods   b. politics   c. education

---

36. The subjects in both sentences seem different: "Congress" and "the new bill." However, we know that it is Congress that proposes and votes on new bills, so the general idea of the subjects of both sentences is the same.

2. New York City has a population of approximately 7.3 million people. What percentage of these would you guess are foreign-born? What other cities in the United States have high percentages of foreign-born residents?

3. What cultural differences could possibly cause problems or misunderstandings between new immigrants and longtime residents?

Vocabulary Practice

Match the underlined words in the sentences with the synonyms or definitions in the list below. Use the context of the sentence to help you guess the meaning.

_____ fall behind   _____ total involvement
_____ conflict   _____ make a sudden attack
_____ hidden motivation   _____ humble; unimportant
_____ hold back   _____ something that causes anger
_____ force out   _____ bring back to life
_____ push gently   _____ continuous, meaningless sound
_____ widespread, everywhere

1. The (a) *babble* of foreign languages on the streets is so (b) *pervasive* that the English speaker often feels like the foreigner.

2. Many immigrants take *menial* jobs and work long hours just to survive.

3. Immigrants have been crucial in *revitalizing* and stabilizing many neighborhoods.

4. The influence on politics usually *lags* a generation behind each new wave of arrivals.

5. The school system's response is to combine bilingual education with the *immersion* approach of English-as-a-Second-Language.

6. In some ways the toughest challenge for New Yorkers already here is cultural and social. (a) *Friction* as new groups move in, (b) *nudging* and (c) *displacing* those already here, is as old a pattern as immigration itself.

7. A shopper born in Haiti insisted that she was (a) *assaulted* without (b) *provocation* in January 1990 by the owner.

8. Often there is a strong economic *undercurrent* to such friction.

9. New immigrant groups pose a challenge for the city's schools and, some say, could *hinder* the progress of American-born blacks.

Newcomers Alter Society, Politics of the Big Apple

By LUCIA MOUAT   (from the *Christian Science Monitor*)

New York City continues to be enriched by new immigrant groups; the latest waves have bolstered the labor force and housing market. But they pose a challenge for the city's schools and, some say, could hinder the economic progress of American-born blacks.

New U.S. citizens taking a naturalization oath.

It's as if the boundaries of the United Nations had suddenly expanded to include all of New York City. The babble of foreign languages on the streets and in coffee shops is so pervasive that the English-speaker often feels like the foreigner. A full one third of all New Yorkers—up from one fourth 10 years ago—are now foreign-born.

The faces change. Over the last 25 years, the Caribbean, Latin America, and Asia have largely replaced the nations of Europe as points of origin, but New York City remains the destination of choice for one of every six immigrants to the United States.

Hispanics account for the largest numerical increase. Greater New York now has the second largest Hispanic community in the U.S., after southern California.

New York is one of the few frostbelt[37] cities to actually grow during the 1980s,

---

37. the northern part of the United States (as opposed to the Sunbelt, or the southern part)

rising from about 7 million to 7.3 million people, according to preliminary 1990 census figures. The new immigrants, arriving at a rate of roughly 90,000 a year, are considered a major factor. Many move into housing and jobs vacated by earlier immigrants, who have been moving steadily to the suburbs for the last two decades.

Some of the newcomers find the American dream lives up to its promise. Most find making a life here much tougher than they were led to believe by television and word-of-mouth[38] success stories. Many take menial jobs and work long hours just to survive.

In addition to enriching the culture in everything from cuisine[39] to music, the new immigrants have had a powerful and largely positive economic and social impact on the city.

"Immigrants have been critical in revitalizing and stabilizing many New York neighborhoods," says Mitchell Moss, director of New York University's Urban Research Center.

The influence on New York politics usually lags a generation behind each new wave of arrivals. Yet neighborhood ethnicity is playing a major role in the redrawing of City Council districts now under way.

When the Soviets crack down on Armenians or cyclones batter Bangladesh, a sympathetic community of immigrants in the U.S. now invariably sends up a cry of concern. Congress and U.S. foreign policymakers listen.

"The newcomers are a much more diverse group than has come to New York at any other period of our history . . . and it's changing our awareness of the rest of the world," notes Carol Stix, a professor of sociology at Pace University. "Taking a page from the Civil Rights movement, they recognize that they have to speak up and organize to be heard and have their needs met."

---

38. orally; by speech; not written   39. style of cooking (usually by nationality or region)

New York City schools face one of the strongest challenges posed by the new immigrants. On the enrichment side, teachers are being retrained and given new materials on the theory that every subject at every grade level should note contributions made to it by a variety of cultures; it's termed multicultural education.

Yet the English language gap remains a persistent problem for the schools. Currently, some 110,246 children—more than one of every nine in the school system—have only limited English proficiency.

[. . .]

The New York school system's response is often to combine bilingual education, when teachers are available and low test scores indicate a need, with the English immersion approach of English-as-a-second-language (ESL).

Students with very limited English ability are often taught history, math, and science for a time in their own language, in addition to their English language training. As Bob Terte, a spokesman for the city school system explains, "The purpose is to make the kids competent in English as soon as possible and also give instruction in the native language so they don't fall behind."

Yet those speaking less common languages, such as Urdu and Bengali, often must make do with ESL training only. Not knowing in advance which groups to expect, (children of Soviet refugees are the largest group of new students this year) and the high mobility rate of many immigrant families changing neighborhoods complicate the schools' job.

In some ways the toughest challenge for New Yorkers already here is cultural and social. Friction as new groups move in, nudging, and sometimes displacement of those already there, is as old a pattern as immigration itself.

Recent incidents in both New York and Washington, D.C., stand as sharp reminders of the need for increased sensitivity to cultural differences.

- When a Washington policewoman shot at a man resisting arrest for public drunkenness a few weeks ago, the response of Hispanics in his Mt. Pleasant neighborhood was fiery and defensive. They charged that local officials, who are predominantly black, discriminate against them.
- The boycott by blacks last year in Brooklyn's Flatbush section of a grocery owned by a Korean immigrant is another case in point. A shopper born in Haiti insisted she was assaulted without provocation in January 1990 by the owner. The owner, who says the woman did not pay for all her purchases, has been acquitted[40] of the charges against him but now faces a new $6 million damage suit filed[41] by the woman.

Often there is a strong economic undercurrent to such friction. Many blacks, for instance, say they, rather than any immigrants, should reap the job and spending benefits[42] in "their" neighborhoods. Yet cultural differences also play a strong and largely unrecognized role. The common Asian tendency to avoid looking anyone directly in the eye and the lack of a welcoming smile or small talk is sometimes interpreted as rudeness or arrogance. Some Asians try to mask their inability to speak English well.

Many immigrants have been criticized for not making stronger efforts to learn English. Many work such long hours that they have little time. Also, public funding for ESL programs is sharply down. "I don't think New York City and the suburban areas have more than 100,000 slots for this kind of thing—the problem grows more serious each year," says Regina Armstrong of the Regional Plan Association.

"We have a long waiting list," notes Linda Morona, an assistant with ESL programs at New York's McBurney YMCA.

One way in which the New York City Police Department has tried to increase cultural sensitivity is by assigning officers, where possible, to neighborhoods where their own ethnic or racial backgrounds may help. "I think it's been one of the more effective safety valves,"[43] observes James Shenton, a Columbia University history professor who specializes in New York City issues.

---

40. give a decision of not guilty   41. begin a court action for loss or harm   42. collect or enjoy the rewards or benefits

43. way of releasing pressure; a method to help avoid explosion

Comprehension and Discussion

Answer the following questions as completely as possible.

1. How does New York City differ from other cities in the North? Why?

2. The article states that the countries of origin of immigrants have changed, that Europeans are being replaced by people from the Caribbean, Latin America, and Asia. In your opinion, what effects might this change have on life in the United States in general or on the cities in which these immigrants tend to settle?

3. The article mentions that each of the following areas is significantly affected by immigration. Explain in detail how each area is affected. Use examples where possible.

   a. population stability
   b. neighborhood stability
   c. politics
   d. culture/society
   e. education

4. Are there any other areas of life not mentioned in the article which you feel are, or can be, affected by immigration? These may be positive, negative or both.

5. The article talks a great deal about English and English training for immigrants to the United States.

   a. What responsibility do you think the government has to provide training in English for immigrants? For children? For adults?
   b. Should the schools provide instruction in academic subjects in the native language for children?

6. What cultural differences are there between your country and the United States that could possibly cause friction between immigrants from your country and longtime residents of the U.S.?

   Custom / Tradition   Possible Conflict

7. What do you think can and should be done to reduce friction between recent immigrants and longtime residents?

Word Forms

Working with a partner, complete the following chart with the different forms of the words. Use your knowledge of other words and their different forms to help you. Do not be afraid to guess. A dash means there is no form.

Noun	Verb	Adjective	Adverb
	assault	—	—
babble		—	—
	displace	—	—
	hinder	—	—
immersion		—	—
	lag	—	—
—	—	menial	
	nudge	—	—
		pervasive	
provocation			
	revitalize	—	—

Vocabulary Building

The words below follow specific word-building rules. What are the rules? Working in small groups, see how many other words you know that follow the same word-building rules. Give the different forms. Discuss the meanings of the words with your group and then with your teacher.

Verb	Noun	Rule	Other Words (Verb - Noun)
revitalize			
immerse			

Vocabulary Practice

Complete the sentences below with the correct words from the following lists. You may have to use different word forms and tenses. Do not use a word more than once.

Paragraph 1	Paragraph 2
displace	immerse
revitalize	hinder
pervade	nudge
undercurrent	lag
friction	menial
assault	babble
provoke	

1. (a.) _____ between new immigrants and longtime residents can be a common fact of life in big cities in the United States. Although actual physical (b.) _____ on the immigrants is rare, resentment towards them sometimes builds up. This can happen not only when the immigrants are poor but also when they come to the United States with money to invest. Poorer residents may feel a sense of (c.) _____ as immigrants with money open up businesses in neighborhoods in which they do not live. The immigrants, on the other hand, at times complain of an (d.) _____ of racism towards them. They are confused about the negative feelings towards them when all they feel they are doing is bringing about a (e.) _____ of the neighborhood. Cultural differences, while totally innocent on either side, may seem (f.) _____ and at times can cause trouble. However, by no means do negative feelings between new immigrants and citizens (g.) _____ the society. On the contrary, it is amazing that so many people from so many different places can get along so well and that there are so few problems.

2. The problem of learning the language of the new country is usually more difficult for parents than for children. The lack of language skills is often a (a.) _____ in employment for the adult immigrant. Even highly educated people may be forced to take (b.) _____ jobs, often with people from their own countries, so they do not have the opportunity to practice English at work or at home. The children, on the other hand, attend school and are immediately (c.) _____ in the language. In

addition, their younger age gives them greater facility in acquiring the new language. What starts off as nothing but (d.) _____ to them very soon can become the language which they use to study and to play. Children also tend to adapt to the new culture more easily. This (e.) _____ in the adaptation process of the children and the parents can even cause problems at home as the children take up the customs of the new country while the parents keep those of the old. The children may try (f.) _____ the parents into the new culture, but the effort is often rejected.

Focus on Form: Past Perfect and Past Perfect Continuous

had (not)+ Past Participle *(-ed)* (Active)
had (not) + been + Past Participle (Passive)
had (not)+ been + Present Participle *(-ing)* (Continuous)

The past perfect is used to express a situation that happened before another situation in the past. The two past situations are connected in some way, and it is necessary to show this connection in time. (With the words *before* and *after*, the simple past is often used instead of the past perfect because the time relationship is obvious.) The past perfect continuous is used to show a continuing action before another action in the past.

By 1835, fewer than 250,000 people *had immigrated* to the United States in any five-year period. (This means before 1835. But in the period 1835-1840, immigration exceeded 250,000.)

The Chinese *had been working* here for many years when the exclusionary law was passed. **(Continuous)** (Here *when* means *before.* They had been working here first, and then the law was passed. When the action in the main clause happens *before* the action in the *when* clause, the past perfect is used in the main clause.)

VS.

Many Chinese wives *were* not able to join their husbands when the exclusionary law was passed. (Here *when* means *after.* The law was passed first, and then the women were not able to join their husbands. In talking about the past, when the action in the main clause happens *after* the action in the *when* clause, the simple past is used in both clauses. The past perfect is never used after *when.*)

> Up until the U.S. Immigration Act of 1882, no group *had been excluded* from immigrating to the United States strictly because of nationality. **(Passive)** (This changed with the Immigration Act of 1882.)

Grammar Practice

Simple Past vs. Past Perfect. Complete the sentences with the correct verb tense of the words in parentheses. Use the continuous when possible. Be careful of irregular verbs and the passive voice. Use time words and the context of the entire sentence or passage to help you decide which tense to use.

Chinese Laundry Workers in the United States

The settling of the west coast was due in large part to the discovery of gold. When gold (1. discover) _was discovered_ in California in 1848, few Chinese (2. travel) _had traveled_ to the west coast to make their fortune. However, when they (3. start) _____ arriving in large numbers after the Gold Rush, they (4. encounter) _____ prejudice and discrimination. The Chinese (5. play) _____ a major role in building the foundation of the west coast. They (6. prohibit) _____ from prospecting for gold and (7. exclude) _____ from many skilled jobs. Consequently, many (8. hire) _____ to build roads and the railroad. When the railroad (9. complete) _____, the Chinese who (10. build) _____ it (11. lose) _____ their jobs.

The only work that was available or allowed for the Chinese was traditional "women's" work—washing clothes, cooking, or working as servants. By the time California (12. become) _became_ a state, Chinese laundries (13. open) _____ in San Francisco. However, even in this venture, the Chinese (14. face) _____ discrimination. Many Chinese (15. turn) _____ down for licenses to open laundry businesses. In addition, although steam-driven machines (16. use) _____ by white laundry operators since the 1850s, it was not until the 1930s that the Chinese (17. allow) _____ to buy large washing machines. Up until that time, all washing, ironing, and folding (18. do) _____ by hand in the individual Chinese laundries. _had been done_

In addition to the Chinese, hundreds of thousands of immigrants from Europe arrived on the west coast looking for work. As the economy (19. expand) _____ and (20. contract) _____, many people (21. become) _became_ unemployed. Increasingly, Chinese workers (22. blame) _____ for the region's hard times. By the 1880s, anti-Chinese sentiment (23. grow) _had grown_ to such an extent that Congress, in 1882, (24. pass) _passed_ the first exclusionary immigration laws. The law specifically (25. forbid) ~~was forbidden~~ the immigration of Chinese laborers, excluding merchants and students. It was not until 1943 that the Chinese Exclusion Acts (26. repeal) ~~met~~ _was/repealed_ _forbad_ _were_

Grammar Practice

Integration. Complete the sentences with the correct form of the verbs in parenthe-ses—simple past, present perfect, or past perfect. If either the present perfect or the present perfect continuous is possible, give both. You may have to use the passive voice.

The United States (1. be) _____ a haven for refugees since its beginning. The original settlers (2. leave) _____ Europe mainly for political and religious reasons, but later immigrants from Europe (3. tend) _____ to come for economic reasons. Socio-economic upheavals in Europe (4. cause) _____ massive exoduses to the New World. By the time the Irish Potato Famine (5. start) _____ in 1845, no more than 500,000 people (6. immigrate) _____ here in any five-year period. But when the famine (7. be) _____ over, immigration in the five-year period before its end (8. go) _____ up to about 1,700,000. After this period, it (9. begin) _____ to go down again.

World problems (10. reflect) _____ always _____ in the immigration patterns to the U.S. For example, pogroms against the Jews in Russia in the years 1903-1907 (11. bring) _____ about a great increase in the number of Jews coming here. Likewise, poor living conditions in southern Italy at that time (12. mean) _____ a mass immigration from Italy to the United States and Argentina. The major exodus started in 1899, and by 1924 more than four million Italians (13. leave) _____ their homeland.

It should be noted, however, that nobody is sure exactly how many of those early immigrants (14. return) _____ home. Experts (15. estimate) _____ that for every eight that (16. enter) _____ the country during the 19th century, one (17. leave) _____. Between 1908 and 1924, a period that offers some documentation, 3,573,974 people are known to have left—roughly a third of the number that (18. enter) _____ in that period. By the 1880s, cheap steamship fares (19. make) _____ it pos-sible for workers to think of America as a place of short-term employment.

The United States (20. accept) _____ millions of people over the years, those who (21. seek) _____ a better life and those who (22. flee) _____ oppression or natural disaster. Official sources show that by 1981, a total of 50 million people (23. come) _____ into the area now encompassed by the United States. At times, fear (24. emerge) _____ among the citizens that these immigrants would overwhelm the civilization they found or take jobs from those already here. Yet consistently the newcomers (25. accept) _____ the ideal of citizenship, and each group (26. contrib-ute) _____ to the culture of its adopted land. And the antiforeign mind-set (27. undermine) _____ by recent studies which show that immigrants contribute more than they take from the society.

Grammar Practice

Open Practice. Write sentences using the simple past, the present perfect, and the past perfect tenses. Try to write three to five sentences for each tense. These can be separate sentences, not a paragraph. The sentences can be based on the information in the graph on page 6 or in the readings. They can also be personal, about you and either your immigration or your visit to the United States. For example,

I *decided* to come to the United States when I was 20 years old.

So far, I *haven't traveled* outside of this city, but I plan to.

Before I came, I *hadn't* really *realized* how varied the population of the country was.

Class Project

Work on one or more of these projects individually or in groups of two or three students. Then present your findings to the class.

1. In groups of two or three students, interview Americans whose families have immigrated to the United States within the past 150 years. You could ask your teachers, neighbors, or friends who are American or longtime residents of the United States, other students at your school, etc. Ask them if they have any photographs or articles of their immigrant ancestors. Where in the graph presented with Reading 1 do these immigrants fall? Why did they leave "the old country?" What were their experiences when they first came to the United States? If you are an immigrant, how do their experiences compare with yours? If not, how do they compare with the experiences of any classmates or friends who are recent immigrants. Present your "case study" to the class.

2. According to "We, the People," Canada, Australia, Argentina, and Brazil are countries which also had a great deal of immigration. Do library research on the immigrant experience in one of these countries or in any other country which has been greatly affected by immigration. What different types of people immigrated to those countries? What is the situation regarding immigration today? How was the immigrant experience similar to or different from that of the United States? Present your findings to the class.

3. The chart of "Total U.S. Immigration from 1821 to 1980" with Reading 1 notes a number of events which affected immigration to some degree. Pick one of these historical events and do research on it. Be prepared to explain this event to the class and tell how it affected immigration.

Discussion and Writing

Discuss the following topics, first in pairs or small groups, then with the teacher and the entire class. After your discussion, pick one (or more) of the topics and write an essay about it.

1. Discuss immigration to the United States as it is today. How is it different from the way it used to be? What effect is this having on the country and what might it mean for the future of the United States?

2. Has immigration (or emigration) ever had an effect on your country in any way? When did it occur? Why did it occur and what have the effects of it been?

3. Whether or not one feels that the present immigration policy in the United States is good, everyone concedes that immigration on a large scale brings about certain problems. What are some of these problems, and what can be done to overcome them? Pick only one or two of these problems and develop or explain them in detail. Be as specific as possible in your recommendations.

4. Write a personal history with as much details as possible of someone you know or have heard about who immigrated to a new country. This could be yourself, a relative, or a friend. Try to give as much background information as possible about the person (or persons).

Word List

Below is a list of the new words, and their different forms, presented in this chapter.

Noun	Verb	Adjective	Adverb
absorption	absorb	absorbent absorbable apt to	
assault	assault		
babble	babble		
diminishment	diminish		
displacement	displace flee		
friction			
haven			
heritage	inherit		
hindrance	hinder		
immersion	immerse		
lag	lag		
		menial	menially
nudge	nudge		
opulence		opulent	opulently
	overwhelm	overwhelming	overwhelmingly
perniciousness		pernicious	perniciously
pervasiveness	pervade	pervasive	pervasively
(precedent)	(precede)	unprecedented	
provocation	provoke	provocative	provocatively
revitalization	revitalize		
		rough	roughly
	seek		
sparseness		sparse	sparsely
	stem (from)		
turmoil			
undercurrent			
upheaval	heave		

CHAPTER 2

Issues
in Education

Reading 1: "Classrooms of Babel"

Prereading Questions

1. Babel was a city in which, according to the Bible, a tower was built to try to reach heaven and in which there came about a confusion of languages. Babel has come to mean people not understanding each other. What do you think the title of this article refers to?

2. What are some of the problems schools in the United States might face because of immigration?

3. What, in your opinion, are some possible solutions to these problems?

Vocabulary Practice

Circle the correct synonym or definition for each of the italicized words in the sentences below. Use the context of the sentences to help you guess the meanings.

1. A record number of immigrant children *pose* new problems for schools.

   a. get ready for photographs
   b. are normal
   c. present

2. At least two million children, or five percent of the total kindergarten-through-12th grade population have limited *proficiency* in English.

   a. exposure to
   b. competence
   c. problems

3. In most schools, it's not economically *feasible* to hire bilingual teachers unless there are 20 or more students who speak the same language in the same grade.

   a. possible
   b. worthwhile
   c. a problem

4. There aren't many math, chemistry or biology teachers who can *handle* Vietnamese or Tagalog.

   a. touch
   b. understand
   c. control

5. Opponents see total immersion as a *euphemism* for the "good old days" when non-English speaking students either succeeded or failed in mainstream America without special treatment.

   a. inoffensive term
   b. definition
   c. offensive term

6. These centers mix children of all ages and offer comprehensive services such as *immunization* and other health care.

   a. special classes for immigrants
   b. social service help from social workers
   c. making safe from disease though an injection into the body

7. The aim is to provide a *nurturing* atmosphere for a year while the children, many of whom carry psychological scars from living in war-torn countries like El Salvador, learn some fundamentals of English.

   a. caring
   b. normal
   c. natural

8. "Unfortunately," says Laurie Olsen, a project director for an *advocacy* group, California Tomorrow, "the real norm is far less optimistic than what you see happening in the newcomer school."

   a. support (for a cause)
   b. opposition to a cause
   c. lawyers'

9. Classes in the voluntary *enrichment* program encourage mixed groups of native speakers and English speakers to acquire new vocabulary.

   a. money-making
   b. make more meaningful
   c. programs for the rich

Classrooms of Babel

By CONNIE LESLIE with DANIEL GLICK and JEANNE GORDON   (from *Newsweek* magazine)

A record number of immigrant children pose new problems for schools

For picture day[1] at New York's PS[2] 217, a neighborhood elementary school in Brooklyn, the notice to parents was translated into five languages. That was a nice gesture, but insufficient; more than 40 percent of the children are immigrants whose families speak any one of 26 languages, ranging from Armenian to Urdu.

At the Leroy D. Weinberg Elementary School in Miami, a science teacher starts a lesson by holding up an ice cube and asking "Is it hot?" The point here is vocabulary. Only after the students who come from homes where English is not spoken learn the very basics will they move on to the question of just what an ice cube might be.

---

1. a day in elementary schools when class photographs are taken   2. Public School

The first grade at Magnolia Elementary School in Lanham, Md. is a study in cooperation. A Korean boy who has been in the United States for almost a year quizzes[3] two mainland Chinese girls who arrived 10 days ago. Nearby, a Colombian named Julio is learning to read with the help of an American-born boy.

In small towns and big cities, children with names like Oswaldo, Suong, Boris, or Ngam are swelling the rolls in U.S. public schools, sitting side by side with Dick and Jane.[4] Immigration in the 1980s brought an estimated 9 million foreign-born people to the United States, slightly more than the great wave of 8.8 million immigrants that came between 1901 and 1910. As a consequence, at least 2 million children or 5 percent of the total kindergarten-through-12th-grade population have limited proficiency in English, according to a conservative estimate from the U.S. Department of Education. In seven states including Colorado, New Mexico, New York and Texas, 25 percent or more of the students are not native English speakers. And all but a handful[5] of states have at least 1,000 foreign-born youngsters. As a result, says Eugene Garcia, of the University of California, Santa Cruz, "there is no education topic of greater importance today."

How to teach in a Tower of Babel? Since a 1974 Supreme Court decision, immigrant children have had the right to special help in public schools. But how much? And what kind? Many districts have responded by expanding the bilingual education programs they've been using for the past two decades. In these classes, students are taught subjects like social studies, science and math in their native language on the theory that children must develop a firm foundation in their mother tongue before they can learn academic subjects in a new language. Proponents say that even with bilingual educa-

tion it takes between four and seven years for a non-native to reach national norms on standardized tests of most subject material.

In most schools, it's not economically feasible to hire bilingual teachers unless there are 20 or more students who speak the same language in the same grade. Even then, there aren't many math, chemistry or biology teachers who can handle Vietnamese or Tagalog.[6] In addition, critics like author and former Newton, Mass., teacher Rosalie Pedalino Porter argue that the typical bilingual programs for Spanish speakers used over the last two decades haven't worked. The clearest indication of the failure, she charges, is the high dropout rate for Hispanic children—35.8 percent compared with 14.9 percent for blacks and 12.7 percent for whites.

Bilingual classes aren't an option in a classroom where a dozen languages are spoken. In schools such as Elsik High in Houston and New York's PS 217, all immigrant children are mixed in ESL (English-as-a-second-language) classes on their grade level. ESL teachers give all instruction in English. Their special training helps them work with kids who start out not knowing a single word. Some students remain in ESL classes for three or four years. Others move into regular classes but return to an ESL room for remedial periods.

Still other schools such as Houston's Hearne Elementary School use the "total immersion" method. With 104 of Hearne's 970 students speaking one of 23 languages, principal Judith Miller has encouraged all of her teachers to take ESL training so that immigrant youngsters can remain in classes with their native English-speaking peers. "The limited-English children are able to interact with their peers better and learn social skills. They also seem much happier," says Miller. Opponents see total immersion as a euphemism for "the good old days" when non-English-speaking students sank or

---

3. asks questions   4. names considered typically American   5. almost everyone

6. language spoken in the Philippine Islands

swam[7] in mainstream America without special treatment.

Nurturing atmosphere. Some schools have found that immigrant parents can be a great resource, either as volunteers or hired aides. When members of New York's PS 217 Parents Association noticed that non-English-speaking families rarely made any connection with the school, they won a $10,000 grant and hired five mothers of immigrant students as outreach workers. One day each week these women, who speak Urdu, Chinese, Russian, Haitian-Creole or Spanish, do everything from acting as interpreters at parent-teacher conferences to helping families find city services.

California is experimenting with "newcomer" schools that act as a one-year stopover for foreign-born children before they move on to a neighborhood school. These centers mix children of all ages in a given classroom and offer comprehensive services such as immunizations and other health care. Bellagio Road Newcomer School for grades four through eight is one of two such schools in Los Angeles. While most classrooms are Spanish bilingual, other students are taught in English. Teaching assistants who speak a variety of languages help out with translating. Principal Juliette Thompson says the aim is to provide a nurturing atmosphere for a year while the children, many of whom carry psychological scars from living in war-torn countries like El Salvador, learn some fundamentals of English. The newcomer schools seem to be working well, but they don't reach many kids. "Unfortunately," says Laurie Olsen, a project director for an advocacy group, California Tomorrow, "the real norm is far less optimistic than what you see happening in the newcomer schools."

A method borrowed from Canada recognizes that the problem is not one-sided. Called "two-way immersion," the program requires students to learn subject matter in both languages. Classes in the voluntary enrichment program encourage mixed groups of native speakers and English speakers to acquire new vocabulary. Public schools like PS 84 in Manhattan also use two-way immersion to attract upper-middle-class parents. Lawyer Holly Hartstone and her husband, a doctor, enrolled their 9-year-old son Adam in PS 84, where nine of the school's 25 classes are involved in voluntary Spanish two-way immersion. When Adam grows up, his parents expect that he'll live in a global community and need more than one language. These programs are catching on around the country. Two-way immersion in Japanese, which began three years ago in a Eugene, Ore., elementary school has spread to Portland, Anchorage and Detroit. And the French program at Sunset Elementary School in Coral Gables, Fla., recently received a grant from the French government.

Young Yankees. Being a stranger in a strange land is never easy. "All the English-speaking kids should learn a foreign language. Then they'd know how hard it is for us sometimes," says 17-year-old Sufyan Kabba, a Maryland high school junior, who left Sierra Leone last year. But here they are, part of the nation's future, young Yankees who, in the end, must rely on the special strength of children: adaptability.

---

7 fail or succeed on your own; no help given

Many-Tongued Classes
- More than 5 million children of immigrants are expected to enter U.S. public schools during the 1990s.
- About 3.5 million schoolchildren are from homes where English is not the first language.
- More than 150 languages are represented in schools nationwide.
- In seven states, 25 percent or more of students are language minorities.
- By current estimates, 73 percent of language-minority children are Hispanic.

Comprehension and Discussion

A. *Circle the correct answer. If the answer is false, tell why.*

1. Proponents of bilingual programs use the high dropout rate of Hispanic students as an argument to show why bilingual programs are needed.

    True   False ✓

2. In 1974, the Supreme Court decided that immigrant children had the right to special help and that bilingual education had to be offered whenever there were 20 or more students who spoke the same language and were in the same grade.

    True   False ✓

3. One of the problems with bilingual education, particularly for languages that are still less common in the United States, can be finding someone fluent in those languages to teach the academic subjects.

    ✓ True   False

4. What happens in the newcomer schools is typical of what happens for most foreign-born children in California.

    True   False ✓

5. Most states have one thousand or more foreign-born children.

    ✓ True   False

B. *Answer the following questions as completely as possible.*

1. What is the writer doing in the first three paragraphs of the article? Do you feel it is an effective way to start? Why or why not?

2. In one or two sentences, summarize the main idea or thesis of the article. What is the problem and, in general terms, what are the solutions?

3. What are the benefits and the problems of bilingual education, according to the article?

4. The article lists five possibilities which can be used in addition to or as an alternative to bilingual education. Explain them giving the pros and cons for each.

5. Which of the programs mentioned in the article do you feel would be most beneficial for foreign-born students in American schools? Can you think of any other programs which might be helpful? Would there be any difference if the students were adults (university-level) instead of children?

Word Forms

Working with a partner, complete the following chart with the different forms of the words. Use your knowledge of other words and their different forms to help you. Do not be afraid to guess. A dash means there is no form.

Noun	Verb	Adjective	Adverb
1. advocacy*		—	—
2. ...			
enrichment		—	—
euphemism	—		
immunization			—
proficiency	—		
	—	feasible	
—		nurturing	—

Vocabulary Building

The words below follow specific word-building rules. What are the rules? Working in small groups, see how many other words you know that follow the same rules. Give the different forms. Discuss the meanings of the words with your teacher.

Noun	Adjective	Rule	Other Words (Noun - Adjective)
proficiency			
feasibility			
euphemism			

Vocabulary Practice

Complete the sentences below with the correct words from the following list. You may have to use different word forms and tenses. Do not use a word more than once.

pose	handle	nurturing
proficiency	euphemism	advocacy
feasible	immunization	enrichment

1. It is doubtful whether children who are not _____ enough in English will learn anything about an academic subject just by sitting in the class.

---

* Pronunciation Note: The verb *advocate* has two noun forms, *advocacy*, the act of advocating or supporting, and *advocate*, a person who supports. Many other verbs ending in -*ate* also have a noun and/or adjective form that ends in -*ate*. However, the pronunciation of these forms is different. The verb form is pronounced as a "long a" (/ey/), as in the word *late*. The noun and adjective forms are pronounced with the sound / i/, as in *hit, bit, sit.*) Some common words that follow this rule are: advocate (v., n.), estimate (v., n.), and graduate (v., n., adj.). Practice the pronunciation of these words, and try to find others which follow the same rule.

2. _____ of immersion programs say that children will be able _____ regular courses if they also have special ESL classes.

3. In hard economic times, many school districts worry about the _____ of special programs for students of so many different language backgrounds.

4. All children must _____ against certain diseases before they are allowed to attend school.

5. Both longtime residents of the United States and newcomers can _____ by each other's presence in schools and neighborhoods.

6. "U.S. English," a movement to make English the language of the United States by law, is said by opponents to be a _____ way of outlawing the use of other languages in any official business.

7. The current situation in our city schools _____ many questions as to how children can both learn a second language and not lose time with their school subjects.

8. For the future of the country, it is important that we _____ the children of immigrants so that they have a better chance of growing up to be educated, productive citizens.

Reading 2: "Asians Question Admissions"

Prereading Questions

1. What are the admissions requirements for undergraduate degrees in colleges or universities in your country? What do the universities take into account when they decide who will be admitted?

2. In a multicultural society like the United States, do you feel that colleges should make an attempt to have an ethnically diverse group of students? If so, how should this be done? If not, why not?

Vocabulary Practice

Match the italicized words in the sentences with the synonyms or definitions in the list below. Use the context of the sentence to help you guess the meaning.

Sentences 1 - 6
_____ rapid increase or rise
_____ solve; find a solution; understand a problem
_____ causing to admire
_____ have great affection for
_____ overwhelm in number; flood
_____ close inspection; examination

Sentences 7 - 10
_____ unwilling; hesitant
_____ reject
_____ obeying a demand or regulation
_____ make consistent; make opposing ideas agree
_____ gather; come together in groups
_____ unclear

1. Chen, a 4.0 grade point student with an *impressive* extracurricular high school record, was rejected by Harvard.

2. *Deluged* by a great wave of Asian-American applicants, have the elite American colleges tried to keep their numbers down?

3. Asians have traditionally *cherished* education as a means of upward mobility.

4. But despite dramatic *upsurges* in Asian applications to selective schools, Asian admit rates lagged behind those of white admit rates.

5. After years of government *scrutiny* of admissions policies, elite schools do seem to be paying attention to such concerns.

6. They can't *figure out* why people think they are not impressed with Asian-American candidates.

7. The government is reviewing the school's admissions record to insure *compliance* with the Civil Rights Act.

8. Some administrators explain the admissions lag by saying that a science orientation tends to (a.) *cluster* Asian-Americans in particular majors and so more Asians than whites are (b.) *turned down* when admissions for certain departments are filled.

9. Asian Americans have a tough time (a.) *reconciling* the failure of purely academic accomplishments with the somewhat (b.) *murky* requirements of putting together a freshman class.

10. Critics are *reluctant* to give elite schools an A+ just yet.

Asians Question Admissions

By SUSAN GERVASI
(from *The Washington Post*)

He was one of only two Asian Americans at his Butler, Pa., high school. But Herald Chen, 20, had grown up with no sense of being "different." Then, in 1988, Chen, a 4.0[8] grade point student with an impressive extracurricular[9] high school record, was rejected by Harvard. He believes he was turned down because of his race.

"The big question I had was about my last name being obviously Chinese," said the University of Pennsylvania sophomore. "I wondered that if everything else I'd put in my application was the same, but I'd put someone else's name on it, would I have been accepted?"

---

8. having grades of all A's (an A = 4 points)   9. extra school activities, such as clubs or sports

Choosing the right college can be a very difficult but important decision for a student to make.

Posed in broader terms, Herald Chen's question has troubled the Asian-American community for nearly a decade. Deluged by a tidal wave of Asian-American applicants, have the nation's most elite colleges and universities tried to keep their numbers down through ceiling[10] quotas and/or racially discriminatory selection policies?

"We believe there's evidence of discrimination against Asian Americans in college admissions policies, and on a number of campuses," said Paul Igasaki of the Japanese-American Citizens League.

For Asians, who have traditionally cherished education as a means to upward mobility, the idea that America's best schools may not want them—or may not want so many of them—is particularly painful.

Ironically, Asian Americans, who constitute about 3 percent of the nation's population, seem well represented at elite schools. They comprise[11] 17 percent of 1989's entering freshman class at Harvard, 12 percent at Yale, 11 percent at Brown, 18 percent at Stanford, 9 percent at Princeton, 25 percent at the University of California at Los Angeles and 28 percent at UC Berkeley.

"I think the notion of bias is foolish," said Princeton Dean of Admissions Fred Hargadon. "We all sit around and are pretty impressed with Asian-American candidates, and we can't figure out why people think we're not."

---

10. an upper limit or a maximum number   11. make up

During the 80s the number of Asian Americans in colleges more than doubled. According to Vance Grant, a specialist in educational statistics for the government's National Center for Education Statistics, Asian-American college students in 1976 represented 1.8 percent of all collegians. As of 1988, the most recent statistics available, they numbered 491,000—some 3.8 percent of America's college population.

But despite dramatic upsurges in Asian college applications to selective schools and their current impressive numbers on such campuses, Asian "admit rates" during the 1980s (the percentage of Asian students admitted of all Asian applicants) lagged behind those of white and/or of the total applicant pool at highly selective schools.

In the mid-1980s activists in the Asian-American community began to focus on admissions policies and admission rate differences. Now, after years of individual protests, congressional complaints and government scrutiny of admissions policies, elite schools do seem to be paying closer attention to such concerns. But Asian Americans still believe their growing numbers have led some institutions to view them as a threat to the time-honored ideal of campus "diversity." Some politically conservative Asians also charge that affirmative action[12] programs that give preference to blacks and other minority groups (with Asian Americans no longer generally seen as needing such preferential treatment) affect them unfairly.

"It's a complex issue," said Herald's father Andy Chen, a professor of educational psychology at Slippery Rock University and former president of the Organization of Chinese Americans. "The problem for Asians is double-edged, an upper ceiling on admissions at the top, and at the bottom, affirmative action."

Igasaki said, "We haven't heard anyone admit there were ceilings. We can't say what goes on behind closed doors. But we believe there have been conscious decisions to reduce the numbers of Asians, and they've come up with ways to do it. Even if that's not a 'quota,' that's racial discrimination."

Harvard's admissions office did not respond to repeated requests for comment, but the school has denied allegations of racial bias in its admissions policies. Based on the Chen case and others, the Department of Education's Office of Civil Rights (OCR) is reviewing the school's admissions records to ensure compliance with Title VI of the 1964 Civil Rights Act, which prohibits discrimination on the basis of race or national origin by schools that receive federal funds. A report could be forthcoming this spring. OCR is also reviewing UCLA's compliance with Title VI (based on evidence from sources an OCR spokesman would not specify) and is examining several cases involving Berkeley's admissions policies.

One is the case of Yat-Pang Au, 21, who was denied Berkeley admission in 1987 despite a high school record that included straight As and a number of extracurricular awards. His father Sik-Kee Au, a San Jose businessman and Berkeley graduate, believes his son was victimized by attempts to restrict Asian numbers on campus.

Berkeley spokesman Ray Colvig denied Berkeley ever set quotas.

Though his son was recently admitted to Berkeley as a transfer student, Au remains concerned about the issues at stake.[13] "We Chinese Americans value

---

12. providing equal opportunity in job hiring or school admissions for members of groups, usually minorities or women, who had previously been discriminated against   13. at risk

education a lot," said Au. "We are not asking for special treatment, we're asking for equal treatment."

Though a 1987 state audit[14] of Berkeley found Asians admitted at lower rates than whites throughout its colleges—though the Asians had higher GPAs[15] and standardized test scores—some administrators explain admission-rate lags by arguing that a science orientation tends to cluster Asian Americans in particular majors—like engineering and pre-med[16]—and so more Asians than whites are turned down when admissions quotas for certain departments are filled. Ivy League admissions officers also stress the need to put together academically diverse freshman classes.

"I wouldn't say Asian-American students are not diverse enough, but it's clear that at this stage they are not considered along as many dimensions—such as alumni[17] children and varsity athletes—as some other groups of applicants," said Princeton Dean of Admissions Fred Hargadon.

Like other select schools, Princeton has attributed admit-rate lags to the absence of Asians in the categories of athletes and alumni relatives. Harvard Dean of Admissions William R. Fitzsimmons in a 1988 statement attributed a nearly 4 percent admissions rate difference to the fact that "Asians are slightly less strong on extracurricular criteria . . . (and) there are very few Asian Americans in our applicant pool who are alumni/ae children or prospective varsity[18] athletes."

Such alumni "legacy"[19] programs, whereby relatives of graduates get special consideration on the admissions process, upset some Asians.

"We sort of see the legacy programs as affirmative action programs for whites," said Melinda Yee, executive director of the Organization of Chinese Americans. "It seems elitist."

Don Nakanishi, a UCLA professor of education who has studied select schools' admissions policies, wrote last year in *Change* magazine: "Like their predecessors who dealt with the upsurge in American Jewish applicants, [administrators at elite schools] have found themselves defending their institutional need to enroll good football players and the siblings[20] of loyal and wealthy alumni rather than a meritocratic[21] ideal of choosing the best of the brightest."

But admissions officers say Asians are accustomed to the purely meritocratic tradition of Asian institutions and don't understand that American schools are different.

"We're obliged to select a class that will be diverse and keep the faculty happy," said Brown University Dean of Admissions Eric Wider. "I think Asian Americans have a tough time reconciling the failure of purely academic accomplishments [as admissions criteria] with the somewhat more murky requirements of putting together a freshman class. We need a football team. We need to pay attention to our alumni. This combines to make admissions a very creative and judgmental process."

---

14. an official examination of records   15. grade point average; the average of all of a student's grades   16. pre-medicine   17. alumni/alumnae (plural masculine/feminine; singular = alumnus, alumna): graduate of a school   18. the principal teams of a school   19. something that is handed down to you from an ancestor   20. brothers and sisters   21. based solely on merit or accomplishment

Princeton's Hargadon also believes that a greater percentage of highly qualified Asian Americans applies in greater numbers to the select colleges than non-Asian applicants. "I think that, in general, education has a higher priority in Asian-American families across-the-board,[22] and with that there's a slightly greater 'name-brand' attraction" to select schools, said Hargadon.

Hargadon also points out that schools like Princeton—to which "in one year, 1,500 or 2,000 high school valedictorians[23] apply"—are swamped with academically superior students. He attributes the Asian-American complaints in part to the fact that when select schools reject them, "it's human nature" to try to blame the schools.

"I'm not sure the anxiety of Asian Americans is worse than that of other groups that get rejected," said Hargadon, who added that he gets a variety of letters from rejectees accusing Princeton of rejecting them for the wrong reasons. "Everybody tends to generalize from their particulars, and that's what upsets me about the Asian-American thing."

Though critics like Melinda Yee agree things may be improving (especially at Berkeley, where officials eventually admitted last spring that their admissions policies had unfair impact on Asian Americans), they're reluctant to give elite schools an A-plus just yet. Where improved admit rates are concerned, for instance, "numbers can be misleading," said Yee. "We want to make sure these are long term effects. We need to see a pattern over a number of years."

Given their demographics,[24] Paul Igasaki speculates Asian Americans could eventually find even community colleges harder to get into. But civil rights leaders emphasize they're not asking for favored treatment—just equality.

"What we see people complaining of is a sense there are too many Asian Americans," said Igasaki. "But we don't feel that's something that should legitimately cause anybody concern."

---

22. affecting or touching everybody or everything equally   23. a student, usually the one with the highest grades, who gives the farewell speech at graduation   24. the study of human populations

Comprehension and Discussion

A. *Circle the correct answer. If the answer is false, tell why.*

1. The rate of Asian-American students in all American universities is higher than the rate of Asian Americans of the total population of the United States.

True   False

2. A greater percentage of the total population of Asian-American students apply to the elite universities than do whites.

True   False

3. Even though Asian Americans are a racial minority, they are not given preference in affirmative action programs.

True   False

4. The fact that Asian Americans constitute three percent of the population of the United States, but in some cases over twenty percent of the population of elite schools, shows that they are admitted at a rate higher than that of whites.

True   False

B. *Answer the following questions as completely as possible.*

1. List the various criteria that American colleges and universities use for admission. Which ones do you think are valid? Are there any which you feel should not be used in admitting students?

2. How do these criteria differ from those used in your country?

3. What reasons are given for the possible rejection of Asian-American students with outstanding academic records by American colleges and universities?

4. Explain the alumni "legacy" programs and why minority groups, including Asians, might think they are unfair. Does the fact that a student has close relatives who are alumni of a school mean anything in being admitted to that school in your country?

5. In your opinion, is a college or university justified in accepting a student whose grades or test scores are lower than those of another student who has been rejected in order to keep the student population diverse?

6. What does football have to do with college admissions?

Word Forms

Working with a partner, complete the following chart with the different forms of the words. Use your knowledge of other words and their different forms to help you. Do not be afraid to guess. A dash means there is no form.

Noun	Verb	Adjective	Adverb
	cluster	—	—
compliance			
	deluge	—	—
scrutiny		—	—
upsurge		—	—
	—	murky	—
	—	reluctant	

Vocabulary Building

The words below follow specific word-building rules. Working in small groups, see how many other words you know that follow the same rules. Give the different forms. Discuss the meanings of the words with your teacher.

Verb	Noun	Rule	Other Words (Verb - Noun)
comply			
scrutinize			

Vocabulary Practice

Complete the sentences below with the correct words from the following list. You may have to use different word forms and tenses. Do not.use a word more than once.

impressive	upsurge
deluged	scrutiny
cherish	compliance
figure out	cluster
reconcile	turn down
murky	reluctance

Many Asian-American students feel that the elite colleges and universities in the United States do not accept them simply because of their race. The schools, on the other hand, deny that racism plays a part in their admissions policies. The following are some feelings and explanations of both sides:

The universities:

1. Asian-American students are often (a.) _____ to accept the fact that American universities have different standards of admission from those of Asian schools. When the students (b.) _____ by the school of their choice, they may have trouble (c.) _____ why.

2. Admissions officers say that they receive a (a.) _____ of applications, many of which (b.) _____ them a great deal. They say that they (c.) _____ each application and, while (d.) _____ with federal guidelines concerning racism, try to compose a freshman class with that characteristic which is (e.) _____ by American universities—diversity. They add that the (f.) _____ of applications by Asian Americans in the past decade makes admissions more competitive for everyone.

The students:

3. Asian-American students feel that the universities have not (a.) _____ themselves to the fact that, although the students have Chinese surnames, they are Americans and only wanted to be treated as such. They feel that the admissions requirements are (b.) _____

and can be used by the schools to protect themselves. According to Asian Americans, saying that these students tend (c.) _____ in certain majors is stereotyping them.

Focus on Form: Noun Clauses

"We . . . are pretty impressed with Asian-American candidates, and we can't figure out *why people think we're not*."

A clause is a group of words that has a subject and a complete verb. A noun clause (. . . *why people think we're not*):

- is a clause that can function like a noun.
- cannot stand alone in a sentence.

There are three types of noun clauses:

1. *That* noun clauses—often derived from a statement.

That + Subject + Verb

It is interesting *that many Asian Americans do well in school.* (OR *That many Asian Americans do well in school* is interesting.) (**Statement:** Many Asian Americans do very well in school.)

2. *Wh-question* noun clauses—often derived from an information question.

Wh-word + Subject + Verb

Where the school districts will find the money for these programs is a problem. (**Information Question:** Where will the school districts find the money?)

3. *Yes-No question* noun clauses—often derived from *Yes/No* questions.

Whether (or not) + Subject + Verb

(*If* may be used in place of *whether* when the noun clause is not first in the sentence. *If* may not be directly followed by "or not." The "or not" is optional.)

Whether (or not) bilingual education is better than other programs for non-native speakers is unclear.

It is unclear *if (whether) bilingual education is better than other programs.* (**Yes/No Question:** Is bilingual education better than other programs?)

Grammar Practice

Change the following statements and questions to sentences with noun clauses. Use the information in parentheses to complete the sentence. If there is more than one way, give both.

1. The rising rate of immigration to the United States will bring new challenges for our school systems. (This is apparent.)

2. How should we teach children from so many different language backgrounds in one classroom? (No one knows for sure.)

3. Can affirmative action undo past discrimination? (This is the question being debated.)

4. Many immigrants put their hopes for their children in education. (This is not surprising.)

5. Will the school of their choice accept them? (Students are naturally worried about this.)

6. Why are American schools so interested in extracurricular activities? (I don't understand this.)

7. Do American universities put a quota on the number of international students they accept? (I wonder.)

8. How long does it take to find out if you are accepted to a university? (I have no idea.)

Focus on Form: Functions of Noun Clauses

A noun clause is a clause that acts or functions like a noun. Remember:
- a noun can be the subject of a sentence, the object of a verb, the object of a preposition, a subject complement (after the verb *to be*), or an object complement.
- a noun clause fulfills these same functions. It can also be the complement of an adjective.

Grammar Practice

Underline the noun clauses in the following sentences.

1. *Subject of the Sentence*

   a. What many Asian Americans wonder is why the universities don't just look at their records.

b. That a person's admission to college may depend on club activities amazes me.

2. *Object of a Verb*

Then they'd know how hard it is for us sometimes.

3. *Object of a Preposition (that* noun clauses cannot come directly after a preposition. They must be preceded by "the fact.")

   a. He is worried about the fact that a TOEFL score of 600 is required.
   b. Only after students who come from homes where English is not spoken learn the very basics will they move on to just what an ice cube might be.

4. *Subject Complement* (After the verb *to be*)

The question is whether students can learn academic subjects if they have not mastered the basics of English.

5. *Adjective Complement*

It is obvious that something must be done about our schools.

6. *Object Complement*

The admissions officer told the student what he wanted to hear.

Grammar Practice

Read the following sentences. Then, using this information, write sentences containing noun clauses in the spaces below. (This information comes from an article titled "Foreign Students Under Fire." After this exercise you will read the article.)

a. The Massachusetts legislature passed a bill in 1988 which raised the tuition of foreign undergraduate students in public colleges.

b. Massachusetts is not the only state to have raised tuition for foreign students.

c. In 1988, 41 percent of the doctoral degrees in engineering awarded in the United States were awarded to foreign students.

d. Foreign students account for less than three percent of the total college population of the United States.

e. Some Americans have fears about the foreign graduates.

f. A large number of the foreign **students** in the United States do not receive any money from the colleges.

g. Foreign students bring benefits to **the** economy of the United States and to the graduate programs of many universities.

h. Some foreign students encounter resentment from Americans.

i.   We are hurting ourselves by keeping foreign students out of our universities.

j.   Americans tend to go directly into the job market with only a B.A. degree.

k.   Foreigners tend to be motivated by goals which are different from those of Americans.

l.   Are foreign students taking the place of Americans in graduate school?

(In this exercise, all of the examples are based on the sentence "Americans tend to go directly into the job market with only a B.A. degree." Use information from different sentences for each of your examples. You do not have to use the exact words of these sentences. Just use the ideas. For variety, try not to use the same words as the ones in parentheses.)

1.   *Noun Clause as Subject*

   Example: That Americans tend to go directly into the job market with only a B.A. degree (surprises me).

   a.
   b.

2.   *Noun Clause as Object of Verb*

   Example: (I wonder) why Americans tend to go directly into the job market with only a B.A. degree.

   a.
   b.

3.   *Noun Clause as Object of Preposition*

   Example: I'm (interested in) why Americans don't tend to go to graduate school.

   a.
   b.

4.   *Noun Clause as Subject Complement*

   Example: (The question) is why they don't go to graduate school before starting to work.

   a.
   b.

5.   *Noun Clause as Adjective Complement*

   Example: It's (surprising) that Americans tend to go directly into the job market with only a B.A. degree.

   a.
   b.

Reading 3: "Foreign Students Under Fire"

Prereading Questions

1. The expression "under fire" means "being criticized" or "being blamed" for something. Why might foreign students in the United States be under fire?

2. What are some possible benefits of foreign or international students studying in American universities? These can be benefits to the students, to the universities or to the United States.

3. Why might some American citizens, rightfully or wrongly, resent the fact that many foreign students are studying in the United States?

4. If you are studying in an American college or university, have you personally felt any positive or negative feelings towards you because of this?

Foreign Students Under Fire

By JAMES N. BAKER with RENEE MICHAEL, TOM SCHMITZ, and JOANNE HARRISON
(from *Newsweek* magazine)

Resentment rises as more come to the U.S.

Massachusetts likes to call its capital city the "cradle of liberty"[25] and compare it to ancient Athens. But these images of enlightenment[26] have come under challenge in Boston's gold-domed Statehouse. The number of foreign students coming into Massachusetts, state Rep. Roger Tougas said, has "gotten out of hand."[27] He argued that the students have been "poshly[28] subsidized[29] by tax dollars," even if they were from countries associated with terrorism. To discourage foreign students, Tougas introduced legislation to raise their tuition at public colleges. His bill passed easily, and Gov. Michael Dukakis signed it into law last June. Starting in 1988, foreign undergraduates have to pay as much as 38 percent more than American youngsters from out of state. "Foreign students are not productive citizens," said Tougas. "If they are going to reap the benefits, I just want them to pay for it."

Scattered episodes—large and small—indicate that resentment of foreign students is also rising around the country. Louisiana increased tuitions this year, and Tougas says he's gotten inquiries[30] from legislators in other states. An embarrassing incident took place at the University of Rochester in up-

25. where liberty began. A cradle is a baby's bed
26. period or time of knowledge; freedom from beliefs which have no basis in fact   27. out of control   28. extravagantly; in luxury   29. to give financial assistance, usually from a government to a person or institution

30. questions

state New York. Because the university's graduate business school had accepted a Japanese employee of Fuji Photo Film, Inc., the Eastman Kodak Co., fearful of corporate spying at its Rochester headquarters, threatened to withdraw the 230 students it provided yearly to various programs at the school. The school caved in[31] and rescinded[32] the young man's acceptance, but last month, after a public outcry, invited him back. (He had already enrolled at the Massachusetts Institute of Technology.)

Five years ago, when the number of foreign students hit 300,000, concerned college administrators predicted a backlash[33] of quotas, prohibitive tuition hikes,[34] and growing xenophobia.[35] The resentment has been building gradually, though foreigners account for less than 3 percent of the total college population. Fears that foreign graduates will snatch away[36] good jobs from Americans—particularly engineers whose profession draws the most foreigners—persist despite evidence to the contrary. The Immigration and Naturalization Service says the majority of foreign students return home, and the Department of Labor reports that non-Americans constitute only 4 percent of the country's engineering work force.

Statistics also show that the 343,777 foreign students now in the United States—two-thirds of whom pay their own way—are a good national investment. Not only do they pump[37] $2 to $3 billion into the economy every year, they bring distinction to second-rate colleges, keep graduate programs afloat,[38] and contribute to U.S. technology. Making foreign students welcome has always been a source of good will. Under the

best of circumstances, the policy makes life-long, sometimes influential, friends for the United States—for example, both Corazon Aquino and Zachary Onyonka, Kenya's foreign minister, graduated from U.S. colleges. Proponents of an open-door policy expect the same not only from the Malaysians and Taiwanese who are here in large numbers now, but also from the students from oil-rich Iran and Nigeria who flocked[39] here in the early 1980s.

Why then do foreign students encounter resentment from Americans? Perhaps it's because they're highly visible in certain disciplines. They earn from 27 to 41 percent of the doctorate degrees awarded in engineering, life sciences, architecture, computer science, and mathematics. Some schools have consciously set out to lure[40] talent from overseas to enhance[41] the reputation of their graduate programs. The University of Southwestern Louisiana in Lafayette, for example, built an $8 million computer system for studying factory automation—the only one of its kind on an American college campus—knowing it would attract the best minds in the world to study computer science there.

Bachelor's degree. Still, foreign students are not supplanting[42] Americans in graduate schools; they're filling empty spaces. Americans simply aren't going to graduate schools anymore. At Syracuse University, where foreigners account for 70 percent of the graduate engineering enrollment, dean Theodore Bickart admits, "Quite frankly, they are sustaining our higher education." Eager to make money, Americans tend to rush into the marketplace armed with only a bachelor's degree. "Financially, it was foolish of me to carry on," says Texan Michael Schuh, a Ph.D candidate in mechanical engineering at the University of California, Berkeley. "Someone who's been working for as long as I've been

---

31. to give in; accept without protest 32. to void; to abolish something that had already been given 33. a strong reaction against a political, legal, or social practice 34. increase 35. unwarranted fear of foreigners, strangers, or outsiders 36. to grab or grasp quickly; to steal 37. to give a lot of money to 38. literally "floating"; to keep financially stable

---

39. to travel in large numbers 40. to attract or tempt with promise of an award or prize 41. to make better in cost, value, or reputation 42. to take the place of; replace

in grad school will be making the same money." More patient foreigners tend to be motivated by other goals. Schuh's classmate Ching Bin Liaw of Taiwan says, "In Chinese society, a higher degree means people respect you, and your family will be proud."

As the debate about foreign students heats up, educators, professionals and legislators offer controversial—and often contradictory—images for the 1990s. Some imagine university faculties clogged[43] with foreigners; others envision important scientific research left undone because all the Ph.D.'s went home after all. The problem boils down[44] to the absence of qualified Americans, a situation that can be remedied only over time by

recruiting bright students for careers in scientific fields. "We're shooting ourselves in the foot if we send foreigners home," says Robert Weatherall, job-placement director at MIT. "It's because of them we're not further behind." His point is hard to dispute. Imagine what might have happened if we'd booted out[45] Chinese-born Paul Chu in 1968, right after he received his Ph.D. in physics from the University of California, San Diego. Earlier this year Chu stunned the world when he used yttrium to make a high-temperature superconductor. The news may have reached the Massachusetts Statehouse: last week a legislative committee recommended repealing[46] last summer's tuition hike.

---

43. to block   44. to summarize or reduce to the basic reason

45. to throw out or expel   46. to change a law or other official act that had already been enacted

Comprehension and Discussion

A. *Circle the correct answer. If the statement is false, tell why.*

1. Americans who are not residents of Massachusetts pay higher tuition in public colleges than residents of the state do.

   True   False

2. Foreigners who are residents of Massachusetts would have to pay more tuition under this new law.

   True   False

3. The lack of Americans who are willing and/or able to study in scientific fields is one of the reasons why there are many foreign students in these fields in American universities.

   True   False

4. This article is generally favorable towards foreign students in American colleges and universities.

   True   False

B. *Answer the following questions as completely as possible.*

1. What are the possible arguments, based on fact or not, for charging foreign students higher tuition rates or even for limiting their numbers in American universities? Explain each one as thoroughly as possible. If the article is not specific about these arguments, you may have to make inferences. Give at least four arguments.

2. What are the arguments in favor of having foreign students in American universities?

3. In your own words, explain the difference between the motivations of American students and foreign students and how this affects the ratio of American to foreign students in graduate programs in the United States.

4. If foreign students account for only three percent of the total population of students in the United States, why is resentment against them growing?

5. Are there many foreign students in the universities in your country? If so, where do they come from? What do they usually study? Is the tuition for them the same as the tuition for citizens of your country?

6. Most public colleges in the United States have low tuition because they are supported by state taxes. Students from out of state, whether American citizens or not, usually have to pay higher tuition at a state school than residents of that state. Should foreign students, therefore, pay even more tuition since they or their families do not pay taxes in any state? Support your answer.

   (**Note:** The charging of higher tuition for international students has not been implemented in the state of Massachusetts.)

Vocabulary Building

A. *Look at the following sentences from the readings.*

"..The notice to the parents was translated into five languages. That was a nice gesture, but *insufficient*."

"...their admissions policy had had *unfair* impact on Asian-American students."

The prefixes in- *and* un- *are ways of giving the opposite or negative idea of an adjective or its other forms. Other ways are with the prefixes* il-, *and* ir-.

il- *with (many) words that begin with the letter "l"* —*illegal, illiterate*

ir- *with (many) words that begin with the letter "r"* —*irregular, irrelevant*

Unfortunately, with un- *and* in-, *there are no rules which tell us when to use one or the other.*

B. *Look at the following list of words and, working in groups of two to four, decide whether to use* un-, in-, il-, *or* ir- *for each one. (Remember that* in- *changes to* im- *before "m," "p," or "b.") Discuss the meanings with your group members and then with your teacher.*

1.   able   _____

2.   fertile   _____

3.   possible   _____

4.   employed   _____

5.   appropriate   _____

6.   moral   _____

7.   sanitary   _____

8.   official   _____

9.   prudent   _____

10.   principled   _____

11.   trustworthy   _____

12.   licit   _____

13.   reliable   _____

14.   conceivable   _____

15.   comprehensible   _____

16.   determined   _____

17.   determinate   _____

18.   deniable   _____

19.   definable   _____

20.   decisive   _____

21.   decided   _____

22.   lucky   _____

23.   foreseen   _____

24.   legible   _____

25.   questionable   _____

26.   excusable   _____

27.   explicable   _____

28.   lawful   _____

29.   perceptible   _____

30.   premeditated   _____

31.   manly   _____

32.   movable   _____

C. *How may other adjectives you can come up with that begin with* un-, in-, *or* im-?
*Only choose words which have a corresponding positive form. For example, the
adjective "immaculate," which means "pure," begins with* im-, *but it is not a
negative form. There is no corresponding positive form.*

Focus on Form: Some Uses of Noun Clauses

1. Noun clauses are commonly used to show emotion, emphasis, or
interest.

> *What amazes me* is the number of international students in
> engineering programs.

> *What I find interesting* is *how international students can do so
> well in courses given in a foreign language.*

(Note that the second sentence contains two noun clauses, one as the
subject of the sentence and the other as the subject complement.

Some commonly used verbs in noun clauses to show emphasis, emotion, or interest are:

amazes	annoys	astonishes	bothers
fascinates	frightens	interests	irritates
puzzles	scares	worries	

> What *frightens* me is the backlash against foreign students.

dislike	enjoy	find (fascinating, surprising, etc.)
hate	like	love

> What I *enjoy* is a plate of Mexican food.

can't	believe
	condone
	forgive
	understand

> What I *can't condone* is war.

2. Noun clauses are used in indirect questions. The use of an indirect question can make the question softer, more polite.

> **Direct Question**—Why do some Americans resent foreign students?
> **Indirect Question**—Do you have any idea . . . ?
> **Direct Question**—Is the admissions officer in?
> **Indirect Question**—Can you tell me . . . ?

Some common introductions for indirect questions are:

do you know	would you happen to know
do you have any idea	would you have any idea
can you tell me	would you mind telling me
would you mind if I asked	I wonder

Grammar Practice

Complete the following sentences using noun clauses. Use any of the information from the articles in this chapter or questions you may have about education. Change the words to fit your feelings. For example, in number 4 you might want to say "irritating" instead of "fascinating." After you have finished the sentences, discuss the content of them with the class.

1. I don't understand . . .

2. I'm very (interested in) . . .

3. . . . is (apparent) to me.

4. It is (fascinating) . . .

5. What (annoys) me is . . .

6. I find it (unusual) . . .

7. What . . .

8. That . . .

9. Why . . .

10. . . .

Grammar Practice

Ask your teacher any questions you may have about education in the United States. Use indirect questions. You may also ask other students in the class about education and admission requirements in their countries.

Class Project

Work on one or more of these projects individually or in groups of two to three students. Then present your findings to the class.

1. Investigate the admission requirements in the school which you are attending or which you would like to attend. What scores are required? Are extracurricular activities important? If so, is an exception made for an international student from a country where such activities are not important or are unavailable? If possible, obtain an appointment to interview an admissions officer. If not, look at the school's catalogue. Report your findings to the class.

2. Make a presentation to the class about the system of education in your country. Compare it to the system of education in the United States. How are they alike; how are they different? What are the advantages and disadvantages of both?

Discussion and Writing

Discuss the following topics, first in pairs or small groups and then with the teacher and the entire class. After your discussion, pick one (or more) of the topics and write an essay about it.

1. What is the purpose of a college education? Is it to broaden the students, make them better citizens of their country and of the world or is it to prepare them for a good job and a good living?

2. Although not all students may get into the college of their choice, the United States has one of the highest rates in the world of students who enter college after high school. In some other countries, admission to college is much more competitive, and the percentage of high school graduates who go on for higher education is much lower. What are the advantages and disadvantages of both systems?

3. Discuss the issue of "student diversity" in college admissions. Should colleges and universities take ethnicity, race, geography (what part of the United States a student comes from, so as not to have too many east or west coast people, too many big city people, etc.), for example, into account in order to have a more diverse student body?

4. If you are not an immigrant and if you plan to study for an academic or professional degree in the United States, explain why. Why didn't you study in your own country? What advantages do you think an American education will give you? If you plan to return to your country after your education, what effect do you think having an American degree will have?

5. What are the benefits and the problems of bilingual education?

6. Discuss admission standards of universities in your country. What would you change about these requirements if you could?

7. Some people believe that a college education should be open to everyone, that anyone who graduates from high school should have the right to attend college. Discuss "open admissions," its benefits and its possible problems.

8. Discuss the issue of foreign students in American colleges and universities. Should there be limits placed on the number of foreign students allowed to enroll? Should foreign students be required to pay higher tuition in public colleges?

Word List

Below is a list of the new words and their different forms, presented in this chapter.

Noun	Verb	Adjective	Adverb
advocacy	advocate		
advocate			
	cherish		
cluster	cluster		
compliance	comply	compliant	compliantly
deluge	deluge		
enrichment	enrich		
euphemism		euphemistic	euphemistically
feasibility		feasible	feasibly
	figure out		
handle	handle		
immunity			
immunization	immunize	immune	
impressiveness	impress	impressive	impressively
murkiness		murky	
nurture	nurture	nurturing	
pose	pose		
proficiency		proficient	proficiently
reconciliation	reconcile		
reluctance		reluctant	reluctantly
scrutiny	scrutinize		
	turn down		
upsurge	surge		

The American Character

Reading 1: "Busybodies: New Puritans"

Prereading Questions

1. A busybody is a person who minds other people's business, who has too much interest in other people's lives. From what you have seen or heard of the American people, do you think they are "busybodies" or do you think they basically respect other people's privacy?

adj. puritanical

2. What do you know about the Puritans? Brainstorm with a group of three or four students. List as many adjectives as possible which you think would describe Puritans. How many of these adjectives do you think would apply to present-day Americans?

3. What rights does an employer or the government have in determining what a person can or cannot do? In groups of three or four, look at the following statements and tell whether you agree or disagree with them. Try to come to a consensus or an agreement for each one. Be prepared to explain why you agree or disagree. You may basically agree or disagree with a statement but offer exceptions.

   a. A company sometimes has the right to tell its employees what they can do, or how they should live on their own time.
   b. Expression of ideas which are intolerant of others can be repressed for the good of the society.
   c. It is reasonable not to buy the products of a company because of the political views of the owners.

boycott

   d. The government has the right to limit or control personal behavior if it affects the environment.
   e. A company can require female employees to wear makeup.

Vocabulary Practice

Circle the correct synonym or definition for each of the italicized words in the sentences below. Use the context of the sentences to help you guess the meaning.

1. The United States is also the home of dedicated neo-Puritans, humorlessly imposing on others *arbitrary* (meaning their own) standards of behavior, health, and thought.

   a. very harsh or strict
   b. determined by personal opinion, not fact
   c. legal

neo-
(new)

2. Civil libertarians *concede* that companies have a right, not to mention a moral obligation to shareholders, to protect themselves from ruinous medical bills.

   a. strongly disagree; deny
   b. reluctantly agree; admit
   c. hope

3. If society requires corporations to pay for most of workers' health-care costs, society cannot object if those companies *intrude* on employee life-styles.

   a. go where one is not wanted, without invitation
   b. like; strongly favor
   c. are not interested in

4. How can a corporation demand that an employee *refrain* from smoking away from work?

   a. allow oneself to
   b. repeat
   c. keep oneself from

5. Most Americans appear to *endorse* the view that the only thing that should be considered is job performance. According to a poll by the National Consumers League, 81 percent of Americans believe an employer has no right to refuse to hire an overweight worker.

   a. approve; support
   b. criticize; deny
   c. motivate; push

6. One useless and unenforceable regulation is the one that *bars* flu sufferers from going out in public.

   a. punishes
   b. places where people drink
   c. prohibits

7. The Wall Street Journal reported last week that a woman was arrested, handcuffed, and forced to spend six hours in jail on Easter Sunday. The woman, who had no previous police record, was *apprehended* picking flowers from an office park for her grandmother's grave.

   a. arrested; seized
   b. seen; discovered
   c. worried about

8. Their efforts have received a great deal of publicity but they remain, in many cases, *undaunted*.

   a. afraid
   b. unknown
   c. not discouraged

9. You're talking about something a person did, something he certainly has a right to do, and something that a public institution should certainly not *penalize* people for.

   a. award
   b. punish
   c. ignore

10. In both spiritual and *secular* appearance, intolerance has been a recurring theme in U.S. history.

    a. of the church
    b. about sex
    c. not of the church

11. Surprisingly, the censors and the neo-Puritans belong to two *disparate* groups. One group is working-class in origin and feels that its status is being threatened by differing life-styles. The other consists of cause-oriented activists, such as animal rightists and environmentalists.

    a. very similar
    b. completely different
    c. separate

[handwritten: or /er/ an /ian   people]

Busybodies: New Puritans

By JOHN ELSON   (from *Time* magazine)

Repent! The hour of the meddlers[1] is at hand![2] *[handwritten: right now]* **And they are putting other Americans' views, behavior and even jobs at increasing risk.**

[1] Consider, for a moment, these twin signs of our scrambled[3] times:

• In Los Angeles, Jesse Mercado was dismissed from his job as a security guard at the *Times* despite an excellent performance record. The reason? Mercado was overweight.

• In Wabash, Ind., Janice Bone lost her job as an assistant payroll clerk at the Ford Meter Box Co. The reason? The firm, which will not let its employees smoke either on the job or at home, insisted that she take a urine test, which proved positive for nicotine.

[2] Welcome, readers, to the prying[4] side of America in the 1990s. The U.S. may still be the land of the free, but increasingly it is also the home of dedicated neo-Puritans, humorlessly imposing on others arbitrary (meaning their own) standards of behavior, health, and thought. To a number of concerned observers, the busybodies—conformity seekers, legal nitpickers[5] and politically correct thought police—seem to have lost sight of a bedrock[6] American virtue: tolerance, allowing others, in the name of freedom, to do things one disagrees with or does not like, provided they do no outright harm to others.

[3] "There should be limits to what we are prepared to tolerate," says president Ste-

---

1. people who interfere in other people's business 2. near; soon 3. mixed up 4. looking closely into other's affairs

5. one who is concerned with small, often insignificant details 6. foundation; basic principle

phen Balch of the National Association of Scholars, based in Princeton, N.J., which is dedicated to fighting lockstep[7] leftism in academia. "But in a free society where people
35 are going to get along, those limits have to be pretty wide." Balch is concerned that the very definition of tolerance is changing: more and more people see it as "requiring others to do the kinds of things that they consider
40 enlightened." On many campuses, the prevailing standard these days would appear to be that of Marxist philosopher Herbert Marcuse, a guru[8] for many flower-power[9] youths during the rebellious '60s. In his
45 dense treatise, *One-Dimensional Man,* Marcuse argued that tolerance for the expression of intolerant attitudes, like racial discrimination, should be repressed for society's good.
50 One key battleground in the tolerance war is life-style. These days, smoking, drinking or noshing[10] on high-cholesterol snacks isn't just a health risk. It can endanger your job as well. Concerned about the ever rising
55 (about 15% annually) cost of health insurance, at least 6,000 U.S. companies, including Atlanta-based Turner Broadcasting, refuse to hire smokers, and in some cases fire those who don't beat the habit, even
60 when it is only practiced off the job. For similar insurance reasons, corporate discrimination against the overweight is so widespread that some of the obese have formed a lobbying group called the National Associa-
65 tion to Advance Fat Acceptance.

Meanwhile, corporate busybodies are ingeniously finding new things to ban—all in the interest, naturally, of slimming health-care costs. One company in Pennsylvania,
70 according to the American Civil Liberties Union, has barred its managers from riding motorcycles: too risky. A Georgia firm has warned its employees to stay away from such life-threatening activities as cliff climbing and
75 surfing.

Civil libertarians concede that companies have a right, not to mention a moral obligation to shareholders, to protect themselves from ruinous medical bills. But some
80 critics argue that the punitive[11] firings of Mercado and Bone represent a throwback[12] to the early 1900s, when spies from the Ford Motor Co.'s notorious Sociological Department invaded autoworkers' homes to search
85 for forbidden booze[13] or unmarried live-ins. (Ford's Big Brother[14] approach was intended partly to protect its employees from Detroit's legions[15] of prostitutes and grifters,[16] who preyed[17] on the kind of ill-educated new im-
90 migrants who often worked on the assembly lines.)

A counterargument is that if society requires corporations to pay for most of workers' health-care costs, society cannot object
95 if those companies intrude on employee lifestyles. But as Lewis Maltby of the A.C.L.U.[18] notes, the question then becomes, Where do you draw the line?[19] It is generally legal for a company to declare its workplace a smoke-
100 free environment and to punish violators. How, though, can a corporation or government agency demand that employees like Bone refrain from lighting up away from work, especially since smoking itself is not a
105 crime? High cholesterol levels can lead to heart disease and other health problems. But what right does an employer have to demand that a worker refrain from eating fried chicken or ice cream?

7. without thought; just following an ideology
8. spiritual leader and teacher 9. slogan of the hippies in the 60s—use of peaceful methods
10. eating snacks

11. punishing 12. going back to an former characteristic; a regression 13. alcoholic drinks 14. a reference to the name used for the dictatorial government in George Orwell's *1984*
15. large numbers (of people) 16. swindlers; people who make money by cheating others
17. to hunt and cause great trouble for; victimize 18. private legal organization dedicated to protecting civil liberties and constitutional rights 19. How far can you go? Where will it end?

"The only thing that should be considered is job performance," says law professor Irwin Schmerinsky of the University of Southern California. "If the courts allow firms to make decisions on potential costs, it's hard to know where the restrictions will end." Most Americans appear to endorse that view. According to a poll by the National Consumers League, 81% of Americans believe an employer has no right to refuse to hire an overweight person and 76% feel companies should not be allowed to ban smoking off the job.

The nation's lawmakers are beginning to listen: 19 states, including New Jersey, Colorado and Oregon, have passed some form of legislation that bars employers from discriminating against workers because of their lifestyle. (Despite Indiana's new smoker-protection law, Bone has not got her former job back, and has filed a claim against the company. Overweight Mercado sued, won, and got a judgment of more than $500,000, plus a return to his old post.)

[. . .]

More than anyone else except the French, Americans have been infected by the delusion that strict laws are necessary to protect people from themselves. The nation's statute books are crammed with[20] millions of useless and largely unenforceable regulations, like the one in Seattle that bars flu sufferers from going out in public. Most of the rules are ignored, but their existence is a constant source of inspiration to the puritanically minded.

Yet perhaps out of frustration that serious crime seems to be leaping out of control, some guardians of the law have taken to enforcing these juridical[21] minutiae[22] with singular determination. Consider Cobb County, Ga., where serious crimes like robbery have increased since 1990. The *Wall Street Journal* reported last week that Re-

becca Anding of Marietta was arrested, handcuffed and forced to spend six hours in jail on Easter Sunday. Anding, who had no previous criminal record, was apprehended picking tulips from an office park to place on her grandmother's grave. Another Marietta resident, Linda Judson, spent four hours in jail in May after she was apprehended for failing to return two overdue rental tapes to a local video store.

Finally, of course there are the academic enforcers of political correctness, or "p.c.,"[23] whose efforts have received widespread publicity but who remain, in many cases, undaunted.

[. . .]

Hardly a week goes by without some new example of attempts to enforce conformity on campus. At the California State University at Northridge, an offer by the Carl's Jr. fast-food chain to install a branch in the newly expanded bookstore was rejected last May. The reason was not the quality or price of the chow[24] but student and faculty objections to the conservative views of the chain's owner, Carl Karcher, who financially supports antiabortion groups such as the National Right to Life Action League. To Stephen Balch, Northridge's decision was outrageously intolerant. "You're not talking about Karcher doing anything on campus," he says. "You're not even talking about anything the fast-food chain did as a corporation. You're talking about something its owner did, certainly something he has a right to do, and something that a public institution should certainly not penalize people for."

The weary truth is that busybodyness is, as black radical H. Rap Brown once said of violence, as American as cherry pie. The Puritans, who began it all, had "a desperate and intolerant wish to cleanse the world of

---

20. filled or stuffed with
21. having to do with the law or the legal system
22. trivial, unimportant details

23. social or political statements or actions which are in accord with or are not offensive to women, social, ethnic, religious or racial minority groups, the handicapped, ecologists, etc.   24. food (slang)

its "impurities," editor Lewis Lapham of *Harper's* has written, and their ambition was to build a New Jerusalem on earth despite all of life's uncertainties. In both spiritual and secular guise,[25] that has been a recurring theme in U.S. history, from the Great Awakening of the early frontier days to the noble experiment of Prohibition.

To sociologist James Jasper of New York University, today's would-be[26] censors and neo-Puritans belong to two disparate groups. One consists of those, frequently working class in origin, who feel their status threatened by differing life-styles—hence their hostility to drugs and casual sex and their sympathy for the goals of decency-obsessed media baiters[27] like the Rev. Donald Wildmon[28] or Senator Jesse Helms.[29] The other group, Jasper says, consists of cause-oriented activists, such as animal rightists and environmentalists, who are intent on making people think about the consequences of letting endangered species die out or contaminating the atmosphere with hair spray.

Both groups have contributed to what sociologist Jack Douglas of the University of California at San Diego calls "a degree of self-centered moralism that is unprecedented in American history." Douglas worries whether the pendulum[30] will ever swing back the other way. Among other things, he notes, the new forms of personal intolerance occur at a time when the common bonds of U.S. society—our shared values, our political understandings—seem weaker than ever. "Maybe," he glooms, "America is too large and diverse to be one country under democracy any longer."

Even those who reject Douglas' perspective might reasonably conclude that the long war against the busybodies has to be won—if it is to be won—a skirmish at a time, tiny battles at the perimeter of individual privacy and choice. One hero in this ongoing conflict is Teresa Fischette, 38, a ticket agent for Continental Airlines at Boston's Logan International Airport. Eager to establish a new image for its ground personnel, the carrier last May decreed that its female ticket agents must wear makeup. Fischette refused, was fired, but was then offered a job where she would not be in contact with customers. No way: Fischette filed suit. With the case gaining national publicity, Continental gave Fischette her job back (with back pay) and shaded back[31] its new cosmetics code to a guideline.

No hard feelings, Continental. But we say, Hats off to her!

---

31. cut back or reduced

---

25. appearance (usually meant to deceive) 26. wanting to be   27. one who attacks the media with criticism, insults, etc.   28. conservative Protestant minister who has led a campaign against what he considers to be pornography   29. conservative Republican U.S. senator from North Carolina   30. the part of a clock that swings back and forth to regulate the time. Will the pendulum ever swing back the other way? = Will public opinion change and go the other way?

Comprehension and Discussion

A. *Circle the correct answer. If the answer is false, tell why.*

1. One the basic principles of the United States is allowing people to do things that we disagree with as long as nobody is hurt.

   True   False

2. Civil libertarians say that although companies have a right and a duty to protect their financial standing, if we start intruding on people's private lives, we do not know where it will end.

   True   False

3. The student and faculty rejection of the installment of a fast-food chain on a California campus because of the political views of the owner is an example of "political correctness."

   True   (False)

4. The writer of this article feels that "busybodyness" is a new characteristic of the 1990s.

   True   (False)

5. The great diversity of American society today may contribute to this new form of intolerance because we have fewer shared values.

   (True)   False

B. *Answer the following questions as completely as possible.*

1. Stephen Balch, of the National Association of Scholars, says that the definition of tolerance is changing, that people see it as "requiring others to do the kinds of things that they consider enlightened." What do you think he means by this? What examples of this type of thinking are given in this article?

2. Do you feel that any of the examples given in the article are not examples of "busybodyness" but are necessary actions for a just, efficient society? In other words, do you agree completely with the writer's examples as support for his thesis or not? Either way, support your stand.

3. The "busybodies" are put into three major categories. What examples are given for each category? Some examples may overlap into different categories. Explain each in your own words.

   a. conformity seekers
   b. legal nitpickers
   c. politically-correct thought police

4. Can you think of any examples in your country of what the writer would consider "busybodyness"? Which of the writer's categories ("conformity seekers, legal nitpickers, and politically correct thought police") would they fall into?

5. Explain the difference between the two major groups of "neo-Puritans." Why is a point made of these two groups?

6. One person quoted in the article says, "There should be limits to what we are prepared to tolerate. But in a free society where people are going to get along, those limits have to be pretty wide." What, in your opinion, are those limits? Where does one draw the line as to what is tolerated and what is not? Be as specific as possible.

7. What characteristics of American society do you feel are shown by this article? Are these characteristics positive, negative, or neutral for you? Look at the following list and explain if and how these characteristics are shown in the article. You may add any other characteristics which you feel are represented by the article or the information in it.

puritanical	permissive
self-critical	self-contented
conservative	liberal
open-minded	close-minded
sophisticated	unsophisticated

Word Forms

Working with a partner, complete the following chart with the different forms of the words. Use your knowledge of other words and their different forms to help you. Do not be afraid to guess. A dash means there is no form.

Noun	Verb	Adjective	Adverb
	apprehend	—	—
	—	arbitrary	
	concede	—	—
	endorse	—	—
	intrude		
	penalize	—	—

Vocabulary Practice

Complete the sentences below with the correct words from the following list. You may have to use different word forms and tenses. Do not use a word more than once. Try to do this without looking back at the definitions.

arbitrary	concede	intrude	refrain
endorse	penalize	bar	apprehend
undaunted	disparate	secular	

1. In 1620, when the Puritans arrived in what is now the state of Massachusetts, they found a cold, harsh wilderness. However, (a. not discouraged) _undaunted_, they stayed and established the Massachusetts Bay Colony. Although they came to this country for religious freedom, the society they created was far from (b. non-religious) _secular_. Their laws were not (c. on personal opinion, without basis on fact) _arbitrary_ decided
   rally

but were based on the Bible. For example, on the Sabbath, the day of rest, people were (d. prohibited) _____ ~~barred~~ _____ from working. They also had to (e. keep themselves) _____ refrain _____ from dancing, playing cards, smoking or enjoying music on Sundays. Anyone who was (f. seized) _____ apprehended _____ breaking any of the laws was severely (g. punished) _____ penalized _____. Although many political freedoms were granted, any deviation from the Puritan way was not accepted.

2. Because of its Puritanical history and also because of its Bill of Rights, which defines the rights of the people, the United States is often seen as containing two completely (a. different) _____ disparate _____ societies, as being both puritanical and permissive. For example, although conservatives might (b. reluctantly agree) _____ concede _____ that we have the right to read or see whatever we want, they might draw the line at pornography. Liberals, on the other hand, would see this as (c. going without invitation) an _____ intrude _____ into one's privacy. The problem that many politicians have is that nobody wants to be seen as (d. supporting) _____ endorsing _____ censorship or pornography.

     (r) intrusion   stop

Focus on Form: Modal Perfects

May/Might Have, Must Have, Could Have, and Should Have

The first example in the article "Busybodies: New Puritans" is about Jesse Mercado, the security guard who lost his job because he was overweight. We do not know very much about him or his situation, but let's imagine the following:

1. *should have been*
    He was not given a second chance.

2. He did not try to lose weight. He did not diet or exercise.   *He could have*

3. *could*
    We do not know what his weight was before he started working.

4. The company has a strict weight policy about the weight of its security guards.

5. We do not know why they were worried about his weight.

Read the sentences about Mr. Mercado. Remember that they all refer to the past. Decide which of the following meanings the sentences express and put the number before each group.

1. Possibility (One of many, and we do not know if it happened or not.)

2. Possibility (But we know it did not happen.)

3. Advice, unfulfilled obligation, or regret

4. Strong probability, assumption

A. I think they were wrong to fire Mr. Mercado.

_____ He had a good record. He *should have been given* another chance. They *shouldn't have fired* him.

B. Why do you think they were so worried about his weight?

_____ I don't know. They *might have been* afraid that he wouldn't be able to protect them because of his weight. They *may have thought* that he would have a heart attack if he had to run after someone.

C. Why do you think they hired him in the first place?

_____ He *must not have been* heavy when he first started working there. I think he had worked there for quite a while. They *must have liked* him or they wouldn't have kept him. He *must have been doing* a good job.

D. He knew that he was overweight and that there was a policy against it.

_____ He *could have tried* to lose weight. He *could have gone* on a diet. He *could have exercised*.

Modal Perfects

may		
might	**+ have + Past Participle *(-ed)* (Active)**	
must (not)	**+ have + been + Past Participle (Passive)**	
could	**+ have + been + Present Participle *(-ing)* (Continuous)**	
should		

Short statements or answers = **Modal + have.**

Modal + have been (When the main verb is *to be* or the passive is used.)

- **Possibility in the Past**—One of many. We do not know if it happened or not.

    May or Might (Not) Have + Past Participle

    They *might have been* afraid that he wouldn't be able to protect them because of his weight. It's a possibility. We don't know. He *might have been hoping* they would change the rules. **(Continuous)** (Had he *been* warned about his weight? I don't know. He *might have been.* = He *might have been warned* about his weight.)

- **Probability in the Past**—We are almost sure. We are making an assumption or a deduction from the facts we have.

Must (Not) Have + Past Participle

They *must have liked* him. We are not 100 percent sure, but we are making a strong guess or an assumption from what we know of the facts. (Did they like him? They *must have*. = *They must have liked him*.) (*Was* he well-liked? He *must have been*. = *He must have been well-liked*.)

- **Possibility in the Past that Did Not Happen**—One of many possibilities, but we know it did not happen.

Could Have + Past Participle

He *could have tried* to lose weight. He *could have gone* on a diet.

Could have is frequently used when there was a possibility but we know it did not happen. Here we know or we are assuming that he did not try. *Could have* is also sometimes used by native speakers like *may* or *might have* just to mean a past possibility. However, *may/might have* cannot be used for a possibility if we know it did not happen.

He didn't even try to lose weight. He *couldn't have been* too worried about his job. *Could not have* means "impossibility." We may be sure of this or it may be an assumption.

- **Past Obligation or Advice**—Something you did not (or did) do and you had an obligation to do (or not to do). An unfulfilled obligation. Regret or advice about a past action with which you disagreed.

Should Have + Past Participle

He *should have been given* another chance. = He wasn't.

They *shouldn't have fired* him. = They did.

I *should have tried* to lose weight. = I didn't.

Grammar Practice

Read the following situations. Using the verb in parentheses, complete the sentences with the correct modal perfect. If no verb is given, use the short form. You may have to use passive or continuous. In some sentences more than one modal may be possible. Be prepared to explain what your choice means. Read the entire situation before making a decision, and keep in mind the information from the reading.

1. Janice Bone lost her job because she smoked at home. Her company insisted that she take a urine test, which tested positive for nicotine. The article does not say why she had to take the test. It just (be) _____ a routine test, they (suspect) _____ that she smoked, or she (see) _____ smoking by a supervisor.

2. It is difficult to keep a secret in a small town or city. Everybody eventually knows everything. She (know) _____ that one day the company would find out that she smoked.

3. When she learned that she had been fired for smoking away from the workplace, she (be) _____ furious.

4. Indiana passed a smoker-protection law, but Bone didn't get her job back. She _____.

5. Teresa Fischette (agree) _____ to wear makeup, but she decided to fight the rule. The airlines (consider) _____ only _____ her job performance.

6. Mercado (surprise) _____ and (thrill) _____ by the court award of $500,000 as well as the return to his job. I wonder if he ever returned to the job after getting so much money. Who knows? He (neg.) _____. With so much money, he (decide) _____ to retire.

7. He (be, neg.) _____ overweight when he started working there because the company has strict rules about weight for its guards.

8. We usually think of police as taking care of important crime issues. The police who arrested the woman for not returning two overdue tapes (have, neg.) _____ too much to do if they were able to spend their time on such an unimportant issue.

9. The woman who was arrested for picking tulips from public property (do, neg.) _____ it. If everyone picked flowers from public property, there wouldn't be any flowers left. However, the police also (handcuff, neg.) _____ and (arrest) _____ her. They (give) _____ her a fine or even just (give) _____ her a lecture instead. Critics of this police action feel there are many other more important things they (do) _____ at the time instead of wasting time arresting a flower picker.

10. The people who worked for the Ford Motor Company in the early 1900s (hate) _____ it when the Sociological Department entered and searched their homes. Since they had no choice, they (feel) _____ like slaves instead of workers. Ford said it did this to protect the workers from bad outside influences. Perhaps this was true, but it (try) _____ also _____ just to force the workers to follow its own code of decency.

Focus on Form: *Must have* vs. *Had to*

The modal *must* can have two different meanings in the present: obligation (also expressed by *have to* or *have got to*) and probability.

> She was fired. She *must* be very upset. **(Probability)**

> I smoke too much. I really *must* quit. **(Obligation)**

Although the present forms of these words are the same, the past forms are different and often cause confusion.

	Present	**Past**
Probability	She *must be* very upset.	She *must have been* very upset. (She lost her job. We can assume she was upset.)
Obligation	I *must* quit smoking.	I *had to* quit smoking. (I had an obligation and I did it; a fulfilled or completed obligation.)

Grammar Practice

Complete the sentences with either must have (been) *or* had to. *Use the correct form of the verb in parentheses. If no verb is given, use the short form. Read the entire situation before making a decision.*

1. Did the company give Mercado his job back? Yes, they did. They _____had to_____. That's what the court ordered.

2. The Ford Motor Company workers (let) ___had to let___ the inspectors into their homes if they didn't want to be fired.

3. Ms. Fischette (be) __must have been__ very much against the idea of being told how she had to look if she was willing to fight her employer and even go to court.

4. She probably felt that she (fight) __had to fight__ in order to protect her personal freedom.

5. The woman who was arrested for not returning the video tapes to the store (be) __must have been__ shocked when the police appeared at her door.

6. Mercado's company (pay) __had to pay__ an award and (give) ___give___ him back his job.

7. The video store owners (complain) __must have complained__ to the police about the woman with the two overdue tapes.

Reading 2: "Loving America"

Prereading Questions

1. What is patriotism to you? What do you love your country for?

2. Do you think there is any difference in how or why you love your country and how or why Americans love theirs?

Word Analysis

Look at the words in the chart below and discuss the meanings of them with your teacher. They are all possible characteristics of the people of a country. Do these words have positive, negative, or neutral meanings for you? Check one category for each word. Discuss the connotations these words have for you and how they are seen in your culture. Then put a check after each one if you feel it is a characteristic of the American people and/or of the people of your country.

	Positive	Negative	Neutral	U.S.?	Your country?
patriotic	____	____	____	____	____
materialistic	____	____	____	____	____
collectivist	____	____	____	____	____
individualistic	____	____	____	____	____
self-critical	____	____	____	____	____
optimistic	____	____	____	____	____
pessimistic	____	____	____	____	____
idealistic	____	____	____	____	____
cynical	____	____	____	____	____
naive	____	____	____	____	____
fatalistic	____	____	____	____	____
freedom-loving	____	____	____	____	____
arrogant	____	____	____	____	____
contradictory	____	____	____	____	____
aggressive	____	____	____	____	____
bureaucratic	____	____	____	____	____

Vocabulary Practice

Match the italicized words in the sentences with the synonyms or definitions in the list below. Use the context of the sentence to help you guess the meaning.

Sentences 1-8

_____ giving a feeling of strength; making one feel good
_____ great in size
_____ almost completely
_____ unavoidable
_____ anger at an offense
_____ insult
_____ unreachable
_____ born with (a quality)

Sentences 9-15

_____ come together from different points, intersect
_____ free; not stopped or hindered
_____ limitation; restriction
_____ agree or decide to do
_____ two opposing views, both of which contain some truth
_____ cannot be untied or separated
_____ confusion
_____ loss of one's dreams

1. It is possible to be moved by the endless American plains and the homes defiantly set down in the middle of this *vastness*.

2. Each nation had a firm belief in the *innate* superiority of its own people.

3. On its 200th anniversary, America *virtually* demands that we face the question: Just why do we love America?

4. In the middle of corruption and commercialism, violence and disorder, *resentment* and confusion, just what are the country's qualities that we cherish?

5. Americans insist on dominating fate. This is *invigorating* and liberating for "fate" is only too easily used as a justification for inaction.

6. Indeed, even nature must be put in its place through technology, and even death is somehow considered an *affront*, a failure of medicine, or of right living.

7. We are reluctantly willing to accept as *inevitable* natural disasters, but little else.

8. Where is the line between making the most of one's potential and reaching for the *unattainable*?

9. There is little sense that evil is a constant presence and *inextricably* mixed with good.

10. It is sometimes difficult to contemplate how much freedom we Americans have *undertaken* to bear.

11. What is the line between education as a tool and education as a kind of magic? The line is not clear so when education fails, *disillusionment* is bitter.

12. All American forces, including money, *converge* in the passion for freedom.

13. The great source of our current *bafflement* is that we somehow expect a wildly free society to have the stability of a tradition-guided society.

14. We somehow believe that we can have freedom from community (a.) *constraints,* but also freedom from smog, freedom from economic controls, freedom from the ups and downs of an (b.) *unhampered* economy.

15. Both conservatives and liberals are living examples of this *paradox.*

Loving America

By HENRY GRUNWALD
(from *Time* magazine)

Part I

Loving America is a very special task. No other country makes quite the same demands in being loved, nor presents quite the same difficulties.

In most other nations, patriotism is essentially the love of family, of tribe, of land, magnified. There may well be an ideological admixture.[32] The France of the Revolution and Napoleon, for instance, proclaimed the rights of man. Liberty, equality, fraternity were useful enough to overthrow an order and kill a king. But France's love of her earth and her produce,[33] her landscape, her language and her money—those are the things French patriotism is really about. So it is with other European nations. The songs and the poetry of patriotism are filled with scenery: with rivers and mountains, with cities longed for, with valleys lost, with castles conquered. American patriotism has much less of this specific sense of place. "From sea to shining sea" or "purple mountain majesties"[34] are somewhat unconvincing.

It is possible to be deeply moved by the endless American plains, and the settlements[35] defiantly set down in the midst of this vastness, by the coast of Maine or the Rockies or the desert. But that is not loving America. Loving America means loving what it stands for as a political and social vision. Although the great American epic[36] is the conquest and taming[37] of a continent, American patriotism is not concentrated on geography but on a historic event and an idea. The event is the creation for the United States as a fresh start, a different dispensation.[38] The idea is freedom. Both notions have been distorted or perverted at times—that happens with all patriotism. But even when it is misused, American patriotism remains ideological more than racial or ethnic.

When the French carved up Germany or the Germans carved up France, it was done for the greater glory of each nation, with firm belief in the innate superiority

---

32. (formal) a mixture; something which is mixed together   33. (accent on first syllable) farm products—fruit and vegetables   34. words from the song "America the Beautiful"   35. small communities, particularly in an unpopulated area   36. story of bravery; great deeds   37. to bring something wild under control   38. freedom not to follow a rule   39. chauvinism or extreme patriotism

of their own people. Whenever Americans went to war, they may have been seized by jingoism[39] to some extent, but more than anything else Americans believed they were fighting for ideas, for a system. It may have been naive to think that other countries were waiting to be given the blessings of democracy, free enterprise and individualism, but that is what Americans did believe.

The U.S. was not born in a tribal conflict, like so many other nations, but in a conflict over principles. Those principles were thought to be universal, which was part of the reason for the unprecedented policy of throwing the new country open to all comers. That not only served to make the U.S. a world power in sheer[40] numbers (compared, for instance, with Canada, which kept its population small and has complained ever since about being overpowered by its southern neighbor). It also greatly reinforced the abstract and ideological nature of American patriotism. The millions from other lands and other cultures had different loves for many different plots of earth, languages, traditions. The unifying love had to be for America as an idea.

In part, this helps to explain the unusual stability of American institutions. In Europe it is possible to shift loyalties from king to republic from democracy to dictatorship, and still love one's country. In the U.S. loyalty must be to the institutions themselves. At the same time this explains the extraordinary degree of American unease, self-criticism, dissatisfaction with leadership. If Congress functions badly, if politicians are corrupt, if Presidents do not inspire, this is seen as a breakdown of the whole American enterprise.

We still perceive America as something unprecedented in history, as an experiment, and as such, something that must "work" in order to prove itself over and over again. Hence America demands that love be given not once and for all, but that it be constantly renewed and reaffirmed. That is why both American patriotism and American self-criticism can be so shrill.[41] Attacks on America from within are usually prompted by disappointed love. "My country, right or wrong" is not a very American slogan.[42] We Americans have a hard time accepting a situation in which our country is wrong, not because we are more arrogant than other people, but because our country's rightness is our soil, our home. One loves one's birthplace or one's parents because they *are* one's birthplace or one's parents, regardless of whether the place is especially attractive or the parents especially worthy. One loves them because they exist. America demands to be loved not because it is, but for what it is—and not only for what it is, but for what it does. By its own insistence, to love the U.S. is also to judge it.

Thus, amid the chorus of congratulations on this Bicentennial, America virtually demands that we face the question: Just why do we love America? Amid corruption and commercialism, violence and disorder, resentment and confusion, just what are the country's qualities that we cherish?

Part II

One loves America both for its virtues and its faults, which are deeply intertwined.[43] Indeed, one loves America for the virtues *of* its faults. One loves the almost obsessive American need to believe, the resistance to cynicism, even if that

---

40. complete and pure; nothing else involved   41. unpleasantly loud and sharp sounding
42. a motto or saying for a group, also used in advertising   43. twisted together or connected

Are Americans more nationalistic than citizens of other countries?

sometimes means oversimplification and moralizing. One loves the unique American restlessness,[44] the refusal to settle for what is, even if that sometimes means a lack of contemplation and peace. One loves the fact that America sees itself as the shaper of its own destiny, both private and public. While psychology, sociology and determinist historical theories have become massively fashionable, there is still a strong strain of resistance to the notion that man is formed by environment, by outside powers, or that the nation is in the grip of immutable[45] forces. This rejection of fate, this insistence that everything is possible, is surely the dominant American characteristic, and the heart of its genius. Other nations cringe[46] before fate, endure it nobly, or outlast it patiently. America insists on dominating, on bullying, fate. This is very invigorating and liberating, for "fate" is only too easily used as a justification for inaction, for maintaining an old order no matter how miserable.

In rejecting fate, the U.S. is the ultimate incarnation[47] of Western, Faustian[48] man. But that posture[49] toward the universe also has immense dangers. There is no shifting of blame, no relief in the notion that "this is the way things are". We are reluctantly willing to accept as inevitable natural disasters, but little else. Indeed, even nature must be put in its place through technology. Even death is somehow

---

44. inability to relax or stay in one place 45. unchangeable 46. bow down or move back, out of fear or shame 47. the humanization of an idea; a perfect example of 48. power-hungry, with no concept of morality (from the character of Faust, a magician who sells his soul to the devil for power) 49. attitude; way of standing or sitting

considered an affront, a failure of medicine, or of right living. Disease, poverty and other ancient afflictions simply are not accepted as part of the human condition. Perhaps rightly so—and yet the conviction that they can be banished[50] completely is a tremendous burden because each setback,[51] each delay, is seen as a personal or national failure. That is partly why we Americans are so impatient with the study of history—because history is a reminder of fate. We would rather learn to do than learn to know.

One must love this American view of learning as the tool by which man transforms himself. We Americans believe that everything can be learned, including, to a very large extent, to be what you are not. You can learn to be pretty if you are plain, charming if you are dull, thin if you are fat, youthful if you are aging, how to write though you are inarticulate, how to make money though you are not good with figures. There is something admirable about this, yet nagging[52] questions remain: Where is the line between making the most of one's potential and reaching for the unattainable? Where is the line between education as a tool and education as a kind of magic? The line is blurred,[53] and that is why when education fails, disillusionment is so bitter.

One loves—with some misgivings[54]—the deep American belief in human perfectibility and goodness. Yet an element of this belief is the fact that America lacks an adequate sense of evil. In the Enlightenment tradition, evil is explained away as a curable flaw. But even in the puritan and evangelical traditions, the American sense of evil is curiously shallow[55] and optimistic; more concerned with behavior (sex or drink, for example) than with the deeper states of sin. The devil can be banished, and evil can be fought; evil is seen almost as a mere "problem" to be solved. There is little sense that evil is a constant presence and inextricably mixed with good. That is why every new American generation seems to discover evil as if it had been invented only yesterday—and by the older generation. There is not much of the insight that man and society are permanently imperfect.

Hence the shock and surprise when we find out that evil is being done by us or in our name. Hence, also, a kind of inverted pride, a mirror image of boosterism;[56] if one side of the American chorus proclaims that the country is the best, the greatest ever or anywhere, the other side asserts that it is the worst ever, the worst anywhere. Both attitudes are equally false and provincial.

Part III

The American self-image similarly hovers[57] between idealism and materialism. Can one love the American attitude toward money? Can one love America in the throes[58] of selling, a country wrapped in one endless, all-intrusive commercial? Can one love America in those moments when the immeasurable is measured in the balance sheet,[59] when the ultimate goal becomes the bottom line?[60]

The American spirit is deeply divided about money. In one sense the faith in money is pure, it need not, as it does in so many older societies, apologize for its existence. Money is what it is—good in its own right, a sign of success, if perhaps

---

50. to force to leave; send into exile   51. a stopping or slowing down of progress
52. constantly annoying or bothering   53. not clear; indistinct   54. doubts or feelings of
uncertainty   55. superficial; without depth   56. the act of supporting or promoting a
cause   57. move back and forth, in a state of uncertainty   58. in the effort of; struggling
with   59. bookkeeping, amount of money earned or lost   60. profit

no longer of divine grace. Yet this view is at war with an older tradition from which, even in a country that slights[61] history, the imagination is never quite free: whether in the Bible or in fairy tales or in great works of fiction, money is held in contempt.[62] The great callings are not trade commerce but the state or the military or the church or scholarship. The great legendary virtues are not thrift—and its explosive extension, profit—but courage, kindness, and faith.

[. . .]

Ultimately all American forces, including money, converge in the passion for freedom—and that is, above all things, what one loves about the U.S. No country carries the belief in freedom farther, the belief that the individual must be free to make of himself what he can, that citizens must be free as far as humanly possible from government. There is about most Americans an attitude toward authority which is immensely bracing[63] and which both dazzles[64] and frightens people of other nations. Most Americans show a self-confidence which to others often appears to be mere swagger,[65] but which is the characteristic of a country that never had either a formal aristocracy or a peasantry.

We tend to think of freedom as a positive and unalloyed[66] good. We speak of "enjoying" freedom. Yet we fail to understand that freedom is not only a blessing but a burden. It is sometimes dizzying to contemplate how much freedom we Americans have undertaken to bear. In politics, in government, in business but also in education and in our private lives, we place immense responsibility on the individual. It can be argued that we bear freedom for much of the rest of the world—not only in the sense of material and military support for the cause of freedom as the West understands it, but in the sense of experimenting with freedom in a kind of vast social laboratory.

Our experiments are not often appreciated by the rest of the world, nor are they necessarily comforting even to ourselves. We have broken or bent all the traditional framework of rules: in religion, in family, in sex, in every kind of behavior. Yet we are surprised when the result is both public and personal disorder. We have not grasped[67] the cost accounting of freedom. The great source of our current bafflement is that we somehow expect a wildly free society to have the stability of a tradition-guided society. We somehow believe that we can simultaneously have, to the fullest, various *kinds* of freedom: freedom from discipline, but also freedom from crime; freedom from community constraints, but also freedom from smog; freedom from economic controls, but also freedom from the inevitable ups and downs of a largely unhampered economy.

Both American conservatives and liberals are embodiments[68] of this paradox. Liberals are forever asking state intervention in the economy for the sake of social justice, while insisting on hands-off in the private area of morals. Conservatives take the opposite view. They demand self-determination in politics, but suspect self-determination in morals. They demand laissez-faire[69] in business, but hate laissez-faire in behavior. In theory, there is no contradiction between these positions. For freedom to be workable as a political and social system, strong inner

---

61. pay little attention to; ignore   62. have disrespect for; look down on   63. stimulating
64. amaze; inspire admiration   65. boasting, bragging, proud way of walking   66. complete and pure   67. understand; comprehend (usually a concept)   68. to put into bodily form; to be a perfect example of   69. non-interference by the government (usually in the economy)

controls, a powerful moral compass and sense of values, are needed. In practice, the contradiction is vast. The compass is increasingly hard to read, the values hard to find in a frantically open, mobile, fractioned[70] society. Thus a troubling, paradoxical question: Does freedom destroy the inner disciplines that alone make freedom possible?

It is an ancient question, and the way America struggles with it—fitfully,[71] painfully, earnestly, in millions of minds and thousands of communities—is deeply moving. It is the most important struggle going on in the U.S., and its outcome is far from assured. The people willing to undertake this struggle, or even capable of understanding it, are in a clear minority in today's world. Almost everywhere we see arising a new political feudalism that once again promises a fixed society, an order in which everyone is taken care of—the only price being the loss of freedom.

So one must love America, most of all and most deeply for its constant, difficult, confused, gallant and never-finished struggle to make freedom possible.

One loves America for its accomplishments as well as for its unfinished business—and especially for its knowledge that its business is indeed unfinished. One should never love America uncritically, because it is not worthy of America to be accepted uncritically; the insistence on improving the U.S. is perhaps the deepest gift of love. One ultimately loves America not for what it is, or what it does, but for what it promises. True, we know that every national promise sooner or later fades and that fate cannot be forever dominated or outmaneuvered. But we must deeply believe, and we must prove, that after 200 years the American promise is still only in its beginning.

---

70. disconnected and fragmented; not whole   71. not restfully

Comprehension and Discussion

A. *Circle the correct answer. If the answer is false, tell why.*

Part I

1. When Americans went to war, they did it because they believed that people in other countries wanted the same things they did.

    True   False

2. American governmental institutions are very stable because Americans are very loyal to their country.

    True   False

3. The love Americans have for their country is similar in nature to the love they have for their parents.

    True   False

Part II

4. Americans believe strongly in fate or destiny as a determiner in their lives.

True   False

5. Americans have difficulty believing that both good and evil are inevitable aspects of life.

True   False

Part III

6. Having money was once seen as sinful in the United States.

True   False

7. America can be seen as an experiment in democracy for the rest of the world.

True   False

B. *Answer the following questions as completely as possible.*

Part I

1. How did Americans' feelings towards the principles on which the United States was founded affect its immigration policy, and how did the immigrant experience affect the special way of loving America?

2. In your own words, summarize how American patriotism differs from that of other countries.

Part II

3. What is the dominant American characteristic, and how is this "the heart of its genius"? What problems might it also cause?

4. The writer says that Americans think they can transform themselves through learning, that they can learn to be pretty and charming, how to write, and how to make money. What does this say about the American character, and how do these examples relate to the "insistence that everything is possible"? Have you seen any other example of this characteristic in Americans?

Part III

5. Explain the conflict Americans have between materialism and idealism.

6. How can freedom be both a blessing and a burden, and what are some of the problems which result from this great emphasis on personal freedom? How do conservatives and liberals embody this paradox?

7. The writer asks what he calls a troubling question: "Does freedom destroy the inner disciplines that alone make freedom possible?" What do you think he means by this? Can too much freedom destroy freedom? If so, what can be done to preserve freedom?

8. The writer is giving his analysis of the American character. Are there any aspects of this analysis with which you particularly agree or disagree?

Word Forms

Working with a partner, complete the following chart with the different forms of the words. Use your knowledge of other words and their different forms to help you. Do not be afraid to guess. A dash means there is no form.

Noun	Verb	Adjective	Adverb
bafflement		baffling	—
constraint		—	
	converge	—	—
	—	inevitable	
paradox	—		
	—		reluctantly
resentment			
		(un)attainable	—
—		(un)hampered	—

Vocabulary Practice

Complete the sentences below with the correct words from the following list. You may have to use different word forms and tenses. Do not use a word more than once.

Sentences 1-8	Sentences 9-14
resentment	(un)attainable
undertake	innate
paradox	disillusionment
vastness	converge
virtually	affront
constraints	hamper
invigorating	inevitable
inextricable	bafflement

1. Probably no other country in the world has had such a major influence on worldwide popular culture as the United States has had. At times American culture and international popular culture seem _____ connected.

2. This _____ influence is both widely accepted and strongly criticized at the same time.

3. It seems _____ that many people criticize American policy and culture while wearing American jeans, listening to American music or watching American television programs, and drinking American soft drinks.

4. To some, American popular culture is vital and _____; to others it is decadent and demoralizing.

5. _____ everyone in the world has heard of Coca-Cola and Pepsi-Cola and of many of the popular American television programs.

6. In many countries, the great number of American television programs shown is causing the governments to _____ special efforts to increase the number of local programs.

7. Consequently, many governments are putting _____ on the percentage of foreign programs which can be broadcast in a day.

8. These restrictions are naturally _____ by American television companies.

9. These companies do not understand why they should be _____ in their efforts to give people the programs they seem to want.

10. One of the criticisms of American television is that there is an emphasis on programs showing very wealthy people. People who learn about the United States through its television programs are often _____ when they visit the United States and see the reality.

11. Poor Americans may also feel frustrated at viewing life-styles which they feel they will never be able to _____.

12. Another criticism of American television is the _____ violence on almost every drama.

13. People who have never visited the United States but only know it from television could easily come to think that Americans are _____ violent.

14. A third criticism is that the cultures of many countries are becoming too Americanized. Some Americans see this criticism as an (a.) _____ to American culture. Others may just find it (b.) _____ that people would object to the spread of American culture. Still others see all of these criticisms as an excuse to exclude American programs simply for reasons of profit.

15. Whatever the reason, when the motives of morality, national pride, and profit _____, the result may indeed be the limitation of American programs on foreign televisions.

Vocabulary Building

"Other nations cringe before fate, endure it nobly, or *outlast* it patiently."

The prefix *out-* can mean "to do more or to a better or superior degree." Therefore, "to outlast" means to last longer. This prefix can be used with many verbs to show this level of superiority.

Pronunciation Note: When nouns and adjectives begin with *out-*, the accent is usually on the first syllable.

Since they put in the new machinery, the *out*put of the factory has doubled.

She's a very *out*going (extroverted) person.

When a verb begins with *out-*, generally speaking, the accent is not on the first syllable. If the verb that is attached to the prefix *out-* has more than one syllable, the accent is in the same place as it would be without the prefix.

He takes such good care of his car, it will out*last* him.

He was so out*dis*tanced in the race that he could never catch up.

Vocabulary Practice

Complete the following sentences with one of the verbs in the list below. Use each word only one time. Pay close attention to the context to decide which one to use.

outwork	outlive	outsmart (fox, wit)	outnumber
outdo	outplay	outweigh	outshine
outrun	outsell	outwear (stay)	outbid

1. One of the criticisms of Americans is that they always seem to have to _____ everyone else. This can be seen in their love for superlatives—the tallest building, the biggest cars, the greatest baseball team, the highest standard of living, etc.

2. Many manufacturers are worried because some imported products are _____ American products in the United States. The question is why. For example, do Americans buy imported cars because they are cheaper, or better?

3. One of the differences between Canada and the United States is that the United States _____ Canada by a great deal. Considering its size, the population of Canada is quite small.

4. When trying to buy a house, you have to be careful that someone doesn't _____ you. If this happens, you will lose the house.

5. He joined the marathon just for the fun of it. He didn't expect to win because he knew he could never _____ everyone else.

6. The police have been trying to catch that criminal for years, but they have never been able to because he always _____ them.

7. The fight wasn't really fair. The winner _____ his opponent by 20 pounds.

8. (Same word as #7.) Even though he may have a lot of faults as a politician, I still think that the good _____ the bad.

9. When you visit people, you shouldn't stay too long. You could _____ your welcome.

10. My brother makes a great deal of money. He gets paid for how much he produces, not how long he works, and he's very fast. He can _____ anybody.

11. He was picked the most important athlete of the year. No other player even came close. He can _____ anyone else on the team.

12. It is very common for women to _____ their husbands. Consequently, there are far more widows than there are widowers.

13. Even though all of their children are good in school, the one everyone notices the most is the youngest. She _____ all of her brothers and sisters.

Grammar Practice

Modal Perfects—May/Might, Must, Could, Should Have

A. *Review of Meanings:* Imagine that a crime has been committed, and Mr. X is a suspect. *Depending on the situation, each of the sentences in Column A could be said about him, but each has a different meaning. Match the sentence in Column A with the explanation in Column B which would justify the use of the modal.*

A	**B**
1. Mr. X must have done it.	_____ He felt he had no other choice. His children were starving. He doesn't regret it.
2. He might have done it.	_____ He wasn't even near the scene of the crime, and he can prove it.
3. He had to do it.	_____ Why not? He had the motive.
4. He shouldn't have done it.	_____ It was a stupid thing to do. Now he'll have to spend years in jail.
5. He could have done it.	_____ There was nobody else around. He had the motive, the means, and the opportunity.
6. He couldn't have done it.	_____ He was there. He had the opportunity. But we know he didn't do it.

B. *Read the following situations and complete the sentences about each situation. Then, using modal perfects, write at least one sentence of your own, and if possible more, about each situation. Try to use all of them and all forms—passive, continuous, and negatives.*

1. The Puritans arrived in the New World in the winter after having spent months crossing the ocean. They had to start life all over. They (suffer) _____ a great deal that first winter.

2. It is amazing to think how the Puritans ever even expected to survive the first winter in this strange land with no one here to help them. The winter here was probably harsher than any winter they had ever experienced in England. Do you think they had realized how difficult it was really going to be? They (neg.) _____.

3. Crossing the Atlantic in a small boat in winter is very dangerous. They (kill) _____ all _____.

4. They (be) _____ very happy with their situation in England if they were willing to take such risks.

5. Many people feel that the strong American character that we inherited from the Puritans has become one of always being a "victim" or of always trying to get as much money as possible for our injuries. Many examples seem to support this hypothesis. A woman who smoked heavily for more than 40 years and developed lung cancer sued the tobacco companies that made the cigarettes she smoked. After she died, her family continued the suit. She (stop) _____ smoking. Nobody forced her to smoke.

6. A psychic who made a living by telling the future said that she lost her powers after a CAT-scan (X-ray) of her brain to see if she had a brain tumor. She sued the doctor. The jury awarded her a million dollar settlement. (This award was later reversed on appeal; the woman received nothing.) She (tell) _____ the truth. I doubt it, but you never know. Yes, she _____, but I doubt it too.

7. A man accused of murder used the argument that he had gone temporarily insane because of eating too much sugar and junk food. The jury (accept, neg.) _____ that line of defense! (Notice the exclamation point.)

8. The police raided a fraternity house at a major university and arrested students for possession of drugs. The father of one of the students said that the police (go) _____ after major drug dealers and not someone like his son, who used drugs but didn't sell them.

9. In California, a 19-year-old woman who was obviously drunk wanted to buy gas for her car. The gas station attendants gave her coffee, tried to persuade her not to drive, and even offered to call her mother to come and pick her up. Finally they sold her the gas. After leaving the gas station, she got into an accident and killed two people. The family of one of the victims sued the gas station for liability in the accident. Since the woman was under 21, perhaps the family (sue) _____ the person who gave her or sold her the alcohol.

10. A woman in Texas bought a car for her son, who was in the Marine Corps in North Carolina. The Marine lent the car to a friend, who got into an accident. The victim's family sued the mother for having given the car to her son, who might lend it to someone who was negligent. Before this happened to the mother, she (think) _____ it was impossible to be sued for something she herself did not do.

Grammar Practice

Short Modal Perfect Forms

Below are two sets of questions/statements and answers to be answered in pairs. Student A will ask Student B the questions in the A list. Using the information given, Student B will answer the questions with a short modal perfect. Student A corrects Student B after each question. Next, reverse roles, with Student B asking the questions, Student A answering, and Student B correcting the answer. Listen carefully to the content of the questions and look at the clues that are provided to help you decide which modal to use. Be careful of negatives and the passive voice. Note: The correct answers are in parentheses.

Student A Questions/Statements

1. Did you study last night? (No, but I *should have. [could have]*)

2. Did John go to the concert yesterday? (I don't know. *He might have.*)

3. Were Ted and Alice at the party? (They *might have been.* I arrived late, and lot of people had already left.)

4. Guess what? I think I saw the President walking down the street yesterday. (You *couldn't have.* I read that he's out of the country.)

5. Did Albert arrive at the airport on time last night? (He *must have* because he didn't come back to my place, and he doesn't know anyone else here.)

6. I'm surprised that I didn't see you at the party last night. Did you stay home to study? (Yes. I *had to.* I had a big test today.)

7. I really appreciate all the help you gave me yesterday. I bought you a little present for your trouble. (You *shouldn't have.* It was no trouble.)

Student A Answers

1. It _____. They went to wonderful places, and they had a lot of time and money to spend.

2. Yes, but he _____. That's why he failed the test today.

3. Yeah. She _____. Her mother is very sick.

4. I'm not sure, but he _____. He wasn't feeling well yesterday morning.

5. Yes, but you _____.

6. He _____. He's not smart enough.

7. You never know with him. He _____. He's a pretty strange guy.

8. I'm surprised Marie didn't go home for vacation. (So am I. She certainly could have. She has enough money.)

9. Do you think he was the one who committed the murder? (He *couldn't have been.* He's so gentle he wouldn't hurt a fly.)

10. I'm sorry I wasn't there for the sunset. (You *should have been.* It was beautiful.)

8. I didn't talk to her, but she _____. She looked very happy when I saw her.

9. That's really too bad; you _____. She was very upset.

10. I _____. I had no other choice!

Student B Answers

1. No, but I _____.

2. I don't know. He _____.

3. They _____. I arrived late, and a lot of people had already left.

4. You _____. I read that he's out of the country.

5. He _____ because he didn't come back to my place, and he doesn't know anybody else here.

6. Yes. I _____. I had a big test today.

7. You _____. It was no trouble.

Student B Questions/Statements

1. They're so lucky. I bet it was a great trip. (It *must have been.* They went to wonderful places, and they had a lot of time and money to spend.)

2. Was your brother at the party last night? (Yes, but he *shouldn't have been.* That's why he failed the test today.)

3. Did she really go back home? (Yeah. She *had to.* Her mother is very sick.)

4. I wonder if John went to the meeting. (I'm not sure, but he *may [might] not have.* He wasn't feeling well yesterday morning.)

5. I don't know why you're so upset that I went swimming alone at night. Nothing happened to me. I didn't drown. (Yes, but *you could have.*)

6. Do you think he planned that robbery all by himself? (He *couldn't have.* He's not smart enough. [He *must not have.*])

7. Do you think he really did that? It sounds like such a crazy thing to do. (You never know. He *may [might] have.* He's a pretty strange guy.)

8. So am I. She certainly _____. She has enough money.

8. I hear that Yoko got a letter from the university. Was she accepted? (I didn't talk to her, but *she must have been.* She looked very happy when I saw her.)

9. He _____. He's so gentle he wouldn't hurt a fly.

9. I was going to call my sister last night, but then I decided not to. (That's too bad. You *should have.* She was very upset.)

10. You _____. It was a beautiful sight.

10. Why did you do that? (I *had to.* I had no other choice!)

Class Project

Work on one or more of these projects individually or in groups of two to three students. Then present your findings to the class.

1. Do library research on the Puritans and the Puritan experience in the New World. Who were they? What were their beliefs? What effect did their beliefs have on their daily lives? What effect did they have on education and on the democratic principles of the United States?

2. "Political correctness" or "p.c." is a topic which has generated a great deal of controversy in the United States in recent years and about which there have been many newspaper and magazine articles. Being politically correct is particularly an issue on college and university campuses. Find specific examples of "p.c." and explain them to the class. What did some of these issues involve, and, for those which took place on campuses, how did the school administrations solve them? Show how this concept is affecting language.

3. Pick one of the cases mentioned in Reading 1 of this chapter. Look up old newspaper or magazine articles about the case. Find out exactly what happened in this case and explain it in detail to the class.

Discussion and Writing

Discuss the following topics, first in pairs or small groups and then with the teacher and the entire class. After your discussion, pick one (or more) of the topics and write an essay about it.

1. What does patriotism mean to you? What doesn't it mean? Define this word as completely as possible.

2. Write an essay titled "Loving *(name of your country).*" If you see a difference between why people in your country love their country and other people love theirs, explain this difference.

3. In the essay "Loving America," the writer states that the belief that everything is possible is the dominant American characteristic. What is the dominant characteristic (or one of the most dominant characteristics) of the people of your country? Explain it in as much detail as possible. Are there both positive and negative consequences of this characteristic? If possible, tell why you think the people have this characteristic, and then show how it is manifested in daily life.

4. The American culture is seen as being both puritanical and permissive. Does your culture have two sides which seem contradictory (for example, very traditional and very modern at the same time)? Explain these two sides, and show how this contradiction at times causes confusion or problems within the society.

5. The Puritan background, immigration, geography—all of these factors have had an effect on the American character. Pick two or three factors which you feel may have had an effect on the character of your people. Explain these factors in as much detail as possible and tell how you think they may have been the cause for a certain general characteristic of the people. (Possible factors might be religion, geography, philosophy, the economy, weather, etc.)

6. Discuss the question of whether too much freedom can ultimately destroy freedom.

7. The article "Busybodies: New Puritans" is quite critical about what the writer sees as a trend in the United States. He supports his view with many examples. Is there any trend going on in your country which you do not like? Write an essay criticizing this trend. Use as many examples as possible to get your point across. Or is there a trend which you do like? If so, write an essay in favor of this trend.

8. Discuss the effect of American culture on your country. Pick one aspect, such as television, clothing, food, or music, and tell what the effect has been and why you think this has happened? Do you feel this effect is positive, negative, or neither?

Word List

Below is a list of the new words, and their different forms, presented in this chapter.

Noun	Verb	Adjective	Adverb
affront			
apprehension	apprehend		
arbitrariness		arbitrary	arbitrarily
attainment	attain	(un)attainable	
bafflement	baffle	baffling	
	bar		
concession	concede		
constraint	constrain		
convergence	converge		
disillusionment	disillusion		
disparateness			
disparity		disparate	
endorsement	endorse		
	hamper	unhampered	
inevitability		inevitable	inevitably
inextricability		inextricable	inextricably
innateness		innate	innately
intrusion	intrude	intrusive	intrusively
	invigorate	invigorating	
paradox		paradoxical	
penalty	penalize		
refrainment	refrain		
resentment	resent	resentful	resentfully
		secular	
		undaunted	
		(daunting)	
	undertake		
vastness		vast	vastly
			virtually

CHAPTER 4

Parents–
Rights and
Responsibilities

Reading 1: "The Custody Case that Went Up in Smoke"

Prereading Questions

1. What are a parent's rights and responsibilities concerning a child's health?

2. When parents get divorced or separated, on what basis should custody of the child be decided?

3. Can you think of a situation in which a parent's life-style or habits could be seen as dangerous to a child? If so, what, if anything, can or should be done to protect the child?

The Custody Case That Went Up in Smoke

By BARBARA KANTROWITZ with ALDEN COHEN and MEGAN DISSLY   (from *Newsweek* magazine)

Anna Maria De Beni Souza never thought her less than half-a-pack-per-day cigarette habit was anybody else's business. But last week a California Superior Court judge thought otherwise[1] when he ordered the Sacramento woman to stop smoking in front of her 5-year-old son Maximilian. She cannot light up[2] again until the boy turns 18—or the ruling is overturned. Judge David Stirling included the ban in a preliminary ruling on a custody dispute between De Beni Souza and the boy's father, Manfred Kallweit. The father had complained to the court that his son's health could be hurt by inhaling secondhand smoke.

The judge's unusual ruling has turned what should have been a fairly routine custody fight into another battleground in the war over smokers' rights. Both sides have been deluged by phone calls from as far away as Germany and Japan. Charles Asbury, Kallweit's attorney, defends the decision. "The courts have regularly forbidden people to drink alcohol and consume drugs in child-custody cases," he says. "This was a logical extension of the court's power." But De Beni Souza thinks the ban is absurd: "Can he sit next to someone in a restaurant who is smoking? Or can we visit friends who smoke? Is that bad, or is it just my smoke?"

While the smoking ban is now law for De Beni Souza, the custody dispute is still up in the air.[3] She and Kallweit never married and no longer live together. De Beni Souza thinks it will take time to work out all the details of their agreement. In the meantime, she'll have to hope that a higher judge overturns the ban—or else she'll have to take up chewing gum.

---

1. the judge thought differently 2. to smoke

3. undecided

Comprehension and Discussion

A. *Circle the correct answer. If the answer is false, tell why.*

1. The judge's ruling in this case is final.

True   False

2. The court has not ordered the mother to quit smoking completely.

True   False

3. Until the custody case is settled, Ms. De Beni Souza cannot smoke in front of her child.

True   False

B. *Answer the following questions as completely as possible.*

1. How do you feel about Ms. De Beni Souza reaction to the ruling? Do you agree or disagree with her?

2. The father's attorney says that this ruling is "a logical extension of the court's power" in custody cases to prohibit certain activities, such as drinking alcohol and consuming drugs. Do you agree? If you agree, tell why. If you do not agree, do you agree that the court has this power in the cases of alcohol or drugs? If so, what is the difference? Either way, support your statements.

3. In general, what do you think about the ruling in this custody case?

4. What are some possible consequences of this ruling?

Reading 2: "In Child Deaths, a Test for Christian Science"

Prereading Questions

1. When, if ever, does the state have the right or responsibility to intervene or interfere in the care of a child?

2. If a family's religious beliefs conflict with what the government feels the parents' responsibilities are for the health and the education of the child, what can or should be done?

3. Do you know of any religions which use prayer to heal or cure illness? Are these religions common in your country? Are there any special laws concerning them?

Vocabulary Practice

Match the italicized words in the sentences with the definitions or synonyms in the list below. Use the context of the sentence to help you guess the meaning.

Sentences 1 - 6

_____ a belief, usually of a religion
_____ take over another's rights
_____ produce
_____ complete; not lessened in any way
_____ oppose; meet an attack with another attack
_____ by the nature of a person or thing
_____ free from; allow not to have to do something
_____ causing great anxiety or pain

Sentences 7 - 14

_____ avoid by going around
_____ secondary; with inferior rank
_____ believe something to be the result of
_____ forgiving; merciful; not strict
_____ ability to achieve results
_____ go or turn to when help is needed
_____ say or affirm something to be true
_____ express a belief
_____ something that holds back, stops or blocks

1. This was only the latest of a number of successful prosecutions of Christian Scientists whose children died *agonizing* deaths after spiritual healing failed.

2. The *tenets* of the church remain fundamentally unchanged since Mary Baker Eddy founded it in Boston in 1879.

3. Christian Scientists (a.) *counter* that by seeking to kill a crucial belief of their faith, law enforcement officials are (b.) *infringing* on their religious liberties.

4. The decision against the parents was called an *unmitigated* attempt to undermine the Christian Science way of life.

5. Defense lawyers argue that because most states specifically (a.) *exempt* those who rely on prayer from charges of child abuse or neglect, the prosecutions are (b.) *inherently* unfair.

6. Far from discouraging Christian Scientists from practicing their faith, the prosecutions were *generating* renewed interest from outsiders.

7. To *circumvent* those statutes which exempt parents from charges of neglect, prosecutors have generally chosen to charge the parents with putting the health of the child in danger.

8. The principal *impediment* against overturning those laws is the power of the church.

9. Your right to practice your religion is *subservient* to your child's right to live.

10. Church doctrine *holds* that all illnesses are rooted in fear and alienation from God.

11. Various testimonies by church members (a.) *attest* to the (b.) *efficacy* of prayer in curing various diseases.

12. To Mrs. Swan, the more *lenient* treatment of the Christian Scientists is a function of how much political influence they have.

13. Christian Science practitioners *attributed* the boy's illness and his failure to improve to Mrs. Swan's decision to have surgery a few months earlier.

14. She *resorted to* spiritual healing when her son became sick.

In Child Deaths, a Test for Christian Science

By DAVID MARGOLICK   (from the *New York Times*)

David and Ginger Twitchell, a Christian Science[4] couple from Massachusetts who relied on prayer rather than on doctors as their young son lay dying from an obstructed[5] bowel,[6] were convicted of involuntary manslaughter[7] last month. It was a stunning[8] verdict, coming as it did in the very shadow of[9] the Mother Church in Boston.

But the death of 2-year-old Robyn Twitchell and the conviction that followed was only the latest of a number of successful prosecutions of Christian Scientists whose children died agonizing deaths after spiritual healing failed.

The prosecutions, like many historic constitutional cases, represent a clash of apparent absolutes: of religious liberty and parental autonomy on the one hand and the right of the states to protect children—and the rights of the children themselves—on the other.

While the tenets of the church, particularly its reliance on prayer in lieu of[10] standard medical treatment, remain fundamentally unchanged since Mary Baker Eddy founded it in Boston in 1879, they have come under intense attack in courtrooms and state legislatures.

In the last 15 months, Christian Scientist parents have been convicted of involuntary manslaughter, felony[11] child abuse or child endangerment in two California cities, as well as in Arizona and Florida. Other prosecutions, in Santa Monica, Calif., and Minneapolis, have been dismissed, although prosecutors in Minnesota have appealed.

"The message has been sent," said John Kiernan, the prosecutor in the Twitchell case. "Every parent of whatever religious belief or persuasion is obligated to include medical care in taking care of his or her child."

Major Challenge for Church

Rita Swan of Sioux City, Iowa, a former Christian Scientist, has led the campaign for such

---

4. a religion whose doctrine states that illness can be healed through prayer and meditation
5. blocked 6. intestine that carries waste matter out of the body 7. the crime of killing someone unintentionally 8. shocking; surprising 9. very close to; in the same city or neighborhood

---

10. in place of 11. a serious crime, one for which punishment could be imprisonment in a state or federal institution

prosecutions after being convinced that her reliance on spiritual healing was largely responsible for the death of her infant son. "I'm sure the church has never faced a challenge like this in its history," she said. "The church has been so sophisticated and so smooth that coroners[12] and prosecutors and social workers have just assumed that Christian Scientists have the right to do this."

Christian Scientists counter that by seeking to smother[13] a crucial tenet of their faith, law enforcement officials are infringing on their religious liberties. Nathan Talbot, chairman of the church's committee on publications, said, "They are trying to prosecute out of existence this method of treatment."

The chief lawyer for the church, Theodore E. Dinsmoor of Gaston & Snow in Boston, has called the Twitchell case "nothing short of a gross intrusion on the First Amendment" and "an unmitigated attempt to undermine[14] the Christian Science way of life."

Faith vs. the Law: A Special Report

Fighting the Prosecutions

Defense lawyers appealing the convictions also argue that because most states specifically exempt those who rely on prayer from charges of child abuse or neglect—exemptions written into the law at the behest of[15] the Christian Science church—the prosecutions are inherently unfair. To circumvent those statutes,[16] prosecutors have generally chosen to charge the parents either with manslaughter or endangerment, where no such exemption applies.

The American Academy of Pediatrics[17] is leading a campaign to overturn these ex-

emptions, now in effect in more than 40 states. But only in South Dakota has it succeeded. The principal impediment, the doctors say, is the considerable lobbying power[18] of the Christian Science church.

Power Is Not in Numbers

The denomination—officially the Church of Christ, Scientist—says it has 500,000 members in this country; its critics call that an exaggeration. In any case, the church's power lies not in numbers but in influence. Its members are largely middle- and upper-class people who participate fully and successfully in American society. They include luminaries[19] like William H. Webster, the Director of Central Intelligence, and Adm. Stansfield M. Turner, a former director, Representative Christopher Shays, Republican of Connecticut, Judge Thomas P. Griesa of the United States District Court for the Southern District of New York, and Jean Stapleton and Carol Channing, actresses.

Dr. Norman C. Fost of Madison, Wis., who recently retired as head of the pediatrics academy's committee on bioethics,[20] said, "We're interested not just in kids who die. What we're concerned about are the hundreds and hundreds more who suffer from inadequate medical treatment."

Some Reconsidered Positions

Several prosecutors who say they were initially sympathetic to the Christian Science legal position say they reconsidered. "The first bell that went off in my head was 'religious freedom,'" said K. C. Scull, the attorney who handled the prosecution of John and Katherine King of Phoenix for the death of their 12-year-old daughter, Elizabeth. "But then I got to thinking, 'Wait a minute. You can't let kids die. Your right to practice religion is absolutely subservient to your child's right to live.'"

---

12. a doctor, usually employed by a city or county, who investigates deaths that may not be due to natural causes 13. kill; suffocate 14. weaken or injure, often slowly by small degrees 15. at the request of (formal) 16. laws 17. branch of medicine treating children

---

18. the power to influence members of Congress to make (or not make) laws 19. notable or famous people 20. the study of the ethical aspects of medicine

Would a mother have the right to take her child out of the hospital if she wanted?

These prosecutors nonetheless say they sympathize with the parents.

"On the one hand, it's hard for me to understand how someone could sit by and watch their child die without doing everything to attempt to save his child, including prayer," said John O'Mara of Sacramento, the prosecutor in one of the California cases. "On the other hand, these people are nice, middle-class, and well-intentioned. They're not drug-crazed psychotics, like an awful lot of the people I see."

The Debate: Healing, Power and a Crusade

Spiritual healing lies at the theological heart of Christian Science. Church doctrine holds that all physical ailments are rooted[21] in fear, alienation from God and other mental factors, and that real healing is brought about by a spiritual breakthrough that takes place through prayer, study, and introspection, usually with the assistance of the church's "practitioners," those members considered expert in helping patients cope with what they consider the mental roots of their disease.

Various testimonies by church members appearing in Christian Science literature over recent years attest to its efficacy in curing arthritis, gallstones, asthma, appendicitis, goiter, polio, pneumonia, cancer, epilepsy,[22] multiple sclerosis, cataracts, glaucoma, diabetes, mental retardation, venereal disease and other ailments that medicine considers congenital,[23] incurable, or terminal.[24]

---

22. a brain disease   23. a disease existing at one's birth   24. a disease that will cause death

---

21. originate in; have a beginning in

Mother Blamed for Problems

The campaign against spiritual healing has been fueled by growing concern over child abuse and recognition of children's rights. It has also been propelled—at times, almost single-handedly[25]—by Mrs. Swan.

Mrs. Swan resorted to spiritual healing when her 2-year-old son, Matthew, took sick[26] in November 1976. Christian Science practitioners attributed the boy's illness and his failure to improve to Mrs. Swan's decision to have surgery a few months earlier to remove a cyst[27]—which had failed to respond to faith healing—as well as on a feud[28] she was having with her father.

The boy died of meningitis in July 1977. Within days, Mrs. Swan broke with the church, and in 1983 she founded Child, an organization whose name is an acronym for Children's Healthcare Is a Legal Duty.

Acting as friends of the court in various cases, the Christian Science church has spent lavishly on legal fees, hiring lawyers from some of the most respected firms in the country. It has also mounted costly advertising campaigns, including full-page newspaper advertisements asserting that it is being "persecuted for prayer."

Although parents who belong to other denominations, including the Church of the First Born, the Faith Assembly, and the True Followers of Christ, have gone to jail for failing to provide their sick children with medical care, no Christian Scientist has thus far. Instead, like the Twitchells, Christian Scientists have received a combination of probation, mandatory community service and fines. They have also pledged to provide medical care for their surviving children.

Whether these sentences are just is a matter of debate.

"I didn't want to see the Kings go to prison," Mr. Scull said of the defendants in the Phoenix case. "These people absolutely loved that girl, and they absolutely believed in their religious teachings. What's the point of taking a childless couple who are outstanding citizens in every other way and putting them in prison?"

To Mrs. Swan, however, the more lenient treatment is a function of how much political influence Christian Scientists have. "I think it's the power, prestige, and respectability of the Christian Science church and the money they have to spend," she said. "Otherwise, I don't see any difference. Dead is dead."

The Legal Clash: A Difficult Decision Between Rights

The debate highlights the inherent tension between First Amendment guarantees that, on the one hand, say government cannot inhibit the free exercise of religion, and on the other, say government cannot be seen as giving preferential treatment to any particular religious group.

Prosecutors argue that courts have long empowered states to regulate religious conduct, as opposed to religious beliefs. They cite cases upholding laws against polygamy[29] as well as court-ordered transfusions and vaccinations.

"Parents may be free to become martyrs of themselves, but it does not follow they are free to make martyrs of their children," the United States Supreme Court held in *Prince v. Massachusetts,* a 1923 ruling involving a Jehovah's Witness prosecuted for violating child labor laws by having her 9-year-old daughter peddle[30] religious tracts.

The Christian Scientists, conversely, invoke *Wisconsin v. Yoder,* a 1972 decision

---

25. alone; by oneself   26. became sick (usually seriously)   27. a growth on the body that usually contains a liquid   28. hostility or argument over a long period of time

29. marriage with more than one spouse
30. sell on the street or from door to door

that held that the Amish[31] had the right to keep their children out of public schools. The First Amendment, the court held, protected not just religious beliefs but "a way of life."

---

31. a religious sect established in Switzerland in the 17th century. They came to the United States in the 19th century in search of religious freedom. The Amish do not believe in modern progress—they use horses instead of cars, they do not use electricity, etc.

Far from discouraging Christian Scientists from practicing their faith, the prosecutions were generating renewed interest from outsiders, said Mr Talbot, chairman of the church's publications committee. //

"We are having dozens and dozens and dozens of examples of people coming to our churches and reading rooms who have heard about the Twitchell case and are asking if Christian Science can heal them," he said. "Something is happening here, and it's not what the prosecutors intended."

Comprehension and Discussion

A. *Circle the correct answer. If the answer is false, tell why.*

1. The Twitchell case is the first time a Christian Scientist has been successfully prosecuted for the death of a child who had been ill and had not received medical care.

   True   False

2. Rita Swan is a government prosecutor specifically involved in children's healthcare issues.

   True   False

B. *Answer the following questions as completely as possible.*

1. Explain, in your own words, the problem presented in this article. What is the basic clash and how does it highlight the tensions inherent in the First Amendment?

2. Explain how Mrs. Swan became involved in the prosecutions of Christian Scientists.

3. No members of the Christian Science church have gone to jail for not providing proper health care for their children, but people of other religions have. Give as many reasons as possible why Christian Scientists have not received this punishment.

4. According to the writer, what are the arguments *for* and *against* the prosecution of parents who withhold medical care on religious grounds? Can you add any more?

5. The prosecutor in the King case says, "What's the point of taking a childless couple who are outstanding citizens in every other way and putting them in prison?" Do you agree that there would be no point in sending these parents to prison? If you agree, what punishment do you think they should receive? If you disagree, explain why.

6. Explain the exemptions that exist in many states concerning prayer for illness and what prosecutors and organizations are trying to do about them.

7. What previous rulings argue First Amendment guarantees of freedom of religious beliefs and/or lifestyles?

8. The First Amendment to the Constitution states that Congress cannot prohibit the free exercise of religion or pass laws which would stop people from following their religion. Is the free exercise of religion being infringed upon in this case? If so, explain how it is and what should be done. If not, explain specifically up to what limits people have the right to exercise freedom of religion. In either case, support your statements with examples and/or explanations.

Word Forms

Working with a partner, complete the following chart with the different forms of the words. Use your knowledge of other words and their different forms to help you. Do not be afraid to guess. A dash means there is no form.

Noun	Verb	Adjective	Adverb
	exempt	—	—
		agonizing	
	infringe	—	
	circumvent	—	—
impediment		—	—
efficacy	—		
	—	subservient	
	—	lenient	

Vocabulary Practice

Complete the sentences below with the correct words from the following list. You may have to use different word forms and tenses. Do not use a word more than once.

Sentences 1 - 4	**Sentences 5 - 10**
counter	attribute
generate	hold
infringe (on) upon)	lenient
agony ized	resort
tenet	circumvent
unmitigated	impediment
exempt	subservient
inherent	attest
	efficacy ious

1. Christian Scientists feel that the government is (a.) ___infringing on___ their right to practice their religion, one of the basic (b.) ___tenets___ of which is healing through prayer.   belief

2. The government (a.) ___counters___ this argument by saying that the Constitution does not (b.) ___exempt___ religions from punishment if a law is broken.

3. Many people feel that parents who have lost children (a.) ___have agonized___ enough and that a verdict of guilty against them would only compound the tragedy. Opponents feel that letting a child die without consulting a doctor is (b.) ___unmitigated___ murder.

4. An (a.) ___inherent___ problem of a society composed of many different nationalities, races, and religions is that there will sometimes be misunderstandings and disagreements among the groups. Nothing seems to (b.) ___generate___ such strong emotions as religion.

5. Many religions (a.) ___hold___ that prayer is (b.) ___efficacious___ in healing illness, and followers of those religions (c.) ___attest___ to the number of cures they have witnessed. Those who don't believe in faith healing (d.) ___attribute___ these cures to more natural causes.

6. In the United States, where there is separation of church and state, church laws are ___subservient___ to state laws.

7. Traditionally, the courts have shown great ___leniency___ towards these parents and have not sent them to prison.

8. Although freedom of religion is a basic right of Americans, the government does not allow religions to ___circumvent___ the law for religious purposes.

9. People who believe in faith healing feel that if the government forces them to use doctors, it would ___impede___ them in practicing their religion.

10. When faced with a major illness, people often will ___resort___ to methods they may have never even considered using before, from traditional medicine to prayer to alternative types of medicine.

Focus on Form: Adjective Clauses

Adjective clauses are clauses that work like adjectives; they modify or give more information about a noun or a pronoun. There are two types of adjective clauses—essential and non-essential.

An essential adjective clause:

- must contain a subject and a verb.
- is essential to the meaning of the sentence.
- restricts the noun it modifies.
- is not separated by commas.
- begins with *who, which, that, whose, whom, Ø,* or the adverbials *when* or *where.*
- comes as close as possible to the word it modifies.
- must modify a specific word, not an idea.

Grammar Practice

The following sentences all contain essential adjective clauses. Underline the clause in each sentence. The first one has been done for you.

1. The church's members are largely middle- and upper-middle class people <u>who participate fully and successfully in American society.</u>

2. The first bell that went off in the prosecutor's head was religious freedom.

3. The death of 2-year-old Robyn Twitchell and the conviction that followed was only the latest of a number of successful prosecutions of Christian Scientists whose children died agonizing deaths after spiritual healing failed.

4. Various testimonies by church members appearing in Christian Science literature in recent years attest to its efficacy in curing arthritis, gallstones, asthma, . . . and other ailments medicine considers congenital, incurable or terminal.

5. The person on whom the tenets of this church are based is Mary Baker Eddy.

6. The verdict is particularly surprising because it happened in the state where Christian Science was founded.

7. It comes at a time when prosecutions of Christian Science parents for involuntary manslaughter or child endangerment have been on the increase.

The adjective clauses in the sentences above restrict the nouns they modify. For example, the church members are not just middle- and upper-middle class people. They are middle-class and they participate fully. This implies that not all middle-class people participate fully and successfully in American society but these people do. Also, Christian Science not only says that prayer can cure ailments. It can cure ailments (that) medicine considers congenital, incurable, or terminal. The adjective clauses are essential to the meaning.

Grammar Practice

The relative pronoun that one uses to begin an essential adjective clause depends on the function of the word in the clause. Working in pairs or small groups, decide which words can be used in each of the following adjective clauses. The number of blanks indicates the number of possibilities.

1. *Relative Pronoun as Subject of the Adjective Clause—Person:*

   They are middle-class people ___ ___ participate fully in life.

2. *Relative Pronoun as Subject of the Adjective Clause—Thing:*

   The first bell ___ ___ went off in my head was "religious freedom."

3. *Relative Pronoun as Object of the Adjective Clause—Person:*

   The parents ___ ___ ___ they are prosecuting are well-intentioned people.

4. *Relative Pronoun as Object of the Adjective Clause—Thing:*

   It cures other ailments ___ ___ ___ medicine considers congenital.

5. *Relative Pronoun as Possessive—Person or Thing:*

   This is the latest of a number of successful prosecutions of Christian Scientists ___ children died agonizing deaths.

6. *Relative Pronoun as Object of Preposition—Person:*

   The person on ___ the tenets of this church are based is Mary Baker Eddy.

   The person ___ the tenets of this church are based ___ is Mary Baker Eddy.

   The person ___ the tenets of this church are based ___ is Mary Baker Eddy.

   The person ___ the tenets of this church are based ___ is Mary Baker Eddy.

7. *Relative Pronoun as Object of Preposition—Thing:*

   The disease for ___ he is being treated used to be incurable.

   The disease ___ he is being treated ___ used to be incurable.

   The disease ___ he is being treated ___ used to be incurable.

   The disease ___ he is being treated ___ used to be incurable.

Focus on Form: Relative Adverbs for Time or Place

Nouns of time and place cannot always be followed by *when* or *where*. These two relative adverbs can be used to substitute for:

- **a time**   **+ in + which** (more formal)
    + when

    It comes at a time *when (in which)* prosecutions are on the increase.

- **a place**   **+ in or at + which** (more formal)
    + where

    The town *where (in which)* it happened is only a few miles from here.

    The place *at which (where)* I saw him is only a few miles from here.

- (But only: The town *which (that, Ø)* he mentioned is in Massachusetts.)
- When the relative adverbs are used, the words they refer to can be deleted in an essential adjective clause:

    He did it at a time in which few people had ever heard of it.
                                    BUT:
    He did it *at a time* when few people had ever heard of it.

    He did it when few people . . . .

Grammar Practice

Each of the following sentences contains an essential adjective clause. Complete the sentences with the correct relative pronoun or adverb (who, which, whose, whom, that, when, where, or Ø). If more than one can be used, give all possibilities.

1. Parents _____ children go to non-traditional schools must be careful to choose one _____ meets state regulations concerning education.

2. Sending a child to a school _____ the state has not accredited or approved could cause criminal charges to be brought against the parents.

3. Children _____ the state identifies as studying in unauthorized schools could even be institutionalized.

4. To the surprise of many people, the United States is a country _____ compulsory school attendance laws are determined by the

individual states. However, these states may not deny the constitutional rights of its citizens.

5. Over the years, the United States Supreme Court has been trying to find a balance between state laws _____ were too restrictive, such as those _____ required attendance only in public schools, and the interests of children _____ were not being properly educated.

6. The cases _____ the courts must have had difficulty deciding were those involving schools _____ were run by religious groups and _____ did not meet state standards.

7. Since children, the people for _____ state laws on education were intended, cannot decide for themselves about their education, the state feels a responsibility for them.

8. Opponents feel that it is the parents _____ must decide what is better for their children. Some even say that local communities are only concerned about losing state aid _____ is based on enrollment.

Reading 3: "Can Choosing Form of Care Become Neglect?"

Prereading Questions

1. Do you know of any forms of medical treatment which do not involve a medical doctor or "traditional" medical care? Are these treatments used in your country? Do you think they can be effective?

2. Do people have the right to choose their own forms of medical care even if this form of medicine is not recommended by their doctor?

3. Are physical therapy, massage, acupuncture, or herbal medicine ever used as options in your country? If they are, explain who would use them and when they would be used.

Vocabulary Practice

Match the italicized words in the sentences with the synonyms or definitions in the list below. Use the context of the sentence to help you guess the meaning.

___ criticize	___ arrogant
___ keep; own	___ belittle
___ prevent	___ take away; ignore
___ accusation	___ evidence

1. The *allegation* of neglect rests with Ms. Cheng's refusal to agree to surgery for her daughter.

2. The lawyer is seeking *testimony* by Asian as well as Western physicians.

3. The State Department of Children and Youth Services has been criticized for what people have called a series of inadequacies and is being *rebuked* in hearings throughout the state.

4. Ms. Cheng's lawyer said that case, in which Ms. Cheng only wants to try traditional Chinese medicine for her daughter first, is an example of how the medical establishment in the United States totally *disparages* alternate forms of medicine.

5. The lawyer added that the throwing away of a brand of medicine practiced by two-thirds of the world is *cavalier*.

6. "Western medicine has made great advances, but we don't *harbor* all medical knowledge in the world."

7. Doctors say it is not an issue of hospitals trying to (a.) *override* the rights of the mother. They say that since the child's illness could (b.) *preclude* her from getting out of a wheelchair, the parent does not have the right to deny treatment that could help.

Can Choosing Form of Care Become Neglect?

By JAMES FERON   (from the *New York Times*)

BRIDGEPORT, Conn., Sept. 27—When Juliet Cheng was called in to Newington Children's Hospital in July, she thought it was for a final consultation about the health of her 7-year-old daughter, who suffers from severe juvenile[32] rheumatoid arthritis,[33] before they returned to China for medical treatment there.

Instead, a security man and social workers charged her with neglect and placed her daughter, Shirley, into temporary state custody.

The allegation of neglect rests with Ms. Cheng's refusal to agree to surgery for her daughter's legs. Without it, the hospital says, Shirley will never be able to walk. But Ms. Cheng, who was born in China and is a naturalized United States citizen, says she does not trust American doctors. She wants to return to her native country to try more traditional and familiar options first, like physical therapy and herbal medicine.

A juvenile court judge has authorized surgery on the child's hips, knees, and ankles, but the procedure has been twice scheduled and postponed as Ms. Cheng's lawyer, George Athanson, takes the case through state and federal courts. He is seeking a full hearing, with testimony by Asian as well as Western physicians.

---

32. having to do with young people
33. a disease characterized by swelling, pain and burning of the *joints*, the areas where the bones join

The case is now in Federal District Court in Hartford, where Judge T. Emmet Clarie is deciding whether it is a federal matter and, if so, whether to grant a temporary restraining order.[34] "If he grants the order," Mr. Athanson said, "we'll have a full hearing on a preliminary injunction,[35] and then we'll bring in the doctors."

Ms. Cheng, 39, moved to this country in 1980. She has a mother and a sister living in the Poughkeepsie, N.Y., area, where she lived until moving to Newington for her daughter's treatment. She is separated from her husband, whom she met in the United States.

Although the case recalls medical confrontations over the rights of parents to withhold treatment from their children, this incident deals with what Ms. Cheng and her lawyer say is the right of a parent to choose a particular form of treatment.

Ms. Cheng says she is not opposed to medical intervention and has consented to physical therapy, the use of casts and anti-inflammatory[36] medication prescribed by specialists including her physician, Dr. Lawrence Zemel. Newington doctors, for their part, have permitted Ms. Cheng to continue to administer Chinese medication and to have her daughter treated by a practitioner of homeopathic medicine.[37]

Agency Is Said to Be Insensitive

The dispute comes at a time when the State Department of Children and Youth Services, which has temporary custody of Shirley Cheng, has been criticized for what people have called a series of inadequacies and is being rebuked in hearings throughout the state. A three-member panel is hearing testimony in a class action suit[38] that the Connecticut Civil Liberties Union brought nine months ago on behalf of nine children.

At a hearing in the class action suit Carolyn Richter, a lawyer for Connecticut Legal Services, offered examples Wednesday night of what she said were the agency's overbearing and insensitive operations. After the hearing, she said the Cheng case "is an example of the medical establishment deciding they have the truth of the matter and totally disparaging alternate forms of medicine."

Ms. Cheng "only wants to try other options first," Ms. Richter said. "What is outrageous is that powerful people—the institutions and the doctors—are throwing away a brand of medicine practiced by two-thirds of the world. That's cavalier."

"If there is still time, as we understand it, the state should not have stepped in," Ms. Richter said. She was referring to testimony that Dr. Zemel was said to have given in juvenile court, where proceedings are closed to the public, that the operation need not take place for two years. Mr. Athanson said he had a transcript of Dr. Zemel's testimony to that effect.

Hospital's View

Mr. Athanson also argued that "western medicine has made great advances, but we don't harbor all medical knowledge in the world. Some of the things that have been used in China for thousands of years may be helpful here."

Dr. Zemel, a specialist in pediatric rheumatology, has declined to discuss the case or to respond to the statement that Mr. Athanson said he made in closed court, but

---

34. a court order that stops an action 35. a court order to stop temporarily an action until a court decision has been made about that action 36. against inflammation, i.e., the heat, swelling, and pain caused by injury or infection
37. a system of medicine using small quantities of a treatment which in large doses would cause symptoms similar to the ones of the illness being treated. It is considered to be a more natural method of treatment.

---

38. a lawsuit by a plaintiff on his own behalf and on the behalf of other plaintiffs who have the same complaint against the defendant

Dr. Julius Landwirth, vice president for medical affairs at Newington, spoke for him and for the hospital.

"When Shirley was referred to us, she was absolutely crippled," Dr. Landwirth said. He said that physical therapy and medication had proved unsuccessful because "her joints were so contracted, so frozen, that it was impossible to straighten them out using the usual procedures."

"The problem arises when the only opportunity to prevent this child from living with a lifelong crippling condition is being denied her," he said. "It is then appropriate, when either a life-threatening condition or a condition with lifelong crippling implications exists, that a physician and an institution need to raise the question of possible medical neglect."

"It's not up to us to decide that," he said. "It's up to the child protection agency and the court to answer that question." Dr. Landwirth also asserted that it was "not the same as saying we have a culture gap because the child has been receiving care with nontraditional medicines in addition to the traditional ones."

Best Interests of the Child

"Nor is it an issue of physicians and the hospital overriding the rights of a mother to make decisions. The question is, given a serious, lifelong, irreversible handicapping condition that will preclude this child from ever getting out of a wheelchair and with treatment available to relieve that condition, does a parent have a right to deny that or is that denial a form of medical neglect."

He said the surgery would relieve the tightness around the girl's joints. "We don't really go into the joints; it's a matter of releasing the tension on the ligaments and tendons that surround the joint. They are all tightened up and shortened—they need to be released and lengthened."

A spokesman for the Department of Children and Youth Services, Tom Moriarty, said, "What the Newington doctors and we are saying, and to what the courts have so far agreed, is that what the mother wants to do is not in the best interests of the child."

Ms. Cheng, who visits her daughter twice a day: "Shirley is very upset in the hospital. Every time she sees me she asks me to take her out of her chair. She doesn't want to do the surgery. I just want her back so we can return to China."

Comprehension and Discussion

A. *Circle the correct answer. If the answer is false, tell why.*

1. Ms. Cheng's doctors are against any use of non-traditional medicine on Shirley.

   True   False

2. Ms. Cheng says she will allow surgery, but she wants to try traditional Chinese medicine first.

   True   False

3.   Reporters at the court proceedings quoted the doctor as saying that physical therapy had proved unsuccessful.

True   False

4.   A trial was held and surgery was ordered for Shirley.

True   False

B.   *Answer the following questions as completely as possible.*

1.   How does Ms. Cheng's case differ from the cases of the Twitchells and the Kings in the previous article?

2.   What arguments do Ms. Cheng and her lawyers give for her actions? What arguments does the prosecution give? List as many as possible.

3.   Since Ms. Cheng is trying to get her daughter treatment, why has the issue of neglect come up?

4.   In your opinion, can choosing a form of treatment become medical neglect or do people have the right to choose whatever form of treatment they wish for themselves or for their children?

5.   In your opinion, are the doctors, social workers, and courts who are trying to keep Shirley here being arrogant about other non-traditional forms of treatment?

6.   If you were the judge, how would you rule in this case? Explain your ruling.

(**Note:** A panel of three doctors appointed by the court later ruled that Shirley Cheng would not have to undergo surgery.)

Word Forms

Working with a partner, complete the following chart with the different forms of the words. Use your knowledge of other words and their different forms to help you. Do not be afraid to guess. A dash means there is no form.

Noun	Verb	Adjective	Adverb
allegation		alleged	
testimony		—	—
	rebuke	—	—
	disparage	disparaging	
—	—	cavalier	
	preclude		—

Vocabulary Practice

Complete the sentences below with the correct words from the following list. You may have to use different word forms and tenses. Do not use a word more than once.

allegation	testimony	rebuke	disparage
cavalier	harbor	override	preclude

1. The use of alternative forms of medicine which have not been tested in the United States, especially for serious diseases such as cancer and AIDS, often causes great debate and sometimes results in court cases. Doctors who use medicines which have not been tested and approved by the Food and Drug Administration will be strongly _____ and may even lose their license.

2. If these cases go to court, expert witnesses are often called in to give _____.

3. When medicines used in other countries are not available in the United States, this may be seen by some as a _____ of the medical system of the other country.

4. Sick people who are denied the use of alternative medicines often (a.) _____ that their rights are being (b.) _____ and that these restrictions (c.) _____ them from taking advantage of medicine that may help them. They say that the United States does not (d.) _____ all of the knowledge of medicine and that non-traditional types of medicine should be allowed.

5. The government counters this by saying that they are not being _____ about people's illness. They say that they are only trying to protect sick people from medicine that has not been proven to work.

Vocabulary Building

The prefix *over-*, as in "override," has several, sometimes opposite, meanings. For example, it can mean "to do in excess" (*overdo*), "to do unintentionally" (*overhear*), "to show superiority" (*oversee*), "to put in an inferior position" (*overturn*), etc. It is very often used, particularly with the meaning of "excess."

Using different forms of the words below, and the prefix over-, *complete the following sentences. Some of the words may not be obvious. Try to guess the meanings.*

time	lap	sleep	due	look	draw
come	sight	throw	joy	charge	eat

1. When they heard that they were not going to be prosecuted, they were _____.

2. That restaurant was wonderful last night, but I think I _____. I couldn't fall asleep for hours, and then, of course, this morning I _____ and got to work late.

3. I'd better get this book back to the library. It's _____.

4. I can't believe how high the lawyer's fees were. Joe was really
   _____.

5. My brother is glad he got the promotion, but he has to work incredible
   hours. And since he's not paid by the hour, he doesn't even get paid
   _____.

6. My boss told me he would _____ my mistake this time, but that if
   I did it again, I could be fired.

7. Fortunately, the plot to _____ the government did not succeed.

8. I'm sorry I can't lend you the money, but my bank account is already
   _____ and I don't get paid until next week.

9. They are always having problems at work because their jobs _____
   and they don't really know who is responsible for what. Consequently,
   sometimes important work doesn't get done or it gets done twice.

10. I'm sorry I didn't mention your name in the thank-you letter. It was a
    horrible _____ on my part.

11. It's very inspirational to read about those immigrants who _____
    all sorts of language, cultural, and economic problems and became incred-
    ible successes.

Vocabulary Building

*Working with a partner or in a small group, list as many other words as possible that
begin with the prefix* over-. *Discuss the meanings and give a sentence for each word.*

Focus on Form: Non-essential Adjective Clauses

Non-essential Adjective Clauses give extra or non-essential information. They:
- may be omitted without changing the meaning of the noun or of the
  sentence.
- must be separated from the rest of the sentence with commas.
- begin with *who, which, whose, whom (or a preposition + whom), where or
  when*.
- *cannot* begin with *that or Ø*.
- can be quantified with words such as *all, half, some, etc. (all of whom, half
  of which)*
- must modify a specific word, not an idea.

Grammar Practice

Each of the following sentences contains a non-essential adjective clause. Underline these clauses and separate them from the rest of the sentence with commas. The first one has been done for you.

1. Ms. Cheng, <u>who was born in China and is a naturalized U.S. citizen</u>, says she does not trust American doctors.

   (*who* = subject of clause—Person)

2. This comes at a time when the Department of Children and Youth Services which has temporary custody of Shirley Cheng is being criticized . . . .

   (*which* = subject of clause—Thing)

3. She is separated from her husband whom she met in China.

   (*whom* = object of clause—Person)

4. The operation the doctors describe as necessary would release the tension on the ligaments.

   (*which* = object of clause—Thing)

5. Ms. Cheng whose daughter was born in the U.S. was born in China.

   (*whose* = Possessive)

6. Dr. Zemel to whom Ms. Cheng went for medical advice declined to discuss the case.

   (*whom* = object of preposition—Person)

7. Chinese medicine about which little is known in the United States has been used for thousands of years in China.

   (*which* = object of preposition—Thing)

All of the adjective clauses in the previous section give extra information and may be omitted without changing the meaning of the sentence or of the noun they modify.

Ms. Cheng, *who was born in China*, says she does not trust...

If we say, "Ms. Cheng says she does not trust American doctors", the meaning of the sentence does not change. "Was born in China" is extra information.

Note: Generally speaking, adjective clauses that come after proper nouns (Ms. Cheng, America, China, for example) are non-essential.

Grammar Practice

Using adjective clauses, combine the following sentences to form one sentence for each group. To help you, the sentences have been marked E for essential and NE for non-essential adjective clauses. Remember that the essential clauses do not need commas but the non-essential ones do. If there is more than one way to combine the sentences, give both ways.

This exercise will give you some background information about the Amish. Remember that this is not a paragraph. A paragraph would not have adjective clauses in every sentence. This is just practice in using adjective clauses. After completing the exercise, discuss this group of people. Have you heard about them before? Have you seen photographs of them? If so, describe them and tell what you know about them.

1. Throughout the centuries, the Amish have held tightly to a biblical command. This command states that we should not conform to the world. (E)

2. In the 1800s, the Amish went to Pennsylvania. They were being persecuted for their religious beliefs. They found religious freedom in Pennsylvania. (NE)

3. The Amish call all the non-Amish "English." There are only two types of people for them. (NE)

4. The Amish are also called Pennsylvania Dutch. Many of them live in Pennsylvania. (NE)

5. The name was a mistake. The "English" gave them this name. (NE)

6. They were originally from the German part of Switzerland and spoke German. The word "German" in the German language is "deutsch." This was misunderstood as Dutch. (NE)

7. When a number of cases of polio broke out in Pennsylvania, the Amish would not let their children take the polio vaccine. Their religion prohibits the use of modern medicine. (NE)

8. The problem was to get the Amish to agree to take the vaccine so that no more people, Amish or non-Amish, would get the disease. The state government had this problem. (E)

9. Finally the Amish agreed to take the vaccine. The Amish do not like to make problems for their "English" neighbors. (NE)

10. The Amish are gentle people. Their values are totally unlike those of most Americans. (NE) Many admire these people for their simple life-style. (E)

Grammar Practice

Each of the following sentences contains an adjective clause. Decide whether it is essential or not. If it is not essential, separate the clause with commas. Then give the correct relative pronoun or adverb. If more than one can be used, give all possibilities. Use Ø to show that no relative pronoun is necessary.

Remember that none of the information in these sentences is new to you. Use your knowledge from the readings to help you decide which clauses are essential and which are non-essential.

1. Ms. Cheng thought the meeting was for a final consultation about the health of her daughter _____ doctors are treating for severe rheumatoid arthritis before their return to China.

2. Mr. Zemel has declined to respond to the statement _____ Mr. Athanson said he made in court.

3. Ms. Cheng _____ visits her daughter twice a day said, "Shirley is very upset in the hospital."

4. The dispute comes at a time _____ the State Department of Children and Youth Services _____ has temporary custody of Shirley Cheng has been criticized for what people have called a series of inadequacies.

5. She has a mother and a sister both of _____ live in the Poughkeepsie, N.Y. area.

6. The death of two-year-old Robin Twitchell and the conviction _____ followed was only the latest of a number of successful prosecutions of Christian Scientists _____ children died agonizing deaths after spiritual healing.

7. The doctrine _____ spiritual healing is based on holds that all physical ailments are rooted in fear, alienation from God, and other mental factors.

8. What's the point of taking a childless couple _____ everyone has described as outstanding in every other way and putting them in prison?

9. Rita Swan _____ son died of meningitis in 1977 founded CHILD, an organization _____ name is an acronym for Children's Healthcare Is a Legal Duty.

10. The Twitchells _____ have three other sons are described by their lawyer as loving parents _____ tragedy should never have been compounded by this prosecution.

Class Project

Work on this project individually or in groups of two to three students. Then present your findings to the class.

The United States has a number of small religious sects which differ greatly in beliefs (and often in dress or customs) from the majority of the people of the country or even within their general religious grouping (Christian, Jewish, Muslim). Go to the school or public library and see what you can learn about one of the following religious groups. If you know of a similar group that is not listed here, one in your country, for example, which differs a great deal from the rest of society, feel free to do research on it. Finding pictures or drawings of your group would be very helpful. Make a presentation to the class about the group you have chosen. Two or three students may wish to work together.

Amish   Mennonites
Chassidim (Hassidim)   Shakers

Discussion and Writing

Discuss the following topics, first in pairs or small groups and then with the teacher and the entire class. After your discussion, pick one (or more) of the topics and write an essay about it.

1. The First Amendment to the Constitution states that the government cannot prohibit the free exercise of religion or make laws that stop people from following their own religion. Up to what limit do you think people should be allowed to practice their own religion without interference from the government? When would governmental interference be required?

2. Do parents have total control of their children or does the government have a right and a responsibility to intervene in the care of children? If you feel that the government could and should intervene in certain cases, tell specifically when this should happen. Can this right also be extended to unborn children, as, for example, in cases of pregnant women who take drugs or other substances which could harm the child?

3. Discuss the case of Ms. De Beni Souza, the California woman who was ordered by a judge to stop smoking in front of her son. In a custody case, is the law within its rights in telling a parent what he or she can or cannot do? Do you feel that the law has gone too far in this case? If so, explain why and tell what the limit of governmental interference should be in these cases. If not, support your agreement.

4. Are there any religious groups in your country which are in a minority and which are in conflict in some way with the government or the laws of the land? Explain the background of the problem and what the government does or does not do about it. What solution do you see to the problem? If there is a minority religious group but no problem, explain why. What have the people or the government done to avoid problems of this kind?

5. Some religions forbid certain medical practices which could help people from contracting a disease or which could even save a life. The Amish are against immunization, for example, and Jehovah's Witnesses are against blood transfusions. Do the Amish have a right to refuse to be immunized (or have their children immunized) even if it means they might get or spread an illness? If they do refuse, should they be forced to take the vaccine? Or if a Jehovah's Witness is in an accident and will die without a blood transfusion, does the doctor have the ethical and moral duty to obey his or her wishes and not give the transfusion, or should this be done against the patient's wishes? What if the patient is a child whose parents are against the transfusion on religious grounds? Comment on either or both of these situations.

Word List

Below is a list of the new words, and their different forms, presented in this chapter.

Noun	Verb	Adjective	Adverb
allegation	allege	alleged	allegedly
	attest		
attribution	attribute		
		cavalier	cavalierly
circumvention	circumvent		
	counter	counter	
disparagement	disparage	disparaging	disparagingly
efficacy		efficacious	efficaciously
endangerment	endanger	endangered	
exemption	exempt		
generation	generate		
harbor	harbor		
	hold (that)		
impediment	impede		
infringement	infringe (on, upon)		
		inherent	inherently
leniency		lenient	leniently
obstruction	obstruct	obstructive	obstructively
	override		
preclusion	preclude	preclusive	
rebuke	rebuke		
resort	resort (to)		
subservience		subservient	subserviently
testimony	testify		
		unmitigated	
	(mitigate)	(mitigating)	

CHAPTER 5

Drunk Driving: Whose Responsibility Is It?

Reading 1: "Employers Becoming Court Targets in the Fight to Halt Drunken Driving"

Prereading Questions

1. What part, if any, does alcohol play in making business deals in your country? When people work for a company, do they ever feel an obligation to drink?

2. What are the drinking laws in your country? What happens if a person is found driving under the influence of alcohol?

3. If a person drinks too much and has an accident, whose responsibility is it? What if the person is not an adult?

4. Generally speaking, do you think that a person who sells or serves alcohol to someone who is obviously drunk or getting drunk has any moral or legal responsibility for the actions of that person?

Vocabulary Practice

Circle the correct synonym or definition for each of the italicized words in the sentences below. Use the context of the sentences to help you guess the meaning.

1. Donna Waldrop won an $800,000 judgment against the company that employed the drunken driver who killed her son in an accident. She said she wanted corporate America to get the message that they had to be *accountable.*

   a. able to show where their money is
   b. responsible
   c. free of care

2. This may be a trend towards *holding* companies legally *liable* when drinking and doing business are mixed.

   a. making responsible
   b. making truthful
   c. making free from guilt

3. In the 80s the courts said that the establishments that sold the liquor had a duty and a responsibility, but the corporations got through the 80s *unscathed.*

   a. with responsibility
   b. unharmed
   c. dutifully

4. Even if the Florida case is overturned on appeal, it has made an *indelible* impression on the way in which corporations think about these issues.

    a. controversial
    b. can't be argued
    c. can't be erased

5. Expense reports would show that the man who bought the drinks was *reimbursed* by the company for those purchases.

    a. not allowed
    b. paid back
    c. not paid

6. Florida does not have a law establishing social host liability for guests who *overindulge* and then have accidents.

    a. buy others too many drinks
    b. act responsibly
    c. do or have something to excess

7. There is a social responsibility that we as sponsors of events where alcohol is served have to be *cognizant* of.

    a. legally responsible for
    b. aware of
    c. careless about

8. Often we see others drinking and we know they are going to drive and we *disassociate** ourselves from it. (* This word is also spelled "dissociate.")

    a. take responsibility for
    b. separate
    c. interest

Employers Becoming Court Targets In the Fight to Halt Drunken Driving

By RONALD SMOTHERS (from the *New York Times*)

Brenda Greenbaum and Donna Waldrop are not financiers,[1] corporate raiders[2] or giants of industry. But the mere mention[3] of their names may send shivers[4] through the corporate suites[5] of companies that give Christmas and New Year's parties or sponsor functions that combine business and liquor.

Mrs. Greenbaum, a nurse in Boca Raton, Fla., said that her 23-year-old son, Raymond Fields, was killed six years ago by a drunken

---

1. people who control large amounts of money
2. people who take over large corporations
3. just saying 4. cause to be afraid

5. executive office

driver coming home from a business and social gathering. Three months ago, she won an $800,000 judgment against the company that employed the driver.

"I wanted corporate America to get the message that they had to be accountable," she said. "I still have a lot of unresolved grief, but maybe some of those executives will think about this and realize that it could have been their loved ones who got killed."

As for Donna Waldrop of Euless, Tex., there is still a bitter edge in her voice[6] when she talks about her husband, Dudley, who was killed nearly four years ago as he was driving home from a night of what she said was business-related drinking. Last month she and her husband's three children reached an $11 million out-of-court settlement with his employer, a Fort Worth beer distributor.

"If they are going to send them out drinking and expect them to drive, they ought to take the responsibility," Mrs Waldrop said.

Mixing Drinking and Business

Even though the two cases do not yet have the weight of legal precedents, together their impact has been enough to get the attention of many companies. Some fear that the cases may represent the leading edge[7] of a trend toward holding companies legally liable when drinking and doing business are mixed.

To be sure, the number of alcohol-related automobile deaths has declined in the last 10 years, to 39.7 percent of all accident deaths in 1990, from 46.3 percent in 1982. But at the same time, courts throughout the country have been broadening the liability of bars, of the hosts of private parties where liquor has been served, and now, of companies paying for liquor at business functions.

"In the 80s the focus in these cases was on the liquor licensee,[8] the bar or restaurant which sold the liquor to the person who went out and had an accident," said Ronald Beitman, a Massachusetts lawyer and expert on liquor liability. "The courts said that those establishments had a duty and a responsibility in those cases, but the corporations got through the 80s unscathed. These cases are telling them that in the 90s they are going to be subject to the same sort of scrutiny and that they have a special duty."

Jay A. Winsten, director of the Harvard Alcohol Project at the university's School of Public Health, said, "The message here is that if the company pays for the alcohol, they have a duty and responsibility in the event of an accident. The implication is that every isolated instance of business drinking constitutes corporate drinking, and by putting the company's deep pockets[9] at risk that means it might spur changes."[10]

In interviews, corporate meeting planners said companies have long been aware of the risks inherent in alcohol consumption linked to the job. Many, they say, have long since changed policies and practices to cut down on drinking at business meetings, and some have canceled seasonal parties and celebrations altogether.

A survey by the Harvard Alcohol Project showed that the Procter & Gamble Company, the Campbell Soup Company, and the Goodyear Tire and Rubber Company are among many large corporations that have eliminated Christmas or holiday parties because of their concern about employee drinking. Other companies, among them the International Business Machines Corporation, the State Farm Mutual Automobile Insurance Company, and the General Motors Corporation, still hold the parties but substitute cake and coffee or fruit baskets and other food items for alcohol.

Kate Dane, a meeting planner with Cincinnati Bell Information Systems, said the company now limits the liquor available at

---

6. a bitter sound to   7. have the lead; be ahead of   8. person who holds the license

9. the financial assets of the company
10. cause or force change to happen

business functions, both because its employees have a greater health consciousness and because the company is more cost conscious.

'Whole New Can of Worms'

But Serena Leiser, who was a meeting planner for the Data General Corporation, a software company based in Westborough, Mass., said the Florida and Texas cases "open up a whole new can of worms."[11]

Mr. Beitman, the Massachusetts lawyer, said he has been getting calls from corporate lawyers seeking his advice on what they should do in light of[12] the Florida and Texas cases. Even if the Florida decision is overturned on appeal, he said, it has made an indelible impression on the way in which corporations think about these issues.

Forty-three states and Washington D.C. have passed laws or their courts have repeatedly found that negligent commercial servers of alcohol can be held liable in some accidents by their intoxicated patrons, a recent survey by the National Highway Traffic Safety Administration found. Twenty-three states extend this same liability to non-commercial settings and to social hosts. But in 12 of those 23 states, social hosts can only be held liable if they serve alcohol to minors.[13] And in at least three states—Missouri, Washington, and Colorado—the courts have specifically said that social hosts and, by extension, corporate hosts cannot be considered in the same way as those who sell drinks.

The Florida Case

The Florida case dates back to 1985. Not only did Mrs. Greenbaum lose her son in the car accident in Fort Lauderdale, she also lost her best friend.

On the night of Sept. 20, John Mills, a heating and refrigeration systems salesman with Carroll Air Systems of Tampa, was attending an industry seminar at a hotel in Fort Lauderdale and, some witnesses later said, drinking and talking to potential customers. His boss, James Carroll, was there as well, buying drinks for Mr. Mills and others. Mr. Carroll's expense reports would show that he was reimbursed by the company for those purchases.

Shortly after midnight, Mr. Mills left the hotel for the 20-minute drive home. Minutes later he plowed[14] into the back of Mr. Fields' car at a speed that the police later estimated at 86 to 97 miles per hour in a 45 m.p.h. zone. Mr. Mills survived the accident.

Jeffrey D. Fisher, Mrs. Greenbaum's lawyer, said he built his case around the idea that the company "fostered and encouraged" Mr. Mills to do business over drinks at the seminar and "looked the other way in regard to an inherently dangerous business practice."

Florida does not have a law establishing social host liability for guests who overindulge and then have accidents, and that factor made the ruling in the Carroll Air Systems case all the more significant, some experts say.

"The significant relationship in this case was employee/employer and not host and guest or bar and customer," Mr. Fisher said. "We proved that what was happening, the entertainment was part of the business and that the employer had a duty to supervise its employees."

Mark Boyd, Carroll Air Systems's lawyer, called the jury decision in the case "outrageous" and said that the connection between Mr. Mills's attendance at what he called a dinner dance and the conduct of business was "a bit strained."[15]

---

11. open up new, unexpected problems which will be difficult to control　12. considering
13. legally not an adult

14. ran into, usually at great speed　15. taken to an extreme; hard to prove

The Texas Case

In the Texas case, Dudley Waldrop, a brands manager for B. E. Keith Distributors, was involved in a practice called "night calls" in which marketing teams from both local distributors and the Anheuser-Busch Companies, Inc., visit bars in an area, buying drinks for patrons in a bid to build brand loyalty. On the way home, Mr. Waldrop drove his car into a parked car and was instantly killed.

Although both the distributor and the beer company maintained in court papers that Mr. Waldrop got drunk in the course of visiting other bars not on that night's schedule and on his own time, the local distributor nevertheless settled the case out of court.[16] David Greenlee, general counsel for the distributor would not comment on the settlement or confirm the amount. He said the company continues to maintain that Mr. Waldrop "was stone cold sober"[17] when his company duties ended that night and he went off on his own to visit other bars.

Mrs. Waldrop and other family members have also filed suit against Anheuser-Busch. No trial date has been set for that suit, and Anheuser-Busch the nation's largest brewery, would not comment on the case.

Many companies like the Control Data, a computer manufacturer based in Minneapolis, have been aware of their potential liability for some years. Kevin Johnston, national manager for marketing and incentive programs at Control Data, said the company has policies aimed at preventing problems. Liquor is not served at company functions on company property, he said. When the company has meetings outside its property, he said, it hires professional bartenders trained to spot problems, does not offer open bars and uses a system of drink tickets to control drinking.

In addition, Mr. Johnston said, when the company holds meetings at resorts, all events are held on resort property to cut down on the need to drive. And, he said, if the need for an event outside the resort does arise, there is always a plan in place to have employees transported by bus or van.

"Every state views the law differently, but we all see what these lawsuits can do," Mr. Johnston said. "There is a social responsibility that we, as sponsors of these events, have to be cognizant of. Wherever there is the opportunity for something to go wrong, you have to be careful."

Julie Rochman, an official at Health Communications, a consulting firm in Washington that specializes in alcohol-related issues, said that such measures as those being used by Control Data are not as widespread as they should be. Still, her company gets calls from corporations when they are about to have a Christmas party or when they are in the midst[18] of lawsuits over some alcohol-related accident involving their employees.

"They either want a quick fix[19] or they want us to help them get out of trouble," she said. "The motivation of a lot of companies is more fear than concern. But we are getting a lot more interest since the Florida decision alone, because it is a new wrinkle."[20]

"You know, this isn't a problem only with your 'problem drinkers'," Ms. Rochman said. "It's anybody, including the company vice president, who some are afraid to approach and tell he's drinking too much. It just takes people skills." Mrs. Greenbaum agreed.

"So often we see others drinking and we know they are going to drive and we disassociate ourselves from it," she said. "But then something happens, people come around[21] for a while afterward, and then they stop. But your grief goes on. People ought to be more aware of this."

---

16. come to an agreement in a civil case before the case begins or ends 17. completely sober; not at all drunk

18. in the middle of 19. an easy answer or solution 20. a new possible problem
21. people do the right thing and act as they should

Comprehension and Discussion

A. *Circle the correct answer. If the answer is false, tell why.*

1. The plaintiffs in both of these cases are family members of men who died in accidents after drinking for business purposes.

    True   False

2. In alcohol-related accidents, the tendency now seems to be for the courts to hold the giver or seller of alcohol liable rather than the drinker.

    True   False

3. Three states have specifically exempted corporations from liability.

    True   False

B. *Answer the following questions as completely as possible.*

1. What has been the change of attitude between the 80s and the 90s concerning drinking and responsibility?

2. How are different corporations reacting to this trend? List as many different policies as possible.

3. Explain the following sentence from the article: "The motivation of a lot of companies is more fear than concern."

4. What is the special significance of the Florida decision?

5. Do you see any major differences between the Florida case and the Texas case? If not, why do you see them as the same? If so, does this difference make you see the two suits against the companies in a different light?

6. What are your opinions on both of these cases? Should companies be held responsible when drinking and doing business are mixed and an accident occurs?

7. In this article, a statement is made which is neither proved nor explained. It could leave the reader looking for an explanation or wondering what the writer meant. Is there any sentence that left you with this feeling?

Word Forms

Working with a partner, complete the following chart with the different forms of the words. Use your knowledge of other words and their different forms to help you. Do not be afraid to guess. A dash means there is no form.

Noun	Verb	Adjective	Adverb
—		accountable	—
—		cognizant	—
—		indelible	
—		liable	—
	reimburse	—	—
	overindulge		

Vocabulary Practice

Complete the sentences below with the correct words from the following list. You may have to use different word forms and tenses. Do not use a word more than once.

overindulge	reimburse	hold liable
accountable	cognizant	indelible
unscathed	disassociate	

1. If you have expenses for a job, very often you have to pay for them yourself and then submit a request for _____.

2. The possible _____ of a company when one of its employees is in an accident after drinking for business purposes is a fairly new idea.

3. It is not uncommon for a drunk driver to walk away from an accident completely _____ while others are seriously injured or even killed.

4. During holiday times, _____ in food and drink is common. Therefore, one must be extra careful when driving during those periods.

5. One who has lost a loved one because of a drunk driver will probably be _____ affected by the accident.

6. In the past, it was easier for companies to (a.) _____ themselves from an employee's behavior. Now that there is a possibility of being (b.) _____ for an employee's actions, companies have to be more aware of possible problems. This (c.) _____ could save lives and money.

Vocabulary Building

"But at the same time, courts throughout the country have been *broadening* the liability of bars . . ."

The italicized verb in the sentence above *(to broaden)* follows a specific wordbuilding rule. What is the rule? Working in small groups, list other words you can think of that follow the same rule. Discuss the meanings of the words with your teacher.

Rule : _____ + *-en* = _____

Focus on Form: Verb + Gerund or Infinitive

The company *refused to acknowledge* having any responsibility for the accident.

refuse + **infinitive (to. . .)**   *acknowledge* + **gerund (-ing)**

A. Gerunds or Infinitives

When two verbs come together in English, sometimes the second one is a gerund and sometimes it is an infinitive. This is a problem for people learning English because there does not seem to be any reason for using one or the other. One possible explanation is that the gerund is used to talk about something that is a fact while the infinitive is used to talk about something in the future.

She enjoys having a drink after work.—She knows she enjoys it because she has done it. It's a fact.

She hopes to open her own bar and restaurant.—She has a hope about the future.

However, there are many cases where the rule does not work, and there are many exceptions. Most people feel it is easier just to be aware of the words and to practice using them whenever possible.

B. Negatives and Passives

- the negative of the infinitive or the gerund is formed with *not*
- the passive is formed with *to be* or *being* + *past participle*

  He resolved *to drink* less at parties this year.

  He resolved *not to drink* so much at parties this year.

  He expected *to be served* whatever he wanted.

> She contemplated *serving* only non-alcoholic drinks at the party.
>
> She contemplated *not serving* alcohol at the party.
>
> She resented *being told* what she should or shouldn't serve at the party.
>
> **Note:**
>
> 1. She didn't contemplate serving alcohol at the party = She never thought about serving alcohol. It was never even a question.
> 2. She contemplated not serving alcohol. = She thought about the idea of not serving alcohol. She thought about a negative action.

Grammar Practice

Complete the following sentences using a gerund or an infinitive in each blank. You may have to use negatives or passives. Try to do them as quickly as possible without thinking about them too much. Which one sounds better to you? After you have finished, check the answers by looking at the lists of words (pages 127-128) that are followed by gerunds or infinitives.

1. In California a gas station sold gasoline to a drunk woman who then had an accident, killing two people. The court ruled that selling her gasoline was the same as giving her the key to the car. The service station attendants later admitted (know) _____ that the driver was drunk, but still they agreed (serve) _____ her and (sell) _____ her gasoline. They feel that they had done enough by spending a great deal of time (try) _____ to sober her up and that they don't deserve (hold) _____ liable for the accident.

2. Most people can't imagine (sell, neg.) _____ a drink in a bar if they are old enough and if they can afford (pay) _____. They may even demand (serve) _____. However, bartenders can refuse (serve) _____ anyone they want if the person appears (be) _____ drunk. Bartenders may have difficulty sometimes (decide) _____ who has had too much to drink, but someone who can barely manage (sit) _____ up at the bar cannot be expected (drive) _____ away safely. Although people resent (tell) _____ they have had too much, and many bartenders may hesitate (say) _____ this, the bars have to avoid (involve) _____ in a lawsuit. And, of course, no one wants (risk) _____ (be) _____ the cause of injury or death to anyone else.

3. Both bars and private hosts should spend some time (think) _____ about what they can do to help people who tend (overdrink) _____.

Restaurant and bar associations advise (keep) _____ a large stock of snack foods and non-alcoholic drinks available at all times. They even recommend (give) _____ free non-alcoholic drinks to designated drivers. Hosts of private parties should resist (fill) _____ up a glass every time they see that it is empty, and they should arrange (have) _____ intoxicated guests driven home.

4. The judge considered only (give) _____ the drunk driver a warning when the driver promised (drive, neg.) _____ under the influence of alcohol again. However, when the judge happened (learn) _____ that the driver had failed (appear) _____ for counselling after a previous drunk-driving case, he sentenced the driver to three months community service and threatened (revoke) _____ the driver's license for two years if he dared (do) _____ it again. Although the defendant knows he will miss (drink) _____ a few cocktails before he returns home at night, he realizes that he has to give up (stop) _____ at the local bar for "happy hour." If he loses his license, he'll have to quit (work) _____. He knows that he needs (learn) _____ some self-restraint.

Focus on Form

Verb + Gerund

acknowledge	escape	recommend
admit	finish	regret*
advise	give up	resent
appreciate	have a good time	resist
avoid	have fun	resume
be busy	have trouble	risk
can't help	imagine	spend time
consider	keep on	spend ten minutes (a day, a week, etc.)
discuss	miss	suggest
dislike	picture	take up
don't mind	postpone	understand
encourage	put off	
enjoy	quit	

*Regret + *infinitive* is used to give bad news in a formal way.
("We regret to inform you that the show has been cancelled.")

Verb + Infinitive

afford	endeavor	plan
agree	expect	pretend
appear	fail	promise
arrange	happen	refuse
ask	hesitate	resolve
attempt	hope	seem
care	intend	tend
choose	learn	threaten
dare	manage	want
decide	mean**	wish
demand	need	would like
deserve		

** *to mean* = to intend = + infinitive; I *meant to go* home early.
to mean = have as a consequence = + gerund; Drinking too much now
means having a headache tomorrow morning.

Verb + Gerund or Infinitive
(No Change in Meaning)

begin	hate	neglect
can't stand	like	prefer
continue	love	start

He *hates to see* people drink too much.

He *hates seeing* people drink too much.

Reading 2: "Now Barkeepers Join Drive for Safer Drinking"

Prereading Questions

1. What responsibility do bartenders or waiters have to watch the level of sobriety or intoxication of their customers?

2. Can people who serve alcohol refuse to serve someone who has already had too much too drink? Can or should they also encourage people to drink less?

3. What else can bars and restaurants do to keep people from getting drunk?

4. Do bars in your country do anything to get people to drink more, such as offering snacks or lowering the price of drinks at certain times?

Vocabulary Practice

Circle the correct synonym or definition for each of the italicized words in the sentences below. Use the context of the sentences to help you guess the meaning.

1. The police chief is *toasting* the bartenders because they didn't serve drinks.

   a. punishing
   b. drinking to the health or well-being of
   c. criticizing

2. When summertime visitors *swell* the population of Martha's Vineyard to 85,000, vacationers fill the beaches and bars looking for a good time.

   a. improve the quality of
   b. make more friendly
   c. increase the size of

3. *Rowdiness* was so reduced that the season turned out to be one of the quietest in years.

   a. loud, disorderly behavior
   b. happiness
   c. crime

4. A TIPS video-taped restaurant scene (A.) *depicts* a woman, to the embarrassment of her husband, complaining (B.) *caustically* to the waitress that her cocktail is weak.

   (A.) a. define
          b. represent
          c. criticize
   (B.) a. sarcastically, unpleasantly
          b. politely
          c. jokingly, in a friendly way

5. Most people would just put her down as *obnoxious*, but a trained person would see that she has had too much.

   a. right to complain
   b. drunk
   c. offensive, disagreeable

6. The goal is to avoid *confrontation* and an ugly scene.

   a. hostile opposition
   b. losing customers
   c. seeing her face to face

7. As a further *incentive*, they are giving away a car.

   a. criticism
   b. approval
   c. motivation

8. The bartender schools also recommend that bars *stock* plenty of nonalcoholic beverages.

   a. invest in the stock market
   b. not carry
   c. keep a supply of

9. Behind the (A.) *proliferation* of bartender programs is (B.) *sustained* national anger over abusive drinking.

   (A.) a. success
         b. rapid increase
         c. complaints about
   (B.) a. continuous
         b. weak
         c. lack of

10. Courts are awarding ever bigger damages against businesses serving drunk patrons who later *maim* or kill someone.

    a. insult
    b. cripple, disfigure
    c. crash into

11. Shortly before the accident, the man *staggered* up to the bar and said loudly, "Give me one for the road."

    a. walk unsteadily
    b. walk proudly
    c. run

Now Barkeepers Join Drive for Safer Drinking

By STEVE HUNTLY
(from *U.S. News and World Report*)

It's none for the road at many bars since courts made drink servers pay damages in drunk-driving cases.

The police chief is toasting the bartenders these days in Edgartown, Mass. All because of drinks they didn't serve.

That made 1985 different. Normally, when summertime visitors swell the population of the Martha's Vineyard town to 85,000, vacationers clog[22] beaches

---

22. to cause to become full or blocked

"Happy Hour" after work. Or should it be called "Dangerous Hour"?

and bars looking for a good time and sometimes—after a few too many drinks—finding trouble.

But this year, drunken-driving arrests in June and July numbered only a third of last year's. Rowdiness was so reduced that the season turned out to be one of the quietest in years. To Chief George Searle, the reason was clear: "The bars cleaned up their act."[23]

Taverns[24] and restaurants in Edgartown joined the growing numbers of bars and eateries[25] across the country responding to lawsuits over drunk driving by encouraging "responsible drinking" by patrons and by training bartenders, waiters and waitresses to spot clues[26] that an imbiber[27] is nearing the limit and to steer him or her away[28] from alcohol.

In Edgartown's case, the school for bartenders came in a program called TIPS—Training for Intervention Procedures by Servers of Alcohol—which was developed by Dr. Morris Chafetz and is marketed by Health Communications, Inc., of Washington, D.C. Other training projects have been produced by the National Restaurant Association and the National Licensed Beverage Association, a tavern trade group.

---

23. to improve or change for the better one's actions   24. bar   25. restaurants (slang)
26. to recognize signs   27. drinker (formal)   28. to gently guide away

The programs can include instruction manuals, videotape presentations and role-playing sessions on cues betraying potentially troublesome drinking and how to handle it. A TIPS video-taped restaurant scene. for example, depicts a woman, to the embarrassment of her husband, complaining caustically to a waitress that her Rob Roy, a cocktail of Scotch and vermouth, is weak. "Most people would just put her down as obnoxious," says master trainer Scott Mueller. "But someone who can't taste the Scotch has had too much." The way to handle her: get water and snacks to the table and seek her husband's help.

The goal is to avoid confrontation and an ugly scene. Jim Lambert, manager of Rumors restaurant in Washington, D.C., credits the training for an estimated 25 percent drop in the number of times Rumors has to "shut someone off."

Rumors also instituted a designated-driver[29] project to give drinkers a safe ride home. Patrons signing up as drivers get free nonalcoholic drinks each time they come in with a group. As a further incentive, Rumors and a local auto dealer are giving away a car in drawing[30] for designated drivers.

Shirley Temple[31] returns. The bartender schools also recommended that bars stock plenty of nonalcoholic beverages, offer "mocktails,"[32] alcohol-free cocktails such as a daiquiri[33] without the rum, give away high-protein and greasy snacks such as boiled eggs, peanuts, ribs and shrimp that slow the absorption of spirits, and end such "happy hour"[34] features as two drinks for the price of one.

The schooling causes some businesses to rethink their operations. Don Clark, owner of the Colony Bar in Port Huron, Mich., doubled to six his number of waitresses so each one would have fewer people to watch for signs of trouble.

The training was relatively rare only two years ago. Now, it is found across the country and has won the endorsement of big brewers,[35] including Anheuser-Busch, Miller, and Stroh. Seminars for the National Restaurant Association's program are available in 35 states. More than 12,000 people have taken the tavern association's course. In eight months on the job, TIPS master trainer Mueller visited 40 states. TIPS' expertise has been passed on to 1,850 trainers—often bar and restaurant owners or mangers who instruct their employees. For instance, Nancy Sage, administrator of Sage's restaurants in Chicago, has tutored 350 people.

Behind the proliferation of bartender programs in sustained national anger over abusive drinking, blamed for at least 43 percent of last year's 46,200 traffic fatalities. Massachusetts, Connecticut, Rhode Island, and North Carolina are among states that have banned "happy hour" cheap drinks, and other states are considering restrictions.

Courts are awarding ever bigger damages against businesses serving drunk patrons who later maim or kill someone. In January, a restaurant agreed to a 3.9-million-dollar out-of-court settlement for the family of a Mattapoisett, Mass., woman killed by a drunken driver. Shortly before the accident the man had staggered up to the restaurant's bar and said loudly, "Give me one for the road."[36]

---

29. a person in a group who promises not to drink alcohol and to be the driver for the rest of the group   30. a type of lottery   31. a drink that looks like a cocktail but has no alcohol; a "cocktail" for a child, named after a famous child movie star   32. mock, or fake, cocktail; cocktail with no alcohol   33. a cocktail made of rum, fruit juice, sugar and ice.   34. limited time, for example from 4:00 to 6:00 PM, during which a bar gives food or sells drinks at a special price   35. companies that make beer   36. the last drink before leaving

Reported decisions against alcohol servers soared 300 percent in the past two years, says Ronald Beitman, a Falmouth, Mass., lawyer and publisher of *Dram Shop and Alcohol Reporter* newsletter. Dispensers of alcoholic beverages are liable in such cases in 35 states and the District of Columbia.

The bottom line. Alcohol-awareness training programs can help restaurants in some states cut costs of hard-to-come-by[37] liability insurance. The CIGNA Corporation's INA and Aetna Insurance subsidiaries offer a 10 percent discount on liquor-law liability rates to businesses where three fourths of alcohol servers have passed TIPS exams.

Insurance and legal costs make the fees for the training programs cheap. TIPS charges $500 for teaching trainers and $12.50 for each server subsequently instructed by the trainer.

Costs aside, the hospitality industry see bartender schools as a way to protect a vital part of business. Says a Chicago restaurateur, "If we don't sell alcohol, the price of food goes up and we're in lot trouble."

---

37. difficult to obtain or find

Comprehension and Discussion

A. *Circle the correct answer. If the answer is false, tell why.*

1. People who serve alcohol are being trained to be able to determine when a person is drunk.

   True   False

2. The TIPS training program is so successful partly because it is the only one of its kind in the United States.

   True   False

3. The major beer companies are against the programs because people will drink less and the companies will lose money.

   True   False

B. *Answer the following questions as completely as possible.*

1. Briefly, and in your own words, explain how and why the summer of 1985 was different from other summers in Edgartown, Massachusetts. What led to the efforts to bring about a change?

2. In addition to bartender training programs, such as TIPS, what other recommendations or methods are used to discourage people from drinking and driving or from getting drunk? Give four and explain each one fully.

3. What are the reasons, both on the part of the bars and of the public, for this strong interest in drunk driving?

4. In what different ways do these programs help bars and restaurants?

5. How successful has the TIPS program been?

6.   Do you feel that a bar or restaurant should ever have responsibility for an accident caused by a driver who got drunk in that bar or restaurant?

7. The article mentions a case in which an out-of-court settlement was reached. Why do you think the restaurant agreed to this settlement of $3.9 million? What would have been the main argument against them?

8. Would these types of programs and courses be possible, or probable, in your country? Would they be necessary or helpful?

Word Forms

Working with a partner, complete the following chart with the different forms of the words. Use your knowledge of other words and their different forms to help you. Do not be afraid to guess. A dash means there is no form.

Noun	Verb	Adjective	Adverb
—	—		caustically
confrontation			—
	depict	—	—
	—	obnoxious	
proliferation		—	—
rowdiness	—		
	stagger	staggering	—
	stock	—	—
		1. sustained	—
—	—	2. . . .	—
	swell		—
	toast	—	—

Vocabulary Practice

Complete the sentences below with the correct words from the following list. You may have to use different word forms and tenses. Do not use a word more than once.

Sentences 1-5	Sentences 6-11
toast	caustically
rowdiness	maim
depict	sustained
swell	stagger
confrontation	stock
proliferation	incentive
	obnoxious

1. Because of age requirements and strong laws about drinking and driving, juice bars are starting _____ in many urban areas.

2. Even though the old woman's neighbors were being (a.) _____ and were keeping her up at night, she was afraid (b.) _____ them about it.

3. In the past, drunks were often _____ in films as funny and harmless.

4. Let's drink a _____ to the newlyweds!

5. The man's face was all _____ from drinking too much alcohol.

6. Even when customers are (a.) _____, a bartender usually has to be polite and has to avoid making (b.) _____ comments to them.

7. The statistics on drunk-driving accidents are _____. I couldn't believe it when I read how many alcohol-related accidents occur every year.

8. Groups such as MADD, Mothers Against Drunk Driving, are working _____ the efforts against drunk driving.

9. One of the difficulties in opening a bar or a restaurant is that it can cost a great deal of money to acquire a good _____ of alcohol.

10. Lower insurance rates are an _____ for bars to use bartender-training programs.

11. If a person _____ in an accident, he or she may sue for the loss of income resulting from the disability.

Focus on Form: Gerunds and Infinitives— Different Times

Normally when two verbs come together, the first verb happens first and the second one happens second or they happen at the same time. For example:

She agreed to go. = She agreed first and then she went.

She considered stopping. = She considered it first.

Sometimes, however, it is necessary to show that the second verb happened first.

She appears to have drunk a lot. = It appears *now* that she drank a lot before.

Grammar Practice

Look at the following sentences; put a 1 over the verb (or group of verb forms) that happened first and a 2 over the verb (or group of verb forms) that happened second.

1. She *didn't appreciate having to tell* him to stop drinking.

2. He *claimed to be* sober.

3. He *regrets* very much *having drunk* too much.

4. I *don't appreciate having had* to stop him.

5. The public *seems to have decided* that they have had enough of drunk driving.

6. They *appear to have been arrested* for drunk driving.

7. He *claimed to have been* sober when the accident happened.

8. She *resented not having been told* that he was an alcoholic.

9. He *regretted having to tell* his guests not to drink any more.

Focus on Form: Gerunds and Infinitives— Different Times (continued)

A. DIFFERENT TIMES

When the second verb happens before the first, the auxiliary *have* + the past participle of the verb are used with the second verb to show the time difference. Infinitives (after appear, claim, seem):

- to have + past participle is used for infinitives. *Examples 5, 6, 7*
- (Passive = to have been + past participle. *Example 6*)

> He claimed *to be* sober. = He claimed then that he was sober then.
>
> He claimed *to have been* sober. = He claimed then that he had been sober before.
>
> He appears *to have been* arrested = It appears now that he was arrested before.

Gerunds

- *having* + past participle is used for gerunds. *Examples 3, 4, 8*
- (Passive = *having been* + past participle. *Example 8*)

> I don't appreciate *having* to tell him. = I have to tell him and I don't like the fact that I have to.
>
> I don't appreciate *having had* to tell him. = I had to tell him, and now I don't like the fact that I had to do it.

I resented *having been told* that I was drunk. = I resented that they had told me earlier that I was drunk.

Note: Since we normally regret what we did or did not do in the past, the past form must only be used if the time is not clear from the context. For purposes of practice, use *having* + *past participle* after "regret" if the second verb happened before the "regret."

B.   VERB + GERUND OR INFINITIVE (CHANGE IN MEANING)

Remember and Forget **+ Infinitive or Gerund**

- An infinitive shows that the first verb happened first.
- A gerund shows that the second verb happened first.

+ Infinitive

I always *remember to go.* = I go because I remember first that I am supposed to go.

I *remembered to call* her. = I remembered first that I was supposed to call her, and then I called.

He *forgot to call* me. = He forgot first, so he didn't call me.

+ Gerund

I *remember going.* = I went and now I remember the action.

I *don't remember* (I forget*) *calling* her, but my wife is sure that I did. = I called her first. Now I don't remember that I called her.

(*Forget* is rarely used in this way. Instead we would say, "I don't remember.")

Stop **+ Infinitive or Gerund**

- The infinitive after *stop* means "in order to."
- The gerund after *stop* means "to quit."

   I *stopped to have* a drink. = I was doing something else, and I *stopped in order to* have a drink.

   I *stopped drinking.* = I quit. I don't drink any longer.

Try **+ Infinitive or Gerund**

- The infinitive shows ability or lack of ability.
- The gerund shows the use of an alternative. We know it can be done.

   Try to walk. = You have hurt your back and I know it is difficult for you to walk now, but see if you can do it.

   Try walking. = You want to do some exercise, and you don't like jogging. Try walking as an alternative. I know you can do it.

   He *tried to eat.* = But he couldn't. He was too sick.

   He *tried eating.* = He ate, but it didn't help. He still felt sick.

Grammar Practice

Complete the sentences with the correct form of the verb in parentheses.

1. If the police stop your car and you appear (drink) _____ too much alcohol, they may ask you to try (walk) _____ a straight line to prove you are not drunk.

2. If you know you are going to be driving, it's good advice to stop (think) _____ before you drink.

3. A group of friends who go out partying should always remember (pick) _____ a designated driver.

4. If you feel you've had too much alcohol to drink, try (drink) _____ fruit juice to help sober you up. It's better than coffee.

5. I was surprised when I woke up this morning and had a slight hangover. I don't remember (drink) _____ very much last night.

6. The Massachusetts bar that agreed (give) _____ a multi-million-dollar settlement to the family of a woman who was killed by a drunk driver probably regrets very much (serve) _____ him when he asked for "one for the road."

7. It often takes time before the effects of alcohol are felt. Don't wait until it's too late. Stop (drink) _____ before you feel the effects.

8. They appeared (be) _____ in good condition to drive when they left.

9. He seems (lose) _____ his car keys, and it's a good thing. He's in no condition to drive.

10. I always forget (carry) _____ the car registration with me, but this weekend I really have to try (remember) _____ (put) _____ it in my wallet. There are going to be a lot of police out on the roads because of the holidays.

widower

Reading 3: "Loan Puts Widow, 91, In Jeopardy"

Prereading Questions

1. Can you imagine a situation in which loaning money to someone could get you into trouble for what the person did with the money?

2. How old do you have to be to get a driver's license in your country? What is the procedure? Are there special classes that you have to take? What kinds of tests are required?

Vocabulary Practice

Match the italicized words in the following sentences with the definitions in the list below. Use the context of the sentence to help you guess the meaning.

_____ leave out; eliminate
_____ build up; amass
_____ extremely poor
_____ triumph; overcome
_____ someone who lives through great suffering or who dies for a belief
_____ argue; assert; maintain
_____ a difficult situation or condition
_____ admit
_____ cause someone to judge prematurely or unfairly

1. Mrs. Wilson is not seen, as she fears, as a symbol of the evils of drunken driving. To the contrary, she has been perceived as a kind of living *martyr*.

2. There is some dispute about the seriousness of Mrs. Wilson's immediate *plight*.

3. The plaintiff's lawyers (a.) *contend* that Mrs. Wilson's claims of poverty are exaggerated. He says that she is not (b.) *destitute* and that her supporters are trying (c.) *to prejudice* potential jurors.

4. Mrs. Wilson *acknowledges* that she knew that her grandnephew did not have a driver's license.

5. The Vermont Supreme Court ruled that the judge had been wrong to *exclude* the auto dealer from the case and ordered a retrial.

6. Mrs. Wilson once had a bank account of more than $500,000 that she and her late husband had *accumulated* over a lifetime.

7. If Mrs. Wilson *prevails* in court, she might be able to reduce the amount of her liability.

Loan Puts Widow, 91, In Jeopardy

SPECIAL TO *THE NEW YORK TIMES*

NORTH BENNINGTON, Vt., Oct. 27—Even in the glow of Indian summer[38] Luella Wilson rarely goes outdoors anymore. She does not like to sit in the warm sunshine on her
5 front porch because she fears that the neighbors will look at a tiny 91-year-old woman and see a criminal.

A Vermont jury has found Mrs. Wilson liable for a car accident in which alcohol was
10 a factor that maimed a young man. But she is not seen, as she fears, as a symbol of the evils of drunken driving.

---

38. a period of warm weather in late autumn

To the contrary, since word got out that Mrs. Wilson could lose her life savings, and her house because of the ruling, she has been perceived as a kind of living martyr to the heavy hand[39] of the law.

"An elderly man called to ask if I wanted an apple pie," Mrs. Wilson said as she showed off dozens of cards of support, many of them stuffed with crumpled $1 bills. "I told him I loved apples. He said he'd bring it down."

A Dispute Over Responsibility

While there is some dispute over the seriousness of Mrs. Wilson's immediate plight, many Vermonters say she should not have been held responsible for an accident involving a car she neither owned nor drove. On the grounds that she had lent the driver, her grandnephew, the money to buy the car, she was ordered to pay the victim $950,000.

The plaintiff's lawyer, Rolf Sternberg, contends that Mrs. Wilson's claims of poverty are exaggerated and that her supporters are deliberately spreading false information to prejudice potential jurors shortly before a retrial is scheduled to begin.

"She is not destitute," Mr. Sternberg said. "The court order said that her assets are to be frozen[40] except for what she needs to live adequately. Somebody is trying to make it difficult to pick a fair and impartial jury."

And he said the judgment is consistent with established legal doctrines that hold people responsible for the consequences of knowingly giving dangerous tools to people who are likely to misuse them.

Passenger Injured in Crash

"You cannot give property to someone who, by reason of inexperience or incompetence, is likely to cause harm to someone else," Mr. Sternberg said.

Mrs. Wilson was asleep on the night of April 24, 1984, when her 18-year-old grandnephew, Billy Stuart, drove off a railroad bridge in a 1981 Chrysler that he had just purchased with money she had lent to him

One of his passengers, Mark Vince lost a leg in the accident. Mr. Vince sued both Mrs. Wilson and Ace Auto Sales, the Bennington car dealership where Mr. Stuart bought the car.

In a three-day trial held in Bennington Superior Court in February 1987, Mr. Stuart, who was not prosecuted on criminal charges, acknowledged that he and his companions had been drinking heavily and smoking marijuana on the night of the accident. And Mrs. Wilson acknowledged in an interview that she knew her grandnephew did not have a driver's license.

Victim Awarded $950,000

She did not appear at the trial, both because of poor health and because her lawyer felt certain she could not lose.

Although the judge, Arthur O'Dea, ruled that the auto dealer could not be held liable for the accident, the jury held that Mrs. Wilson owed Mr. Vince $950,000 for his injuries.

"I didn't give him the car and I didn't sell him the car," Mrs. Wilson said. "I just loaned him the money to buy the car. They told me at the bank there could never be any trouble over that check."

Mrs. Wilson's lawyer, Manfred Ehrich, called the judgment "an outrageous precedent," and added, "She didn't even own the car. It was never in her name."

Earlier this year the Vermont Supreme Court ruled that Judge O'Dea had been wrong to exclude the auto dealer from the case before the trial began and ordered a retrial, tentatively scheduled to begin Nov. 6 in Bennington Superior Court.

Insurance Company Sued

At the same time, Mrs. Wilson has sued her insurance company, Vermont Mutual, which refused to represent her at the 1987 trial.

The retrial has been a long time coming for Mrs Wilson, who once had a bank account

---

39. overly harsh   40. She would be unable to spend or move her savings.

of more than $500,000 that she and her late husband, Harry Wilson, had accumulated over a lifetime. Over the years the Wilsons had raised horses and had owned a nightclub in Troy, N.Y., a motel in Miami and a grocery store in Bennington, four miles south of this village in southwestern Vermont.

She said she spent some of her savings on annual trips to Florida and Cuba, but much of it went to friends and relatives as loans and gifts.

Now, Mrs. Wilson said, she is destitute, eating a hot meal once a day provided by Meals on Wheels,[41] for which she pays $1 a week.

---

41. a charitable organization that delivers hot meals to old people in their homes

"She has no income except rent from me and $158 a month from Social Security," said Mike Madden, Mrs. Wilson's tenant and companion. "She doesn't know how she'll pay her property taxes."

The taxes, estimated at more than $2,400, are due early next month.

As it stands now, if Mrs. Wilson prevails in court she might, at best, hope to reduce the amount of the award and share the responsibility with the car dealer. If she loses, she will lose everything, including her house and antique silver.

"If she loses this case, they'll auction everything off and put her in a nursing home for a crime she didn't commit," Mr. Madden said.

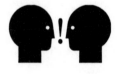

Comprehension and Discussion

A. *Circle the correct answer. If the answer is false, tell why.*

1. The prosecution feels that Mrs. Wilson's lawyer is exaggerating her financial situation in hopes of getting sympathy from prospective jurors.

    (True)   False

2. Although he was not sued for damages, Mr. Stuart was charged with driving without a license and while under the influence of alcohol and drugs.

    True   (False)

3. In the retrial, the auto sales dealer will probably be included.

    (True)   False

B. *Answer the following questions as completely as possible.*

1. How are Mrs. Wilson's fears contrary to reality?

2. Why might it be difficult to pick an impartial jury in this case?

3. What is the theoretical basis of the case against Mrs. Wilson?

4. What was probably a major mistake that Mrs. Wilson's lawyer made in the original trial? Why?

5. What are the arguments for and against the responsibility of Mrs. Wilson in this case?

6.   What is your opinion of this case? Who should be held liable? Why?

Note: The Vermont Supreme Court ruled that Mrs. Wilson and the auto dealer were both responsible. It was also ruled that her insurance company had to represent her. An out-of-court settlement was reached between the insurance company and Mr. Vince. The amount of the settlement was not disclosed.

Word Forms

Working with a partner, complete the following chart with the different forms of the words. Use your knowledge of other words and their different forms to help you. Do not be afraid to guess. A dash means there is no form.

Noun	Verb	Adjective	Adverb
	accumulate		
	contend	—	—
	—	destitute	—
	exclude		
	prejudice		—

Vocabulary Practice

Write a summary of the article using as many of the new words in this section as possible. If possible, include words from the previous sections in this chapter.

Vocabulary Building

"The auto dealer *had been excluded* from the case at first."

A. *The word* exclude *comes from the Latin root* claudere, *to shut or close, and the prefix ex-, out. Therefore,* exclude *means "to shut or leave out." Look at the different prefixes below. Some of then can combine with the root* clude, *or one of its forms, and some cannot. Working in small groups, decide which ones can be used to form words based on this root, and then match them with the definitions. Remember that not all words will have the same forms.*

a - *not*	re - *again*	post - *after*
in - *in*	de - *reverse*	con - *with, together*
se - *apart*	pro - *in favor of*	pre - *in front of, before*

	Word	Definition or Synonym
1.	exclude	leave out; eliminate
2.	_____	end; come to believe or decide through reasoning
3.	_____	prevent; make impossible by another action
4.	_____	person who withdraws from the world; a hermit (no verb form)
5.	_____	have as a part; be made up of; make part of
6.	_____	set apart or away; hide (verb form exists but is rare)

B. *Give the different forms of the words in the list above. Put them in alphabetical order. Forms that are rarely used are not included. A dash means there is no form.*

	Noun	Verb	Adjective	Adverb
1.				—
2.	exclusion	exclude	exclusive	exclusively
3.				—
4.				—
5.		—		—
6.			a.	—
			b.	

Vocabulary Practice

Complete the sentences below with the correct forms of the words from your list above.

1. After the trial, Mrs.Wilson went into _____ because she was afraid that people would see her as a criminal.

2. Her age did not _____ her from going to the trial, but her lawyers did not think her appearance was necessary.

3. Cases such as Mrs. Wilson's are difficult because many people feel there is no _____ proof about whose responsibility the accident was.

4. Sometimes people who are maimed in accidents have difficulty adjusting to their condition. Some do not want to be seen, and they become _____ for a while. With time, most people adjust and take part in normal activities again.

5. The (a.) _____ of the auto dealer in the retrial is almost certain because of the Vermont Supreme Court's ruling that it had been wrong to (b.) _____ him in the first place.

Grammar Practice

Complete the following sentences using either a gerund or an infinitive in each blank. Try to do them as quickly as possible without thinking about them too much. Which one sounds better to you? After you have finished, check the answers by looking at the lists of words that are followed by gerunds and infinitives. Be careful of the passive voice, negatives, and differences in time.

Walking the Fine Line at Holiday Office Parties

Don't expect (1. hear) _____ "last call" for drinks at this year's holiday office party. Companies are not going to encourage (2. drink) _____ this year—and with good reason. They are hoping (3. avoid) _____ (4. get) _____ involved in lawsuits and (5. hold) _____ liable for damages caused by employees who get drunk at office parties. They cannot afford (6. be) _____ careless. Companies began (7. worry) _____ when, in 1985, a restaurant in Cambridge, Ma., agreed (8. pay) _____ a $1 million settlement to a man who was injured by one of the restaurant's employees after an open-bar Christmas party at the restaurant. Many company officials acknowledge (9. be) _____ worried and some are even considering (10. neg.,have) _____ holiday parties.

However, a victory in court against an employer may not be easy or fast. Lawyers may have difficulty (11. prove) _____ employer liability. But to avoid possible problems, experts recommend (12. take) _____ certain precautions at holiday parties:

A.   Endeavor (13. hold) _____ office parties in bars or restaurants with professional bartenders. Do not risk (14. let) _____ guests serve themselves.

B.   Do not be afraid to refuse (15. serve) _____ drinks to anyone who seems (16. have) _____ too much to drink.

C.   If someone appears (17. be) _____ inebriated, arrange (18. have) _____ him or her driven home in a taxi or by a fellow guest. If necessary, offer (19. pay) _____ the cab fare.

D.   Do not neglect (20. provide) _____ snacks which are high in protein and low in salt. These are good alcohol absorbers.

E.   Give people alternatives. Try (21. serve) _____ a wide variety of interesting non-alcoholic drinks, such as fruit punch, so that non-drinkers do not feel left out.

F.   When it is getting close to the end of the party, experts suggest (22. neg., announce) _____ "last call." Instead, quietly close the bar and quit (23. serve) _____ drinks.

G.   Do not fail (24. supply) _____ time for guests to get sober. Offer coffee and dessert as a way of getting them to stay for a while without taking in more alcohol.

Although one can see why company officials, and even hosts of private parties, might resent (25. have) _____ to follow such strict guidelines, refusing (26. do) _____ so could result in injured employees and friends and possible lawsuits. And no one wants, or can afford, (27. hold) _____ liable for injury to another person.

Grammar Practice

Think about the situations in the three articles in this chapter. Then write as many sentences as you can about the people and the situations using words from the lists of words which are followed by infinitives or gerunds. You may also write sentences about your feelings about the general situation of drinking, driving, and responsibility. See how many sentences you can write in 15 minutes. Work for speed, but keep the reality of the situations in mind. Use negatives, the passive voice, and different times. Look at the following examples:

The Texas company feels they don't deserve *to be held* liable for Mr. Waldrop's accident because they say he was on his own time.

Now Mrs. Wilson avoids *going* out on the porch.

It seems that the courts want *to help* the victims of drunk drivers.

People in the United States tend *to blame* others for their actions.

People who cause accidents because of drunk driving should have to spend time *working* in hospitals with accident victims.

Suggested Grammar Practice

There are many words in the lists of verbs given in this chapter. In addition, a student learning English will not have the intuition that a native speaker has about when to use a gerund or an infinitive. Studying lists of words does not help very much because it is often difficult to remember what is right when you are speaking—even if you can recite the list. The best way to remember something is to use it. Try writing five sentences with these words every day, sentences that have meaning for you, about your own life. When you have some extra time, sitting on a bus, for example, read your own sentences to yourself and try to make new ones in your mind.

Class Project

Work on one or more of these projects individually or in groups of two to three students. Then present your findings to the class.

1. Make a presentation to the class about the role of alcohol in your country. What are the laws concerning alcohol? What role does it play in work, in social functions? Has this role changed? Do any traditions, such as holiday celebrations, involve alcohol? Students from the same country can make joint presentations. If you are from a country where alcohol is forbidden, explain your feelings about the social use of alcohol. Do you seen anything hypocritical about a society which forbids the sale of drugs but allows the sale of alcohol and sometimes even glorifies its use?

2. Divide the class in half. Each half will pick one of the situations described in this chapter and hold a trial to decide who is liable. As an alternative to the cases discussed so far, the class can make its own situation. Do not be afraid to be imaginative or funny. The purpose is to practice free speaking. For example, imagine a student who has gained too much weight eating every day at a fast-food restaurant. Each side should choose students to play the following roles, depending on the number in the class. If there are not enough students for two groups, only one group will do the role-play.

1 plaintiff	2 lawyers (1 for each side)
1 defendant	2-6 members of the jury
1 judge	witnesses for each side

   The class should discuss with the teacher the responsibility of each person involved and the general procedure of an American trial. Generally speaking, and in simple terms, a civil case proceeds in the following way:

   a. The judge opens the case, briefly explaining what it is about and what the responsibilities of the jurors are.

b. The attorney for the plaintiff begins questioning the witnesses for the plaintiff's side.

c. The attorney for the defendant cross-examines each witness before the next one begins.

d. When the plaintiff's side has been presented, the defendant's attorney may call witnesses to prove his or her case.

e. While the lawyers are questioning the witnesses, the opposing lawyer may object if the question is felt to be irrelevant, unfair, based on hearsay, etc. The judge rules if the question can be asked ("Objection overruled.") or not ("Objection sustained.").

f. When all the evidence has been presented, the lawyers, starting with the defendant's side, summarize the main arguments in favor of their clients.

g. The jury deliberates and comes to a decision.

Each side should practice its trial before presenting it to the entire class. Each jury will decide, based on the evidence, the law, and the presentation of the other students, who is liable. If the jury decides in favor of the plaintiff, the jury and the judge will decide on a financial settlement to be awarded to the plaintiff.

Discussion and Writing

Discuss the following topics, first in pairs or small groups and then with the class. After your discussion, pick one (or more) of the topics and write an essay about it.

1. Pick one of the situations described in this chapter, and decide who should be held responsible. Explain the case, and then give the reasons for your decision.

2. Discuss the idea of the responsibility of the seller and the consumer. You may use one of the cases in this chapter as an example. Remember that the essay is to be about the general issue.

3. What are some possible ramifications of these cases? Think in terms of general product or manufacturer liability. You may view this as either positive or negative.

4. Defend or oppose laws concerning the responsibility of people other than those directly involved in drunk-driving accidents.

5. How might the cases presented in this chapter be similar to or different from what would happen in your country? Explain in detail the situation in your country concerning drinking and responsibility.

6. Some critics have seen these types of cases as examples of one of the problems of American culture today, that is, blaming others and refusing to take responsibility for one's own actions. Others see them as a way of guaranteeing that the sellers or givers of potentially harmful tools take responsibility for what they do. Which way do you see the issue?

Word List

Below is a list of the new words, and their different forms, presented in this chapter. Only forms which have the same general meaning as the words used in the articles are given. Forms which are rarely used have not been included.

Noun	Verb	Adjective	Adverb
accountability		accountable	
accumulation	accumulate	accumulative	accumulatively
	broaden	broad	
		caustic	caustically
cognizance		cognizant	
conclusion	conclude	conclusive	
confrontation	confront	confrontational	
contention	contend	contentious	
depiction	depict		
destitution		destitute	
disassociation	disassociate		
(dissociation)	(dissociate)		
exclusion	exclude	exclusive	exclusively
inclusion	include	inclusive	inclusively
		indelible	
incentive		incentive	
liability		liable	
	maim	maimed	
martyr	martyr		
martyrdom			
obnoxiousness		obnoxious	obnoxiously
overindulgence	overindulge	overindulgent	overindulgently
plight			
preclusion	preclude	preclusive	
prejudice	prejudice	prejudiced	prejudicially
		prejudicial	
	prevail		
proliferation	proliferate		
recluse		reclusive	
reimbursement	reimburse		
rowdiness		rowdy	rowdily
rowdyism			
seclusion	seclude	secluded	
		seclusive	
stagger	stagger	staggering	staggeringly
stock	stock		
sustainment	sustain	sustained	
		sustainable	
swelling	swell	swollen	
toast	toast		
	(resolve)	unresolved	
		unscathed	

Part I Review

Grammar

Circle the best answer for each of the following sentences. Use only the information given in each sentence.

1. Anyone who is planning to work as a bartender should consider _____ TIPS course.

   a. take
   b. to take
   c. taking
   d. to take/taking

2. When the Europeans came to this country, the Native Americans _____ lived here for thousands of years.

   a. had already lived
   b. already lived
   c. have already lived

3. I didn't go with them because I _____ home to watch my little brother.

   a. should have stayed
   b. must have stayed
   c. had to stay
   d. could have stayed

4. I can't believe that you walked across that highway at night. You _____ been killed.

   a. should have
   b. may have
   c. could have
   d. must have

5. The Chinese _____ prohibited from immigrating to the United States for many years.

   a. have been
   b. were
   c. had been

6. Congress is not planning to cut down on the number of immigrants who can enter the United States. _____, the new bill would increase the number of visas for immigration.

   a. In contrast
   b. On the contrary

7. Q: Have they been given the mail yet?
   A: I'm not sure. They _____.

a. might have
b. might have been
c. must have been
d. should have

8. She is very concerned about _____ her daughter hasn't returned home yet.

   a. that
   b. whether
   c. the fact that
   d. if

9. The U.S. Immigration Act of 1921 was a law (A.) _____ gave preference to immigrants based on their national origin. (B.) _____, the U.S. Immigration Act of 1965 favored family reunification.

   (A.) a.   , which
         b.   that
         c.   which/that
         d.   , which/that
   (B.) a.   In contrast
         b.   On the contrary

10. _____ international students can work is something I have to find out.

    a. whether/if
    b. if
    c. whether

11. Acupuncture _____ is a traditional type of Chinese treatment using needles_ is now commonly used in the United States.

    a. , that...,
    b. that
    c. , which...,
    d. , which

12. I hope the police don't stop me. I can never remember _____ the car registration with me.

    a. to take
    b. taking
    c. to have taken
    d. having taken

13. A: Look at that building. Isn't it beautiful?
    B: If you really want to see a beautiful sight, just try _____ your head and _____ at that sunset.

    a. to turn, look
    b. turning, look
    c. turning, looking
    d. to turn, to look

14. The place _____ he mentioned __ is not too far from here.

    a. that/ which/Ø
    b. , which...,
    c. that/ which/ Ø...,
    d. where/in which/Ø

15. From 1985 until 1991, he _____ in a small room near school.

    a. had lived
    b. has lived
    c. lived
    d. has lived or has been living

16. From what people tell us, she doesn't seem _____ sick when she arrived.

    a. to have been
    b. to be
    c. being
    d. having been

17. A: It's too bad he didn't come.
    B: Yes. He _____. He would have loved it.

    a. must have
    b. should have
    c. might have
    d. had to

18. I really wonder _____

    a. why do they do it.
    b. the fact that they do it.
    c. why they do it.
    d. that they did it.

19. The brother _____ I met last January_ is the one he gets along with the best.

    a. , whom/that...,
    b. whom/that
    c. whom/that/Ø
    d. ,whom...,

20. _____ A/a TOEFL score of 550 is required for admission.

    a. That
    b. The fact that
    c. Ø
    d. Whether or not

21. He always has trouble (A.) _____ (B.) _____ that.

    (A.) a. to try
            b. to have tried

      c. trying
      d. having tried
(B.) a. doing
      b. do
      c. to do
      d. to have done

22. When she refused (A.) _____, the children began (B.)

    _____.

    (A.) a. to leave
          b. leaving
          c. to leave/leaving
          d. to have left
    (B.) a. to scream/screaming
          b. to scream
          c. screaming

23. Q: Was he given a second chance?
    A: No. He _____.

    a. should have
    b. must have been
    c. should have been
    d. might have been

24. Q: Do you think he did it?
    A: He _____. There was nobody else around.

    a. had to
    b. must have been
    c. shouldn't have
    d. must have

25. It's too bad that the buses stop (A.) _____ so early. I really resent
    (B.) _____ to take a taxi home when I come home from school.

    (A.) a. to run
          b. running
          c. to run/running
    (B.) a. having had
          b. to have
          c. to have had
          d. having

26. By the time they (A.) _____ back, they (B.) _____ for
    almost a year.

    (A.) a. had gotten
          b. got
          c. have gotten
          d. were gotten

(B.)   a.   were traveling
       b.   have been traveling
       c.   had been traveling
       d.   traveled

27.   Even though he's 50 years old, he still resents _____ to work while his younger brothers went to college.

a. having
b. having had
c. having had/to have had
d. to have had

28.   They _____ the Atlantic ten times in 15 years at a time when it took weeks to make the trip.

a. had crossed
b. crossed
c. have crossed
d. have crossed/have been crossing

29.   It was a time _____ people came here expecting to find the streets paved with gold.

a. when
b. in which
c. when/in which
d. when/in which/Ø

30.   When steamship fares became cheap, many people _____ back and forth various times between Europe and the United States.

a. have traveled
b. had traveled
c. traveled
d. have traveled/have been traveling

31.   I don't recommend _____ too long on that machine if this is the first time that you've done it.

a. to exercise
b. you to exercise
c. exercising
d. exercise

32.   The Puritans came to the New World for religious freedom. _____, most immigrants in the late 19th century came for economic reasons.

a.   In contrast
b.   On the contrary

33.   In the past 30 years, most immigrants _____ to the United States from Asia and Latin America.

a. have come
b. have come/have been coming

c. come
d. are coming

34. This is not a religion _____ tenets most people would find unusual.

   a. which/that/Ø
   b. whose
   c. whose/Ø
   d. , whose

35. Would you happen to know _____ he's going or not?

   a. if
   b. whether
   c. what
   d. whether/if

Vocabulary

Circle the word which best completes the sentence.

1. When he started to look for an acting job, he was afraid that his accent would be a/an _____, but it turned out to be an asset. He played the role of a foreign tourist.

   a. opulence
   b. provocation
   c. hindrance
   d. rebuke

2. Very often immigrants have to take _____ jobs to begin with, jobs which are below their level of education.

   a. pernicious
   b. compliant
   c. preclusive
   d. menial

3. His parents had always _____ his poor grades in school to lack of intelligence, but later they found out that he had a hearing problem.

   a. attributed
   b. disparaged
   c. prejudiced
   d. precluded

4. Even though she was 80 years old, she was _____ by the thought of traveling alone all over Europe.

   a. unattainable
   b. unprecedented
   c. reluctant
   d. undaunted

5. The _____ of advertising about men's hair coloring perhaps says something about modern man's desire to look young.

   a. perniciousness
   b. feasibility
   c. pervasiveness
   d. depiction

6. The police made some very serious _____ against his gang.

   a. undercurrents
   b. allegations
   c. disparagements
   d. detentions

7. "Passing away" is a/an _____ for dying.

   a. advocate
   b. preclusion
   c. disparagement
   d. euphemism

8. Perhaps the _____ of the United States has something to do with the individualistic character of the people.

   a. disparity
   b. vastness
   c. murkiness
   d. plight

9. After the accident, a feeling of great sadness _____ the atmosphere of the office.

   a. endorsed
   b. provoked
   c. pervaded
   d. rebuked

10. The complete _____ of the ruling is what made most of the students so angry. They felt there was no reason for it.

    a. innateness
    b. inevitability
    c. arbitrariness
    d. perniciousness

11. When their house burned down, they were left with _____ nothing.

    a. innately
    b. overwhelmingly
    c. cavalierly
    d. virtually

12. The _____ of the criminals allowed the people in the town to sleep better at night.

a. endangerment
b. apprehension
c. assault
d. prevalence

13. Although they had been separated for two years, he still could not _____ himself to the possibility of a divorce.

    a. reconcile
    b. rebuke
    c. refrain
    d. concede

14. After the fire, the church was _____ with offers of help.

    a. nudged
    b. assaulted
    c. deluged
    d. harbored

15. Please _____ from speaking in a loud voice. The students are taking a test.

    a. concede
    b. comply
    c. refrain
    d. preclude

16. The politician was overheard making a/an _____ remark about an ethnic group. Consequently, he lost many votes.

    a. disparaging
    b. pernicious
    c. unprecedented
    d. inebriated

17. She thought the idea was interesting; she was just worried about its _____.

    a. pervasiveness
    b. liability
    c. feasibility
    d. inextricability

18. When I first arrived in New York, I was _____ by the number of people everywhere.

    a. immersed
    b. reconciled
    c. refrained
    d. overwhelmed

19. When their team won the game, all of the students left the dormitories and _____ in the middle of the campus.

a. intruded
b. deluged
c. converged
d. constrained

20. I don't think that diet will hurt you, but I have doubts about its
     _____.

a. proficiency
b. revitalization
c. efficacy
d. feasibility

21. The children had become so _____ that the party was stopped.

a. arbitrary
b. paradoxical
c. rowdy
d. abstinent

22. I always find a long morning walk to be _____.

a. immersing
b. scrutinizing
c. disparaging
d. invigorating

23. In movies today, the heroes are _____ as very clean-living. They
     never smoke or drink.

a. contended
b. hindered
c. nurtured
d. depicted

24. The parents complained to their neighbors because the dog attacked their
     child with no _____.

a. ramification
b. provocation
c. diminishment
d. resentment

25. Since there is no precedent for this court decision, no one knows what the
     _____ of it will be on future similar cases.

a. concessions
b. immunity
c. ramifications
d. turmoil

26. When his visits to the doctor didn't help, he _____ to herbal
     medicine.

a. reconciled
b. scrutinized

c. rebuked

d. resorted

27. Her lack of a high school degree was an _____ in getting a promotion.

    a. impediment
    b. exclusion
    c. incentive
    d. endorsement

28. He lived a very _____ life—no cigarettes, no alcohol, and no coffee.

    a. exclusive
    b. abstinent
    c. destitute
    d. preclusive

29. Howard Hughes, the famous businessman, was a _____. He only saw the people who worked for him.

    a. destitution
    b. euphemism
    c. rebuke
    d. recluse

30. The judge gave him a light sentence because of the _____ circumstances of the crime.

    a. mitigating
    b. inebriating
    c. overwhelming
    d. intrusive

Definition Game

The class is divided into four to five groups of three to four students each. Each group draws lots to decide who will be first, second, third, and fourth to play. Each group in turn picks a category and a number of points. The more points there are, the more difficult the word. When the first group has chosen a category and point value, the teacher gives the clue. Students have 15 seconds to discuss among themselves and give an answer. If they are right, they get the points, and it becomes the next group's turn. If they are wrong, the next group can try. If the second group gets the right answer, they get the points and another chance. The game continues until all the words have been given. The group with the most points wins.

Points	Immigration	Education	Americans	Parents	Drunk Driving
10					
20					
30					
40					
50					

The Smoking Controversy

Reading 1: "Why Smoking Bans Are Dangerous"

Prereading Questions

1. In the United States, laws concerning smoking vary from city to city and from state to state. What are the laws concerning smoking in your city and state? If you are not now living in the United States, what American laws about smoking have you heard or read about? How do these laws differ from laws in your country? Look at the following list and check the places where smoking is prohibited. Add explanations or qualifiers if necessary.

	City/State in the United States	Your City or Country
public transportation (buses, subways)	_____	_____
taxis	_____	_____
restaurants	_____	_____
bars	_____	_____
elevators	_____	_____
offices	_____	_____
sports stadiums (indoor and outdoor)	_____	_____
public buildings (bank, post office)	_____	_____
restrooms (toilets)	_____	_____
movie theaters	_____	_____
supermarkets/food stores	_____	_____
long-distance buses	_____	_____
department stores	_____	_____
national flights	_____	_____

2. Do you think that the laws concerning smoking are too strict, too lenient, or all right in your country and in the city or state you are living in the United States? Explain.

3. How would you change the laws, if you feel a change is necessary?

4. Smokers: How do you feel about the efforts to restrict smoking? Do you feel you understand the feelings of many nonsmokers?

    Nonsmokers: Do you feel that smokers have rights concerning smoking that should be respected?

5. Are attitudes towards smoking changing in your country? If so, how? Are these attitudes having any effect on the number of people who smoke?

6. Even if you are a nonsmoker, can you see any reasons why smoking bans could be thought of as dangerous?

7. Can you think of any other bans or recommendations, either in the United States or in your country, against personal behavior other than smoking? Can you imagine any possible bans in the future?

Vocabulary Practice

Match the italicized words in the sentences with the definitions in the list below. Use the context of the sentence to help you guess the meaning.

_____ deliberately and constantly avoid
_____ acting on a sudden inclination or urge
_____ pass a law
_____ peculiarities; characteristics peculiar to a person
_____ harmful; dangerous
_____ without change; constantly
_____ hate
_____ outgoing; preferring to be with others instead of alone
_____ position or attitude
_____ not consider; disregard
_____ staying away from or denying oneself pleasurable things such as alcohol, tobacco, or sex

1. Across the United States, municipal authorities are *enacting* anti-smoking laws.

2. As someone who *detests* cigarettes, I should be pleased at these developments.

3. Cigarette smoke disgusts me, and in a restaurant, office, or airplane full of the stuff, the fumes *invariably* find their way to my "nonsmoking" seat.

4. Employees who do not join gyms and nutrition workshops sometimes find themselves (a.) *shunned* by colleagues and (b.) *passed over* for promotions.

5. We nonsmokers who believe that we have a right to our own *idiosyncrasies* have an obligation to defend smokers' rights as well.

6. To oppose a ban on smoking is to object to the demand upon a group of people to give up their particular (a.) *stance* toward life—one that, for all its (b.) *noxious* qualities, has contributed much to the American character.

7. Smokers are far more likely to be (a.) *impulsive*, (b.) *extroverted* risk-takers. They take chances in a variety of areas of their personal lives that (c.) *abstinent* types like me shy away from.

Word Analysis

The following three characteristics are discussed in the next article. Do these words have positive, negative, or neutral meanings for you? Check one category for each word. Discuss the connotations these words have for you and how they are seen in your culture. If possible, discuss these in small groups of mixed cultures first and then with the entire class.

	Positive	**Negative**	**Neutral**
idiosyncratic			
extroverted			
impulsive			

Why Smoking Bans Are Dangerous

By **BARRY GLASSNER**
(from the *New York Times*)

The tobacco companies, at long last, are getting theirs.[1] Across the United States, municipal authorities are enacting anti-smoking laws. One third of all American corporations have instituted non-smoking regulations, and the number is rapidly growing.

As someone who detests cigarettes, I should be pleased at these developments. Cigarette smoke disgusts me, and in a restaurant, office or airplane full of the stuff, the fumes invariably find their way to my "non-smoking" seat. Never once—not even as a rambunctious[2] adolescent—can I remember having the slightest inclination to smoke.

So why do I find myself concerned rather than relieved that Hunter College, where I spend a good bit of time, has just instituted tough new regulations against smoking? Frankly, I worry that one day the college authorities may well go after me, too. While I won't smoke, I also don't do some of the things that many who oppose smoking think I should do—for example, I do not get very much exercise nor do I maintain a low cholesterol diet.

Already some insurance companies offer lower rates to people who exercise and reduce their cholesterol levels. How would I feel if my employees removed egg products and fried foods, both of which I eat regularly, from the menu at the staff lunchroom. Or if I were forced to weigh in[3] or work out[4] each morning before I went to the office? Such scenarios[5] are not so farfetched.[6] Recent studies of so-called wellness programs at work sites have documented the existence of corporate environments in which pressures to shape up and eat right have become extreme. Employees who do not join gyms and nutrition workshops sometimes find themselves shunned by colleagues and passed over for promotions. If they become ill, colleagues blame them for having brought the illness on themselves.

One might support a ban on smoking while opposing certain other restrictive measures, of course, on the grounds that smoking, unlike eating an egg salad sandwich or flaunting[7] a rotten physique,[8] hurts others as well as oneself. But sustaining such an argument is not easy. Health economists have shown convincingly that everyone pays, through higher insurance premiums and an overtaxed health system, for everyone else's unhealthy behavior.

I accept the fact that I may be harming myself and others by my actions. Like those who smoke, what I do not accept is that this potential harm is greater than the hardship required to change my ways. It might not be a terrible burden to give

---

1. receiving punishment, bad news (implying that it is deserved) 2. loud; disorderly but not dangerous or bad 3. take one's weight at the beginning of an event (as boxers do before a fight) 4. exercise 5. a hypothetical series of events or happenings 6. unbelievable; improbable 7. show off; excessively exhibit one's own characteristics 8. form of the body

up fatty **foods** and to strap oneself into a rowing machine. No doubt some people accomplish such things easily. As for myself, every low cholesterol diet I have ever tried has left me hungry and frustrated, and I've yet to meet an exercise machine I've liked.

In surveys, the major reasons smokers give for their habit is that they enjoy it and find it relaxing. Those are exactly the reasons I eat what I do and spend my spare time with a book or in front of a television screen. These choices fit my personality and life style. To oppose a ban on smoking is to object to the demand upon a group of people to give up their particular stance toward life—one that, for all its noxious qualities, has contributed much to the American character.

Social psychologists have found that, as a group, smokers differ from non-smokers. Smokers are more likely to be impulsive, extroverted risk takers. They take chances in a variety of areas of their personal lives that abstinent types like me shy away from. Smokers tend to drive faster, for instance, and to make more venturesome business decisions.

We all take unnecessary risks at times and behave in ways that upset others. Smokers may do so in more areas of life, or in different ways, than nonsmokers. But we nonsmokers who believe that we have a right to our own idiosyncrasies have an obligation to defend smokers' rights as well.

Comprehension and Discussion

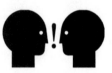

A. *Circle the correct answer. If the answer is false, tell why.*

1. The writer has never had any desire at all to smoke.

    True   False

2. The writer is against smoking bans for purely political reasons.

    True   False

3. According to the writer, because eating poorly does not affect anyone else, we do not have to worry about restrictions on eating or other life-style habits.

    True   False

4. The writer admits that the examples of having to do exercises or be weighed before working are extreme but that he uses them to make a point.

    True   False

B. *Answer the following questions as completely as possible.*

1. Although the writer of this article is not a smoker and he hates smoking, he feels that bans against smoking are dangerous. Summarize, in general

terms, why he takes this position, and explain the following two arguments: He is afraid that they may go after him next, and he objects to a demand on a group of people to change their life-style.

2. An argument generally anticipates opposing arguments and then tries to refute or disprove those arguments. The writer anticipates that someone might say that his arguments are farfetched. What is his refutation?

3. A good argument often concedes or admits that the opposition has a good point. However, this concession is usually followed by a reason to show why the argument is still valid. Look at the two concessions that the writer makes. Explain in your own words how he tries to show that his argument is still valid.

Concession	**Explanation**
A. One might support a ban on smoking while opposing certain other restrictive measures on the grounds that smoking . . . hurts others as well as oneself.	
B. I accept the fact that I may be harming myself and others by my actions.	

4. Generally speaking, do you agree or disagree with the premise that smoking bans are dangerous? Whether you agree or disagree, are there any opposing viewpoints which you would agree with?

5. Do you feel that the writer makes a good argument? Why or why not? Whether you agree or disagree with this essay, which argument do you find the most convincing and which one do you find the least convincing?

Word Forms

Working with a partner, complete the following chart with the different forms of the words. Use your knowledge of other words and their different forms to help you. Do not be afraid to guess. A dash means there is no form.

Noun	**Verb**	**Adjective**	**Adverb**
—	detest		
	enact		
	—	extroverted	—
idiosyncrasy	—		
	—	impulsive	
	—		invariably
	—	noxious	

Vocabulary Practice

Complete the sentences below with the correct words from the following list. You may have to use different word forms. Do not use a word more than once.

enact	detest	invariably
shun	pass over	idiosyncrasies
abstinent	noxious	stance
impulsive	extroverted	

1. The United States has always been considered a country of individualists. We are seen as people who not only tolerate but also admire individualism. The heroes of American films are often not the characters who plan their actions carefully but those who act (a.) _____ and basically do what they want. However, the reality can be somewhat different. Now some people fear that we are being pressured to conform to be like everyone else and that (b.) _____ behavior is becoming less and less tolerated.

2. Behavior in and out of the workplace is being monitored, and many companies are taking a strong _____ against lifestyles that they consider unhealthy.

3. Few people deny that nonsmokers should not be subjected to the _____ fumes of another person's cigarettes.

4. And most people, smokers and nonsmokers alike, find the actions of those few smokers who don't respect the rights of others to be _____.

5. However, it is not only the careless smoker who bothers others who may _____ when it comes time for promotion or even a job.

6. For some employers, _____ from certain behaviors on the job, such as smoking, is not enough.

7. A woman in Indiana was fired not because she smoked at the workplace but because nicotine showed up in a routine urine test given by her employer. The state legislature later passed a law making it illegal to fire someone for smoking off the job. Although the _____ of this law prevents future occurrences of this type, the Indiana woman who lost her job did not get it back.

8. Americans have always been known as outgoing people. For now it seems that the famous American _____ is being directed at telling others what they should or should not do.

9. But (a.) _____ the pendulum swings the other way. Perhaps some day soon it will be the finger-pointers who (b.) _____ by others.

Focus on Form: Subjunctive Noun Clauses

Look at the following sentences. Following the pattern in the example, complete the other sentences by circling the correct answer. Work in pairs or small groups.

Example: The California Medical Association (CMA) is proposing that the state *ban* smoking in all indoor public facilities. *(Active)*

1. The CMA also suggests that cigarette sales from machines ____. *(Passive)*

    a. are banned
    b. be banned
    c. banned
    d. ban

2. According to Glassner, it is important that we ____ bans against smoking.

    a. don't make
    b. didn't make
    c. not make
    d. have not made

3. The tobacco industry has made the recommendation that vending machines ____ in the ban. *(Passive, Negative)*

    a. have not been included
    b. were not included
    c. are not included
    d. not be included

Grammar Practice

The previous sentences all contain a main clause and a noun clause. Underline the main clause and circle the noun clause in each sentence.

Focus on Form: Subjunctive Noun Clauses

1. When a main clause containing words of urgency, advisability, recommendation, request, etc., is followed by a noun clause, the subjunctive (or base form) of the verb of the noun clause is used. This form, known as the *uninflected form*, is the same as the infinitive (to do) without the to.

   Notice the following about the verb in subjunctive noun clauses:

   • There is no *inflection*, that is, no final *-s*, *-ed*, or *-ing*.

   • This form is used regardless of the tense of the verb in the main clause or the subject in the noun clause. (See examples below.)

- The negative is formed with *not*.
- The passive voice is formed with *be* (which is the base form of *to be*) + the past participle.
- The word *that* usually (but not necessarily always) precedes the noun clause.

The following verbs are followed by subjunctive noun clauses:

demand	propose*, **
insist*	recommend*
move***	request**
prefer**	suggest*

- (With all of these verbs, *that* is optional.)

His parents	are demanding demand have demanded demanded will demand etc.	(that)	I you he, she we they their children	*stop* smoking. *not smoke*.

2. What other forms follow the same rules? Look at the list below.

- _____ or _____ forms of these verbs are also followed by the base form.

suggestion	proposal
insistence	recommendation
insistent	demand (noun)
preferable	request (noun)

---

* *Insist, propose* (when it means *suggest*), *recommend* and *suggest* can also be followed by a gerund.

  He insisted on smoking.

  They proposed *going* to the Cancer Society for help.

  She recommended *not trying* to go cold turkey.

  We suggested *cutting* down little by little.

  Insist and suggest can also be used to mean "say," i.e., insist = say strongly; suggest = say indirectly or imply. With these meanings, the subjunctive is not used.

  He insisted that he *was* right.

  Are you suggesting that he *did* it?

** *Prefer, request*, and *propose* (when it means *intend*) can also be followed directly by an infinitive. They *cannot* be followed by an object and an infinitive.

  I prefer *to stop* all at once. (I prefer *not to sit* in the smoking section.)

  He requested *to sit* in the smoking area.

  She proposes *to quit* soon.

  BUT: I prefer that *you stop* all at once.

*** Move in this sense means to propose formally, as in a meeting. (I move that we take a vote.)

Grammar Practice

Complete the following sentences with the correct form of the words in parentheses.

1. The proposal that the government completely (prohibit) _____ the sale of cigarettes was vetoed.

2. The student government moved that smoking only (allow) _____ in designated areas.

3. The passenger was insistent that he (give) _____ a seat in the smoking section.

4. Her doctor has been suggesting for a long time that she (attend) _____ a special group that helps people quit smoking.

5. Some people believe that it is preferable that the government (enact, neg.) _____ laws about smoking but that we (rely) _____ on common courtesy.

Grammar Practice

In his essay, "Why Smoking Bans are Dangerous," Barry Glassner admits that he does not have what might be considered a healthy diet today and that he does not exercise very much. Imagine that Mr. Glassner went to a doctor for an annual checkup. Look at what a doctor might have told him. Then imagine telling a friend what the doctor said to Glassner. Use one of the following words and a subjunctive noun clause in each sentence. Use a different word in each sentence, and be careful of the meaning and of the level of strength of the word you use. You do not have to use every word from the original sentence in your sentences.

request	propose
insist	recommend
move	suggest
prefer	demand

1. "You have to cut down on foods that are high in cholesterol."

   The doctor . . .

2. "Get some exercise!"

3. "Why don't you try walking to work once in a while?"

4. "You could eat more green vegetables and fewer fried potatoes."

5. "Could you please pay the nurse on your way out?"

Mr. Glassner told a friend about the visit to the doctor. The friend had been thinking about changing his habits also.

6. "Maybe if we jog together we'll stay with it."

   The friend . . .

7. Mr. Glassner: "Okay, but please don't tell anybody that we're doing this."

8. Despite his new habits, Mr. Glassner still feels that people should have the right to do what they want. At the next faculty meeting, he brings up the idea of establishing a smoking room. He says, . . .

Reading 2: "Cigarette Ads: A Matter of Life"

Prereading Questions

1. Are ads for any products prohibited in your country? If so, what are the products? Are the ads prohibited on TV, newspapers, or radio?

2. Is there any justification for prohibiting ads for a product that is legally available?

3. Think about ads for cigarettes that you have seen, either in the United States or in your country. What do they try to do? Is there any difference between the ads in the United States and those in your country? How do ads try to get people to smoke or to change brands of cigarettes?

4. How are people normally depicted in ads for cigarettes or alcohol? Describe them and what they are usually seen doing. Then look at the following cartoon. What do you think it is saying? Describe how a similar type of ad for smoking would be.

Vocabulary Practice

Circle the correct synonym or definition for each of the italicized words in the sentences below. Use the context of the sentences to help you guess the meaning.

1. Imagine what would happen if someone came up a new product that had no notable benefits, was addictive, and could be considered the cause of death of 350,000 Americans each year? Would the Food and Drug Administration give his *brainchild* a seal of approval?

    a. sons and daughters
    b. great idea
    c. document

2. Would the government allow it to be *extolled*?

    a. praised
    b. criticized
    c. thrown out

3. What do you do once cigarettes are in the marketplace? What do you do once you have a *hooked* population?

    a. robbed
    b. unhappy
    c. addicted

4. This is the question that *plagues* the anti-tobacco coalition.

    a. annoys greatly
    b. makes sick
    c. pleases

5. The actions of the anti-smoking people can be seen as an attempt to gradually get the country to stop smoking without going *cold turkey*.

    a. special programs
    b. stopping without pain
    c. stopping at once

6. Nothing has *elicited* quite the level of controversy as the proposal to ban all forms of cigarette advertising and promotion.

    a. stopped
    b. brought out
    c. made illegal

7. Anti-smoking groups *are backing* legislation to raise cigarette taxes.

    a. supporting
    b. opposing
    c. stopping

8. Opponents of bans on cigarette advertising are against these bans because they say that censorship is *contagious*.

    a. sometimes necessary
    (b) can be spread
    c. can be stopped

9. I have watched the argument about censorship with some *trepidation*.

    a. amusement
    (b) fear
    c. agreement

10. An ad that portrays the glamour of smoking is *intrinsically* false.

    (a) in its nature
    b. not at all
    (c) obviously

11. Do we have to allow the tobacco industry to keep their (A.) *constituency* intact, to maintain the smokers' (B.) *clout*?

    ex.) Karry's constituency

    (A.) (a) people they represent
          (b) profits
          c. losses
    (B.)   a. addiction
          (b) influence (passive)
          c. diseases

Cigarette Ads: A Matter of Life

By ELLEN GOODMAN
(from *The Washington Post*)

Imagine what would happen if some modern entrepreneur came up with a nifty[9] idea for a new consumer product. It was an item that had no notable benefits, was addictive and would be implicated[10] in the deaths of some 350,000 Americans a year.

What precisely would be the response of his corporate superiors? Beyond stunned silence? Would the Food and Drug Administration[11] give his brainchild a seal of approval? Would the government allow it to be extolled and sold to citizens? Hardly. If cigarettes did not exist, we might invent them, but never in the wildest scenario would we let them loose[12] on the legal market.

But what do you do once cigarettes are in the marketplace? What do you do once you have a hooked population, a hooked economy? This the raw-throated[13]

to be out of it "rhythm"

big wig
= a powerful person

---

9. very good, interesting (slang)   10. imply that someone is to blame for something; to blame   11. (FDA) Federal agency which tests and then approves or denies the sale of food and drug items   12. allow them to be free   13. a question that is asked over and over so many times that it makes the throat sore

question/that plagues the antitobacco coalition. When you cut right through all the arguments by lawyers and doctors and public-policy makers, what we have are fifty million addicted Americans. We know two things about them with absolute certainty. That smoking is bad for their health, bad for everyone's health, not to mention health bills. That banning cigarettes at this moment in time/would be a social disaster,/turning smokers into criminals and farmers into bootleggers.[14]

The actions of the antismoking people/can be seen as an attempt to get around the central conflict, an attempt to wean[15] the country from smoking without going cold turkey. So far, they have tried putting warnings on cigarettes and rotating those warnings. They are backing legislation to raise cigarette taxes and to eliminate the industry's deduction for advertising. Even the movement toward a smoke-free workplace and public space has, as a subtext,[16] the hope that smoking will gradually become socially unacceptable.

But nothing has elicited quite the level of controversy as the proposal to ban all forms of cigarette advertising and promotion, The latest bill, introduced February 24 by Mike Synar (D-Okla.), would outlaw the whole $2 billion boodle:[17] newspaper and magazine ads, billboards,[18] posters, match advertising, samples, sponsorships of athletic events—virtually anything with a cigarette name on it except the package itself.

Synar, (who smoked for ten years,) became convinced after watching the non-effect of labels that, "You cannot compete with $2 billion worth of advertising and promotion." The ban is seen as a better way to stop companies from recruiting new and young customers, to make up for the ones who haves died or quit. With no new recruits, ashtrays will gradually become heirlooms.[19]

The American Medical Association agrees. The American Bar Association disagrees. First Amendment lawyer Floyd Abrams calls it censorship and warns: "Censorship is contagious." American Civil Liberties Union Director Ira Glasser says, "We have always been against bans of advertising (for) any products that are legal to sell."

I have watched this argument emerge with some trepidation. I no longer worry that banning tobacco ads today will make it easier to ban liquor ads tomorrow and then salt, beef, fat, even automobiles. Tobacco is unique. As Synar puts it, "We are dealing with the only product/ that /when used as instructed is destructive." Moreover, each ad that portrays the glamour[20] of healthy young people smoking is intrinsically false.

But I agree/that there is something contradictory/in the message/that it's okay to sell cigarettes but not okay to tell people about them. The Supreme Court ruled /that Puerto Rico could permit gambling and prohibit advertising for it. Such a duality(is) apparently constitutional but also contradictory.

Nevertheless, what are our choices? Cigarettes are deadly. It isn't okay to sell them in any moral sense, but we allow it. Fifty million addicts make a ban on cigarettes impossible. Does that mean we are stuck forever with this health

---

14. people who make or sell illegal products, especially alcohol   15. gradually remove a person from what he or she is accustomed to (such as a baby from a bottle)   16. secondary message   17. money, gained illegally; bribe; stolen goods (slang)   18. large posters for advertising on roads and highways   19. an old object, usually of a family, often valuable   20. attractiveness; charming and beautiful in a sophisticated way

do away with = eliminate
a shift = change

disaster? Because we can't forbid cigarettes, do we have to allow the industry access to new addicts, allow them to keep their numbers up, keep their constituency intact, maintain the smokers' clout? I don't think so.

This is perhaps the most powerful place to interrupt the cycle. A ban on advertising is an imperfect and unstable compromise. But the alternative is grim in its consistency: the seduction of yet another generation into disease.

Comprehension and Discussion

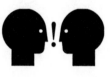

A. *Circle the correct answer. If the answer is false, tell why.*

1. The writer feels that because of the special nature of tobacco she is not worried that a ban on advertising for cigarettes will lead to a ban on advertising for other products which are not considered healthy.

    True   False

    tempation

    appeared

2. The writer is against making cigarettes illegal for moral reasons.

    True   False

3. Of all of the actions taken to try to get people to quit smoking, the most controversial has been the movement toward a smoke-free workplace and public space.

    True   False

4. There is a precedent for banning advertising for a product or activity that is legal.

    True   False

B. *Answer the following questions as completely as possible.*

1. In the first paragraph, the writer uses a hypothetical situation as an attention-getting device. Do you feel this is an effective way to start the essay? Why or why not? What did it make you think? What would happen in this situation?

2. What does the writer mean when she says that we have a "hooked economy?"

3. What have the antismoking activists been doing to get people to quit smoking, and why has the proposal been made to ban all advertising for cigarettes?

4. What are people who say "censorship is contagious" afraid of, and how does the writer refute this argument?

5. Does the writer ever concede a point? If so, what is it? How does she continue to support her argument despite this concession?

6. What is meant by the statement that "A ban on advertising is an imperfect and unstable compromise?"

7. What do you agree or disagree with in this essay? Give as many examples as possible.

Word Forms

Working with a partner, complete the following chart with the different forms of the words. Use your knowledge of other words and their different forms to help you. Do not be afraid to guess. A dash means there is no form.

Noun	Verb	Adjective	Adverb
	back	—	—
1. constituency	—	—	—
2. …	—	—	—
	—	contagious	—
	elicit	—	—
	extol	—	—
—	—		intrinsically
	plague	—	—

Vocabulary Practice

Complete the sentences below with the correct words from the following list. You may have to use different word forms. Do not use a word more than once.

Sentences 1 - 4	Sentences 5 - 9
cold turkey	hooked
extol	contagious
trepidation	clout
plague	elicit
back	brainchild
	intrinsically
	constituents

1. In the past, tobacco _____ as a product which was beneficial to one's health. Now it is seen by many as a _____ on society.

2. There are differing views on the best way to quit smoking—cutting down gradually or going _cold turkey_.

3. Very few people _____ the idea that tobacco should be made illegal.

4. Although most parents do not want their children to smoke, some allow them to, with _____, because they are afraid that a prohibition would make the practice even more exciting.

5. Politicians may hesitate to fight against tobacco if their (a.) _____ work in the tobacco industry. In addition, if these politicians have a great

deal of (b.) _____ , other politicians may hesitate to go against them.

6. Tobaccoless cigarettes are a (a.) _____ that never succeeded. People who are (b.) _____ on nicotine are not interested in smoking lettuce leaves.

7. Risking danger for the desired substance is often an _____ part of addiction of all kinds.

8. Although smoking may not be physically _____ , it is very common for young people to start smoking simply because they see their peers or their parents doing it.

9. In a democracy, talk of prohibitions usually _____ *elicit* a great response, often even from people who are against the substance to be prohibited.

Reading 3: "Asia: A New Front in the War on Smoking"

Prereading Questions

1. Are tobacco companies in your country privately owned and run or are they run by the state? If so, does the state have a monopoly?

2. Which cigarettes are the most popular in your country, local cigarettes, American, or cigarettes from another country? Why? What types of people generally tend to smoke American cigarettes? Do any specific types tend to smoke local cigarettes?

3. As far as you know, is anything done to control the sale of foreign cigarettes in your country?

Vocabulary Practice

Match the italicized words in the sentences with the synonyms or definitions in the list below. Use the context of the sentence to help you guess the meaning.

_____ secret; not open
_____ hard; harsh; unbending
_____ friendly relationship because of a common cause
_____ awkward; clumsy; heavy
_____ wear down because of constant, longterm contact with a force
_____ advance or invasion

_____ reduce or cut down
_____ harsh; bitter; scathing
_____ tempt or attract with promise of pleasure or an award
_____ increase efforts or commitment
_____ happen at the same time (two or more events) without plan

1. The Thai government imposed high import duties, a (a.) *cumbersome* customs clearance procedure, and a (b.) *stiff* ban on cigarette advertising.

2. Thailand relied heavily on an *alliance* of local and international anti-smoking activists.

3. Anti-smoking groups are working to create the kind of opposition throughout Asia that has seriously *eroded* the U.S. tobacco market.

4. The U.S. (a.) *inroads* in Asia are prompting anti-smoking activists to (b.) *step up* their efforts.

5. China is enacting laws to bar tobacco ads and *curtail* smoking in public places.

6. The U.S. companies say the anti-smoking activism is just *covert* protectionism.

7. The lifting of the ban in Korea (a.) *coincided* with an outbreak of (b.) *vitriolic* anti-American outbursts.

8. U.S. companies say that their ads only *lure* those who already smoke.

Asia: A New Front in the War on Smoking

By PETE ENGARDIO with ROBERT NEFF   (from *Business Week* magazine)

An international alliance aims to outflank[21] U.S. tobacco companies

It was a Pyrrhic victory[22] for the U.S. tobacco industry. Last November, the Thai government, bowing to heavy pressure from U.S. trade negotiators, opened its $744 million cigarette market to imports. But not before Thailand imposed high import duties, a cumbersome customs-clearance procedure, and a stiff ban on cigarette advertising. So you won't see Marlboro men rambling across the range[23] on Bangkok's billboards anytime soon.

What sets this effort apart from other campaigns to curb American tobacco imports is that Thailand relied heavily for help on an alliance of local and international anti-smoking activists. 'The Thais came to us and said: 'Your government is trying to force U.S. cigarettes down our throats,'"[24] recounts Alan Davis of the American Cancer Society, an alliance member. Now, these antismoking groups are working to create the kind of opposition throughout Asia that has seriously eroded the U.S. tobacco market.

The activists have their work cut out for them;[25] Philip Morris, R.J. Reynolds Tobacco, and Brown & Williamson export 75 billion cigarettes to Asian countries. That figure

---

21. gain an advantage over (in a war)   22. a victory with great losses (Named after King Pyrrhus of Epirus, an ancient country in what is now part of Greece, who won a battle against the ancient Romans but with such great losses that the value of the victory itself was questionable.)   23. a reference to the Marlboro man in ads, sitting on a horse, going slowly across vast areas of open land

---

24. forcing; allowing no opportunity to resist
25. have a great deal of work to do, and you know that you have it

吸烟危害健康

An anti-smoking campaign in China. Do these campaigns work?

dropped slightly from 1989 to 1990, but mainly because U.S. companies began moving more production to offshore factories.

The U.S. inroads in Asia are prompting antismoking activists to step up their efforts. On Jan. 9, a 14-nation group met in Hong Kong to map out a four-year strategy to combat smoking in the region. The group, called the Asian Consultancy on Tobacco Control, recently linked up with a computer network to get news of U.S. tobacco company activities. Its strategy: train activists and persuade Asian countries to adopt uniform tobacco control.

Already in Hong Kong, where U.S. companies control 80% of the cigarette market, the government has banned all radio and TV ads for cigarettes. And even China, which takes in $5.2 billion in revenues from the state-owned tobacco monopoly, is enacting laws to bar tobacco ads and curtail smoking in public places.

The U.S. tobacco companies are fighting back. "I guess you could say we're at war," says Clive Turner, director of the pro-industry Asian Tobacco Council. That's no surprise; American cigarette makers figure that east Asia, which generates about $36 billion in annual cigarette sales, is one of their most promising growth markets. So Turner's council is helping companies lobby governments to keep them from adopting even stiffer measures. In Thailand, they're pressing authorities to allow sponsorship of sporting events.

'COVERT PROTECTIONISM.' The U.S. companies say that some of the antismoking activism is really part of an effort to discourage foreigners from competing with state-run tobacco monopolies. "It's just covert protectionism," contends Richard L. Snyder, executive vice-president of Philip Morris International, Inc., South Korea, which relies on the government tobacco monopoly for 10% of its revenues, used to threaten citizens with arrest if they so much as lit up an imported cigarette. The lifting of this ban in 1987 coincided with an outbreak of vitriolic anti-American protests. Today, heavy restrictions confine the non-Korean share of the cigarette market to 5%. Even in Japan's relatively open market, the government-owned monopoly, Japan Tobacco, Inc., holds an 84% share.

Asia's most prominent antitobacco crusader, Dr. Judith M. Mackay, concedes that anti-U.S. resentment is "really moving things here." But she says banning cigarette ads is a logical first move, even though it may benefit monopolies. While U.S. companies insist their ads only lure those who already smoke, health officials fear that Madison Avenue-style[26] blitzes[27] create new demand and undermine their efforts.

In markets such as Japan, South Korea, and Philippines, where more than 60% of males light up, activists have a long way to go. But the note that cigarette use in Japan is dropping about 1% a year. Both the activists and the tobacco companies also are mindful of the American experience. Although it took years for antismoking sentiment to catch on, today just 27% of U.S. males smoke, down from 57% in the mid-1950s. Even a little campaign can turn out to be a big threat.

---

26. an avenue in New York City. The term is commonly used to mean the world of advertising   27. a heavy attack or campaign

Comprehension and Discussion

Answer the following questions as completely as possible. Use your own phrasing, but try to use the following words in your answers:

cumbersome	vitriolic	curtail	lure
alliance	inroads	stiff	erode
step up	covert	coincide	

1. How was the Thai government's opening to cigarette imports a Pyrrhic victory for the U.S. tobacco industry?

2. What did local and international anti-smoking activists do in Thailand and what are they working towards?

3. What steps have been taken by some Asian governments in regards to cigarettes and smoking?

4. How are the tobacco companies fighting back?

5. What do the U.S. companies say about the antismoking efforts? What do they mean by this?

6. What happened in South Korea in 1987 and what does the article imply that this means?

7. How do tobacco companies defend their advertising campaigns? What do opponents feel about this?

8. How might the comparison of smokers in the United States and in Asia make activists and tobacco companies both optimistic and pessimistic?

9. What is being done to get people to cut down or quit smoking on your country?

10. Critics of the tobacco companies contend that while a great deal is being done to get people to quit smoking in the United States, stronger efforts are being made to sell more tobacco to Asia. Do you see this as a contradiction? Explain your answer.

Focus on Form: More on Subjunctive Noun Clauses

Look at the following sentences:

The doctor advised *that he cut* down on his smoking.

> or

The doctor advised *him to cut* down on his smoking.
(The doctor advised *him not to smoke* so much.)

The words in the following list can be followed by:

- a subjunctive noun clause.
- an *object* + (not) + an *infinitive*.

(*Two exceptions are *arrange* and *intend* + for + object + infinitive.)

advise	command	order
arrange *	direct	require
ask	forbid	urge
beg	intend*	

- When you have a choice and the subjunctive is used, it sounds formal. It is used in formal writing or speaking.
- *That* is always used after these verbs when a subjunctive noun clause follows.

	advisable	
	essential	
	important	*that we stop* advertising cigarettes.
It is	imperative	
	mandatory	*for us to stop* advertising cigarettes.
	necessary	
	preferable	
	urgent	
	vital	

Note: When other adjectives, such as *apparent, clear, obvious*, which do not imply "urgency," "advisability," etc., are followed by noun clauses, the verbs in these clauses:

- use the inflected form, i.e., they show person and tense and have a final *-s,*

  -ed, -ing.
- form the negative with the auxiliary *(do, does, did, is, was,* etc.) + *not*
- form the passive with the inflected form of *to be (am, is are, was were, been)*

It is *essential* that he quit smoking.

BUT: 1.   It is *apparent* that he doesn't like smoke.
2.   It's *clear* that she is having a lot of trouble quitting.
3.   It was *obvious* that he hadn't been given a promotion simply because he smoked.

Grammar Practice

Complete the sentences with the correct form of the verbs in parentheses. Decide whether to use the base form, the inflected form, or the infinitive. You may have to use the passive voice.

1. Legislation concerning tobacco and alcohol has changed a great deal recently. The U.S. government requires that tobacco companies (put) _____ health warnings on all tobacco products, and alcohol companies must do the same for their products.

2. Many cities require bars and restaurants (post) _____ signs about the danger of alcohol for pregnant women. Although some bars and restaurants complain about this policy, the government feels it is essential that women (make) _____ aware of the dangers of alcohol to the fetus. Most doctors advise pregnant women (neg., drink) _____ alcohol.

3. United States laws forbid cigarette companies (advertise) _____ on television. Consumer activists feel that this prohibition is not strong enough. They are proposing that tobacco companies (neg., allow) _____ to sponsor athletic events. They feel it is obvious that sponsorship of an athletic event, with the name of the tobacco product clearly shown in the background, (be) _____ nothing but advertising in disguise.

4. Opponents say that although it is important that the public (become) _____ aware of the dangers of tobacco, prohibitions are not the way to go about it. It is always preferable for people (change) _____ their habits because they want to and not because they have to. You can order a child (neg., smoke) _____, but this might only make smoking more desirable.

5. Some people ask that the government (set) _____ up educational programs for young children. The suggestion has been made that a tax on tobacco (use) _____ to finance these programs.

6. Many large corporations are arranging for their employees (take) _____ free programs to help them stop smoking. It is apparent that most companies (prefer) _____ that their workers (neg., smoke) _____.

7. Tobacco is not the only product whose advertising is under fire. Some consumer groups are also demanding that makers of alcoholic beverages (neg., allow) _____ to advertise their products on television. Others are recommending that ads for beer and wine (neg., show) _____ during sporting events. These groups feel it is imperative that young people (neg., associate) _____ sports with drinking.

8. Leaders of minority groups feel it is clear that minority groups (target) _____ by tobacco and alcohol companies and they insist that these companies (stop) _____ this practice. Some billboard companies have directed that ads for tobacco and alcohol (neg., place) _____ near schools. Minority groups are demanding that they (receive) _____ the same consideration.

Grammar Practice

Complete the following sentences. Use information from the readings or your own opinions. If a sentence can be completed in two ways, give both.

1. Many nonsmokers are demanding . . .

2. Many smokers are only asking . . .

3. The AMA feels it is essential that young people . . .

4. Many consumer advocates feel it is clear that advertising for cigarettes . . .

5. Ellen Goodman, in her essay on cigarette ads, does not propose that we . . .

6. The U.S. government requires . . .

7. Barry Glassner ("Smoking Bans are Dangerous") feels it is imperative . . .

8. If people are smoking near you and the smoke is bothering you, you could request . . .

9. Some nonsmokers who believe that smoking is a personal decision feel that we can advise . . . , and we can urge . . . , but it is important that . . .

10. Regarding advertising for tobacco and alcohol, my recommendation is . . .

Grammar Practice

Make your own proposals, recommendations, suggestions, etc., about any of the issues discussed in this chapter. The sentences do not have to be connected into a paragraph. They can be separate sentences just to practice the forms about these different issues.

1. It is essential . . .

2. I propose that . . .

3. My recommendation about the rights of smokers vs. nonsmokers is that . . .

4. I think/don't think a private company can demand . . .

5. I would advise that governments . . .

6. If a friend told me that he wanted to quit smoking, I would suggest that . . .

7. Governments should/should not require . . .

8. I think it is (choose one: interesting/vital) . . .

Class Project

Work on one or more of these projects individually or in groups of two to three students. Then present your findings to the class.

1. If you once smoked but stopped, tell the class about your experience. How old were you when you started? Why did you start? What did cigarettes mean to you? When and why did you decide to quit smoking? How did you do it? Had you tried and failed before? Do you still have the desire to smoke? Give as much information as possible about yourself and smoking.

2. What do experts recommend that smokers do to stop smoking? Do research on ways to stop smoking. If possible, speak to someone at a health clinic, the American Cancer Association or some other non-profit group, and find out what they recommend. Present your findings to the class.

3. Look at the issue of advertising for tobacco and alcohol. How has advertising for these products changed over the years? Find ads for cigarettes or alcohol in old issues of magazines in the library. Do you see any differences between these and ads in present-day magazines? Find ads that will support or refute the claims of tobacco companies that the purpose of cigarette advertising is to get smokers to change brands and not to get people to start smoking.

Discussion and Writing

Discuss the following topics, first in pairs or small groups and then with the entire class. After your discussion, pick one (or more) of the topics and write an essay about it. If the essay is argumentative, remember to include a concession and a refutation.

1. Consumer advocacy groups are recommending that advertising for tobacco and alcohol be banned or at least limited. For example, they say that alcohol should not be advertised during sporting events and that these events should not be sponsored by tobacco companies, even if no actual advertising of the product takes place. Support or oppose this proposal or any part of it.

2. Discuss the issue of prohibitions or bans on smoking. What limits, if any, should a government put on tobacco products and smoking? Do laws against smoking infringe on the civil rights of smokers?

3. Discuss the issue of the importation of American cigarettes to Asia. Are the actions of the different Asian governments because of health reasons or are they just "covert protectionism?" Do you agree with the strong measures these governments are taking? Should they be stronger or more relaxed?

Word List

Below is a list of the new words, and their different forms, presented in this chapter.

Noun	Verb	Adjective	Adverb
alliance	ally	allied	
ally			
backing	back		
ban	ban		
brainchild			
	broaden	broad	broadly
clout			
coincidence	coincide	coincidental	coincidentally
cold turkey			
constituency			
constituent			
contagion		contagious	
covertness		covert	covertly
cumbersomeness		cumbersome	
curtailment	curtail		
	detest	detestable	detestably
enactment	enact		
elicitation	elicit		
erosion	erode	erosive	
extolment	extol		
extroversion		extroverted	
	hook	hooked	
idiosyncrasy		idiosyncratic	idiosyncratically
implementation	implement		

Noun	Verb	Adjective	Adverb
impulsiveness	impulsive	impulsively	
inroads			
	intrinsic	intrinsically	
invariability		invariable	invariably
lure	lure		
noxiousness		noxious	
	pass over		
plague	plague		
	shun		
	single out		
stance			
	step up		
stiffness	stiffen	stiff	
sweep	sweep		
trepidation			
unanimity		unanimous	unanimously
vitriol		vitriolic	

CHAPTER 7

Whose Child Is It?

Reading 1: "Whose Baby Will It Be?"

Prereading Questions

1. Cartoons in newspapers or magazines are often political or social commentaries. They use humor to present serious social issues. What does this cartoon say about what is happening in the society of the United States today? Do you find this cartoon humorous? Why or why not?

2. What are some possible legal, ethical, or social issues which might result from using new or non-traditional birth technologies?

3. Why might people use new birth technologies rather than just adopt a child?

4. Is surrogate motherhood legal or possible in your country? If so, are there any laws regulating it? Does it happen frequently?

5. What is the definition of a mother? Can you imagine a situation in which there might be a problem deciding who a mother is?

Predicting Vocabulary

We can assume that certain words have a good possibility of appearing in an article about surrogacy or new birth technologies. These words may have to do with the techniques in these new technologies, for example. Working in small groups, make a list of words which might be used when talking about surrogacy or new birth techniques.

Whose Baby Will It Be?

By BARBARA KANTROWITZ with ALDEN COHEN and MEGAN DISSLY
(from *Newsweek* magazine)

When surrogacy sours

Four years ago surrogate mother Mary Beth Whitehead ignited[1] a national debate when she sued to regain custody of her daughter. Since then, 10 states have passed laws governing surrogacy contracts like Whitehead's, in which birth mothers are artificially inseminated with the father's sperm. But the issue of surrogate motherhood is far from settled. Last week a suit filed by a pregnant California woman raised troubling questions about the uses of even more sophisticated reproductive techniques. For the first time, a judge will have to decide whether a birth mother can keep a child that is not genetically hers, but rather the product of another couple's sperm and egg.

In January, Anna Johnson, a 29-year-old vocational nurse and single mother from Orange County, agreed to bear a child for Mark and Crispina Calvert for a total fee of $10,000. An embryo created through the in vitro fertilization of a sperm and egg from the Calverts was implanted in Johnson's uterus. Crispina Calvert had previously undergone a hysterectomy[2] and could not bear children herself. Under the terms of their surrogacy contract, the Calverts were to pay Johnson $150 monthly and $2,000 every trimester.[3] Johnson claims the relationship soured[4] in June, when she went into false labor and the Calverts refused to drive her to the hospital. She also claims their monthly payments were late. Now she wants to keep the child. Mark Calvert, 34, an insurance underwriter,[5] and his wife, a 36-year-old

nurse, deny Johnson's claims and say the woman is just trying to exploit[6] them financially and emotionally. They contend that they have not only upheld[7] the contract but have gone beyond it, making two $2,000 payments at least a month ahead of schedule.

Surrogate arrangements are still relatively rare. In the past decade, there have been 2000 such births. The vast majority were so-called traditional surrogacies, like the New Jersey case in which Mary Beth Whitehead was artificially inseminated with sperm from the natural father, William Stern. In that suit, the birth mother was granted visitation rights and the New Jersey Supreme Court held that commercial surrogacy contracts are illegal because they constitute baby selling; however, the ruling was based on New Jersey law and applies only to that state. The Johnson case represents an even more unusual arrangement: gestational surrogacy, where a fetus conceived in a test tube is implanted into the surrogate mother's uterus. Experts in surrogate motherhood estimate that there have been between 50 and 80 such births in the United States, although the technology has been available for five years.

California has no law governing either gestational or traditional surrogacy, although several such measures have been introduced in the state legislature in recent years. The civil code defines the mother as the woman giving birth. Beyond the legal issues, experts in reproductive medicine have reservations about gestational surrogacy. In a recent ethical position paper, the American

---

1. set fire to; arouse; start 2. surgical removal of a woman's uterus 3. three-month period 4. to go or become sour or bad 5. a person who works for an insurance company to determine whether people who want insurance coverage are good risks for the company

6. use unethically or unfairly 7. maintain or support; follow regulations or laws

Fertility Society says that there is no research on the long-term psychological effects. The society says the procedure should be considered a "clinical experiment." At this point, it is a social and legal experiment as well. Two months from now, when the Johnson-Calvert baby is born, it will be a judge who decides which mother will take the child home.

Comprehension and Discussion

Answer the following questions as completely as possible.

1. The article begins with the example of Mary Beth Whitehead. Later on in the article it mentions her again. From what you read in this article and from what you may have heard about this case, explain what happened and why she is important here.

2. How is the case of Anna Johnson different from that of Ms. Whitehead?

3. What is the difference between traditional and gestational surrogacy?

4. How does gestational surrogacy complicate an already complicated issue?

5. Civil law in California defines a mother as the woman who gives birth to the child. This code was probably enacted before gestational surrogacy became a possibility. Does the fact that Ms. Johnson has no genetic link to the child make a difference in this case? Who, in your opinion, is the mother?

6. If you were the judge in this case, how would you rule? If you gave Ms. Johnson custody, would you give the Calverts visitation rights? If you gave the Calverts custody, would you give Ms. Johnson the right to visit the child? Why or why not?

7. One aspect of the case that the article does not mention is that Ms. Johnson is African-American, Mrs. Calvert is Asian, and Mr. Calvert is white. Do you think these racial differences will have any effect on the judge's decision? Should they?

8. Custody of a child born to a surrogate mother is always a potential problem. What would happen, for example, if a child were born through traditional surrogacy (the contract father's sperm and the surrogate's egg) and later the couple got divorced? Usually, but not always, women get custody of children after a divorce. In this case, the contract mother would have no genetic link to the child, but the father, as the sperm donor, would. Would this automatically mean that the woman's bid for custody would be rejected? Or what would happen if the contract parents changed their minds and refused to take the child, for example, if the child were born with a birth defect? Comment on these possibilities.

Note: Mr. and Mrs. Calvert were granted custody of the child Ms. Johnson carried for them.

Focus on Form: Present Unreal Conditionals

1. Some people *want* a baby with a genetic link; therefore, they *don't consider* adoption.
2. If people *didn't want* a baby with a genetic link, they *would consider* adoption.
3. Perhaps some people *don't use* surrogacy because it *is* very expensive.
4. More people *might use* surrogacy if it *weren't* so expensive.
5. We *don't have* clear laws about these technologies, so there *are* many legal problems.
6. If we *had* clear laws about these technologies, there *wouldn't be* so many legal problems.

Sentences 1, 3, and 5 are statements of fact. Sentences 2, 4, and 6 are examples of hypothetical or unreal situations in the present. They tell us how something would, could, or might be if something else were different. To show that something is unreal or hypothetical in the present, the following formula is used:

IF CLAUSE	RESULT CLAUSE

IF + Subject + *Past tense*,
   were
   could
(Passive = were + Past Participle)
	Subject + *Would (Could, Might) + Base Form*

Note:

- The *If* clause may be first or second in the sentence. If the *If* clause comes first, it is followed by a comma. There is no comma if the *Result* clause comes first.
- The Base Form is the infinitive without the *to*. There can be no final -*s*, -*ed*, -*ing*.

  Infinitive = *to eat*   Base Form = *eat*
  Infinitive = *to have*   Base Form = *have*
  Infinitive = to be   Base Form = *be*

- *would* = definite (in the speaker's opinion)

  might = perhaps would
  could = would be able

Grammar Practice

Change the following sentences into conditionals. Be careful of which is the If clause and which is the Result clause. Use would, could *or* might *in the Result clause. You may have to change other words so that the sentences make sense and sound logical.*

1. Ms. Calvert can't have her own children so she's in this strange situation today.

2. Ms. Whitehead has visitation rights to her daughter possibly because she has a genetic link with her.

3. The Calvert-Johnson case is probably complicated by the fact that Ms. Johnson and the child she bore are of different races.

4. It isn't easy to decide who the mother is in these cases because many states don't have laws concerning surrogacy.

5. We don't know the psychological problems children born to surrogate mothers might have so we can't prepare the children.

6. (Opponents of surrogacy say that it exploits poor women.) A woman who is poor and unemployed does not have many options; consequently, she may decide to carry another woman's baby.

7. Because the problems of new technology cannot be foreseen, it is not easy to avoid these complicated legal and ethical issues.

Reading 2: "A Custody Fight for an Egg"

Prereading Questions

1. It is becoming more and more common in the United States for a couple to sign a prenuptial contract to plan what would happen to money or property in case of divorce. What do you think of these contracts? Can you think of any other types of contracts that a couple might want to sign?

2. What say does or should a man have in deciding when to become a father? If the child has already been conceived, does he have the right to change his mind and not become a father?

3. Imagine a couple who froze their own fertilized eggs for future implantation. The couple die in an accident. What should be done with these frozen pre-embryos?

Vocabulary Practice

Match the italicized words in the sentences with the synonyms or definitions in the list below. Use the context of the sentence to help you guess the meaning.

_____ taking out; removing (by force)

_____ hold back; control; deprive of freedom

_____ place into; insert

_____ result or period after a misfortune

_____ person who gives or contributes something

_____ on the side; the area far from the center but within the boundary

_____ separate

_____ very unusual; completely unconventional

_____ fall apart

1. The doctors fertilized eggs in a petri dish and tried unsuccessfully twice to *implant* them in Mary Sue's uterus.

2. When the marriage *disintegrated*, the remaining seven pre-embryos became its most dramatic leftovers.

3. Now a Blount County judge has wisely *restrained* access to these fertilized eggs.

4. But when the husband and wife formally *split*, the court must decide the fate of what they joined together.

5. But the questions it raises are at the center, not the *periphery*, of this still new technology.

6. Taking the most logical steps can lead down the most *bizarre* trails.

7. Mary Sue's participation—hormonal treatment, egg (a.) *extraction*, unsuccessful implants—was greater than that of her husband as sperm (b.) *donor*.

8. Six years ago, another couple died in a plane crash leaving no instructions for the fate of the fertilized eggs which are still stored in a clinic in Australia. In the *aftermath*, many clinics drew up agreements, asking couples what they wanted done with the fertilized eggs if they could no longer use them.

A Custody Fight for an Egg

By ELLEN GOODMAN
(from *The Washington Post*)

This is how it happens in ethics class. The teacher begins the morning with a carefully constructed and rather farfetched hypothetical case. Today, it's a doozy.

Imagine, just imagine, says the teacher, that a couple comes to divorce court to split up their property. They are not wrangling over[8] a house or a boat or car. What they each demand is custody of their seven pre-embryos, the creations of his sperm and her eggs that lie frozen at the in vitro fertilization clinic.

The class lets out a collective groan.[9] Come on. Too farfetched. That would never happen. Give us a break.

Well, students, the ultimate hypothetical has now happened in Maryville, Tennessee. The main players in this true story are Mary Sue and Junior Lewis Davis. The outcome[10] is up for grabs.

---

8. fight over; argue about 9. make a low, wordless sound, from pain, grief, disapproval, or disbelief 10. result

During their ten years of marriage, Mary Sue had five tubal pregnancies that finally led the couple to an IVF clinic. There the doctors fertilized eggs in a petri dish[11] and tried unsuccessfully twice to implant them in Mary Sue's uterus. When the marriage disintegrated, the remaining seven pre-embryos became its most dramatic leftovers.[12]

Now a Blount County judge has wisely restrained access to these fertilized eggs, but when the husband and wife formally split, the court must decide the fate of what they joined together.

This is more than a bioethics freak case. There have been well over 4,000 children born from IVF. Only this once have pre-embryos been part of a property claim in a divorce settlement. But the questions it raises are at the center, not the periphery, of this still new technology.

Is an embryo really property? This is one that our ethics class could debate for days. Junior Davis listed these fertilized eggs under the joint property. Mary Sue says, "I consider them life." The head of the IVF clinic, Dr. Ray King, believes "they should be treated like children." Junior Davis's lawyer, Charles Clifford, says, "In the law, if they are not human beings they are property."

If embryos are property under the law, how does the court decide whose property? It cannot, after all, rule for joint custody, one week in his freezer, one week in hers. It could, I suppose, divide these fertilized eggs the way California divides assets, right down the middle: three for Junior, three for Mary Sue and one up for grabs. That hardly solves the puzzle.

Alternatively, the court could decide "ownership" on the basis of what sociologist Barbara Katz Rothman describes reluctantly as "sweat equity."[13] Mary Sue's participation—hormonal, treatment, ova[14] extraction, unsuccessful implants—was greater than that of her husband as sperm donor. The court could also calculate the dollar equity.[15] Whoever paid for the clinic might own the "product." Taking the most logical steps can lead down the most bizarre trails.

The other ways to determine possession do not promise to be easier. Perhaps the pre-embryo should go to the one most in need or most eager to "use" it. Mary Sue, who can only have children through IVF, has said she wants to be a mother, although she is not sure she has the emotional or financial resources to try again. Junior has not said what he would do with the embryos.

There is also the sticky matter of rights. Junior says he doesn't want to father children now. Does he have a greater right to determine the pre-embryos than a man who fertilized an egg in, shall we say, the more traditional way? Mary wants to mother a child. Does she have a greater right to bear her ex-husband's child than another divorced woman? After all, Mary Sue could use these eggs after their divorce. Junior could end up responsible for the child. Whose rights are right?

Lest[16] this ethics class get way out of hand, one other set of possibilities. If the court awards the pre-embryos to one or the other, what is to stop either from donating them to other infertile couples? Or using them in second marriages?

---

11. a shallow dish used in laboratory research   12. normally, food that remains after a meal. Here it means business that remains unfinished   13. who worked hardest 14. eggs or reproductive cells of animals (singular = ovum)   15. value of property or business   16. (formal) to prevent the possibility; to keep from

Life beginning in a petri dish. Is it unnatural?

Hard cases make bad law and dilemmas make bad ethics. The Davis story teaches both those maxims.[17] Not even an advanced seminar could work out a perfect resolution.

But there is a way to prevent such a hypothetical from becoming a reality again. Six years ago, another couple, Mario and Elsa Rios, died in a plane crash, leaving no instructions for the fate of the fertilized eggs which are still stored in a clinic in Australia.

In the aftermath, many clinics drew up agreements, asking couples what they wanted done with the fertilized eggs if they could no longer use them. They could add what I would call pre-conceptual clauses to these agreements. Husband and wife would decide in advance which would control the fate of their biological merger if they uncouple.

The new technology allows us to imitate the act of creation in a laboratory petri dish. But it has devised no biogenetic way to resolve everyday human conflicts. We are left to sweep up after the new technology. This ethics class will meet again.

---

17. a short saying, usually to teach a lesson; a proverb

Comprehension and Discussion

Answer the following questions as completely as possible.

1. Complete the following statement:

   The major theoretical question in this case is . . .

2. Explain the issue of property and what it means for this case.

3. Summarize the possible ways of deciding who should receive the eggs. Can you add any other arguments which could be used in making this decision?

4. Why is Mr. Davis opposed to the use of these eggs by Mrs. Davis?

5. How does the writer propose that similar conflicts be avoided in the future?

6. The writer says that medical technology gives us new possibilities in life. For example, people who could not have their own children before are now able to do so. However, these new technologies also bring us new legal, ethical, and social problems. What other medical technologies have given us both advantages and, at the same time, these types of problems.

7. Explain the two maxims in this essay, and tell how the Davis case teaches both of them.

   "Hard cases make bad laws and dilemmas make bad ethics."

8. In your opinion, who should be given custody of the fertilized eggs? Support your opinion.

Note: Mrs. Davis was granted custody of the seven frozen embryos. However, the Tennessee Supreme Court overturned this decision and ruled that she could not force her ex-husband to become a father. Mrs. Davis was denied the right to use the embryos. The decision did not say what should be done with them.

Word Forms

Working with a partner, complete the following chart with the different forms of the words. Use your knowledge of other words and their different forms to help you. Do not be afraid to guess. A dash means there is no form.

Noun	Verb	Adjective	Adverb
	disintegrate	—	—
donor		—	—
	implant	—	—
periphery	—		
	restrain	—	—

Vocabulary Practice

Complete the sentences below with the correct words from the following list. You may have to use different word forms and tenses. Do not use a word more than once.

restrain   periphery   donor   extract   split
aftermath   disintegrate   bizarre   implant

1. Medical science, law, and ethics are more than just _____ related. They are closely connected.

2. The problem is that there is a _____ between what we can do and what we have laws for, and this can present us with dilemmas we had never imagined before.

3. Medical ethicists often feel that people should use some _____ in dealing with completely new medical advances and that lawmakers should try to predict possible ethical or legal problems.

4. Some people feel that the new birth technologies will lead to a total (a.) _____ of the value placed on human life and on natural reproduction. Others feel that medical advances are a natural part of life and should be taken advantage of but that problems arise afterwards because we do not have laws or ethics to deal with them. Usually it is only the (b.) _____ of a legal dilemma that brings about new legislation.

5. Our attitudes change along with the technical advances but it often takes time. What once might have been considered _____ is now accepted as normal.

6. Not very long ago, just the thought of _____ an organ would have seemed like something from a science-fiction novel. Today it is commonplace.

7. However, even here there are human, ethical, and legal issues to take into account. Although it is possible to give someone else an organ and to go on living a normal life, as in the case of a kidney transplant, (a.) _____ an organ from one person and (b.) _____ it into another is not as easy as removing a tooth and putting in a false one. Many factors, physical, emotional, and ethical, must be taken into account.

Vocabulary Practice

The writer uses many informal words and expressions in this essay. Words and expressions such as these are used more commonly in speech, but they can be used in writing to make a point. The point in this essay is how bizarre the situation is. In addition, the hypothetical situation is a class, where students might use more informal expressions. Look at these words and the situation or context they are in. Then try to guess the meaning within the context. Circle the correct answer.

1. The class usually begins with a farfetched hypothetical situation. Today it's a *doozy.*

    a. about the same as usual
    b. even more farfetched than usual
    c. less farfetched than usual

2.   The class let out a collective groan . . . Too farfetched. *"Come on! Give us a break."*

a. Let's go.
b. Let us have a rest.
c. You're joking. I don't believe it.

3.   The main players in this true story are Mary Sue and Junior Davis, who are fighting over the custody of seven pre-embryos. The outcome of this custody fight is *up for grabs.*

a. a settled issue
b. uncertain; undecided; open to everybody
c. the first one to grab it, gets it

4.   Both parties want the embryos. One side says that they should be treated like children. The other that they should be treated like property. There is also the *sticky* matter of rights. Junior says . . . Mary Sue says . . . Whose rights are right?

a. complex or difficult to decide
b. sticks to you, like glue
c. bizarre

5.   Technology allows us to imitate creation, but it cannot solve everyday human conflicts. We are left to *sweep up after* the new technology.

a. imitate
b. throw out
c. repair the damage

Vocabulary Practice

Complete the conversations with the correct words and expressions from the list below. You may have to write a full sentence containing the expression.

sweep up after	doozy
Come on. Give me a break.	sticky
up for grabs	

1.   A: Have you seen Elvira's new boyfriend?

B: No, but her boyfriends are usually weird, so he won't surprise me.

A: That's what you think! . . .

2.   A: Poor Joe. His brother got into trouble again, and Joe had to go to the police station to get him out. Then he had to pay for everything the brother had broken.

B: . . .

3.   A: Have you heard about the couple who went to a sperm bank and asked for the sperm of a man who was an athlete, played the violin, appreciated good wines, and had a nice voice?

B: . . .

4. A: Who left this cake on the table? Does it belong to anyone?

    B: No, . . .

5. A: What do you think about surrogate motherhood? Should it be prohibited?

    B: I don't know. . . .

Focus on Form: Past Unreal Conditional

Past Condition	**Past Result**
Mr. and Mrs. Davis *didn't sign* a pre-conceptual contract (in the past).	They *had* to go to court (in the past) to decide the custody of the embryos.

If they *had signed* a pre-conceptual contract, they *wouldn't have had* to go to court.

If + Subject + *had* + Past Participle, (Past Perfect)	Subject + *would* + *have* + Past Participle
	might
(Passive = *had* + *been* + Past Participle)	*could*

Grammar Practice

Complete the sentences with the correct verb forms and modals (would, might, or could). Use the verbs in parentheses. Be careful of the passive voice.

1. If Mary Beth Whitehead (sign, neg.) _____ a contract promising to turn the child over to the contract couple, she (be) _____ able to keep the child.

2. She (sign, neg.) _____ the contract if she (know) _____ how difficult it was going to be to give up the baby.

3. If Ms. Whitehead (give) _____ a waiting period in which she was allowed to change her mind before handing over the baby, she (have, neg.) _____ to go to court to try to keep the child.

4. Ms. Whitehead was paid to act as a surrogate. She (fight) _____ the case better if she (accept, neg.) _____ money.

5. If the Sterns, the contract parents, (give, neg.) _____ custody, they probably (appeal) _____ the decision to a higher court.

6. Ms. Whitehead's husband didn't have a job at the time of the case. If he (have) _____ a job, it (be) _____ easier for her to win the case.

7. Many states (make, neg.) _____ laws concerning surrogacy if it (neg., be) _____ for the Whitehead case.

8. Ms. Whitehead said that she and her husband had talked about the situation before she signed the contract and that he agreed with the plans. He probably (agree, neg.) _____, if he (know) _____ how much pain it was going to cause his wife.

Reading 3: "All in the Family"

Prereading Question

1. Try to answer the following riddle:

    Twins are born, a girl and a boy. The girl looks at the boy and says, "I could be your aunt." How could this be possible? (Remember that twins are born at the same time to the same mother.)

Vocabulary Practice

Match the italicized words in the sentences with the synonyms or definitions in the list below. Use the context of the sentence to help you guess the meaning.

_____ to say or express what might be criticized or considered foolish
_____ to exaggerate or say in a way intending to shock or arouse interest
_____ to make unclear or confusing
_____ to destroy
_____ practicality; dealing with events as they are
_____ make up; invent
_____ lessen in importance; diminish
_____ generally accepted; it must be accepted as truth
_____ stimulating and very exciting
_____ deeply religious

1. Arlette Schweitzer imagines the headlines an attention-grabbing newspaper might (a.) *concoct* to (b.) *sensationalize* her (c.) *admittedly* unusual story.

2. "Christa has no...," a reporter hesitantly *ventures*. "That's right," replies Arlette. "Christa has no uterus."

3. When this misfortune was discovered eight years ago, her mother patiently explains, Christa was only 14, and even then she was absolutely *devastated* by the news.

4. Becoming a surrogate mother, stresses Arlette, is sort of like running a race: the experience may be *exhilarating*, but it is not entirely painless.

5. But now a heartwarming situation has come along in which the moral quandaries *pale* before that most basic of human instincts: the desire of a parent to take on and take away the pain of a child.

6. With refreshing down-to-earth (a.) *pragmatism*, Arlette, a (b.) *devout* Roman Catholic, says she had no doubts about her decision.

7. "That made perfect sense to him. Children are very accepting. It's adults who *cloud* the matter."

All in the Family

By J. MADELINE NASH   (from *Time* magazine)

How does that gutsy[18] South Dakota grandma feel about being pregnant with her daughter's twins?

MOM PREGNANT WITH HER OWN GRANDKIDS!

TWO-HEADED MOTHER GIVES BIRTH TO TWINS!

Eyes twinkling,[19] hand folded across her swelling belly, Arlette Schweitzer imagines the headlines a tabloid[20] might concoct to sensationalize her admittedly unusual condition. The exercise amuses her no end—probably because there is nothing the least bit bizarre about this cheerful 42-year-old librarian who lives with her husband Dan, a fluffy white cat named Boom Boom, and a cocker spaniel named Special on a tree-lined street in Aberdeen, S. Dak. What a visitor notices above all in their cozy,[21] split-level house is the photographs of smiling kids: grandchildren, nieces and nephews and, over the living-room sofa, the large color portraits of the Schweitzers' son Curtis, 26, and daughter Christa, 22.

Now that Christa has, well, got her mother in a family way,[22] newspaper writers and TV crews are camped outside. Since the *New York Times* put her on page one, producers for talk shows have kept calling, photographers have continually rung her doorbell, and somehow, through it all, Arlette Schweitzer has continued to radiate a sense of calm. "Christa has no...," a reporter hesitantly ventures. "That's right," replies Arlette, her voice as clear and as strong as a church bell. "Christa has no uterus."

When this misfortune was discovered eight year ago, her mother patiently explains, Christa was only 14, and even then she was absolutely devastated by the news. "When Christa was just a little girl," recalls Arlette, "all she could talk about was becoming a mother." Two years later, during a visit to the Mayo Clinic, Arlette observed to a physician who examined her daughter, "I wish you could transplant my uterus because I certainly have no use for it anymore." The doctor looked at her curiously. "He asked me how old I was. I said I was 36, which I was at the time. Suddenly it was like a light bulb switched on[23] for all three of us. She was born without a uterus. I was young enough to lend her mine."

In February of this year, at the University of Minnesota Hospital and Clinic in Minneapolis, eggs taken from Christa's ovaries

---

18. courageous; spirited   19. shining like a star
20. a newspaper in a small form, of a size usually not folded in half, and often with attention-grabbing headlines   21. comfortable in a warm, intimate way   22. pregnant

23. to get an idea

were fertilized with her husband Kevin Uchytil's sperm, then implanted in Arlette's uterus. Ten days later, Arlette telephoned her daughter and son-in-law, who live in Sioux City, Iowa. "Congratulations!" she triumphantly exclaimed. "*You're* pregnant." Not long thereafter, Christa, viewing an ultrasound picture of her mother's tummy,[24] saw two heartbeats and realized that her mother would give birth to twins. "How lucky could I be!" Christa said. "This just takes my breath away."

Becoming a surrogate mother, stresses Arlette, is sort of like running a triathlon:[25] the experience may be exhilarating, but it is not entirely painless. For 89 days, she had to inject herself with hormones. "I still have scars on both my hips," she says with a grin. "But as long as you know there's an end to it, I think you can bear almost anything. For 89 days, I think you could even walk on burning coals if you had to. I feel so responsible. This really is a one-shot chance, and so I'm trying to do everything right."

Arlette grew up in Lemmon, S. Dak. where her father was a jeweler. At 15, she surprised her parents by dropping out of school to marry Dan, now a sales representative for the Keebler Co. She had her children early and was for years a stay-at-home mom. "I played house, and I loved every minute of it," she says. Then when Christa was in third grade, Arlette went back to school. For the past two years, she has taken charge of the library at Aberdeen's Simmons Junior High. "My whole life," she says impishly,[26] "I've done in reverse. I feel like Frank Sinatra. I've done it my way."

The idea of surrogate parenting has kept professional ethicists and jurists wringing their hands[27] ever since the first case surfaced in 1978. Is it proper to "rent" a womb by paying a stranger to bear a child? What if the surrogate mother changes her mind? But now a heartwarming situation has come along in which the moral quandaries pale before that most basic of human instincts: the desire of a parent to take on and take away the pain of a child.

With refreshing,[28] down-to-earth[29] pragmatism, Arlette, a devout Roman Catholic, says she had no doubts about her decision. "If you can give the gift of life," she asks, "why not? If medical science affords that opportunity, why not take it?" Far more problematic, in her view, is the more typical situation—such as that involving Mary Beth Whitehead in 1987—in which a surrogate mother is also the biological mother. "These are Christa's eggs and Kevin's sperm," Arlette says. "There's no doubt about whose children these are!"

Asked by her seven-year-old grandson whether Grandma was going to have a baby, Arlette replied, "Christa and Kevin's babies are going to use Grandma's uterus until they're old enough to be born." That made perfect sense to him. "Children are very accepting," observes Arlette. "It's adults who cloud the matter. Maybe it's not quite the same old birds and bees.[30] Maybe now there are birds and bees and butterflies too."

So why not go ahead and congratulate the medical butterflies responsible for this unorthodox biological event? That's what Arlette and Dan and Christa and Kevin plan to do when they welcome their miracle babies into the world this October. "Dan will be up there coaching[31] me," imagines Arlette fondly, "while Kevin and Christa will be getting ready to grab the babies and run." Then Arlette and Dan will settle back to their normal role—that of happy grandparents.

---

24. stomach 25. a race or marathon which includes bicycling, swimming, and running; a very rigorous athletic contest 26. playfully 27. twisting and squeezing one's hands (an action that shows worry or distress)

28. unusual or different in a good way 29. sensible 30. a euphemism for sexual reproduction 31. helping; guiding

Comprehension and Discussion

A. *Circle the correct answer. If the answer is false, tell why.*

1. This article in written only to give information. It does not seem to lean either in favor of or against Ms. Schweitzer and what she is doing.

True   False

2. Ms. Schweitzer decided to act as her daughter's surrogate when they found out that the daughter had been born without a uterus.

True   False

3. Ms. Schweitzer did not seem to have any major moral or ethical problems with the idea of acting as her daughter's surrogate.

True   False

4. Christa's brother Curtis has a child.

True   False

B. *Answer the following questions as completely as possible.*

1. How has Ms. Schweitzer done her life "in reverse?"

2. The article mentions that Ms. Schweitzer did not face the usual "moral quandaries" which are often associated with surrogacy. What are these quandaries?

3. How might children look at a situation differently from the way adults do?

4. What do you feel about this situation? Do you feel Ms. Schweitzer was right in doing what she did for her daughter? Do you see any possible moral, ethical, or psychological problems?

5. Ms. Schweitzer says "If medical science affords that opportunity (to give the gift of life), why not take it?" Do you agree that it is all right to take advantage of all of the opportunities that medical science affords or gives us? Are there limits? Support your opinions. Be as specific as possible.

Note: On October 12, 1991, Arlette Schweitzer gave birth to her grandchildren, a boy and a girl.

Word Forms

Working with a partner, complete the following chart with the different forms of the words. Use your knowledge of other words and their different forms to help you. Do not be afraid to guess. A dash means there is no form.

Noun	Verb	Adjective	Adverb
	concoct	—	—
	devastate	—	—
	—	devout	
		exhilarating	—
1. pragmatism	—		
2. . . .	—	—	—
1. . . .	sensationalize		—
2. . . .	—	—	—

Vocabulary Practice

Complete the sentences with the correct words from the list below. You may have to use different word forms. Do not use a word more than once.

exhilarating	concoct	pale	admittedly	devout
sensationalize	cloud	venture	pragmatism	devastate

It seems that almost every day we are faced with a new ethical or legal dilemma which is brought about by advances in medical technology. What is commonplace today would have seemed like the bizarre (1.) _____ of a fiction writer not very long ago. (2.) _____, medical advances have been around for a long time, and many have been the subjects of (3.) _____ headlines and news stories. However, the ethical quandaries of the past seem (4.) _____ by comparison with those of today. One may look at the problem and say that we have to decide it (5.) _____. But we do not live in a vacuum, and emotions often (6.) _____ the issues. When a family member or loved one is affected, even very religious people, people whose (7.) _____ would never be questioned, may go against their religion's policy and take advantage of medical technology previously considered unacceptable. Unless you have experienced it firsthand, it is impossible to imagine the (8.) _____ you would feel on being told of a serious medical problem and the (9.) _____ at then finding out that there is an opportunity, no matter how farfetched it may sound, to overcome it. Although you may (10.) _____ a guess as to how you would react in a given situation, you will never know for sure unless it happens to you.

Vocabulary Building

The article "All in the Family" uses a number of quotes. The verb to say *is the most common word used to quote someone. However, using the same word (She* said, *". . . ." And then she* said...) *becomes repetitive and boring. It addition, the word* said *is neutral. It tells us nothing about how or why something was said. For example, "Christa has no . . . ," a reporter hesitantly* ventures, *is one way to phrase this idea. You could say, "The reporter hesitantly* says," *but it does not give the idea of saying something with fear of criticism or embarrassment. Scan the article and look for different words the writer uses instead of "said." Can you think of any others which are not used here?*

<u>Words Found in Article</u>   <u>Other Words</u>

Word Analysis

Through the use of different words and phrases, a writer can put a person or a topic in a favorable or an unfavorable light. The article "Whose Baby Will It Be?," about a court case, is presented in a neutral or informational style. The reader does not get the feeling that the writer supports either Ms. Johnson or the Calverts. "All in the Family," however, perhaps because it is not a court case and is seen more as a human interest story, puts the subject, Arlette Schweitzer, and the practice, surrogacy for her daughter, in a favorable light. Right from the beginning, when we are told that she is "gutsy" and that her eyes "twinkle," we are given a positive view of her. These are words which would only be used in a positive sense. In addition to the use of "loaded" words, words that carry positive or negative value, what one chooses to write about can affect how the reader sees the subject. For example, in the first paragraph, we learn about the family's "*fluffy white cat* named Boom Boom and a *cocker spaniel named Special* on a *tree-lined street* in Aberdeen." All of this gives us a very distinct, positive picture of an "average" American family.

Scan the article again and look for "loaded" words, words which carry a certain connotation, or phrases, descriptions, etc., which might cause us to view the family or the situation in a favorable light. Are there any words in the other articles which might show favor or disfavor towards the subject?

Focus on Form: Mixed Time Conditionals

- A past condition can bring about a result in the present.

Past Condition	**Present Result**
They *didn't have* a contract (in the past).	They *have* this problem (today).

   If they *had had* a contract, they *wouldn't have* this problem today.

- A condition that caused a result in the past might still exist. To show that the condition exists (and perhaps that the person is still alive), the present unreal conditional is used with the past result.

Present Condition	**Past Result**
She *isn't* able to carry a baby. (She still isn't.)	She *used* a surrogate. (in the past)

   If she *were* able to carry a baby, she *wouldn't have used* a surrogate.

Grammar Practice

Complete the sentences with the correct verb forms and modals (would, might or could). Use the verbs in parentheses. Depending on the meaning, you may have to use the negative. Be careful of the passive voice. Use your knowledge of the situations from the readings as well as the information given in the sentences to help you. Some of the sentences will contain mixed time conditionals. Remember to ask yourself if the condition still exists.

1. It seems that almost every week a new lawsuit concerning some ethical or legal aspect of a new technological advance arises. There (be) _____ so many legal battles going on if we (have) _____ clearer laws about these new medical technologies.

2. Opponents of surrogacy feel that the practice takes advantage of poor or working-class women. For example, Ms. Whitehead and Ms. Johnson probably (agree) _____ to carry other women's babies if they (be) _____ professional women with high-paying jobs.

3. Race might have been an issue in the Calvert-Johnson case. The fact that Ms. Johnson is black and the baby she bore is not made it obvious that the child is not biologically hers. It (be) _____ more difficult to decide this case in favor of the Calverts, particularly since California law states that the woman who bears the child is the mother, if all of the participants (be) _____ the same race.

4. Surrogate mothers are usually required to pass certain physical, emotional, and family tests. Having other children is important. For example, the Sterns (pick) _____ Ms. Whitehead if she (have) _____ other children or if there (be) _____ any incidences of disease or mental illness in her family.

5. The Whitehead case was the first time a child was taken from a surrogate and given to the contract parents against the surrogate's will. If a precedent (set) _____ in the Whitehead case, it (be) _____ more difficult in general for judges to award custody of children in these cases to women who are not the birth mothers.

6. Despite all of the problems they had, the Sterns probably do not regret their decision to use a surrogate. If they (adopt) _____ a child instead of using a surrogate, they (have) _____ a child with a genetic link to one of them.

7. Mr. Davis said that he had the right not to become a father. One of the arguments used against him was that he (be) _____ able to change his mind and force his wife to get an abortion if she (get) _____ pregnant before the marriage disintegrated.

8. If the Davises (have) _____ a preconceptual contract when they split up, the case (have) _____ to go to court.

9. One of the problems in the Davis case is that because of advanced technology we now can create beings that are hard to define. Are they children or are they property? If we (be) _____ able to create these beings, we (be) _____ in this situation today.

Focus on Form: Conditionals in Short Statements

Very often when we are trying to make a point, or when we answer a question, we make a statement and then we give a conditional to show how things would (or would not) be or have been different if. . . However, instead of giving the complete conditional based on the previous sentence, in order not to sound repetitive, we use a shortened conditional. One or two words can substitute for a whole phrase.

Q: Do many states *have* laws about surrogacy?

A: No. If they *did*, there would be fewer legal problems.
   (did = had laws about surrogacy)

What we are saying here is "No, they don't. If they did, . . ."

Grammar Practice

Try to guess the correct shortened conditional in the following sentences. Circle the correct answer.

1. Most surrogates *are* poor women. If they _____, they wouldn't need to do this.

   a. are
   b. do
   c. were
   d. weren't

2. She *can't* carry children. If she _____, she wouldn't have used a surrogate.

   a. couldn't have
   b. can
   c. can't
   d. could

3. The surrogate *didn't have* enough money to hire a good lawyer. If she _____, she might have won the case.

   a. had
   b. did
   c. had had
   d. didn't

4. There *were* no laws for surrogacy in that state at that time. If there _____, it would have been easier to decide who got custody.

   a. did
   b. had been

c. were
d. was

5. She *wasn't given custody.* If she ___, the contract parents would have appealed.

   a. were
   b. had
   c. was
   d. had been

6. She *couldn't* afford to pay for the costly court battle. If she ___, she might have sought custody of the child.

   a. could
   b. did
   c. could have
   d. can

Focus on Form: Shortened Conditionals

For unreal situations, the following substitutions are made. (See the sentences above for each one):

Present Unreal:

Example: *did* (not) - for all verbs (including *to have*) except *to be*

1. *were* (not) - for the verb to *be*

2. *could* (not) - for the modal *can*

Past Unreal:

3. *had* (not) - for all verbs (including *to have*) except *to be*

4., 5. *had* (not) been - for the verb *to be*

6. *could have* - for the modal *could* (meaning past ability)

(In the negative, *hadn't been able to* is more commonly used.)

Grammar Practice

Complete the statements or answer the questions using the shortened forms of the conditionals.

1. It's obvious that Ms. Schweitzer loves her daughter very much. If she _____, she wouldn't have done something so difficult.

2. Arlette Schweitzer is a very healthy woman. If she _____, she wouldn't have volunteered to become pregnant again at her age.

3. A: Did Ms. Whitehead sign a contract promising to turn the child over to the contract parents?

    B: Yes. If she _____, she might have been able to keep the child.

4. A: Did Mr. Whitehead have a job at the time?

    B: No. If he _____, they might have had a better chance.

5. A: Do the Whiteheads have other children?

    B: Yes. If they _____, the Sterns wouldn't have picked Ms. Whitehead to be the surrogate.

6. Ms. Whitehead wasn't living in a state that had laws about surrogacy at the time. If she _____, she would have had more of an idea of the possibility of getting custody of the child.

7. The Davis's didn't have a contract specifying what to do with the embryos in case of a problem. If they _____, things would have been less complicated.

8. Mr. and Mrs. Rios, the couple who died in a plane crash in Australia, were fairly wealthy people. If they _____, there might have been fewer problems concerning the embryos. The courts had a difficult decision to make. If the embryos were implanted in a woman and if the implantation worked and resulted in the birth of babies, would the babies be eligible to inherit the estate of the Mr. and Mrs. Rios?

9. A: Are sperm donors responsible for the welfare of a child born through artificial insemination of their sperm?

    B: No. If they _____, few men would donate their sperm.

10. A: Does the United States have federal laws regulating birth technologies?

    B: No. If it _____, there would be much less confusion.

Grammar Practice

Pair Work: Shortened Conditionals

Below are two sets of questions/statements and answers. Student A will ask Student B the questions in the A list. Using the information given, Student B will answer the questions with short conditionals. Student A corrects Student B after each question. Next, reverse roles, with Student B asking the questions, Student A answering and Student B correcting the answers. The correct answers are in parentheses after each question. Listen carefully to the verb used and to the tense, and look at the clues to help you decide which short conditional to use. Be careful of negatives and the passive voice.

Student A Questions/Statements

1. Is your cold better? (No. If it *were*, I'd go with you.)

2. Did you have a car when you lived there? (No, if I *had*, I would have done a lot more.)

Student A Answers

1. No. If I _____, I would have gone.

2. Yes. If he _____, he would have been very depressed.

3. It's a good thing she went to the hospital. (I know. If she *hadn't*, she might have died.)

4. Was the water warm? (No. If it *had been*, I would have gone in.)

5. Do you have a TV? (No. If I *did*, I'd go out less.)

6. Were they able to have children? (No. If they *had been*, they wouldn't have adopted a child.)

7. Could you lend me $20? (If I *could*, I would, but I'm broke.)

8. Do you live near your parents? (No. If I *did*, I'd visit them more often.)

9. Did you have a bad time at the party too? (Yes. If I *hadn't*, I wouldn't have left so early.)

10. Was he seen leaving the house? (Yes. If he *hadn't been*, they wouldn't have had any proof against him.)

3. No. If I _____, I'd call home more often.

4. No, but if I _____, I'd go to the mountains.

5. No. If he _____, he wouldn't have gotten sick.

6. No. If they _____, they wouldn't have these problems now.

7. No. If he _____, I wouldn't be here.

8. Yes. If she _____, she wouldn't be able to pay the rent.

9. I'm sorry. If I _____, I would, but I have to work.

10. I don't know. If she _____, she wouldn't tell anyone.

Student B Answers

1. No. If it _____, I'd go with you.

2. No. If I _____, I would have done a lot more.

3. I know. If she _____, she might have died.

4. No. If it _____, I would have gone in.

5. No. If I _____, I'd go out less.

6. No. If they _____, they wouldn't have adopted a child.

Student B Questions/Statements

1. Didn't you know about the party? (No. If I *had*, I would have gone.)

2. Was your brother accepted? (Yes. If he *hadn't been*, he would have been very depressed.)

3. Do you have your own phone? (No. If I *did*, I'd call home more often.)

4. Are you going to travel this summer? (No, but if I *were*, I'd go to the mountains.)

5. Did he have the right clothing for the ski trip? (No. If he *had*, he wouldn't have gotten sick.)

6. Did they sign a prenuptial agreement? (No. If they *had*, they wouldn't have these problems now.)

7. If I _____, I would, but I'm broke.

8. No. If I _____, I'd visit them more often.

9. Yes. If I _____, I wouldn't have left so early.

10. Yes. If he _____, they wouldn't have had any proof against him.

7. Isn't he ready yet? (No. If he *were*, I wouldn't be here.)

8. Did she take the job? (Yes. If she *hadn't*, she wouldn't be able to pay the rent.)

9. Can you help me move tomorrow? (I'm sorry. If I *could*, I would, but I have to work.)

10. Is she sick? (I don't know. If she *were*, she wouldn't tell anyone.)

Grammar Practice

Read the following true story and write as many conditional sentences as possible about this information. Try to use all different kinds, including short conditionals. After reading your sentences to the class, give your personal reaction to the case.

One of the most bizarre cases concerning surrogacy took place in the state of Ohio, which, at the time, had no laws about surrogacy. In 1982, a young married couple, Beverly Seymour and Richard Reams, went to a surrogacy service to get help in arranging for a surrogate mother to have a child for them. They believed at the time that Ms. Seymour was infertile, so they planned to have a surrogate inseminated with the sperm of Mr. Reams. In this way, the child would have a genetic link to at least one of them. The couple signed a contract with the agency. Mr. Reams was to be the biological father and Norma Lee Stotsky the surrogate mother. They agreed to pay her $10,000 and all medical expenses. After they signed the contract, Mr. Reams learned that he too was infertile. Instead of cancelling the contract, Seymour and Reams went to a sperm donor. The surrogacy agency did not know about this development. The use of a sperm donor other than the contract father is not allowed by the agency. In 1985, Mrs. Stotsky gave birth to a girl, Tessa.

A year after the birth of Tessa, the couple split up. Since then the participants in this drama have been involved in one of the most complicated custody cases ever seen in the United States, and perhaps in the world. Both Mr. Reams and Ms. Seymour wanted custody of Tessa, but neither one was a biological parent to her. In the beginning, Mrs. Stotsky, as the biological mother, said that she also wanted custody. Being the biological mother, she would have had a good reason to be given custody of Tessa, but the state of Ohio has a law which states that when a parent has had no contact with or support of a child for a year or more, anyone may request to adopt the child. However, Mrs. Stotsky changed her mind and did not ask for custody. One of the reasons was that she felt she did not have the financial resources to fight the costly court battles. The case was further complicated by the fact that on the original birth certificate, Mrs. Stotsky's husband was listed as the father of the child. This was later changed and Mr. Reams was put down as the father. However, the biological father is Leslie Miner, the sperm donor, who does not want custody of the child.

The court finally made a decision and awarded custody of Tessa to Mr. Reams. However, the case does not end there. The complicated custody case turned into a tragedy of even greater proportions. When Mr. Reams tried to take custody of Tessa, Ms. Seymour shot and killed him. She was found guilty of murder and sentenced to prison. Tessa is living (as of this writing) with foster parents. The family of Mr. Reams is asking for custody of the child, but final custody has yet to be decided.

Class Project

Work on one or more of these projects individually or in groups of two to three students. Then present your findings to the class.

1. What are the laws concerning surrogacy in the state in which you are living? What are they in your country? Are there any specific definitions of what constitutes a mother? What are the laws concerning artificial insemination? Does a sperm donor have any rights or responsibilities? Try to find this information in your local or school library. You can also try contacting fertility centers, lawmakers, or government agencies.

2. Do library research on adoption. Who is eligible to adopt? Has there been a change in adoption in recent years? For example, are there fewer children available for adoption? If so, why? Are people going to other countries to adopt children? If so, why? What are the latest trends in adoption?

3. Louise Brown, an English child born in 1978, was the first test tube baby in the world. How was the news of this situation originally greeted? Try to find essays or newspaper articles which were written before or shortly after her birth. Was this birth sensationalized? Were any predictions made about the child or about where this new technology would lead to? Is anything known about Louise Brown today?

4. Pick some other medical advance that was controversial when it first came out and find news reports about it. What was the initial reaction to the advance? What were the ethical, social, or legal problems? Has it since been accepted?

Discussion and Writing

Discuss the following topics, first in pairs or small groups and then with the teacher and the entire class. After your discussion, pick one (or more) of the topics and write an essay about it.

1. Advances in science and medical technology are taking place so fast that they often surpass our current ethics and/or laws. This presents a problem because society may not be psychologically ready for these changes, and situations may occur for which there are neither laws nor precedents. Explain this situation using specific examples to support your statements. Remember that the issue to be discussed or written about is ethics or morality and law in relation to scientific or medical advances. The specific situation is to be used only as an example to prove your point.

2. Does having the technology, medical or otherwise, to correct a situation, to make our lives happier, or just to give us what we normally could not have always justify its use? Are there limits as to how far science can or should go in offering us a better life or in giving us what we were born without? Support your opinions with specific examples. If you feel there are limits, what exactly should those limits be?

3. Pick one of the three cases discussed in this chapter and discuss it from an ethical, legal, social, or psychological point of view.

4. Technological advances often have consequences that were not foreseen when the advance was being developed. Pick a technological advance not related to birth or surrogacy, and show how there have been unanticipated consequences of this advance. Do not feel that the advance must be a very complex or new one. It could be one that took place a long time ago and one that might seem quite acceptable and normal today.

5. Do you feel that surrogate motherhood should be prohibited or limited in any way? If you feel it should be, should the prohibition apply to all types of surrogacy, (traditional, gestational, surrogacy within the family, surrogacy for money, etc.)? If you feel it should not be prohibited, what can be done to prevent possible legal problems such as custody in case of divorce or the surrogate's wish to keep the child or have visitation rights?

Word List

Below is a list of the new words, and their different forms, presented in this chapter.

Noun	Verb	Adjective	Adverb
admission	admit		admittedly
aftermath			
bizarreness		bizarre	bizarrely
cloud	cloud	cloudy	
concoction	concoct		
devastation	devastate		devastatingly
devoutness		devout	devoutly
disintegration	disintegrate		
donor	donate		
donation			
exhilaration	exhilarate	exhilarating	
extraction	extract		
implantation	implant		
	pale	pale	
periphery		peripheral	peripherally

Noun	Verb	Adjective	Adverb
pragmatism		pragmatic	pragmatically
pragmatist			
restraint	restrain		
sensationalism	sensationalize	sensational	
sensationalization			
split	split		
venture	venture		

CHAPTER 8

A National Obsession?

Reading 1

Read the following paragraph. As you are reading, do not worry about new words. Just read for the general meaning. The title of the article that this paragraph comes from is given later. Do not look at the title now.

Every morning at seven, a group of (1.) *doting* adults gather in a west side park to watch their youngsters play. They discuss party plans for an upcoming birthday, teething problems, and what do to about the (2.) *bully* who lives around the corner. The big news today is that everyone's favorite doctor is moving his (3.) *practice* to the West Side—"Thank God," says one woman. "No more late-night cab rides with Dashiell across town." They exchange remedies for eye infections, names of the best sitters, and observations on their young (4.) *charges'* development. "Reuben plays so well (5.) *one-on-one*," a young woman says fondly. "I just wish he didn't get so loud and (6.) *hyper* in a crowd." "Nick's beginning to vocalize, too," says another. An earnest (7.) *bespectacled* man suddenly notices Lily is (8.) *sulking* by herself. "Lily, go play," he shouts in frustration. "Don't be such a (9.) *spoilsport*."

Discussion

1. Who are the people mentioned in this paragraph? What kind of people are they? What are their worries and interests?

2. Would similar people in your country have the same worries and interests?

Vocabulary Practice

Match the italicized words in the previous paragraph with the synonyms or definitions in the list below. Use the context of the sentence to help you with the meaning.

_____ a person one is responsible for

_____ wearing glasses

_____ showing anger, usually by being silent and usually without great cause

_____ a conversation in which only two people are involved

_____ overly active

_____ showing too much fondness or care

_____ one who ruins the fun of other people

_____ a person who uses strength or size to hurt weaker people or make them afraid

_____ a doctor or lawyer's clients or business

The article continues on the next page.

Heavy Petting

By ELLEN HOPKINS
(from *New York Magazine*)

Dashiell is a borzoi, Reuben is a saluki, Nick is an English cocker, and Lily a Welsh terrier.[1] All over the city, play groups for dogs (sometimes called dog runs) are cropping up.[2] "The group around the corner isn't nice at all," Lily's owner confides.[3] "They're all into macho[4] dogs—Dobermans,[5] you know." Young professionals make play dates for their pets, call walkers[6] when they're going to be late, and skip[7] going out for drinks after work in order to provide some quality time. "I got this hot message in the middle of a meeting yesterday—'Dash in park at 6:15'," says Lily's owner. "We all have each other's phone numbers," Dashiell's owner says. "My dog is my schedule. You couldn't pay me to stay at work past 5:30 now. Dash does have his own nanny,[8] but to help me out, though, when things get too busy. He just adores Elizabeth, and if she can't stay with him when I have a business trip, I simply don't go.

---

1. borzoi, saluki, English cocker, and Welsh terrier: breeds or types of dogs 2. appearing 3. tell something personal or secret 4. masculine in an exaggerated way 5. a breed or type of dog 6. people who walk dogs for money 7. not do something or go someplace 8. a woman whose job is taking care of children

1. Does this change your answers to the previous questions? If so, how?
2. Does anything surprise you? Would these people be talking about the same things in your country?

Paraphrasing

Below are anecdotes, or amusing short stories, about pets. All of them are true. Your teacher will assign one anecdote to two or three students. Read your anecdote, and then, with your partner, practice paraphrasing it. When we paraphrase, we take the main ideas and put them in our own words. Give the general idea that the anecdote deals with, and then give specific examples. Read the anecdote a few times until you feel you understand it thoroughly. Then retell it to your partner without looking at it. Your partner will check to see if you have forgotten anything. Imagine that you know the people involved and that you are telling another friend about them. Don't worry about the names of the people involved. Then move into groups of six with each person having a different anecdote, and tell each other what you have read.

Example: Can you imagine that some people won't move or travel because of their pets? I have a friend who . . . . Another friend . . . . I've heard about someone else . . .

1. Animal behaviorist Warren E. believes in enriching a pet's life experience. "Don't take your dog on the same old run on the same old block every day. Take him on a picnic. If he's bored or depressed, getting him into a good exercise program will take his mind off the bad things. Sure they can do puppy push-ups, and it's good for them." One dog owner has a housekeeper who reads French poetry to the dog. She says that one poet in particular (Baudelaire) puts the dog into ecstasy. Some people dance with their animals. But you have to be careful when you try to enrich your pet's life. One woman who tried to get her cat to do aerobic exercises ended up with a cat with a broken back.

2. Finding the right caretaker when you have to be away is a real concern. Katherine J. said that when her dogs, Apollo and Diana, were very young, her social life was a disaster. "I just couldn't leave them. Finally I asked a friend with a baby what to do, and she told me about the Barnard College baby-sitting service and how wonderful all the girls were. I called and asked for a baby sitter for Saturday night. "How many children?" the woman asked. I was too embarrassed to tell her the truth so I just said two. "How old?" "Three months." "Each? You mean they're twins?" "That's right , they're twins," I answered. The nicest girl showed up and she just roared with laughter when she saw my twins. She was my sitter for quite a while. She would come every Saturday night.

3. When it comes to treating a pet in a special way, pet owners rely on food more than anything else. In an east side supermarket, there are more than three times as many brands of pet food as there are brands of baby food. Go to any pet store and you'll find food for allergic pets, high protein diets for the pregnant, and reducing diets. "Light" foods for pets are becoming increasingly common. But for many only Mom's home-cooking is good enough. Katherine J. cooks chicken with herbs for her dogs. Eleanora T.'s cats celebrate special occasions with jumbo shrimp. Patricia H. says, "Sure Yoda and Gigi get filet mignon, but they deserve it. I may serve a TV dinner to everybody else, but not to my dogs." One man chews up food for his birds and then plays mother, feeding them from his mouth.

4. One of the hardest things for any parent to deal with is illness, and the emotional stress can be just as great for a pet owner. If money spent is a sign of love, the city pet owner's commitment may be stronger. Most parents have insurance, but few pet owners do. Yet they gladly pay thousands to keep a pet alive. A cab driver told about his dog, which had hip problems and on which he spent over $5000. The owners of another dog that had kidney problems felt that the dog should die in the familiar setting of home and not in a hospital. A doctor had to visit twice a day for weeks to keep the dog from suffering until it died. And often when pets die, the owners don't forget. Every Saturday morning a young woman visits a New York pet cemetery to lay a red rose on the grave of her dog.

5. In specialty stores for pets, dogs are fitted for fur coats that cost as much as $800. For casual wear there are raincoats and hand-knitted wool sweaters. Another popular item is a carrying sack for dogs that costs almost $500. The sack in some stores is in such demand that customers may have to wait a year on a waiting list to get one. There are also strings of pearls and

14-karat gold identification tags. People used to be embarrassed about buying things for their dogs, but today it is just the opposite. Now people buy jewelry and clothing for their dogs that match their own. One can buy a variety of beauty aids for pets—makeup, special shampoos, breath fresheners, and perfumes. Some artists even specialize in painting portraits of people's pets.

6. The death of a pet can be a great tragedy for pet owners, particularly for people who have had a pet for a very long time and who feel it is part of the family. However, a way has been found to ease the pain of pet owners whose pets have recently passed away. A freeze-drying process has been developed which removes the moisture from the dead animal and leaves it stiff but clean-smelling. There is also no loss of hair. Eyes can be left open and the pets can be placed in any position. One man had his dog freeze-dried in a sitting position so that he could seat the dog next to his easy chair and pet him while he watched television, as he did when the pet was alive. Freeze-dried pets will last for years and years, like a statue with hair, so the family will be able to have its pet with it forever. Freeze-dried pets will last longer than their owners. Costs range from $400 for a small pet, such as a bird, to about $1800 for a large pet, such as a Doberman.

Discussion

After you have finished retelling the anecdotes to each other in small groups , discuss the following questions with the entire class.

1. What are your reactions to these anecdotes? Which did you find the most surprising, which the most understandable?

2. Can you imagine people in your culture doing any of this? If so, what? If not, why not?

Focus on Form: Negative Inversion

Most people outside of the United States, and many within, would find the situations given in the previous anecdotes to be strange. Imagine hearing about these situations and asking friends about their feelings:

Could you imagine yourself not going on a business trip because of a dog?

Possible answers would be:

No, I couldn't. *or* Never! *or* No way!

To strengthen the answer or to emphasize the negative aspect of it, you could repeat the whole sentence, with the negative word first, and say it with a strong emphasis on the first word or phrase:

In no way *could* I imagine myself not going on a business trip because of a dog.

Some possible reactions to the anecdotes are:

> Not until I came to the United States *did* I *realize* what a big business the pet industry was.

> Little *did* I *know* that people could be so crazy about animals.

Notice that:

- All of the answers begin with a negative or near-negative expression
- The word order changes to the word order of a question.

Grammar Practice

Rewrite the following sentences putting the negative expressions in parentheses at the beginning of the sentence. When you add the new negative, you will have to remove the original negative from the sentence..

1. I have not seen people treat pets as they do in New York. (nowhere)

2. I wouldn't spend thousands of dollars to keep a pet alive. (on no account)

3. People don't hire babysitters for their pets. (only in New York)

4. I couldn't let a dog keep me from moving or traveling. (by no means)

5. People should not spend so much money on their pets when others are starving. (under no circumstances)

6. New Yorkers talk to their pets. They also call them on the telephone. (not only . . . but also) (Inversion takes place only in the first clause.)

7. People aren't so crazy about pets in my country. (rarely)

8. I didn't realize that pets could be so important in people's lives. (not until I came to the United States)

9. I won't be surprised by what I hear about New Yorkers. (never again)

10. I had just arrived in the United States when I saw a dog wearing a raincoat, a hat, and boots. (no sooner . . . than)

Reading 2: "Freud Should Have Tried Barking"

Prereading Questions

1. What beneficial effects do you think pets can have on people in general?

2. What beneficial effects might pets have particularly on children or old people?

3. Can you think of any other specific group of people who might also benefit from having an animal to take care of?

4. What do you think the title of this article means?

Vocabulary Practice

Circle the correct synonym or definition for each of the italicized words in the sentences below. Use the context of the sentences to help you guess the meanings.

1. From the cat forgiven for depositing hair all over the house to the parrot indulged even though it cursed guests, pet lovers *put up with* it all in return for unconditional companionship.

    a. elevate
    b. tolerate
    c. complain about

2. If such a (A.) *bond* between people and animals could once be (B.) *ascribed* to secret (C.) *misanthropy,* the bond is now harder to dismiss. Pet lovers now have science on their side.

    (A.)   a.   connection
           b.   investment
           c.   hatred
    (B.)   b.   the cause of
           b.   a description of
           c.   considered the result of
    (C.)   a.   hatred of people
           b.   love of animals
           c.   craziness

3. A lot of the earlier work was done with the assumption that the relationship between people and animals was positive. But the new wave of studies is more *rigorous.*

    a. thorough; demanding
    b. negative
    c. recent

4. Having marital problems? Bring the dog into the counseling room: the dog's unthreatening presence may help resolve *conjugal* conflict.

    a. all kinds of
    b. relating to pets
    c. relating to marriage

5. The meeting was called "the most remarkable event on humans and animals since Noah's Ark." (A.) *Hyperbole* aside, the meeting was nothing if not (B.) *eclectic.*

    (A.)   a.   lies
           b.   exaggeration
           c.   being overactive

    (B.) a. shocking
          b. varied; diverse
          c. boring

6. Researchers believe that children with pets are less aggressive with their *peers* than children who don't have pets.

   a. animals
   b. older relations
   c. equals, of same age or rank

7. Pets may even *yank* the mentally disturbed back to reality.

   a. pull hard
   b. push away from
   c. eventually help

8. The owners of the nearly 100 million cats and dogs in the United States need no convincing that pets are beneficial for humans, but some scientists have been *skeptical* about the benefits of pets.

   a. worried
   b. convinced
   c. doubtful

9. Another study showed that children who had a close relationship with a pet showed greater (A.) *empathy* for others than petless kids did. Whatever it was that (B.) *fostered* this attitude is uncertain, however. Perhaps parents who buy pets have beliefs or personalities that (C.) *instill* it in their children.

   (A.) a. aggression
          b. understanding of another's feelings
          c. fear
   (B.) a. encourage to develop
          b. lessen
          c. destroy
   (C.) a. discourage
          b. teach a lesson in an obvious way
          c. introduce in the mind by slow efforts

10. Perhaps nurturing a pet reinforced the biological *propensity* for caring among humans.

    a. inclination, tendency
    b. fear
    c. inability; lack of

11. As researchers *grapple with* these questionable results, theorists are asking why man domesticated dogs and cats.

    a. believe
    b. understand
    c. struggle; fight

12. The Barasana Indians of Colombia chew food before feeding it to their animals. Even the Victorians, who gave legal rights to animals against beatings, might *blanch* at such devotion.

   a. accept as normal
   b. become white or pale (from shock)
   c. highly praise

Freud Should Have Tried Barking

By **SHARON BEGLEY** with **KAREN FITZGERALD**   (from *Newsweek* magazine)

Man's best friend can also be his best therapist

If there were ever any doubts about the place of dumb creatures in human affections, they were laid to rest in Victorian England, with legislation giving animals a legal right of protection against beating—years before children enjoyed such standing.[9] From the cat forgiven for depositing hair all over the house to the parrot indulged even though it cursed guests, pet lovers put up with it all in return for unconditional companionship. If such a bond could once be ascribed to secret misanthropy, it is now harder to dismiss: pet fanciers have recruited science to their side. Researchers have found that feathered or four-legged therapists can lower blood pressure. They may improve the survival odds of heart patients and may penetrate the isolation of autistic[10] children. They may even yank the mentally disturbed back to reality. Indeed, some say that healthy people, too, benefit from pets. "The importance of pets... has grown [as] an urbanized mankind has become alienated from nature," said Novelist Konrad Lorenz in a message to a meeting last week on pets and people. "Pets for most people are the most important—if not the only remaining—contact with living nature."

The conference, in Boston, was the largest-ever international meeting on the bond between humans and pets. Leo Bustad, president of the sponsoring Delta Society (which supports research on the topic), called it "the most remarkable event on humans and animals since Noah's ark."[11] Hyperbole aside, the meeting was nothing if not eclectic. More than 150 researchers reported on esoterica[12] like "The Influence of the Rural Exodus Phenomenon on the Human-Pet Relationship in Yugoslavia" and informed the 850 attendees of such minutiae as Sweden's prohibition on castrating dogs. They presented data on pets' ability to heal body and soul. Having marital[13] problems? Bring Spot[14] into the counseling room; his unthreatening presence may help resolve conjugal conflict. Does your heart race as you contemplate the return to school? Watch a bowl of swimming goldfish; they'll calm you. Is Dad shy

---

9. position   10. a form of childhood schizophrenia, usually causing withdrawal

11. a biblical boat on which the animals of the earth were saved from the flood which, according to the Bible, covered the earth   12. material of interest to, or understood by, a very small group of people   13. of a marriage   14. a common name for dogs

Just the presence of
an animal can be
therapeutic for elderly
or troubled people.

about **expressing his feelings?** Get him a pet; it draws out men's nurturing and emotional sides.

The owners of the nearly 100 million cats and dogs in the United States need no convincing on these points, but some scientists have been skeptical about the benefits of pets. "A lot of the early work was undertaken with the *assumption* that the [relationship between people and pets] was positive," says animal ecologist Alan Beck of the University of Pennsylvania. But the new wave of studies is more rigorous. Hubert Montagner of the Universite de Franche-Comte, for instance, used videotapes in a painstaking[15] comparison of children reared with[16] dogs. He observed that although two- to five-year-olds often hit, pulled, or otherwise bothered the dog, it usually responded by docilely[17] turning away. This reaction seems to teach children a lesson, Montagner believes they are less aggressive with their peers than are children who didn't have pets.

Does the beneficial effect of pet companionship last? When Michael Levine of Bloomsburg University in Pennsylvania compared college students raised with dogs with those raised without, he found that women who had owned dogs as children scored higher on tests of self-reliance, social skills, sociability and tolerance than did petless women. Men felt a greater sense of personal worth and of belonging and had better social skills if they'd had a dog. Another study showed that children who had a close relationship with a pet showed greater empathy for others than petless kids did. Whether it

15. very careful; taking great pains to be careful and thorough   16. raised with; grew up with

17. easily led or taught; quietly

was the pet that fostered empathy is uncertain, however; perhaps parents who buy pets have beliefs or personalities that instill empathy in their children.

Frisky spaniel: Some 1,100 programs in hospitals and other institutions use pets as therapists, but the effect of the animals is still being studied. As Beck notes, for many patients any kind of change—not specifically the arrival of a frisky[18] spaniel—is cheering. In an Australian nursing home, for instance, a new canine resident made the elderly patients much more sociable, but the effect disappeared after 22 weeks. Still, some experiments suggest that pets exert a real physiological effect. In 1980 researchers led by Erika Friedmann of Brooklyn College found that pet companionship increases the chances of survival for heart attack patients by some 3 percent. Last week she announced how pets exert this happy influence. When 193 college students read out loud—presumably heightening anxiety levels—the presence of a friendly dog decreased the heart rate of both those judged prone to[19] coronary[20] attacks (because they exhibited Type A behavior) and those considered to be less at risk.

As experimentalists grapple with the equivocal[21] results, theorists are asking why man domesticated dogs (about 12,000 years ago) and cats (about 5,000 years ago). According to one popular hypothesis, as humans evolved their offspring demanded an ever-longer period of care before they could survive on their own; perhaps nurturing a pet reinforced the biological propensity for caring among humans. That propensity can take an extreme turn, of course. The Barasana Indians of Colombia suckle[22] many of the baby tapirs, ocelots, peccaries, and dogs they adopt, hand-feed them at weaning and chew food before feeding it to the animals. Even the Victorians might blanch at such devotion.

---

18. playful and energetic

19. having a tendency to   20. of the heart
21. ambiguous; open to various interpretations
22. to nurse; give milk to a baby

Comprehension and Discussion

A. *Circle the correct answer. If the answer is false, tell why.*

1. In the past, the general feeling about people who loved animals was that they hated people.

    True   False

2. It has been proved that having a close relationship with pets will make children show greater empathy towards others.

    True   False

3. Studies have proved that pets have a definite beneficial effect on patients in hospitals.

    True   False

4. Although many of the new studies about pets and humans do not start with the assumption that pets are beneficial to humans, the results are still open to different interpretations.

True   False

B. *Answer the following questions as completely as possible.*

1. Throughout the article the writer lists many possible positive effects of pets on people. Some have been proved, and some have not. List the positive effects that pets *may* have on humans.

2. Of the effects that you gave above, which ones, in your opinion, are logical and probably true? Are there any that seem unbelievable to you? Explain your answers. Can you think of any other effects, positive or negative, that pets may have on a person or a family?

3. How does early research of the effects of animals on humans compare with later research?

6. Explain the relationship between having pets and showing or not showing aggression.

7. If you have a pet, or if you know someone who does, what positive or negative effects can you see that this pet has had on you or on the owner.

Vocabulary Practice

Match the words on the left with the synonyms and definitions on the right. Try to do this without looking back in the chapter.

Word List A

1. put up with   _____ marital (of a marriage)

2. ascribe   _____ exaggeration

3. misanthropy   _____ doubting; disbelieving

4. rigorous   _____ encourage to develop

5. conjugal   _____ severe; thorough; demanding

6. hyperbole   _____ attribute to a cause or origin

7. foster   _____ hatred of humankind

8. skeptical   _____ tolerate

Word List B

9. yank   _____ become white or pale (usually because of a shock or surprise)

10. peer   _____ struggle; fight

11. empathy   _____ pull hard (slang)

12.	eclectic	_____	connection; tie
13.	bond	_____	equal; same age or rank
14.	instill	_____	inclination; tendency
15.	grapple (with)	_____	varied; diverse
16.	blanch	_____	implant in the mind or introduce by slow, persistent efforts
17.	propensity	_____	understanding of another's feelings

Word Forms

Working with a partner, complete the following chart with the different forms of the words. Use your knowledge of other words and their different forms to help you. Do not be afraid to guess. A dash means there is no form.

Noun	Verb	Adjective	Adverb
empathy			—
hyperbole	—		—
	instill	—	—
misanthrope	—		
misanthropy	—	—	—
	—	rigorous	—
1. ...	—	skeptical	
2. ...	—	—	—

Vocabulary Practice

Complete the sentences below with the correct words from the following list. You may have to use different word forms and tenses. Do not use a word more than once.

Sentences 1 - 5	**Sentences 6 - 11**
put up with	yank
ascribe	peer
misanthropy	empathy
rigorous	eclectic
conjugal	bond
hyperbole	instill
foster	grapple (with)
skeptical	blanch

1. When one reads about the extremes that some pet owners go to, one cannot help thinking that they are not completely true, that there is an element of _____ in the articles written about them.

2. Psychologists have reported cases where (a.) _____ relationships have been ruined by pets. If a person marries someone who has a pet, it

may be difficult to (b.) _____ the attention and affection that the partner gives to the animal. However, some couples also (c.) _____ the success of their relationship to an animal.

3. Since some of the research done on the relationship between pets and humans started with positive assumptions, the results of this research has been greeted with _____ by some scientists.

4. A popular but unproven theory about people who are fanatical animal lovers is that they are _____.

5. Taking care of a pet, feeding, walking, cleaning, etc., may (a.) _____ a sense of responsibility in children. However, the (b.) _____ of good training of an animal may be beyond the capacity of a young child.

6. The human _____ to take care of the young may be reinforced by taking care of a pet.

7. One way to study the effects of animals on humans is to look at certain characteristics of people who have pets and compare them with their _____ who do not.

8. Pet owners cannot be stereotyped. They are an _____ group of people.

9. A friend of mine took his cat to a veterinarian. Although he loved the cat, he could not believe how much it would cost to treat the animal. He actually _____ when the doctor gave him the bill.

10. In large cities, people often hire dog walkers to take their dogs out for them. Some will walk as many as six to eight dogs at a time. At times one can see a dog walker (a.) _____ with all the different leashes and being (b.) _____ in different directions by all the dogs.

11. Most parents hope that the (a.) _____ that develops between pet and child will (b.) _____ strong feelings of self-reliance and personal worth in the children and that they will be more (c.) _____ towards other humans.

Vocabulary Building

Words which have the root -scribe (to write) in the verb form, such as ascribe *(to attribute), have a noun form ending in -scription and/or -script and also often have an adjective form ending in -scriptive. Look at the meanings of the prefixes of the following words, and try to guess the meanings of the words. Match the words with the definitions below. The different word forms are given. Forms that are rarely used have not been included.*

Verb	Noun	Adjective
1. ascribe (*a* = in addition)	ascription	
2. circumscribe (*circum* = around)	circumscription	
3. conscript (British) (*con* = with) (no verb form *-scribe*)	conscription conscript	
4. describe (*de* = down)	description	descriptive
5. inscribe (*in* = in or on)	inscription	
6. prescribe (*pre* = before)	prescription	prescriptive
7. proscribe (*pro* = in front)	proscription	proscriptive
8. subscribe (*sub* = under)	subscription	
9. transcribe (*trans* = across)	transcription transcript	

_____ to give as a rule or a guide; to suggest or order as a medicine

_____ to tell about in detail

_____ to contain or limit; restrict; draw a line around

_____ to attribute; to give something as a cause of

_____ to contract to receive and pay for a certain number of issues of a newspaper or periodical; to contribute money; to express approval

_____ the act of forcing into military service; to draft (Am. E.); person who is drafted

_____ to prohibit

_____ to copy; transfer information from one system to another; record of one's grades

_____ to engrave, to write or print on wood, stone or paper; to sign (formal)

Vocabulary Practice

Complete the sentences with the correct forms of the words from the list above. Some words (in different forms and with different meanings) will be used more than once.

1. A debate among linguists is whether grammar should be _____, that is, telling how it should be used, or _____, just showing how it is used by the people who speak a language.

2. There is a theory that some of the works which are _____ to Shakespeare were really written by someone else.

3. The _____ on the tombstone of the pet was so touching that it could have been about a child.

4. When applying to an American university, you need to send a _____ of your grades from all previous schools.

5. I do not _____ to the theory that people who love animals hate people.

6. During wars there is often a _____ against writing about the number of soldiers dead or wounded.

7. There is no longer _____ in the United States. Military service is voluntary.

8. My brother has had a _____ to that pet magazine for years.

9. The medicine that the veterinarian _____ for my cat was more expensive than the medicine I got from my doctor for myself.

10. Whether we are aware of it or not, our culture influences and limits us a great deal. It _____ how we see the world.

11. Every word that is said during a court trial in the United States is _____ so that the exact testimony can be read at a later date if necessary.

Focus on Form: Negative Inversion

Clauses or sentences that begin with negative (or near negative) forms:

- use the question-form word order even though the sentence is not a question.
- emphasize what we say or write.
- are used in both speaking and in writing, but are more common in writing.
- are used very often to exaggerate.

Example: People would have play groups for their dogs *only in Manhattan*.
Only in Manhattan would people *have* play groups for their dogs.

Some of the most common negative introductions are:

Not only...but also	Not only do some people spend a lot of money on food for their dogs, but some also cook for them.
Not until + clause	Not until I read the article did I realize what some people do for their dogs.
Nowhere	Nowhere have I seen people treat dogs the way they do here.
In no way **Under no circumstances** **On no account** **By no means**	} . . . would I treat a dog badly.
No longer	No longer will I think I know everything about New Yorkers.
In no other (place)	In no other country do people act this way.
At no other (time)	At no other time have I been so surprised.
Never (before/again)	{ Never before have I seen people act this way. Never again will I look at a dog in the same way.

Neither	Neither will I.
Nor	I don't have a pet. Nor do I want one.
In none of	In none of the stories I had heard before coming here did I ever hear about pet cemeteries.
In few cases	In few cases have people who own dogs been bitten by them.
(Only) Rarely	Rarely have I seen so many dogs as in New York.
Seldom	Seldom does one see such pampered animals.
Little	Little did I know that pets were so respected.
Hardly ever	Hardly ever have I seen a snake as a pet.
No sooner . . . than	No sooner had I fallen asleep than the barking of the dog woke me up.
Not once	Not once did he tell me he liked my cat.
Only	Only in New York can one see such things.

Grammar Practice

Complete the sentences with the correct verb forms. Use the subject given in parentheses. Think carefully about which tense you should use. In some cases more than one is possible.

1. I like animals a lot, but in no way (I, feel) _____ that they should run my life.

2. Hardly ever (people, let) _____ animals live in the house with them in my country.

3. My brother is allergic to cats, so you can usually be sure that if there are ten people in a room and one cat, the cat will go to him. This happened the other day. He went to a party at a friend's house, and no sooner (he, sit) _____ down than the cat started rubbing up against him.

4. Dick: "I love my dogs, but I would never spend a lot of money on coats or jewelry for them."
   Teresa: "Neither (I) _____."

5. Jason is quite sure that he will be transferred to the overseas office next year. He doesn't mind moving, but he won't leave without his pet bird. In no way (he, leave) _____ that bird behind, job or no job.

6. I always thought that I was a very unsentimental person. Not until my family's cat died (I, realize) _____ how attached I had become to her.

Reading 3: "High-Tech Medicine at High-Rise Costs Is Keeping Pets Fit"

Prereading Questions

1. If animals are kept as pets in your country, do people take them to a veterinarian, an animal doctor, when the animal gets sick?

2. Are veterinarians common in your country? If so, what types of animals are taken to them? If not, why not?

3. How would you feel about spending large sums of money on an animal you loved if it became sick?

Vocabulary Practice

Match the italicized words in the sentences with the synonyms or definitions in the list below. Use the context of the sentence to help you guess the meaning.

_____ spending
_____ sudden, fanciful idea
_____ mercy killing
_____ dilemma; state of uncertainty
_____ strange people
_____ medical opinion or prediction about the outcome or course of an illness
_____ medical opinion about the nature of an illness; telling what is wrong

_____ kill an animal out of mercy
_____ system of therapy
_____ animals on a farm
_____ complain

1. Ahead lay a seven-week *regimen* of chemotherapy and cobalt radiation.

2. Although prize (a.) *livestock* and race horses have always received high-level care because of their value as property, in the last decade, household pets, mostly dogs and cats, have become beneficiaries of medical and technologically advanced (b.) *diagnostic* treatments perfected on humans.

3. Not long ago, $250 was considered a high price for medical services for an animal because advanced treatment was limited and *euthanasia* was relatively common and accepted.

4. From an ethical point of view, aiding an animal may be a more noble *expenditure* than jewelry.

5. Rising costs do pose a *quandary* for animal doctors.

6. Dogs can be put to death on a *whim* or on grounds of economic necessity.

7. Doctors were beginning to (a.) *balk at* an owner's demand that an animal in good health be (b.) *put to sleep*.

8. Despite a poor *prognosis*, many people pursue all sorts of extreme medical treatment for their pets.

9. You only have to be in this business a short time to learn there are a lot of *oddballs* out there.

High-Tech Medicine At High-Rise Costs Is Keeping Pets Fit

By JON NORDHEIMER   (from the *New York Times*)

Should pets receive medical care that is denied to some humans?

For 30 minutes, as much time as it takes to place a patient inside the metal doughnut of a CAT scanner[23] and make a cross-sectioned[24] study of his cancerous throat, the fate of Buster hung in the balance.

Luck was on the side of the 7-year-old West Highland terrier. Pictures from the computer-controlled imaging device showed that the cancer was not widespread. Ahead lay a seven-week regimen of chemotherapy and cobalt radiation[25] and a $4,000 medical bill for Buster's owner. The guarded[26] prognosis: Buster could have good "quality of life" for another year or two. Without treatment, he would die by Christmas.

Although prize livestock and racehorses have always received high-level care because of their value as property, in the last decade household pets, mostly dogs and cats, have become beneficiaries of medical and technologically advanced diagnostic treatments perfected on humans.

The most advanced procedures, like brain and heart surgery, bone transplants and nuclear medicine, are available at regional training hospitals. Advanced skills and treatments less dependent on special training or equipment are making their way into neighborhood clinics.

As the reach of medicine helps more animals at an ever-higher cost, a debate is gaining momentum on veterinary school campuses and in professional journals that veterinary ethics are not keeping pace, especially with changes in social attitudes toward pets.

"What's different is the unbelievable elevation of the importance of the human-animal bond and evidence that humans have benefited emotionally from the presence of pets," said Dr. James Wilson 3d, a bioethicist at the University of Pennsylvania School of Veterinary Medicine. "More than two out of three Americans think of their pets as family members; some 20 percent in surveys say they are as important as a child."

Americans spent nearly $6 billion on veterinary services in 1987, up 20 percent from the previous survey in 1985, said J. Carl Wilse, an economist for the American Veterinary Medical Association, the profession's governing body, which has 49,875 licensed members.

$4,000 Operation on Pet

Not long ago, $250 was considered a high price for veterinary services for an injured or dying pet, because advanced treatment was limited and euthanasia was relatively common and accepted.

Today nearly that much can be spent at a local animal hospital for a single ultrasound examination. Major orthopedic[27] and heart surgery can cost $1,500 to $4,000. Most such services are not covered by insurance.

There are many people, including pet owners, who consider it unseemly,[28] even shocking, to spend thousands of dollars on

---

23. X-ray device to detect cancer or tumors
24. a drawing of a side, inside view, made by cutting through an object   25. treatments for cancer   26. cautious; restrained

27. medicine dealing with the bones   28. not in good taste; something that should not be done

advanced pet care in a society where humans often have little or no access to such help.

But Bruce Jennings, an associate for policy studies at the Hastings Center, a medical ethics research institute in Briarcliff Manor, N.Y., said that kind of reaction was misplaced.

"As long as the money comes out of an individual's pocket and not public resources, it makes no particular sense to single it out from other economic purchases such as jewelry or a fancy car. From an ethical point of view, aiding an animal may be a more noble expenditure than jewelry."

Rising costs do pose a quandary for veterinarians, though. Even as they profit from medical advances, they are coming under pressure to provide for animals from low-income households.

"Many people can't afford anything but euthanasia," said Dr. Michael W. Fox, vice president of the Humane Society of the United States. "The big question for animal doctors is what to do for a loving elderly person with limited resources whose pet needs a $6,000 operation. It suggests the need for community support for a network of full-service animal charity hospitals like the ones provided in England."

Jerrold Tannenbaum, a lawyer who teaches a required ethics course at Tufts University's veterinary school, said rising costs of the new services pose the question of whether veterinarians—who on average earn $51,000 a year, just 40 percent of what physicians make—should offer more low-cost or free care.

Another question for some veterinarians is the kind of moral claim animals—at least a select number of companion animals—have on humans. They say choices about treatment are being made within a social and legal tradition that animals are chattel[29] and can be put to death on a whim or on grounds of economic utility.

About 7.5 million dogs and cats—healthy of disabled, old and young—are killed each year in this country, according to the Humane Society of the United States. Dr. Wilson, the bioethicist, said veterinarians were beginning to balk at an owner's demand that an animal in basic good health be destroyed.

Animal Rights Issues

"They are saying that the pet may be the owner's property, but they won't push the plunger,"[30] Dr. Wilson said. "This is especially true of the younger graduates influenced by the animal rights movement."

He described the situation of a young veterinarian whose identity he would not disclose. "An elderly widow with a terminal disease wanted her pregnant 3-year-old dog put to sleep because she couldn't afford the cost of a Caesarean procedure and she was afraid, in any case, no one would care for her dog after she herself was gone," he said.

The veterinarian offered to drastically cut his fee, but was unable to change her mind. Although he agreed to destroy the animal, he could not bring himself to do so and delivered the litter at his own expense and found homes for the mother and pups. When the dog owner learned what he had done, she was outraged. She sued him and complained to the state licensing board.

"He did the right moral and ethical thing and faces having his license lifted," Dr. Wilson said.

For Dr. Mike Shires, acting dean of the veterinary school at the University of Tennessee in Knoxville, there is another spin in the ethics debate.

"Despite a poor prognosis, many people pursue all sorts of extreme medical treatments for their pets that weren't available a few years ago," he said. "In cases where continued treatment is cruel, we still have the option denied in human medicine and we recommend euthanasia. If they still in-

---

29. personal material property, slave

30. perform the final act of execution

sist, and you only have to be in this business a short time to learn there are a lot of oddballs out there, we tell them to take their pet somewhere else."

Supply of Advanced Equipment

The demand for the best in pet care has created a secondary market for medial technology. CAT scans and ultrasound diagnostic equipment used on humans are sold to animal hospitals at cut-rate prices when hospitals replace them with state-of-the-art equipment. Similarly, $5,000 pacemakers that go unused beyond recommended shelf life[31] are sold for about $100 and implanted into dogs for about $700, compared with $12,000 for the same procedure on a human.

"If expense is not a consideration, veterinary medicine can do anything on dogs and cats that we can do on human patients," said Dr. Michael Garvey, medical chairman of the Animal Medical Center in New York, where Buster was treated. It is one of a score[32] of teaching hospitals around the nation where the latest treatment is available for pets. "I like to say we work out the bugs[33] on humans and when it's safe enough, we adapt the procedures for animals."

The center handles 70,000 pet visits a year. Its surgeons repair defective heart valves, do double hip replacements and use dialysis to get cats through a dangerous kidney infection.

At the University of California at Davis, veterinary students volunteer their time to a telephone counseling line. "Pet owners can't express their grief in the usual ways because some people might think it's silly," said a fourth-year student, Jennifer Martin, 24 years old. "But consciousness is being raised as more and more clients are demanding it from the profession."

Element of Human Nature

"I don't push the advances on owners with geriatric pets or ones without good quality-of-life prospects," said Dr. Jane Mason, of Chantilly, Va., who graduated from Auburn University in 1986. "It's funny how human nature is, but people with lots of money sometimes won't do anything to save a pet and those who have to scrape every dollar together want to go on with the CAT scans and try chemo."

For those who can pay, the price seems worth it.

"Hey, you don't put a price tag on the life of someone in your own family," said Buster's owner, Noel Cooper, of Rego Park, Queens, who owns several laundromats. "He's like our child. How could I do anything less for someone that gives me so much pleasure?"

---

31. length of time a product can be sold before going bad or losing maximum efficiency   32. twenty (one of a score = one out of twenty)   33. problems or defects (work out the bugs = eliminate the problem)

Comprehension and Discussion

Answer the following questions as completely as possible.

1. How have attitudes towards health care for animals changed in recent years? Give at least two changes.

2. Why have these changes come about?

3. Agree or disagree: "As long as the money comes out of an individual's pocket and not public resources, it makes no particular sense to single it out from other economic purchases such as jewelry or a fancy car." Explain your answer.

4. Explain the ethical problems that some veterinarians are facing now. Give at least two.

5. If pet owners want to have their pets put to death, do you think a veterinarian has an obligation to follow their wishes?

6. What is your opinion of the situation in the article in which the veterinarian did not destroy the animal as the owner wanted but found homes for the dog and her puppies? Did he do "the right and ethical thing?"

7. What is the "secondary market" for medical technology?

8. From a moral or ethical point of view, what is your opinion about spending large sums of money for household pets? Explain your feelings and support your statements.

Vocabulary Practice

Complete the sentences below with the correct words from the following list. You may have to use different word forms or verb tenses. Do not use a word more than once.

quandary	regimen
balk (at)	euthanasia
livestock	expenditure
diagnostic (diagnose, diagnosis)	prognosis
put to sleep	whim
oddballs	

In the past, a great deal of money was spent for the health of (farm animals) (1.) _____ but not for pets. Large (spending) (2.) _____ on a pet's health was considered to be a (fanciful idea) (3.) _____ of (strange people) (4.) _____, not something that normal people did. When the (opinion about the outcome) (5.) _____ of the disease of a pet was very bad, the veterinarian simply performed (mercy killing) (6.) _____ on the animal. However, today, pet owners do not (complain) (7.) _____ the high price of health care for their pets. People are spending more just for a doctor to (give an opinion about the nature) (8.) _____ the illness of their pets than they did before for the treatment. More pet owners are willing to put their animals on strict (systems of therapy) (9.) _____, which can be costly and time-consuming, to give them another year or two of life. However, this poses a (dilemma) (10.) _____ for veterinarians. If a pet owner wants to have the pet (killed) (11.) _____ instead of paying for medical care, can the vet refuse? Or if the owner wants the medical help but cannot afford it, should the vet offer cheaper or free care?

Discussion

Answer the following questions about yourself or the people in your country. Explain each one in as much detail as possible. When possible, begin a sentence with a negative phrase or word and use negative inversion.

1. Do the people in your country buy gifts or clothes for their pets or even bring them into the home? (Give the name of your country in the answer.)

2. Is the death of a pet considered a very sad event? If so, would people have a pet buried in a cemetery?

3. Do people take pets to veterinarians (animal doctors) or do they only use these doctors for farm animals?

4. Can people take pets, such as dogs, into restaurants with them? If they did, how would other people react?

5. Have you ever had a pet? If so, how did you act towards it? If not, would you like to have one?

6. Does one see a great deal of advertising for pet products in your country?

7. Is high-tech medicine available for pets?

8. Would people make or buy special food for their pets? Can you imagine special low-fat foods for fat pets or high-protein foods for pregnant ones?

Grammar Practice

How different is life in the United States from life in your country? What were some of the most surprising differences that you noticed when you first came to this country? Tell about your impressions and feelings when you first came here or about how life is different in your country. Use the words given below. Do not forget to do the inversion and to stress the negative expression when you tell the class about your feelings or experiences. Your sentences may be exaggerations.

1. Never before . . .

2. Only in . . .

3. Not until . . .

4. Rarely . . .

5.   No sooner . . . than . . .

6.   By no means . . .

7.   In no other place . . .

8.   Hardly ever . . .

9.   No longer . . .

10.   . . .

Focus on Form: Showing Agreement with Inversion

She's allergic to cats, and *so am* I. (... and I am too.) = ...and I am allergic to cats too.

I don't have a pet, and *neither does* my brother. (...and my brother doesn't either.)

A: I had pet turtles when I was a child.

B: *So did* my brother. (My brother did too.) = My brother also had pet turtles...

A: His father wouldn't let him keep a dog.

B: *Neither would* mine. (Mine wouldn't either.) = My father wouldn't let me keep..

When all of the information in a clause or sentence, except the subject, is in agreement with the information in the previous clause or sentence, this agreement can be expressed in a shortened form with the conjunctions *so* or *too* (for positive verbs) or with *neither* or *either* (for negative verbs).

Agreement with So or Neither

When a sentence or clause begins with *so* or *neither*:

- the subject and verb are inverted. (Question word order is used.)
- the sentence or clause of agreement has the same verb tense or modal as the first verb.
- the following verb substitutions are made:

    — *am, is, are, was, were* if the first verb is some form of *to be* (including the continuous tenses but not the perfect tenses).

    — *do* or *does* (for all other verbs) if the first verb is in the simple present tense.

    — *did* if the first verb is in the simple past tense.

— *have* or *has* if the first verb is in the present perfect tense (active or passive).

— *had* if the first verb is in the past perfect tense (active or passive).

— the same modal form is used.

Grammar Practice

Complete the following sentences using so *or* neither *and a verb form or modal.*

1. My father never liked the idea of keeping pets in the house, and _____ my mother.

2. She has always had a pet, and _____ her husband.

3. They haven't been here long enough to know about the culture, and _____ we.

4. Don't worry. He'll be good to animals, and _____ I.

5. They can help take care of your cats while you're gone, and _____ I.

6. I'd like to see it, and _____ they.

7. The cat wasn't hurt in the accident, and _____ the dog.

8. She couldn't believe what some people will do for their pets, and _____ he.

9. I don't find any of this surprising, and _____ he.

10. She had heard about it before, and _____ he.

Grammar Practice

Pair Work: Showing Agreement with Negative Inversion

Below are two sets of statements. Student A will make the statement in the Student A List. Student B will agree using either so *or* neither *and the pronoun given in the Student B list. Student A corrects Student B after each statement. Next reverse roles, with Student B making the first statement, Student A answering, and Student B correcting. Listen carefully to the verb or modal used and to the tense. Do them as quickly as possible.*

Student A Statements	**Student A Answers**
1. I can't wake up without coffee. (*Neither can* I.)	1. _____ we.
2. I prefer tea. (*So do* I.)	2. _____ I.
3. He's been studying here for a year. (*So has* she.)	3. _____ he.
4. I'd rather leave tomorrow. (*So would* I.)	4. _____ I.
5. He'll help us if we need him. (*So will* she.)	5. _____ we.

6. I'm starved. *(So am I.)*

7. I had never heard about it until she mentioned it. *(Neither had I.)*

8. We're leaving very soon. *(So are we.)*

9. I don't like that restaurant. *(Neither do I.)*

10. We didn't have any pets when we were children. *(Neither did we.)*

11. We were very tired after the trip. *(So were they.)*

12. I haven't been here very long. *(Neither have I.)*

13. He was sick all night. *(So was I.)*

14. She's a good student. *(So is he.)*

15. She doesn't live near school. *(Neither does he.)*

6. _____ I.

7. _____ she.

8. _____ I.

9. _____ I.

10. _____ she.

11. _____ she.

12. _____ I.

13. _____ we.

14. _____ they.

15. _____ I.

Student B Answers

1. _____ I.

2. _____ I.

3. _____ she.

4. _____ I.

5. _____ she.

6. _____ I.

7. _____ I.

8. _____ we.

9. _____ I.

10. _____ we.

11. _____ they.

12. _____ I.

13. _____ I.

Student B Statements

1. We've never eaten there. *(Neither have we.)*

2. I'd really like to go home for vacation. *(So would I.)*

3. She's from California. *(So is he.)*

4. He needs it now. *(So do I.)*

5. We saw him just last week. *(So did we.)*

6. I'll never eat there again. *(Neither will I.)*

7. He can speak English almost perfectly. *(So can she.)*

8. I don't have enough money to go. *(Neither do I.)*

9. I'm not very tired. *(Neither am I.)*

10. He didn't mind the boat trip at all. *(Neither did she.)*

11. He has a very bad cold. *(So does she.)*

12. I could fall asleep right here. *(So could I.)*

13. We had never met him before today. *(Neither had we.)*

14. _____ he.

14. We were here at 10:00. (*So were they.*)

15. _____ he.

15. We were ready to leave an hour ago. (*So was I.*)

Class Project

Work on one or more of these projects individually or in groups of two to three. Then present your findings to the class.

1. Think of a new product for pets. It could be food, a beauty or health product, clothing, whatever you want. How would you market this product? Think of advertising, packaging, a catchy name, your market, etc. With other students, develop a television commercial to sell your product. Give your group presentation to the class. The class will vote on the most successful entrepreneurs.

2. Visit a pet shop or supermarket (pet section) and report to the class on what you learned about the types of products and services available, etc. Compare the pet food section to the baby food section.

Discussion and Writing

Discuss the following topics, first in pairs or small groups and then with the teacher and the entire class. After your discussion, pick one (or more) of the topics and write an essay about it.

1. Why do you think pets are such an important part of American culture? Does the fact that some people spend a great deal of money on their pets and treat them almost as if they were humans say anything about the society or the culture? If so, what?

2. Describe a strong, positive feeling you had (or still have) toward an animal. What does this animal mean to you? Why was (or is) it so important in your life? What beneficial effects did (does) it have on your life?

3. Compare how animals are treated here with how they are treated in your country. What are the major similarities and/or differences? What do you think is the reason for these similarities or differences?

4. Tell about the strangest pet you have ever seen. What was it? Who had it? How did you feel about it and the owner?

5. Pick one of the discussion questions after any of the readings in this chapter and write an essay about it.

Word List

Below is a list of the new words, and their different forms, presented in this chapter.

Noun	Verb	Adjective	Adverb
	ascribe		
	balk		
		bespectacled	
	blanch		
bond	bond		
bully	bully		
charge			
circumscription	circumscribe		
		conjugal	
conscription	conscript		
conscript			
description	describe	descriptive	descriptively
diagnosis	diagnose	diagnostic	
	dote (on)	doting	
eclecticism		eclectic	eclectically
empathy	empathize	empathic	
euthanasia			
expenditure	expend	expendable	
	foster		
	grapple		
		hyper	
hyperbole		hyperbolic	
inscription	inscribe		
instillment	instill		
livestock			
misanthrope		misanthropic	misanthropically
misanthropy			
oddball			
		one-on-one	
practice	practice		
prescription	prescribe	prescriptive	prescriptively
prognosis			
propensity			
proscription	proscribe	proscriptive	
	put to sleep		
	put up with		
quandary			
regimen			
rigor		rigorous	rigorously
skeptic		skeptical	skeptically
skepticism			
spoilsport			
subscription	subscribe		

Noun	Verb	Adjective	Adverb
	sulk	sulky	
transcription	transcribe		
transcript			
whim		whimsical	whimsically
yank	yank		

CHAPTER 9

The Changing Family, the Changing Woman

Reading 1: "Shifting Suburbs"

Prereading Questions

1. What do you imagine is the traditional American family that was idealized in television programs and films? Describe this in as much detail as possible—where they would live, what kind of car they would drive, if they would have any pets, etc.

2. Is there an idealized picture of the traditional family in your country? What is it? Describe it completely.

3. Has this vision of the ideal family been changing in your country? If so, how and why? What effects have these changes had on the society?

4. What is the divorce rate in your country? How do you think it compares to that of the United States? What do you think are the reasons for rising divorce rates in any country? What are the effects?

Vocabulary Practice

Circle the correct synonym or definition for each of the italicized words in the sentences below. Use the context of the sentences to help you guess the meaning.

1. The disintegration of the traditional family has left behind many broken homes and social and psychological *traumas*.

   a. experiences
   b. deep shocks
   c. benefits

2. Experts say that by the close of this decade, fewer than three out of every ten adolescents will have lived in a continuously *intact* family until the age of 18.

   a. unhealthy
   b. working
   c. whole

3. A year later her family got smaller. Her husband *walked out*.

   a. went for a walk
   b. died
   c. left, abandoned (her)

4. In a community where everyone seemed to be married, she was a *pariah*.

   a. socially unacceptable; an outcast
   b. just like everyone else; a conformist
   c. all alone; a hermit

5. She had no job, no income and—she soon discovered—few real friends. "I was *ostracized*," she recalls.

   a. forced to resign
   b. excluded, shunned
   c. independent

6. From the time her eldest was 10, her children had to *fend for* themselves.

   a. have high regard
   b. defend
   c. take care of

7. Where once the single-family house with a lawn was *ubiquitous*, attached housing is suddenly appearing to shelter older folks, childless couples, and an exploding population of singles.

   a. unheard of
   b. seen everywhere
   c. too expensive

8. The school is well-equipped and has sound programs, as *befits* a town where the median income is over $45,000 a year.

   a. is appropriate for
   b. is unexpected for
   c. is fortunate for

9. A caring man who seems to function as a substitute father to many of his students, he is *alarmed* by what is happening to them.

   a. happy
   b. frightened
   c. being warned

10. It's no wonder that such households, with children from different marriages, new houses, new locations, and sometimes new jobs, are *dysfunctional*.

    a. not working
    b. happy
    c. not common

11. She has devoted her life to Jorie, now a *precocious* ten-year-old who is in the gifted students' program at the school.

    a. average
    b. young for her age; immature
    c. highly developed for her age, especially mentally

12. Now that Jorie is a little older, Shelly Grant thinks about dating again, but she still has *reservations*.

    a. high expectations
    b. doubts
    c. interest

13. Mrs. Leonardo has *ambivalent* feelings about her job. She knows she is providing a necessary service, but she worries about the family life and future of her charges.

    a. negative
    b. positive
    c. mixed

Shifting Suburbs

By ANDREW PATNER　(from *The Wall Street Journal*)

The disintegration of the traditional family has left a trail of broken homes and social and psychological traumas

Buffalo Grove, IL—Walking the streets of this exurb[1] 30 miles from downtown Chicago, a patchwork[2] of subdivisions stitched[3] together into a town, you could forget that this is 1990. Even the newest housing developments look as if the Cleavers[4] could live in them—Dad who coaches Little League,[5] the full-time Mom nurturing 2.2 statistical children, the frisky collie,[6] the station wagon[7] in the driveway. The so-called nuclear family, that American totem.[8]

The demographers[9] and social scientists say that it is disintegrating. The demographers say that by the close of this decade, fewer than three of every 10 adolescents will have lived in a continuously intact family until the age of 18. The social scientists speak of the social and psychological traumas that broken families trail in their wake.[10]

It's a vision, however, that many suburbanites prefer to ignore. Sure, there are a lot more divorces where they live, family life is a little tougher. But the consequences can't be that grave.

Or can they?

A Quiet Street

Phyllis Rose moved here, into the American Dream, in 1968. She had a husband, three small children and, suddenly, a $38,000 home on a quiet street lined with other "expanding families." A year later hers contracted. Her husband walked out.

In a community where a wife's first morning duty was to drive her husband to the commuter rail station, where everyone seemed to be married (in 1970, only 69 residents, male and female, had ever been divorced), she found herself a pariah. She had no job, no income and—she soon discovered—few real friends. "I was ostracized," she recalls.

She moved to the next town out, Long Grove. It was the same. She remembers a moment of kindness when a male neighbor tried to help her shovel out her snowed-in car—only to have his wife appear and pull him away from "the divorcee." She found work and moved back into Buffalo Grove. From the time her eldest was 10, her children had to fend for themselves. "It wasn't what I wanted," she says, "but they learned responsibility."

Today Phyllis Rose is the owner of a large real estate business in a town of nearly 35,000, more than triple the population it had when she first came here. It is a town—moderately upscale,[11] predominantly white—where divorce is shrugged at,[12] where increasing numbers of people have never been married, and where many, many children fend for themselves.

---

1. a residential area beyond the suburbs of a city, often semi-rural　2. made up of various pieces or patches, as in a quilt or bed covering　3. to sew (noun = each movement in sewing)　4. a television family of the 50s, the idealized, traditional middle-class American family　5. association of baseball teams for children　6. a breed of dog　7. a type of car with an extended back area for a third seat or for a larger carrying area. It is considered a typical suburban car.　8. a highly respected symbol　9. a person who studies the characteristics of human populations　10. leave behind them

---

11. high socio-economic status　12. paid little attention to or interest in

Her prospective buyers at Re/Max Experts want to know where the grocery stores and the expressways are, but they are equally interested in the day-care centers. Amid ads in the local paper for furniture and window-blind installation, an attorney offers assistance in divorce and child support and custody proceedings.

The traditional nuclear family has by no means disappeared from Buffalo Grove—but its grip[13] on the town's values clearly is weakening, and it is growing increasingly isolated. Where once the single-family home with a patch of lawn was ubiquitous, attached housing[14] now springs up to shelter older folks, childless couples and an exploding population of singles. Another sign of the times: Of the family households in town, about one in eight now is headed by a woman.

There are lots of other numbers. But what do the numbers say about the quality of family life in Buffalo Grove?

* * *

Buffalo Grove High School is well-equipped and has sound programs, as befits a town where the median income is over $45,000 a year. School spirit is high; the Chargers[15] have brought home both football and soccer championships within the past three years. It is impossible to tell that, as one administrator estimates, half of the 1,600 students are children of divorce.

A score of them usually show up every Wednesday at a school sponsored "divorce group," where they share the pain and problems that their parents' split-ups have brought them. "It gives you someone to talk to," says Tina Hirsch, a junior. "I didn't have that when my parents were first divorced."

Tina, who now divides her time between two sets of parents (her mother and father both remarried), comes home to an empty house, whichever house she goes to. So do many others. In a town where Mom once was always home, she is now gone. And Dad is still rarely home.

"This is a two-car, two-career community," says Cathy Schwartz, administrative assistant at the Northwest Suburban Jewish Community Center. "My own children are latchkeys[16]—well, not latchkeys. Electronic codes."[17]

When they are not working, those mothers who have split from their husbands may be out trying to build a new life. "My mom just got divorced, and now she's always at dance class or on a ski trip," says sophomore David Kamilow, who is often left to prepare dinner for himself and his brother.

Some children just drift like shadows, staying at one parent's house sometimes, staying at friend's homes other times. "I have this one friend, I never know where to call him," says Jennifer Peron, 15. "I have another friend who basically lives in her car."

Richard Schnell, associate principal of Buffalo Grove High, has heard so many of these stories. A caring man who seems to function as a substitute father to many of his students, he is alarmed by what is happening to them. He sees a growing detachment, a gulf, opening between them and parents who have grown too involved in their own increasingly complex lives to be a central part of their children's.

Education? The PTA[18] looks good on paper, he says, but actual parent involvement has tapered off.[19] "These kids have to manage their own lives," says Mr. Schnell. "Education is *their* problem to handle." He sees more of the same in the future, adding, "Our challenge in the 90s is going to be how to cultivate and reinforce a sense of worth in these children without relying on the folks at home."

---

13. strong hold, control   14. two (or more) houses built together, with a common wall between them   15. name of the school's teams

16. children who have their own key to the house (often worn around the neck) to let themselves in after school because the parents are working   17. a reference to a type of lock that is opened not by a key but by a code number   18. Parent-Teachers Association 19. lessen, become smaller or narrower

In such a climate, teenagers are even more reliant on their peers than they might otherwise be, and in Buffalo Grove it would be hard to overestimate the importance of the peer group. Many of these children are family to each other, sometimes because there is no one else.

One sophomore girl whose parents divorced not long ago lived with her father while her mother moved back into the city. But when he remarried, his new wife rejected the girl and, she says, her father literally threw her out. Because there are no established social-service agencies nearby, the girl had nowhere to go and stayed with various friends while her grandmother looked for an apartment in Buffalo Grove. "I couldn't have made it without my friends," she says, some of whose parents thought that she was just spending the night.

Teens here complain that the town provides almost nothing in the way of organized youth programs for them. So they party at each other's houses—often empty houses—or, in the spring and summer months, congregate at night in open fields to hang out[20] and drink. Frequently they drink too much. Mr. Schnell, the associate principal, says that, "100 kids a year in alcohol-rehab[21] programs wouldn't be a bad guess" for the high-school population.

J. Harry Wells doesn't have to guess about his end of it. As executive director of Omni Youth Services, Inc., a local juvenile and family-counseling center, his client logs[22] tell him that exactly 563 Buffalo Grove youngsters and their parents sought help at the center last year. No one can know, of course, how many needed to come but didn't.

Quite a few of his clients are from "blended" families—divorced and remarried people who now gather their respective offspring,[23] essentially strangers to each other, under the same roof. Given the strains on everyone involved—a new job and a new location for one spouse at least, tensions among the children—it's no wonder, he says, that such households are so often dysfunctional. "It's not like 'The Brady Bunch'[24] on TV," he says.

* * *

Back at Buffalo Grove High, a visitor asks a group of four students this question: What is the most important wish you have for the future?

All of them speak immediately, in unison. "That there wouldn't be so many divorces," they say.

* * *

Shelly Grant, a lifelong Chicago-area suburbanite, lives with her daughter, Jordana— she goes by Jorie—in a row house[25] in Oak Leaf Village, a development that is in itself a testament to[26] the changing demography of Buffalo Grove. Of the seven other houses in her row, only two are occupied by families. The others are inhabited by an elderly couple, a young childless couple, two single women, and a middle-aged widow.

Ms. Grant's husband left her when Jorie was only a year old, and the girl entered day care at 20 months. "She grew up there," says her mother. But Shelly Grant was determined to make a close and caring home for her daughter despite every obstacle in the way. And she has, paying a price others are unwilling to pay.

She has devoted her life to Jorie, now a precocious 10-year-old who is in the gifted students' program at school. Ms. Grant, a bookkeeper, has never dated. She has spent every hour she possibly could with her daughter, discussing homework, books, their dreams for the future. "I haven't had the

---

20. spend time doing nothing   21. rehabilitation   22. records of the clients, i.e., names, dates, etc.   23. children

---

24. a TV family in which the children of a man and a woman from previous marriages lived together with no major problems   25. a row of houses, three or more, all connected   26. evidence of

most exciting life," Ms. Grant concedes. "But I've been a very good mother. My child is my greatest accomplishment."

Now that Jorie is a little older, Shelly Grant thinks about dating again, but she still has reservations. "My friends tell me that I should," she says. "But Jorie is my family. This is what I'm used to."

Jorie's other family for much of her life was at Sunnie Kiddie Foundation, Inc., in a nearby town. When the girl started at this day-care center, it was one of the only in the area and served 63 children; now it serves 250 offspring of families where both parents work, and 50 more who have single working parents. Demand is so great that Elaine Lombardo, the center's founder and executive director, could sign up many more parents for care ranging up to $120 a week if she wanted to.

She doesn't want to. Mrs. Lombardo has ambivalent feelings about her job. She knows she is providing a valuable and necessary service, but she worries about the family life and future of her charges. Many children are dropped off at 6:15 A.M. and don't see their parents again until 6 at night—even later, sometimes. One parent, a model, left her four-year-old until 8 P.M. It's not unheard of, either, for parents to drop off children who are obviously ill.

Under the circumstances, it's not surprising that the children come to look upon their teachers and Mrs. Lombardo as mother figures. "The kids kiss me good night," she says. "I'm torn. I want them to feel safe and secure, but this is not their home. Parents think that we can substitute for family, but we can't."

A working mother drops by to pick up her son. She is defensive. "I want the best for him," she says. "I want him to go to college. We need two incomes, and he gets social skills here." What is she supposed to do? She and her husband, both professionals, each log four hours of commuting time daily.

Mrs. Lombardo watches her go. "We're in a very materialistic world," she says, "and these parents are under a great deal of pressure to get the toys that they think they need, for themselves and their children. They'll work around the clock for the things they want to give them—when what they really need to give them is themselves."

Comprehension and Discussion

A. *Circle the correct answer. If the answer is false, tell why.*

1. Starting in the year 2000 fewer than three out of 10 adolescents will live in a family with both a mother and a father in the same house until the age of 18.

True   False

2. Ms. Rose implies that although she would have preferred for her children not to have had to take care of themselves, the experience was not completely negative.

True   False

3. Although many of the parents in this community are very busy, education is still considered important and parents still get involved with the school.

True   False

B. *Answer the following questions as completely as possible.*

1. Throughout the article, many "signs of the times" are given. These are common indicators in daily life of how society has changed. List as many of these signs as possible. Give at least four. Then tell what these signs mean. Are there any other signs of the times that you have noticed in the United States that are not given in this article? Are there any signs of the times that you can think of from your country?

Sign	Meaning
house buyers' interest in location of day care centers not just grocery stores	shows that both parents are working and that there is no one home to take care of the children

2. In an effort to add stability and a sense of worth to their lives, what different things do many of the children of divorced parents do?

3. What are some problems children might have when their parents re-marry?

4. What price, in more ways than just money, might some parents have to pay to give their children what they feel the children need?

5. What do you think the role of the school and the community should be for children of divorced or broken families? Does the school have an obligation to help students with social matters or is its purpose strictly educational?

6. How do the situations given in this article relate to what is happening in your country? Are there many "two-career" communities? Is divorce on the rise? If so, what do the families and/or the communities do to help the children deal with the situation? If divorce is not on the rise, why not?

7. What are your feelings about the children and the parents in this article? What surprised you the most? What aspect would be least like the family situation in your country? Are there any similarities?

Word Forms

Working with a partner, complete the following chart with the different forms of the words. Use your knowledge of other words and their different forms to help you. Do not be afraid to guess. A dash means there is no form.

Noun	Verb	Adjective	Adverb
	—	intact	—
	ostracize	—	—
	—	precocious	

	trauma				—
1.	. . .	—	ubiquitous		—
2.	. . .	—	—		—

Vocabulary Practice

Complete the sentences below with the correct words from the following list. You may have to use different word forms and tenses. Do not use a word more than once.

Sentences 1 - 7	**Sentences 8 - 12**
precocious	alarm
befit	trauma
ostracism	ubiquitous
pariah	fend for
walk out	dysfunctional
ambivalent	reservation
intact	

1. In the past, divorce was seen as immoral, so divorced couples were often avoided. This _____ sometimes even extended to their children.

2. Keeping the family together was of the greatest importance. The _____ of the family was so important that many couples who might have gotten divorced did not.

3. Today divorce is much more accepted, and divorced people are no longer the _____ they once were.

4. Whereas once it was felt that a divorced man did not _____ the office of the presidency of the country, the United States has now had a divorced man as president.

5. Although few people would want the situation to go back to one in which divorce was almost impossible and couples, no matter how unhappy, stayed together just for children and society, most people are disturbed by the high divorce rate. There is great _____ about this change in our society.

6. Now many sociologists and psychologists feel that we have gone too far. Perhaps because divorce is so easy and so acceptable, a man or a woman might just _____ without trying to work on the problems in the marriage.

7. In the past, middle-class children were often naive and innocent about love and marriage. They only saw the good side of it. Today, however, the children of divorced parents often develop a _____ about the bad side of relationships that is frightening to see in such young children.

8. In extreme cases, the family as a unit has stopped functioning. Since this is a relatively new phenomenon, no one knows what this will mean for the

future of our society. However, experts are (a.) _____ by the number of (b.) _____ families in our country.

9. In large urban areas, one can see many signs, ads, and television commercials for divorce lawyers. Perhaps the _____ of these ads gives us an idea of how grave the problem really is.

10. Divorce is rarely easy for the people involved, but it can be especially _____ for the children.

11. Even children of parents who stay together often have to _____ themselves because both parents work and no one is at home to take care of them after school.

12. Most parents who leave children home alone are not happy about the situation. They only do so with great _____.

Focus on Form: Wishes—Past, Present, and Future

Look at the following excerpt from the article:

"What is the most important wish you have for the *future*?"

"All of them speak immediately, in unison: "That there *wouldn't be* so many divorces."

Wishes are like unreal conditionals. They are impossible or hypothetical, at least in our minds. Just by using the word "wish," the idea becomes hypothetical.

Grammar Practice

Circle the correct form for each of the following wishes. Think of them as unreal conditionals. Check your answers with another student.

1. His parents got divorced last year. He wishes they _____ together.

    a. stayed
    b. would stay
    c. had stayed
    d. have stayed

2. There was no place for the teenagers to go at night. The young people wished that the town _____ a social center for them.

a. had had
b. would have
c. had
d. have

3. When she first got divorced, the people in the neighborhood avoided her. She wishes that they _____ friendlier to her.

   a. had been
   b. were
   c. have been
   d. would be

4. Because both parents work, nobody is home when he gets there from school. He wishes that he _____ to be home alone.

   a. hadn't had
   b. doesn't have
   c. won't have
   d. didn't have

5. Her parents aren't going to visit her at school this weekend. She wishes that they _____ to come at least for the day.

   a. were going
   b. are going
   c. had gone
   d. be going

6. There were a great many children from broken homes in the suburban schools. The principal wished that there _____ more intact families.

   a. are
   b. would have been
   c. were
   d. had been

7. He can only see his mother on weekends. He wishes he _____ see her more.

   a. can
   b. could have
   c. could be
   d. could

8. She couldn't stay home to take care of her children because she had to work. Now she wishes she _____ spent more time with them when they were young.

   a. could
   b. could have
   c. were able to
   d. can

Focus on Form: Wishes

Wishes take the following forms:

- present wishes — simple past tense
  were—for the verb *to be*
  could (or *were able*)—for the modal *can*

- future wishes — *would* + base form
  were going + infinitive

- past wishes — past perfect tense,
  could have (or *had been able*)—for the modal *could*

Notice that the word *that* is optional after the verb *wish*. You may use it or not.

The word *wish* can be in any tense. The tense of the wish clause depends on its relation to the wish. Is the wish about something before, at the same time, or after the moment of wishing?

When I was a child I *wished*
{
(before) I *had been born* a prince. (past)
(same time) I *had* wings and *could* fly. (present)
(after) I *would become* a movie star. (future)
}

The young girl always wishes
{
(before) her parents *hadn't gotten* divorced.
(same time) her parents *were* still together.
(after) her parents *were going* to be home when she arrived.
}

Grammar Practice

Read the following situations from the article and complete the sentences with the correct verb forms. In some cases, there may be more than one possibility. If there is, give both. You may have to use negatives or the passive voice, so read each one carefully for meaning. Since we do not know the people involved, we cannot know exactly what they wish. We will be making assumptions. However, use what you know of the people in the article to help you decide which form to use.

1. When Phyllis Rose moved into Buffalo Grove, she had everything most American women of the time wanted. A year later her husband walked out on her, and she was left to raise the children alone. She probably wished he (leave) _____. Perhaps she wished he (come) _____ back. Maybe she wished she (never, marry) _____ him. Surely she wished that she (have) _____ to raise the children alone.

2. From the time her oldest child was 10 years old, the kids had to fend for themselves. She couldn't spend much time with them because she had to work to support them. Now she probably wishes that she (spent)

_____ more time with them. Perhaps she even wishes she (be able to go) _____ back in time and see them grow up.

3. In the past, many of the children of divorced parents in Buffalo Grove felt lonely and isolated. They probably wished they (have) _____ somebody to talk to about their problems.

4. Now there are school-sponsored "divorce groups" for the high school students. People who grew up before these groups started wish they (have) _____ them when they were younger.

5. Even though most children understand what divorce is, most probably wish their parents (get) _____ together again.

6. Many of the teachers of children of broken families wish that they (be able to help) _____ the children more, but they know they cannot really substitute for the parents.

7. The teenagers in these communities wish there (be) _____ more to do at night.

8. One woman in the article had to put her daughter in a day-care center when the child was just 20 months old. The mother wishes that she (have) _____ to do that, but she had no choice. Some day the daughter may wish that she (leave) _____ at a day-care center at such an early age, but she will probably also realize why it happened.

9. Children watch television and see families that are almost perfect. Even if there are problems, they are usually solved in half an hour. Children who watch these programs probably wish that their families (be) _____ more like the families they see on television.

10. The article implies that many of the children of broken homes do not have the opportunity to have a simple, uncomplicated childhood so they grow up before their time. Some day, when these children get older, they will probably wish that they (mature) _____ so early.

Focus on Form: Short Answer Wishes

Shortened forms of wishes are frequently used in conversation. These are often used when the speaker shows some regret in the answer to a question or as a follow-up to the speaker's own statement. They are similar to short answer conditionals.

Q: "Do you live with both of your parents?" (*Do you live*—present tense)

A: No, but I wish I *did*. (= I wish I *lived* with both of my parents.)

"I don't have any brothers or sisters. "I wish I *did*. It's lonely being an only child. (*I don't have*—present tense) (I wish I *did* = I wish I *had* brothers or sisters.)

Q. "Did they have 'divorce groups' when you were a child?" (*Did they have*—past tense)

A: "No, but I wish they *had*." (= I wish they *had had* divorce groups.)

Q: "Were you taken to a day care center as a child?" (*Were you taken*—past passive)

A: "Yes. I wish I *hadn't been*." (= Yes, I was. I wish I *hadn't been taken*...)

"I don't think they'll get back together. I wish they *would*." (*they'll get back*—future) (I wish they *would* = I wish they *would get* back together.)

Q: "Are you going to go on vacation with your parents?" (*Are you going* = future)

A: "No. I wish I *were*." (= I wish I *were going* to go on vacation with my parents.)

Short-answer substitutions:

For the verb *to be*, including passives:
- present wish—were, weren't
- past wish—had (hadn't) been
- future wish—would (wouldn't) be, (or *were* if the question is "Are you going to...?")

For all other verbs, including to *have*:
- present wish—did, didn't
- past wish—had, hadn't
- future wish—would, wouldn't

Grammar Practice

Pair Work: Short Answer Wishes

Below are two sets of questions. Student A will ask Student B the questions in the A list. Using the Student B answers as a guide, Student B will answer the questions with wish *and a short answer. Student A corrects Student B after each question. Next, reverse roles, with Student B asking the questions, Student A answering, and Student B correcting the answer. The correct answers are in parentheses after each question. Listen carefully to the tense of the question.*

Student A Questions	**Student A Answers**
1. Does your room have a kitchen? (No. *I wish it did.*)	1. No. _____

2. Are you going home for vacation? (No. *I wish I were.*)

3. Did you see your brother last week? (No, but *I wish I had.*)

4. Were you given a ride home? (No. *I wish I had been.*)

5. Have you seen that movie? (Yes, and *I wish I hadn't.*)

6. Do you think it will be warm tomorrow? (*I wish it would be.*)

7. Do you have to do it now? (Yes, and *I wish that I didn't.*)

8. Can you speak Russian? (No. *I wish I could.*)

9. Were you at the concert last night? (Yes, and *I wish I hadn't been.*)

10. Could you see her from where you were sitting? (No. *I wish I could have.*) (No. *I wish I had been able to.*)

2. No. _____

3. _____, but I'm broke.

4. _____

5. No. _____

6. Yes, and _____

7. Yes. _____

8. No. _____

9. No. _____

10. No. _____

Student B Answers

1. No. _____

2. No. _____

3. No, but _____

4. No. _____

5. Yes, and _____

6. _____

7. Yes, and _____

8. No. _____

9. Yes, and _____

10. No. _____

Student B Questions

1. Did you meet her? (No. *I wish I had.*)

2. Had you been there before? (No. *I wish I had been.*)

3. Do you have $10 you could lend me? (*I wish I did*, but I'm broke.)

4. Do you think he'll leave soon? (*I wish he would.*)

5. Are you going to the party tonight. (No. *I wish I were.*)

6. Do you have her dog this week? (Yes, and *I wish I didn't.*)

7. Were you seen going in? (Yes. *I wish I hadn't been.*)

8. Could you speak French well when you first moved to France? (No. *I wish I could have.*) (No. *I wish I had been able to.*)

9. Do you live near school. (No. *I wish I did.*)

10. Did you have a car then? (No. *I wish I had.*)

Grammar Practice

Write sentences about yourself and your wishes. Try to use all tenses, making wishes about the past, present, and future.

1. When I (was a child; *or any past time*) I wished . . .

2. I wish that . . .

Reading 2: "The Dreams of Youth"

Prereading Questions

1. Are young women, for examples ages 18-25, different from women of older generations—in your country and in the United States? If so, how?

2. How have young men changed in regards to their attitudes towards women and the family?

3. What does being a "successful woman" mean to you?

4. If there has been a women's movement in your country, how do you think this has affected your life and the society of your country?

Taking a Poll

Answer the questions to the following poll. After the entire class has completed the poll, compile the results. What is the percentage of males and females for each question? Record the percentages for each sex in the spaces provided after the questions.

Love and Marriage	**Female**	**Male**

1. Which of the following is an essential requirement for a spouse? (You may check as many as you want, but the important word is "essential.")

   a. Physically attractive ____ ____ ____
   b. Masculine/feminine traits ____ ____ ____
   c. Well-paying job ____ ____ ____
   d. Intelligent ____ ____ ____
   e. Ambitious and hard-working ____ ____ ____
   f. Faithful ____ ____ ____

2. How difficult is it to have a good marriage today? (Check one.)

   a. Very difficult ____ ____ ____
   b. Difficult ____ ____ ____
   c. Easy ____ ____ ____
   d. Very easy

3. Will couples in your generation be more or less likely
   than those in your parents' generation to get divorced?

   a. More likely   ____   ____   ____
   b. Less likely   ____   ____   ____

Bringing Up Baby

1. If you had the opportunity, would you be interested
   in staying home and raising children? (This means
   you would not work.)

   a. Yes   ____   ____   ____
   b. No   ____   ____   ____

2. Would you raise your children in the same way you
   were raised?

   a. Yes, the same   ____   ____   ____
   b. No, very differently   ____   ____   ____

The More Things Change

1. Do you think it is easier to be a man or a woman?

   a. To be a man   ____   ____   ____
   b. To be a woman   ____   ____   ____

2. Which of the following is your single most important
   goal? (Check one only.)

   a. A successful career   ____   ____   ____
   b. A happy marriage   ____   ____   ____
   c. Well-adjusted children   ____   ____   ____
   d. Contributing to society   ____   ____   ____

Analyzing the Poll

1. Look at the differences in answers between males an females. Are there
   any great discrepancies? What do you think this says about the different
   (or similar) attitudes and feelings of men and women?

2. Compare the way males and females in your class answered with the
   results of the same poll given to young American males and females.
   (page 267) Are there any great discrepancies in how you answered and
   how Americans answered these questions? If there are, to what do you
   attribute these differences? If there are not any major differences, does this
   mean anything to you?

Vocabulary Practice

Match the italicized words in the sentences with the synonyms or definitions in the lists below. Use the context of the sentence to help you guess the meaning.

Sentences 1 - 8

_____ an indication of excellence or quality

_____ fall quickly; dive

_____ alike; without distinctive qualities

_____ a quick look

_____ cause to increase in importance or level of controversy

_____ done without preparation

_____ revise; change; renovate

_____ reject; send away or out of one's thoughts

_____ accept or expect without question

Sentences 9 - 15

_____ right or privilege of a person or a group

_____ unprotected; open to injury or abuse

_____ do or give unwillingly; envy someone else's enjoyment

_____ avoid; escape understanding

_____ a feeling of contempt or superiority for someone else

_____ provide anything another wants

_____ dangerously unstable or insecure

_____ an adjective or phrase used to describe a person; often, but not necessarily, an insult

1. A generation from now, a special issue of a magazine devoted to women will seem about as appropriate as a special issue on tall people. That is not to say that by then men and women will have become *indistinguishable*.

2. The debate about what it means to be a successful woman was further *fueled* by the announcement by TV newswoman Connie Chung that she would leave the competition at CBS in a final effort to become a mother at age 44.

3. One measure of success of the women's movement is the ease with which it is *taken for granted*.

4. Today's young adults *dismiss* old gender stereotypes and limitations.

5. In psychology, the old view that autonomy is the (a.) *hallmark* of mental health is being (b.) *revamped*. A sense of "connectedness" to others is now being viewed as a healthy trait.

6. They were born between 1968 and 1974, a tiny but explosive *glimpse* of history in which the women's movement took hold.

7. Studies of women's changing expectations have found that . . . the proportion of young women who planned to be housewives *plunged* from two-thirds to less than a quarter.

8. Raising a child became less a preoccupation than an *improvisation*.

9. Wild optimism is youth's *prerogative*.

10. They assume that the secrets that *eluded* their predecessors will be revealed to them.

11. It is not that older women *begrudge* the younger women their hopes.

12. The earning power of young families fell steadily during the '80s so that two incomes are a necessity, not a luxury, and a *precarious* economy promises only more pain.

13. She saw her own working mother wear herself out *catering* to her father and brother.

14. In most cases it happened when mothers were trying to decide whether to stay home or go to work. And the women were left so *vulnerable*. Careers became a form of insurance.

15. While the goals are applauded by three quarters of young people, the feminist label is viewed with alarm and (a.) *disdain*; the name of an early woman's liberationist is uttered as an (b.) *epithet*.

This article points out some similarities and many differences between young women of today and their mothers and older sisters. Some are stated directly, and some are implied. Some are expressed through the opinions of the younger women and some through the older women. As you are reading, write down any similarities or differences that you find. Make two columns—one for the older generation and one for younger women.

The Dreams of Youth

By NANCY GIBBS
(from *Time* magazine)

A generation from now, if all the dreams of reformers have come true, a special issue devoted to women will seem about as appropriate as a special issue on tall people. This is not to say that by then men and women will have become indistinguishable, their quirks[27] and cares and concerns interchangeable. Rather, the struggles of the last decades of the 20th century will have brought about the freedom and flexibility that have always been the goals of social reform.

Issues like equal pay, child care, abortion, rape, and domestic violence will no longer be cast[28] as "women's issues." They will be viewed as economic issues, family issues, ethical issues, of equal resonance[29] to men and women. A woman heading a huge corporation will not make headlines by virtue of[30] her gender. Half the presidential candidates may be women—and nobody will notice.

But what will it take to get there from here? As the century fades, women find themselves at a critical juncture, a moment, perhaps, for reflection and evaluation. The cozy,[31] limited roles of the past are still clearly remembered, sometimes

---

27. peculiarity of behavior; behavior peculiar to a person   28. put in the part of; be seen as   29. importance   30. on the basis of; by reason of   31. comfortable, safe, and warm

fondly. The future looms[32] with so many choices that the freedom it promises can be frightening.

The opening year of the new decade has richly sketched[33] the dizzying[34] choices of roles and values facing the next generation of American women and men. When Barbara Bush arrived at Wellesley College to celebrate motherhood and wifely virtues, she sparked[35] a national debate among the young about what it means to be a successful woman. That debate was further fueled by the announcement by TV newswoman Connie Chung that she would abandon the fast track[36] at CBS in a last-ditch[37] drive for motherhood at age 44. Meanwhile, male role models are also in flux. Wall Street wonder boy Peter Lynch hung up[38] his $13 billion mutual fund to do good deeds and have more time with his family. What generation in history has enjoyed such liberty to write the rules as it goes along? Over the past 30 years, all that was orthodox has become negotiable.

Young Americans inherit a revolution that has largely been won. One measure of the success of the women's movement is the ease with which it is taken for granted. Few daughters remember the barriers their mothers faced when applying for scholarships, jobs and loans—even for a divorce. Today's young adults dismiss old gender stereotypes and limitations. They expect equal opportunities but want more than mere equality. It is their dream that they will be the ones to strike a healthy balance at last between their public and private lives: between the lure of fame and glory, and a love of home and hearth.[39]

If there is a theme among those coming of age today—and a theme for this issue—it is that gender differences are often better celebrated than suppressed. Young women do not want to slip[40] unnoticed into a man's world; they want that world to change and benefit from what women bring to it. The changes are spreading. Eager to achieve their goals without sacrificing their natures, women in business are junking[41] the boxy suits and one-of-the-boys[42] manner that always seemed less a style than a disguise. In psychology, the old view that autonomy is the hallmark of mental health is being revamped. A sense of "connectedness" to others is now being viewed as a healthy trait rather than a symptom of "dependent personality disorder." In politics, women candidates are finding that issues they emphasize may carry more weight than ever with voters tired of the guns-not-butter[43] budgets of the 1980s.

In many ways the 16 million or so women between the ages of 16 and 22 are the generation that social scientists have been waiting for. They were born between 1968 and 1974, a tiny but explosive glimpse of history in which the women's movement took hold. Studies of women's changing expectations have found that during those years the proportion of young women who planned to be housewives plunged from two thirds to less than a quarter—an astounding shift in attitude in the flick of an apron.[44] Child rearing[45] became less a preoccupation than an

---

32. appear in the mind as magnified or of great importance   33. draw quickly; make a quick presentation   34. enough to make one dizzy   35. started; set off   36. the career path with most possibilities for advancement   37. last strong attempt   38. quit; stopped working (from the expression *He hung up the towel.* = He quit.)   39. literally, the floor of a fireplace. Used to mean the home, the family   40. move in quickly and smoothly   41. throwing out; getting rid of   42. just like everyone else   43. money for defense instead of social issues   44. in no time at all; very suddenly (from the expression *in the flick of a switch*, i.e., a light switch).   45. raising children

7:30 AM. A mother and child leaving for work and daycare. A busy day for both.

improvisation, housework less an obsession than a chore.[46] Young daughters watched as their mothers learned new roles, while their fathers all too often clung[47] to old ones. They were the first generation to see almost half of all marriages end in divorce.

Disheartened[48] by their mothers' guilt during the 70s and their older sisters' exhaustion hauling[49] baby and briefcase through the career traffic of the 80s, today's young women have their own ideas about redefining the feminine mystique.[50] When asked to sketch their futures, college students say they want good careers, good marriages and two or three kids, and they don't want their children to be raised by strangers. Young people don't want to lie, as their mothers did, when a baby's illness keeps them from work; they expect the boss to understand. Mommy tracks,[51] daddy tracks,[52] dropping out,[53] slowing down, starting over, going private[54]—all are options entertained by a generation that views its yuppie[55] predecessors with alarm. The next generation of parents may be less likely to

46. work, usually in or around one's own house, for which one is not paid   47. (to cling) - stayed closely or tightly to   48. discouraged   49. pulling around; carrying (a heavy load)   50. what being a woman means (One of the earliest books on women's liberation was *The Feminine Mystique* by Betty Friedan.)   51. career track for mothers, with lower pay and fewer possibilities for advancement but more flexibility in scheduling.   52. a response by women against the "mommy track."   53. quitting; leaving the work world, the "straight" world   54. starting one's own business   55. young urban professional

argue over who has to leave work early to pick up the kids and more likely to clash over who gets to take parental leave.

Wild optimism is youth's prerogative, but older women shudder[56] slightly at the giddy[57] expectations of today's high school and college students. At times their hope borders on[58] hubris,[59] with its assumption that the secrets that eluded their predecessors will be revealed to them. "In the 1950s women were family-oriented," says Sheryl Hatch, 20, a broadcasting major at the American University in Washington. "In the 70s they were career oriented. In the 90s we want balance. I think I can do both."

It is not that older women begrudge the young their hopes; rather they recognize how many choices will still be dictated not by social convention but by economic realities. The earning power of young families fell steadily during the 80s, so that two incomes are a necessity, not a luxury, and a precarious economy promises only more pain. When factories cut back, women are often the first to be laid off.[60] As Washington battles its deficits, cutting away at food, health, and child-care programs, it is poor women who will feel the hardest pinch.[61]

These prospects are not all lost on young people; there is plenty of room for realism between their dreams and their fears. A TIME poll of 505 men and women ages 18 to 24 by Yankelovich Clancy Shulman found that 4 out of 5 believed it was difficult to juggle[62] work and family, and that too much pressure was placed on women to bear the burdens. But among those with the education to enter the professions, the response often comes in the form of demands. "What's different between these women and my generation," says Leslie Wolfe, 46, executive director of the Center for Women Policy Studies in Washington, "is that they say, 'I don't want to work 70 hours a week, but I want to be vice president, and *you* have to change.' We kept our mouths shut and followed the rules. They want different rules."

And if the economy cooperates, they may just pull it off, with some help from demographics. This baby-bust[63] generation is about one-third smaller than the baby boomers who came before, which means that employers competing for skilled workers will be drawing from a smaller pool.[64] Today's young people hope that that fact, combined with some corporate consciousness raising about the importance of families, will give them bargaining power for longer vacations, more generous parental leaves and more flexible working conditions. Employers who listen carefully will hear the shift of priorities. Many college students, while nervous about their economic prospects, are equally wary[65] of the fast lane. "We have a fear of being like the generation before us, which lost itself," says Julia Parsons, 24, a second-year law student at Georgetown University Law Center. "I don't want to find myself at 35 with no family. It's a big fear." Big enough, it seems, to account for a marked shift away from 1980s-style workaholism. The TIME poll found that 51% put having a long and happy marriage and raising well adjusted children ahead of career success (29%).

---

56. to shake from fear or dislike   57. lightheaded, enough to make one feel light or dizzy   58. almost becomes   59. overly high expectations or pride   60. fired; forced to leave work, usually for economic reasons, not for incompetence   61. suffer the economic consequences   62. keep two or more things going at the same time   63. few babies being born   64. common group of people or resources   65. cautious

The men are often just as eager as women to escape the pressure of traditional roles. "The women's movement has been a positive force," says Scott Mabry, a 22-year-old Kenyon College graduate. "Men have a new appreciation of women as people, more than just sex objects, wives, mothers." TIME'S poll found that 86% of young men were looking for a spouse who was ambitious and hardworking; an astonishing 48% expressed an interest in staying home with their children. "I don't mind being the first one to stay home," says Ernesto Fuentes, a high school student in Los Angeles' working-class Echo Park district. "The girl can succeed. It's cool with me."

For their part, many women fully expect to do their share as breadwinners,[66] though not necessarily out of personal choice so much as financial need. "Of course we will work," says Kimberly Heimert, 21, of Germantown, Tenn., a senior at American University. "What are we going to do? Stay at home? When I get married, I expect to contribute 50% of my family's income."

When asked how family life will fit into their ambitious plans, young people wax creative.[67] Many want to be independent contractors, working at home at their own hours. Some talk of "sequencing": rather than interrupting a career to stay home with children, they plan to marry early, have children quickly and think about work later. "I'll get into my career afterward," says Sheri Davis, 21, a senior at the University of Southern California. "I'm not willing to have children and put them in day care. I've babysat for years and taken kids to day-care centers. They just hang on my legs and cry. I can't do that." Other women claim to be searching for the perfect equal-opportunity mate. Melissa Zipnick, 26, a kindergarten teacher in Los Angeles, saw her own working mom wear herself out "catering" to her father and brother. "I intend to be married to someone who will share all the responsibilities," she vows.

But such demands and expectations are accompanied by a nagging sense of the obstacles. The fear of divorce, for instance, hangs heavily over young men and women. Nearly three quarters of those in the Time poll said that having a good marriage today is difficult or very difficult. More than half would not choose a marriage like their parents', and 85% think they are even more likely to see their marriages end in divorce than did their parents' generation. "A lot of my friends' parents are divorced," says Georgetown's Parsons. "In most cases it happened when the mother was trying to decide whether to stay home or go to work. And the women were left so vulnerable." Careers become a form of insurance. "I don't want to depend on anybody," says Kellie Moore, 19, a U.S.C. junior who plans to get a business degree. "I have friends who have already set up their own credit structure because they watched their mothers try to set one up after a divorce."

Given this combination of goals and fears, young women would appear to be disciples of feminism, embracing the movement as a means of sorting out social change. But while the goals are applauded by three quarters of young people, the feminist label is viewed with disdain and alarm; the name Gloria Steinem[68] is uttered as an epithet. Some young people reject the movement on principle: "The whole women's movement is pushing the career women," says Kathy Smith, 19, a sophomore at Vanderbilt, "and making light of[69] being a homemaker."

---

66. person who is the major supporter of the family   67. grow; become; speak in creative terms   68. editor of Ms. Magazine, the major magazine of the women's liberation movement; a leading figure of this movement   69. not pay great importance to

Others feel that the battle belonged to a different generation, without realizing that the very existence of a debate about family leave, abortion, flextime,[70] and affirmative action is the fruit of an ongoing revolution. Minority women seem to be the group least likely to abandon the feminist label, perhaps because they are most aware of how many critical battles remain to be fought. In fact, argues Stephanie Batiste, 18, a black freshman at Princeton, "Minority women are almost a separate women's movement ... You're very alone. You get a lot less support."

Here, then, is a goal for the women's movement: the education of the next generation of daughters in a better understanding of their inheritance, their opportunities, and their obligations. And there are lessons to learn in return. Speaking of the new generation, Leslie Wolfe of the Women Policy Studies Center says, "I think they are more savvy[71] than we were, about sexism, about discrimination, about balancing work and family, about sex." They may be wiser, too, about seizing fresh opportunities without losing sight of tradition. Historian Doris Kearns Goodwin once wrote of a woman's dream, "The special heritage of values and priorities that have been traditionally associated with women as wives and mothers can be seen as sources of strength to create an enlarged vision of society." A society so enlarged and strengthened will make more room for everyone's dreams.

---

70. flexible time, not the normal 9 to 5 schedule   71. knowledgeable; aware

WHAT YOUTH THINK

LOVE & MARRIAGE

Which of the following is an essential requirement for a spouse?

	Females	Males
Physically attractive	19%	41%
Masculine/feminine traits	41%	72%
Well-paying job	77%	25%
Intelligent	95%	88%
Ambitious and hardworking	99%	86%
Faithful	100%	97%

How difficult is it to have a good marriage today?

	Very difficult	Difficult	Easy	Very easy
Females	18%	56%	23%	3%
Males	22%	55%	18%	4%

Will couples in your generation be more or less likely than those in your parents' generation to get divorced?

More likely **85%**   Less likely **14%**

BRINGING UP BABY

If you had the opportunity, would you be interested in staying at home and raising children?

	Females	Males
Yes	66%	48%
No	33%	51%

Would you raise your own children the same way you were raised?

Yes, the same	56%
No, very differently	43%

THE MORE THINGS CHANGE...

Do you think it is easier to be a man or a woman?

	Females	Males
To be a woman	30%	21%
To be a man	59%	65%

Which of the following is your single most important goal?

	Females	Males
A successful career	27%	32%
A happy marriage	39%	30%
Well-adjusted children	23%	9%
Contributing to society	6%	16%

From a telephone poll of 505 Americans aged 18 to 24 taken for TIME on Sept. 5-11 by Yankelovich Clancy Shulman. Sampling error is plus or minus 4.5%

TIME Chart by Joe Lertola

Comprehension and Discussion

A. *Circle the correct answer. If the answer is false, tell why.*

1. Young women today want to be just like men.

   True   False

2. Young women today simply expect what their mothers had to fight for.

   True   False

3. The women who were born in the years 1968-1974 were the first generation for whom nearly half of their marriages ended in divorce.

   True   False

4. In some ways young women today seem to be returning to the more traditional roles that their mothers had tried to give up.

   True   False

B. *Answer the following questions as completely as possible.*

1. References are made to Barbara Bush's speech at Wellesley College and Connie Chung's decision to work less to try to have a baby. Of what importance were these actions, and what do they have to do with this article?

2. At different places in the article, women of the 50s, 70s, 80s and 90s are mentioned. Briefly describe each group.

3. Explain the role of demographics in the women's movement.

4. Give the differences that you found in the article between the young women of today and their predecessors.

5. Explain the following sentences from the article in your own words. What do they say about the situation of women (and men) in American society today?

   a. "The cozy limited roles of the past are still clearly remembered, sometimes fondly. The future looms with so many choices that the freedom it promises can be frightening."
   b. "What generation in history has enjoyed the liberty to write the rules as it goes along?"
   c. "Gender differences are often better celebrated than suppressed."
   d. "... they (the older women) recognize how many choices will be dictated not by social convention but by economic realities."
   e. "Young daughters watched as their mothers learned new roles, while their fathers all too often clung to old ones."

6. How do the attitudes expressed in this article compare with attitudes of young men and women in your country? How are they similar? How are they different?

Word Forms

Working with a partner, complete the following chart with the different forms of the words. Use your knowledge of other words and their different forms to help you. Do not be afraid to guess. A dash means there is no form.

Noun	Verb	Adjective	Adverb
disdain			
	dismiss	—	—
	elude		—
improvisation			
	—	precarious	
	—	vulnerable	

Vocabulary Practice

Complete the sentences below with the correct words from the following lists. You may have to use different word forms and tenses. Do not use a word more than once.

Sentences 1 - 9	Sentences 10 - 16
revamp	prerogative
vulnerable	elude
fuel	begrudge
hallmark	improvisation
indistinguishable	precarious
glimpse	take for granted
plunge	cater
dismiss	disdain
epithet	

1. During the Second World War, many women took the place of men in the workforce. However, when the men returned from the war, the number of working women _____.

2. In the 1950s, the _____ of success for many women was a clean home and a successful husband.

3. When women worked, lower pay for the same work that men did naturally _____ their anger and their desire for laws guaranteeing equal pay.

4. Lacking economic power, women also lacked political power. In addition, since they had low seniority, they lost their jobs before men in times of economic crisis. This _____ made it difficult to demand change.

5. In the beginning of the women's movement, women's liberationists were _____ by most men, and many women, as crazy radicals.

6. Critics said that these "women's libbers" were trying to make the sexes _____.

7. "Women's libber" became an _____ for any woman who tried to achieve equality.

8. Because of the women's movement, most major corporations have had to _____ their hiring and promotion policies concerning women.

9. Just a _____ at statistics about the percentage of men vs. women in top-level positions will show how much more progress women have to make to achieve equality.

10. Because of the great changes that have taken place in how men and women interact, many young couples have no old rules to go by in their relationships. Many of them are just _____ as they go along.

11. In the past, having a hot meal on the table waiting for him when he got home from work was seen as a man's _____.

12. Today working women do not have the time to _____ to all the needs of the husband and children as they did in the past.

13. However, the fact that women work does not mean that the burdens of housework are shared equally. Women are still the primary cooks and cleaners. Many women have to keep up a _____ balance between being a career-woman and a housewife and mother.

14. Although most women don't have the time to work all day and cook at night, independence from the kitchen is still an _____ goal for many married women.

15. Even modern, liberal men often look on housework (a.) _____, and they (b.) _____ doing work such as cleaning the bathroom or vacuuming the carpets.

16. Many just _____ it _____ that the work will get done.

Focus on Form: Comparison and Contrast— Showing Similarities and Differences

A. Subject	Verb (Prep.) Verb + Adj. + Prep.	Object of Similarity or Contrast
The American family	{ *resembles* *is similar to* }	the European family *in that* (Shows *how*.) both are getting smaller. *(in that + clause)* . . . the European family *in regard to size. (in regard to* + noun or phrase)
American women	{ *differ from* *are different from* }	many Japanese women *in that* the former usually continue to work after they get married *while (whereas) the latter* often do not. many Japanese women *in regard to* work status after marriage.

B. Preposition + Noun (Phrase), Clause

Like their grandmothers, many young American women feel it is more important to stay home with their children.

Unlike their mothers, who often went to work first and then had children, (adjective clause explaining difference) many young women today are thinking of having children first.

C. Clause; Connector, Clause of Similarity or Contrast

American women often live on their own before getting married;

likewise, / similarly,

northern European women do not necessarily stay at home until marriage. (The similarity is restated in different words.)

American women usually continue to work after they get married;

however, / in contrast, / conversely,

Japanese women often do not.

D. Adverbial clause, clause of contrast

While / Whereas Chinese women live at home until marriage, American women often live alone or with roommates before they get married.

Grammar Practice

Combine the following sentences, or the information in them, using the words in parentheses. You will be using the ideas; you may have to change the wording of the sentences.

1. In many European countries, paid maternity leave for women is guaranteed by the government. In the United States, it is not.

   (unlike)
   (differ(s) from . . . in that)
   (whereas)

2. The American family has become smaller in the past 50 years. The German family has also become smaller.

   (is similar to . . . in regard to)
   (like)

3. The previous generation of American women had children later in life. Younger American women are having children earlier.

   (however)
   (unlike)

4. Young people in northern Europe often leave home before they get married. Young Americans often do also.

   (resemble...in that)
   (likewise)

Grammar Practice

Using the structures given below, write sentences comparing and contrasting family values or the role of women in the United States (or in any other country) with those of your country.

1. ... is/are similar to ... in that ...

2. Like ... , ...

3. Unlike ... , who (which) ... , ...

4. ... ; likewise, ...

5. Whereas ... , ...

6. ... differ (s) from ... in regard to ...

7. ... ; conversely, ...

8. ... is/are different from ... in that ... while ...

Grammar Practice

Look at the list of similarities and differences that you found in the article between the young women of today and their predecessors. (#4, p. 271) Using this information, write five sentences with different forms of comparison and contrast.

Focus on Form: Concessive Contrast

> *Despite the fact that* 56 percent of the females in the poll said that it was difficult to have a good marriage today, almost 40 percent saw a successful marriage as their single most important goal.

Unlike an adversative contrast, which shows an opposite, a concessive contrast shows something surprising or unexpected. (The previous sentence shows adversative contrast. It shows how adversative and concessive contrasts are different.)

Adversative: Single women in the United States often live alone. In *contrast*, single Asian women usually live with their families. (This just shows an opposite or a great difference.)

Concessive: *In spite of* her traditional Japanese upbringing, she lives alone in an apartment a few blocks away from her parents. (The *in spite of* tells us that the main clause will not follow our expectations. There is a surprising contrast.)

Concessive contrast is shown by:
- despite
- in spite of   + noun or phrase
- regardless of

- despite the fact that
- in spite of the fact that
- regardless of the fact that   + clause
- although
- even though

Grammar Practice

Following the pattern in the first example, change each of the clauses into phrases in the sentences below. The first one has been done for you.

1. In spite of the fact that she is young, she has very traditional ideas about women's roles.

   In spite of *her being young*, she has very traditional ideas about the role of women in society. (The "her " in this sentence is possessive.)

2. Despite the fact that she has six children, she has a high position and she is a good mother.

   Despite _____, she has a high position and she is a good mother.

3. Regardless of the fact that he *was* at the peak of his career, he quit to take care of his children. (Be careful of the tense.)

   Regardless of _____, he quit to take care of his children.

4. Although Ms. Allen *was not elected*, she will continue to fight for women's rights. (Be careful of the tense, passive voice, and the negative.)

   In spite of _____, she will continue to fight for women's rights.

5. Despite the fact that she has a full-time job, she cleans the house, takes care of the children by herself, and cooks all the meals.

   Despite _____, she cleans the house, takes care of the children by herself, and cooks all the meals.

6. She left her husband in spite of the fact that he had threatened not to pay child support.

   She left her husband in spite of _____.

Note:

- the subject becomes possessive* (If the subject is a thing, the possessive is usually omitted.)
- the past is formed with *having + past participle*
- the phrase can be reduced by substituting a noun for the verb form if a noun form exists and if there is no change in meaning. (See # 6 above.)
- the clause of concession does not have to be first in the sentence.

---

*In speaking and in informal language, the possessive is often not used.

Grammar Practice

*Combine the following sentences using the adverbials of concession in parentheses.
You may have to change word forms and word order in changing from clause to phrase
or phrase to clause.*

1. Although this country has more females registered to vote than males, there are very few women in high political office.

   (*despite*) . . .

2. Regardless of his having been raised in a very traditional household, he was very happy to stay home and take care of the children while his wife worked.

   (*despite the fact that*) . . .

3. Regardless of the fact that she is very ambitious, she always puts her children first.

   (*in spite of*—reduce the phrase) . . .

4. Regardless of his liberal politics, he still refuses to cook, clean, or take care of the children.

   (*even though*) . . .

5. In spite of the fact that she wasn't interested in politics, she was sure to vote if a woman was running for office.

   (*despite*—reduce the phrase) . . .

Grammar Practice

*Write five sentences using concessive contrast. These sentences could be based on two
(or more) pieces of surprising or unexpected information in the survey, "What Youth
Think" (either the one in the article or the one you did in class). They may also be
based on what you know of family life and women's roles in the United States or in
your country. Try to use some reduced phrases.*

1. Despite . . .

2. Even though . . .

3. . . . regardless of . . .

4. In spite of . . .

5. Although . . .

Class Project

Work on one or more of these projects individually or in groups of two to three students. Then present your findings to the class.

1. Conduct the survey, "What Youth Think," on people outside of your class. Try to survey American young people. Compare these results with the results of the class poll. You may also try to survey older people and compare their answers with those of people aged 17-24. In presenting your results to the class, try to use the structures of comparison and contrast practiced in this chapter.

2. Although we tend to think of the women's movement as something relatively new, it is generally thought to have started in the United States in the 1840s. Women's right to vote was not federally guaranteed until the passage of Amendment XIX to the Constitution in 1920. Do research on the history of the women's movement in the United States. Who were the suffragettes? And what role did the following have to play in this movement?

   Susan B. Anthony
   Elizabeth C. Stanton
   Amelia Bloomer

3. What is the history of the women's movement in your country? Are there any women who stand out as having made great contributions to this movement? Do women have the right to vote? How long have they had this right? Do women have the same rights in law as men, for example in property ownership, divorce, etc.? Are there laws which guarantee women equal opportunity in employment and pay? If so, do these laws work in reality?

Discussion and Writing

Discuss the following topics, first in pairs or small groups and then with the teacher and the entire class. After your discussion, pick one (or more) of the topics and write an essay about it.

1. Describe what changes in the family have taken place in your country. What was the family like before? What is it like now? What brought about these changes? What effect do you think these changes have had or will have on the society in general?

2. Is divorce a problem, or is it on the increase, in your country? If so, why is this happening and what effects is it having on the society? If divorce is not a problem, why not?

3. What changes have taken place in the role of women in your country? Pick two or three differences between how women live today and how they lived 20 to 30 years ago and explain them fully. For example, you could focus on attitudes towards marriage and child-raising, careers, acceptance in society, equality under the law, voting rights, etc. The differences you choose should be related somewhat.

4. In your opinion, have the changes in women's roles been positive or negative? Whether you are male or female, how do you think these changes have affected you personally?

5. How is the American family or the American woman similar to or different from the family or women in your country?

Word List

Below is a list of the new words, and their different forms, presented in this chapter.

Noun	Verb	Adjective	Adverb
alarm	alarm	alarming	alarmingly
ambivalence		ambivalent	ambivalently
	befit		
	begrudge		begrudgingly
	cater (to)		
disdain	disdain	disdainful	disdainfully
dismissal	dismiss		
dysfunction		dysfunctional	
elusiveness	elude	elusive	
epithet			
	fend for		
fuel	fuel		
glimpse	glimpse		
hallmark			
improvisation	improvise	improvisatory	
indistinguishability		indistinguishable	
intactness		intact	
ostracism	ostracize		
pariah			
plunge	plunge		
precariousness		precarious	precariously

Noun	Verb	Adjective	Adverb
precociousness		precocious	precociously
prerogative			
reservation	reserve		
	revamp		
	take for granted		
trauma	traumatize	traumatic	
ubiquitousness		ubiquitous	
ubiquity			
vulnerability		vulnerable	vulnerably
	walk out		

CHAPTER 10

The Environment

Reading 1: "The Warming Globe"

Prereading Questions

1. Have you personally noticed any change in weather patterns in your country in recent years? What are these changes? Is the weather any different now from the way you remember it as a child?

2. What are the major sources of energy in your country? Are there any problems with these energy sources? Are any alternative sources of energy being tried?

3. What environmental problems does your country have? Is anything being done about these problems?

4. Is there a "green" movement in your country? If so, what actions have they taken, and what effects do you think they have had—on the environment, on the policies of the country, or on the consciousness of the people?

5. What specific words would you expect to see in an article about global warming? Brainstorm with other students to make a list of as many words as possible that deal with this topic. Be sure that all students in your group have a basic understanding of the terms on your list.

Vocabulary Practice

Circle the correct synonym or definition for each of the italicized words in the sentences below. Use the context of the sentences to help you guess the meaning.

1. The evidence for global warming is still largely *conjectural*. True the temperature has risen since the start of the century, but most meteorologists are not sure that the globe is already warming.

   a. believed
   b. based on a guess
   c. disbelieved

2. *Untangling* the greenhouse effect from other broad movements in the earth's temperature is extremely difficult.

   a. separating
   b. understanding
   c. interpreting

3. Besides, warming will be (A.) *enhanced* or (B.) *offset* in some highly uncertain ways.

   (A.)   a.   stopped
          b.   started
          c.   made greater, better
   (B.)   a.   counterbalanced
          b.   stopped
          c.   started

4. Think of the vast *alterations* in the earth's geography caused by the last ice age.

   a. changes
   b. time sequence
   c. interest

5. The Soviet Union has been *intrigued* by the idea of being able to cultivate regions which previously it had been unable to cultivate.

   a. has lost its interest
   b. has had its interest aroused
   c. has been considering

6. A rise in the sea level could drive over 60 million people from their homes. Just the numbers could *swamp* most efforts at control.

   a. increase
   b. put under water
   c. overwhelm

7. By the time scientists know more about the size and timing of global warming, it will have become more difficult and expensive to *tackle*.

   a. work with and try to resolve
   b. forget about
   c. understand the nature of

8. *Curbing* the use of some gases will be relatively easy.

   a. Increasing
   b. Penalizing
   c. Controlling

9. Mr. Irving Mintzer of the World Resources Institute made several *crucial* assumptions when he tried to show how future warming might be stabilized.

   a. unimportant
   b. unprovable
   c. extremely important

10. Governments are showing a *wary* but growing interest in the concept of putting a tax on fuels depending on the amount of carbon they contain.

    a. superficial
    b. worried
    c. cautious

11. Only one way of generating electricity is now commercially *viable*.

    a. not acceptable
    b. possible but not probable
    c. capable of success, life

12.   But any program to stop global warming will have to include a large expansion of nuclear power. This is *awkward* for many environmentalists, whose first and deepest sentiment is a hatred of nuclear power.

a. acceptable
b. uncomfortable
c. comfortable

13.   Many developing countries, having *embarked* hopefully on nuclear programs in the early 1970s, have found them plagued by delays and cost over-runs.

a. closed down
b. continued
c. started

14.   Just the size of investment needed to build even one plant makes nuclear power *intimidating* for countries with little foreign-borrowing capacity.

a. possible
b. frightening
c. interesting

15.   Above all, developed countries will worry about the security implications of putting more nuclear capacity in countries which may turn out to be hostile, irresponsible, or simply *inept*.

a. incompetent
b. friendly
c. unfriendly

The Warming Globe

By FRANCES CRAINCROSS   (from *The Economist*)

"Everybody talks about the weather, but nobody does anything about it," said Charles Dudley Warner.[1] He spoke too soon. Some of the gases that have built up in the atmosphere since the industrial revolution—carbon dioxide, nitrous oxide, methane and CFCs[2]—have the ability to trap some of the sun's returning rays like the glass of a greenhouse. As a result, many scientists believe, the planet's surface may warm up far more rapidly than at any time in the past. If that happens, the world may eventually be able to support fewer people than it can today.

The evidence for global warming is still largely conjectural. True, the global temperature has risen by about 0.5°C since the start of this century, and the six warmest years on record have fallen in the 1980s. But most meteorologists are not yet sure that the globe is already warming. Untangling the greenhouse effect from other broad movements in the earth's temperature is extremely difficult.

1. 19th century American editor and author
2. Chlorofluorocarbons

Besides, warming will be enhanced or offset in some highly uncertain ways. For instance, a warmer atmosphere will hold more water vapour.[3] Low clouds reflect sunlight, and so help to cool the earth; high clouds let sunlight through but trap returning radiation, so helping to warm the earth. The ocean mops up[4] much of the world's output of carbon, but warm water holds less carbon than cool. As the sea will heat up more slowly than the land, will it become a carbon source, not a sink?

The pace of warming is almost impossible to predict. But at any given time, the actual warming that has taken place will be less than the warming to which the planet is eventually committed. Even if man stopped producing greenhouse gases tomorrow, some warming would still take place. The conventional wisdom[5] is that the global mean temperature will rise by between 1° and 2°C by 2030, and a further 0.5° by mid-century. In 60 years, in other words, the temperature could rise by half as much as the rise of 5°C since the last ice age, 18,000 years ago. Think of the vast alterations in the earth's geography caused by that infinitely slower change. For many of earth's plants and animals, a few degrees make the difference between survival and extinction. "Global warming", thinks Mr. Norman Myers, a British environment consultant, "may prove to be the single greatest threat to our fellow species."

Those who live in cold climates may rather like the thought of warmer winters, and the Soviet Union has been intrigued by the idea of being able to cultivate its uninhabitable steppes.[6] But climate models find it hard to predict the way the weather will change in particular regions. For instance, latitudes nearer the poles may heat up more than those nearer the equator. That will probably change the pattern of ocean currents. A shift in the Gulf Stream could alter the climate of Western Europe or America by more than the greenhouse effect alone.

People, too, will find it hard to adapt. As warm water expands, the sea level might rise. One estimate says that a rise of 1-2°C might cause a 30- to 40-cm rise in sea level. Some of the world's most densely populated areas are most vulnerable to flooding. Nearly one third of mankind lives within 40 miles of the sea, where land tends to be richest—in Bangladesh, the Nile delta, China, Japan, and the Netherlands. Quite a small rise in sea level might cause a growing tide of environmental refugees. Sir Crispin Tickell, Britain's ambassador to the United Nations, draws a hair-raising[7] picture of a world in which changing climate might, at a cautious guess, drive over 60m[8] people from their homes. "Desperation could push Africans into Europe, Chinese into the relatively empty parts of the Soviet Union, and Indonesians into northern Australia. Sheer[9] numbers could swamp most efforts at control."

By the time scientists know more about the size and timing of global warming, it will have become more difficult and expensive to tackle. A vast study of the ocean, that clue to many of the unknowns, will not be complete for a decade; but with every year that passes, the earth may be committing itself to faster warming.

How to cool it

Several countries have already decided to end their use of the most potent group of greenhouse gases, CFCs. Quite apart from trapping heat, CFCs also destroy the layer of stratospheric ozone that shields the world from the sun's harmful ultraviolet rays.

Curbing the use of CFCs will be relatively easy. Production has dropped from its peak in 1974, thanks to bans on most aerosol use in America, Canada, and Sweden. They are produced by few firms in few coun-

---

3. (British English): vapor   4. clean; soak up (act like a cleaning mop)   5. that which is generally accepted   6. a flat, dry area of land with little vegetation; an area in Siberia

---

7. frightening   8. m = million   9. pure; complete

tries (Du Pont and Allied-Signal accounted for three quarters of America's output in 1986). For the biggest uses of CFCs—as refrigerants, aerosol propellants and bubbles in insulating foam—there are possible substitutes. Even so, it is still not at all clear that developing countries can be persuaded to use them.

At least it is clear where CFCs come from. Not so with two other greenhouse gases—both, molecule for molecule, much more important than carbon dioxide. Methane probably comes from rotting waste, flatulent[10] animals, leaking natural-gas pipelines, fermenting[11] rice paddy fields. Nitrous oxide comes partly from the engines of cars and the chimneys of coal-fired power stations, but also from fertilisers[12] and land clearing. Both gases are likely to be far harder to curb, for both technical and economic reason, than emissions of carbon dioxide.

And that will be hard enough. Carbon-dioxide emissions come partly from deforestation,[13] which accounts for 10-30% of man's annual carbon-dioxide emissions to the atmosphere. Almost all the rest comes from the burning of fossil fuels—coal, oil, and natural gas—which, on combustion,[14] release their stored carbon into the skies. So the main way that global warming can be slowed down is by reducing the combustion of carbon-rich fossil fuels.

A meeting of scientists, conservationists, and politicians in Toronto in June 1988 ended with a call for a 20% cut in emissions of carbon-dioxide by 2005, and a 50% cut by 2025. Most people think that cannot be done. Emissions of carbon dioxide by OECD[15] countries grew by about 4% a year between 1960 and 1973. Thereafter, in spite of the massive oil-price rise and the spread of nuclear power stations, carbon emissions still grew by 1.5%

a year. Conventional estimates predict a growth of about 0.75% a year from now on. And while the OECD countries consume just over half of the world's commercial energy, that share is falling fast. The growth in energy use in the future will come almost entirely from developing and eastern-bloc countries.

One attempt to sketch out how the world might stop warming was presented recently by Mr. Irving Mintzer of the World Resources Institute to a meeting at the East-West Centre in Hawaii. The WRI will publish it this autumn. He used a computer model to show how the commitment to future warming might be stabilised[16] by 2060. He made several crucial assumptions:

• World population stabilises at about 8 billion in 2075. This is the United Nations's "low" guess; its central guess is much higher.

• Economic growth per head in 1975-2025 is about 3% globally; for today's developing countries, between 1975 and 2025, real income per head grows at 4.6% a year. By 2025 this raises real incomes in these countries to about the level of Denmark's in 1975.

• An annual improvement in efficiency of energy use of 1.7-2.4% in today's industrial countries, and 1.4-2.3% in the developing world. In the past decade the improvement has averaged just over 1% a year. It could be done with existing best technology, but it will require sharp price increases for fossil fuels. Gas and oil prices quadruple[17] in real terms; coal prices triple by 2025 and then decline, as coal demand falls.

• Coal is largely replaced by 2025 by natural gas, solar, nuclear, and renewable fuels.

• Use of CFCs stops by 2020 in the industrial world, and by 2050 in the developing countries.

"It's technically feasible but politically impossible," Mr. Mintzer believes. His study shows that energy conservation is, beyond a doubt, the most fruitful and cost-effective way to slow global warming. But persuading people to use energy more efficiently will

---

10. having too much gas in the stomach
11. going through a chemical reaction in which sugar changes to carbon dioxide and alcohol
12. (British English): fertilizers 13. removing trees from forests by cutting or burning
14. burning 15. Organization for Economic Cooperation and Development

---

16. (British English): stabilized 17. multiplied four times

need economic incentives. For the more expensive that carbon-rich energy becomes, the greater the incentive to introduce technologies to save it. If governments rely on information alone to persuade people to buy more efficient cars or insulate their homes, people may well use their savings to drive their efficient cars more often, or to turn up the central-heating thermostat.[18] If so, their demand for energy will not decline.

Rich countries shelter energy prices in various ways. ("Look at the cost of sending a 200-ship flotilla to the Persian Gulf to keep the oilways open," grumbles[19] Mr. Mintzer. "That doesn't show up in oil price. it's buried in the defence[20] budget.") Most Third World countries subsidise the consumption of electricity, natural gas, and coal. Countries with subsidised energy use it less efficiently than those where it is expensive. Indeed, Third World countries account for some of the most appalling examples of energy waste. Like Egypt, which uses a quarter of its electricity (subsidised, inevitably) to drive one vast aluminium plant, in a land that produces no bauxite.[21]

The best way to make sure that the price of energy reflects the damage it does to the environment is to tax it. Governments are showing a wary but growing interest in the concept of a carbon fee: a tax that would be levied on fossil-based fuels proportionately to the amount of carbon they contain. The effect would be to make coal dearer[22] than oil, and oil dearer than natural gas. Even in the United States, the administration is worrying increasingly about the effects of allowing the price of petrol[23] to fall to its lowest level in real terms since the Korean war. Next year the United States will again be dependent for more than half its energy on imported oil. It would not be surprising if

something called, perhaps, an "atmospheric users' fee" were prepared for next year's budget.

The scope for saving energy from existing technology is clearly enormous. A switch to greater efficiency could be speeded up by rules to set minimum standards for cars, domestic equipment and the insulation of new buildings, as well as by insisting on the labelling of domestic appliances to show how much energy they use. The more industry and domestic users get clear information on the amount of energy they are using and how they might reduce it, the faster they are likely to respond.

[. . .]

Quite apart from using energy more efficiently, people will need to use different fuels. In particular, they will need to switch away from coal, even though the world's proven reserves of that fuel vastly exceed those of oil and natural gas. But burning oil releases 70% as much carbon dioxide as coal, natural gas, 50% as much.

Only one way of generating electricity is now commercially viable and produces no carbon dioxide: nuclear power. Plenty of evidence suggests that nuclear power is a worse buy in terms of energy efficiency, if only because of its huge capital cost and lengthy payback period. But any programme[24] to stop global warming will almost certainly have to include a large expansion of nuclear power. This is awkward for many greens, whose first and deepest sentiment is a hatred of nuclear power. Several countries now have a moratorium[25] on new nuclear plants. In Sweden the government has even committed itself to phasing out its nuclear stations by 2010.

Many developing countries, having embarked hopefully on nuclear programmes in the early 1970s, have found them plagued by delays and cost over-runs. The sheer size of investment needed to build even one plant makes nuclear power intimidating for coun-

---

18. a device for controlling equipment, such as furnaces or air-conditioning, to regulate temperature   19. quietly express discontentment or unhappiness   20. (British English): defense   21. the principal mineral of aluminum   22. more expensive   23. (British English):

gasoline   24. (British English): program   25. a stop or suspension of an action or a practice tries with little foreign-borrowing capacity. The World Bank refuses to lend for nuclear programmes. Above all, developed countries will worry about the security implications of putting more nuclear capacity in countries which may turn out to be hostile, or irresponsible, or simply inept. With China sitting on one-third of the world's known coal reserves, it will be hard choice.

Comprehension and Discussion

A. *Circle the correct answer. If the answer is false, tell why.*

1. The process of global warming is irreversible.

True   False

2. The increase in oil prices had a major effect on the level of carbon emissions.

True   False

3. The assumptions that Mintzer made about the possible stabilization of global warming were unrealistic.

True   False

4. Although gasoline is cheap in the United States, the price has gone up a great deal from what it used to be.

True   False

B. *Answer the following questions as completely as possible.*

1. How does the cost of gasoline in your country compare with that of the United States? Do you think the cost has anything to do with how much gas people use?

2. Briefly explain why it may be difficult to predict how the greenhouse effect will affect the planet. Explain first in general terms, and then give specific examples.

3. The article gives a number of factors which contribute to global warming and both the possibilities of and problems with trying to do anything about them. Tell how the following are produced and what can and cannot be done (or would be very difficult to do) about them and why:

    a. CFCs
    b. methane
    c. nitrous oxide
    d. carbon dioxide emissions

4. What is the problem with energy conservation as a means of slowing down global warming?

5. Explain how taxes and the use of existing technology could be helpful in the fight against global warming.

6. What are the problems with the use of nuclear energy?

7. What do you feel can and should be done about energy use and global warming?

Word Forms

Working with a partner, complete the following chart with the different forms of the words. Use your knowledge of other words and their different forms to help you. Do not be afraid to guess. A dash means there is no form.

Noun	Verb	Adjective	Adverb
alteration		—	—
	—	awkward	
		conjectural	—
	embark	—	—
	enhance	—	—
	—	inept	
	—	viable	—
	—	wary	

Vocabulary Practice

Complete the sentences below with the correct words from the following list. You may have to use different word forms and tenses. Do not use a word more than once.

Sentences 1 - 6	**Sentences 7 - 13**
awkward	offset
tackle	intrigue
embark	wary
viable	crucial
alter	inept
conjectural	intimidate
enhance	curb
swamp	untangle

1. Many industrialized countries have _____ on a variety of efforts, such as taxes, bans, financial incentives, etc., to cut down on the use of energy.

2. Most Third World countries are too (a.) _____ with the problem of how to feed their people to think about (b.) _____ or cutting down on the type of fuel they use. They are more worried about (c.) _____ the life of their people now than doing something about a problem that may or may not occur in 50 years.

3.   Developed countries might feel a certain degree of _____ in asking developing countries to give up or cut down on using fuels which they have plenty of and which are cheap for them.

4.   Disagreements in international conferences can be difficult _____ because of the different interests, politics, and resources of each country.

5.   Some scientists _____ that by the year 2030, the mean temperature of the world will have risen by almost 2° C.

6.   If global warming and population growth continue according to some of the worst-case scenarios, the _____ of the planet could be in question.

7.   Because so many unpredictable factors are involved, sometimes it can be difficult to _____ facts from guesses.

8.   One of the fears of nuclear power is that great danger could be caused simply by the (a.) _____ of a worker in a nuclear power station. Government and company officials say that this danger is (b.) _____ by controls built into the system to override human error.

9.   Although coal is the dirtiest fossil fuel, _____ on its use would be virtually impossible because it is also the most abundant.

10. Since some developing countries have great reserves of coal, they will need financial incentives, not threats or _____, to cut down or eliminate the use of this highly polluting fuel.

11. Even though environmentalists have been _____ by the use of solar power for many years, it is still considered experimental and has some problems to be worked out.

12. The developed countries are _____ about giving developing countries the ability to have nuclear power.

13. Whether one believes in the negative effects of global warming or not, most people would agree it is _____ that something be done to help the environment.

Vocabulary Building

"Sir Crispin Tickell, Britain's ambassador to the United Nations, draws a *hair-raising* picture of a world in which changing climate might drive over 60 million people from their homes."

What kind of picture is a "hair-raising" one? It is one which *raises one's hair*, or *makes one's hair stand up*, an image we have of what happens when we are frightened—our hair stands up. English uses many of these metaphorical compound adjectives, in which a part of the body (or something related to the body or the self) is connected with a present participle. They are used to convey an image of a feeling or an action and can be more effective than an ordinary adjective.

A. *Look at the following verbs, and make sure that you understand what they mean. Then, working in small groups, look at the list of compound adjectives and try to guess what they mean. Write a synonym or a definition for each. Think of the action and what meaning it might convey. Notice that some of these words require a hyphen and some do not.*

tingle	shatter
wrack	curdle
boggle	

1. eye-opening . . .

2. stomach-turning . . .

*3. spine-tingling . . .

4. heartwarming . . .

5. breathtaking . . .

6. face-saving . . .

7. mouth-watering . . .

8. ear-shattering . . .

9. nerve-wracking (also nerve-racking) . . .

10. mind-boggling . . .

11. bloodcurdling . . .

12. eye-catching . . .

*13. sidesplitting . . .

14. backbreaking . . .

15. heartbreaking . . .

B. *Complete the following sentences with compound adjectives from the list above. In some of the sentences, more than one adjective may be possible. Be prepared to explain why you used each one. Try to use every adjective.*

1. When the accident first occurred at the Three Mile Island nuclear plant in Pennsylvania, nobody knew for sure how bad the possible radioactive fallout would be. For the people who lived in the area, not knowing whether they would be able to return to their homes or whether they had been affected by the radioactivity was a _____ experience.

2. How can he work in that disco and listen to that _____ music every night?

---

* These words are used more often in writing, such as advertising or film and book reviews, than in speaking.

3. It's nice for a change to see a movie that just makes you feel good, one with no crime, no violence or sex, just a good, old-fashioned _____ story.

4. The Grand Canyon is one of the most _____ sights I've ever seen.

5. I don't understand how you can watch those bloody horror movies. To me they are not even scary; they're just _____.

6. Until I spoke with him, I had never realized how dirty politics were. I guess I was just too innocent. That conversation was really _____. He taught me a great deal.

7. You wouldn't believe the _____ aromas that come out of that bakery.

8. Everyone knew that if he didn't resign he would be fired. Allowing him to resign was just a _____ device.

9. Last night I was sitting home alone when all of a sudden I heard this _____ scream. It really scared me, but I never found out where it came from.

10. It was _____ to see the reaction on his face when he found out he had been fired.

11. Whoever does the window designs for that store is great. They're always very _____.

12. I normally don't like comedies, but this movie was _____.

13. Where does she get the energy to do everything? She has a full-time job with a very high position, she takes graduate classes at night, she has three young children, and she's a gourmet cook. It's _____ how she does it all.

14. Working on a farm may sound like fun, but it's really _____ work.

15. The review of her new book, a mystery, called it _____. The reviewer suggested not reading it if you are home alone at night.

C. *All of the words in this exercise, except* spine-tingling *and* mouth-watering, *can also be used as* verb + (possessive) + object. *(The conversation with him really opened my eyes.) Some are used more commonly in this way than others.*

Rewrite sentences 3-6, 8-11, and 13-14, changing the form from compound adjective to verb + object. (The possessive is not used with face-saving. *The article* the *is often used after* boggle. Breathtaking *becomes* take one's breath away.) *You may have to change some other words in the sentences. Just keep the meaning.*

Focus on Form: Count and Noncount Nouns in Comparisons

Comparisons of Proportion

A. *Count and Noncount Nouns*

Nouns in English, as in many languages, are divided into two groups: *count nouns*—those which can be counted and made plural *(people)*—and *noncount nouns*—those which are considered a mass and cannot be made plural *(coal)*. One of the main problems with the difference between these nouns is when we quantify or compare them.

> If that happens, the world may eventually be able to support *fewer people* than it can be today.

> Most scientists agree that one of the first steps is to get people to use *less coal*.

Some nouns may be both count and noncount depending on the meaning. Often the substance is noncount while the type, kind, or material is count. For example:

> Much less *gas* is needed to heat a house if it is insulated. (the substance or general term). (NC)

> Many different *gases* contribute to global warming. (types of *gases*) (C)

> We need to produce cars that don't use much *fuel*. (NC)

> There are many *fuels* that are less polluting than coal. (C)

Noncount Nouns

quantifier	+	*more* or *less*	+	noncount nouns

a little
far
a lot (informal)
much   + more or less + coal
quite a bit
a great deal

<table>
<tr><td></td><td colspan="2">**Count Nouns**</td></tr>
<tr><td>quantifier</td><td>+ *more* or *fewer*</td><td>+ count nouns</td></tr>
<tr><td>a few (+ more)
far
a lot (informal)
many
quite a few
a great many</td><td>+ *more* or *fewer**</td><td>+ people</td></tr>
</table>

_____

* Since *few* means *not many*, using quantifiers such as *many*, *a great many* or *a lot* seems contradictory. Although it is not wrong to say *many fewer*, we would normally say *far fewer*.

Grammar Practice

Decide whether the nouns in parentheses in the sentences below are count or noncount. Remember that this may change from sentence to sentence depending on the meaning. Then, according to the noun and the meaning of the sentence, decide whether to use more *or* less/fewer. *Use quantifying words with each one. If the noun is countable, make it plural. You may have to choose the correct verb form.*

1. If we want to do something to help the environment, we have to start by using (fossil fuel) _____ as energy sources.

2. One problem is that there is/are (coal) _____ in the world than natural gas.

3. If they had to make a choice, (country) _____ would probably do what is economically more important for their citizens than what is good for the environment.

4. Although carbon dioxide emissions are what we hear about the most, natural processes emit (gas) _____ which would be harder to curb.

5. People had (interest) _____ in the environment 40 years ago.

6. The United States uses (energy) _____ per capita than any other country in the world.

7. Generally speaking, a small car uses (gas) _____ than a large one.

8. People in developing countries use (energy) _____ because they have (appliance, and machine) _____. Most work is done by hand.

9. Because of the high cost and the fears of possible dangers, there will probably be (nuclear power) _____ used in developing countries.

10. Today we have (people) _____ and (natural resource) _____ than we did 100 years ago.

11. The industrialized countries have (population growth) _____ than the developing countries do.

12. Industries are producing (chlorofluorocarbon) _____ today than they did before.

13. Critics contend that (research) _____ could be done to find alternative sources of energy.

14. According to the article, some of the countries of Eastern Europe have (pollution) _____ than the United States or Western Europe do.

15. (possibility) _____ must be explored if we want to continue our standard of living and slow down the damage to the planet.

Focus on Form: *few* vs. *a few, little* vs. *a little*

Positive Connotation	**Negative Connotation**
a few = some (Count)	*few* = not many (Count)
a little = some (Noncount)	*little* = not much (Noncount)

Grammar Practice

Decide whether the noun is count or noncount. Then decide from the context of the sentence if the connotation is positive (some) or negative (not many). Choose few, a few, little, *or* a little *for each of the following.*

1. It is true that we have made _____ progress in controlling pollutants, such as CFCs, but much more needs to be done.

2. _____ developing countries are willing to spend money on non-polluting energy. So much that needs to be done for their people now, and pollution is seen as a problem that has been caused by the industrialized nations.

3. _____ countries have already put bans on most aerosol use.

4. If we all just paid _____ more attention to how we used energy, we could help to contain the problem.

5. Although a great deal of focus has been put on the deforestation of the Brazilian rain forest, _____ attention has been paid to the cutting down of trees in Alaska.

6. _____ can be done about the emissions of gases from fermenting rice paddies, rotting waste, or flatulent animals.

7. Although some of what we know about global warming is conjecture, _____ people would say that nothing should be done to protect the environment.

8. Although many countries would suffer from global warming, _____ countries might actually profit from it, at least in the short run.

9. _____ governments would be willing to take measures to protect the future of the environment if it meant causing unemployment now.

10. An increase of _____ degrees in the earth's temperature may seem insignificant, but many experts feel it could have devastating effects.

Focus on Form: Comparisons of Proportion

Comparisons of proportion show how two things are proportionally related to each other. The more or less one thing happens, the more or less another does. As one goes up or down in degree, so does the other.

> *The more expensive* carbon-rich energy becomes, *the greater* the incentive to introduce technologies to save it.

Comparisons of proportion:

- can be used with nouns, adjectives, and adverbs.
- follow the same rules as regular comparisons:
  - *-er* for adjectives of one syllable (or two syllables if they end in *-y, -ow, -er*) (Example 1 below)
  - *more* + adjectives of two or more syllables (Example 2)
  - *more* or *less* + adverbs (Example 3)
  - *less* + noncount nouns
  - *fewer* + count nouns*

    1. The *dearer* gas is, the less we will use.

    2. *The more expensive* that carbon-rich energy becomes, the greater the incentive to save it.

3. The *less efficiently* a car runs, the more pollution it causes.

- Note that the two clauses of proportion are separated by a comma.

---

* However: *The less people use, the better.* Here *the less* is not referring to people. It is referring to an unmentioned but understood noun—energy. The complete sentence would be "The less energy (that) people use..." *Less* may also be used adverbially, answering the questions "how often," "to what extent," "to what degree," etc.

The *fewer people* who use it, the better. (It is better if not many people use it.)

The *less people* use it, the better. (It is better if people use it less frequently.)

Grammar Practice

Using the information in the following sentences, write new sentences with comparisons of proportion. There may be more than one way to express the ideas and you may have to change the words. Keep the same ideas, and try to use a variety of forms. The first one has been done for you.

1. If we don't drive our cars too much, they will not wear out quickly, and we won't have to buy new ones so often.

    The less we drive, the less quickly our cars will wear out and the less often we will have to buy new ones.

    The less often we drive our cars, the longer they will last and the fewer we will have to buy.

2. Because we don't buy new cars very often, car manufacturers do not need to make so many.

3. If car manufacturers lower the production of cars, they won't need to employ so many people.

4. When there is a high rate of unemployment, the crime rate goes up.

5. If the streets become dangerous, people are likely to stay at home.

6. If people don't go out, some businesses will close.

7. If restaurants and nightspots don't do a lot of business, downtown areas will quickly become deserted.

8. When neighborhoods don't have many people, other people don't want to go there very much. Other businesses are also affected a lot.

9. Consequently, if we drive our cars more, the economy will be better.

Discussion

The ideas expressed in the previous exercise take a certain way of thinking to an extreme. Do you agree with these ideas, either totally or to any extent? Do you see any fallacy or faulty logic in this type of thinking?

Grammar Practice

Complete the following sentences with your own ideas. Use a comparison of proportion in each one.

1. The more expensive gasoline is, . . .

2. The less we spend on environmental research now, . . .

3. The larger the hole in the ozone layer, . . .

4. The longer we wait to do something about global warming, . . .

5. The (more/fewer) countries with nuclear power, . . .

6. The more we expose ourselves to sunlight, . . .

7. The richer a country, . . .

8. The better educated people are, . . .

9. The younger children learn about the environment, . . .

10. The greater the economic disparity between . . .

Reading 2: "How Hard Will It Be?"

Prereading Questions

1. Imagine three simple, everyday changes that people can make in their lives, particularly in what they buy and how they use products, that might help the environment. If everyone, or even the majority of people, were to follow these changes, can you imagine any negative consequences that might result?

2. Why might a government hesitate to pass legislation that would be of benefit to the environment?

3. What problems might occur if all of the nations of the world try to sign a treaty to protect the environment?

Vocabulary Practice

Match the italicized words in the following sentences with the synonyms or definitions in the lists below. Use the context of the sentence to help you guess the meaning.

Sentences 1 - 10

___ spread out investments or business activities; vary

___ made impure; polluted

___ basic installations for the functioning of a government, national or local

___ a very large, indefinite number

___ very wasteful; extravagant

___ promise to give up or not to do something

___ be successful; grow well

___ the process of exhausting; using up and taking away

___ lessen in relative importance

___ complete display

Sentences 11 - 20

___ a superficial story to show or illustrate a deeper point

___ difficult position

___ move without any additional effort or acceleration; do the same as before

___ obvious; noticeable

___ abundant; large in number

___ amount produced; profit on an investment

___ stimulate; urge

___ eliminate gradually; one step at a time

___ widely and unfavorably known

___ miserably

1. It's because our *profligate* ways have done so much harm that large-scale change is inevitable.

2. Unemployment anywhere is a *drain* on the country's resources everywhere.

3. If the car company's managers deserve their opulent salaries, they probably will have *diversified* in those directions before the car market dries up entirely.

4. The major manufacturers who convert to new products or technologies, in time, will *flourish*.

5. There's all that national *infrastructure*—the decaying water and sewage systems, the rusted and worn bridges, tunnels and public buildings, which need to be rebuilt.

6. Some of the *myriad* new jobs that open up will not attract the skilled worker who has lost his job.

7. The water will soon be *contaminated* again by airborne pollution.

8. Even the Great Crash of October 1929, might *pale* alongside that sudden fall that might occur in the future.

9. For example, the effects of global warmup—even severe warmup accompanied with the whole *panoply* of ills like high sea-level rise and violent weather—aren't going to affect everybody in the world to the same degree.

10. Do we Americans have any right to ask an African, Asian, or Latin American peasant to *foreswear* any hope of ever owning a car or a dishwasher, or of flying in a jet plane?

11. Few Third World people are going to be willing to abandon their hopes of making their own lives better for the prospect of some abstract future good; not while they can see every day, on their little black-and-white village television sets, that the rest of us are enjoying *copious* quantities of these things already.

12. It is not merely peasants who will be less than overjoyed at the prospect of making economic sacrifices. Some highly industrialized societies are in similar *straits*, if not worse ones.

13. The most *conspicuous* of these industrialized societies that will have to make economic sacrifices are the nations of Eastern Europe.

14. But most of all, the driving force was simply a hunger for a better life, for the good life of material well-being that Communism had promised and so *abjectly* failed to provide.

15. We have already seen that the industries of the countries of the former Warsaw Pact are *notoriously* the dirtiest and most destructive in the world.

16. Hardin expresses the "tragedy of the commons" in an *allegory*, which goes like this: In a certain village twenty families live...

17. And the ultimate effect is that now there are forty cows on a pasture that can't support more than twenty. It isn't just a matter of lowered milk *yields* now.

18. Let's say that in the first legislative bundle are such relatively moderate, preliminary measures as a total ban on CFCs,...., *phasing out* many bombers, missiles, tanks, and warships, reducing troop levels and closing many military bases.

19. Therefore X can *coast* along in the good old-fashioned, high-polluting way.

20. The only thing that *spurs* us on to try to solve the problems is that we don't have a choice.

How Hard Will It Be?

By ISAAC ASIMOV and FREDERIK POHL
(from the book *Our Angry Earth*)

Make no mistake about it, our environmental problems mean that large-scale changes lie ahead. Businesses will be harmed, people will have to change their jobs. The reason for this isn't that do-gooder[26] environmentalists like ourselves insist on it because of some idealistic devotion to "nature" or the spotted owl.[27] It's because our profligate ways have done so much harm that large-scale change is *inevitable.* The only choice we have—the only future we can invent—lies in deciding which *kinds* of change will be best in the long run, the ones that will come about because we try to clean the world up, or the worse ones that will come about on their own if we don't.

The fact that many people will lose their jobs is bad news for them. It isn't good news for anybody else, either. Unemployment anywhere is a drain on the country's resources everywhere. Adding to it is not a plus. This growth in joblessness won't happen because anyone wishes it to. It will happen inevitably, simply because there is no way to avoid it. If we drive our cars less, they will wear out more slowly and fewer cars will have to be built to replace them; therefore jobs will be lost in Detroit (and in Osaka and many other places around the world). If we recycle paper, fewer trees will have to be cut down to make new pulp;[28] whereupon many of the men and women whose jobs depend on lumbering will lose them. If we cut down on the burning of fossil fuel, oil workers and coal miners will be laid off.

But if we *don't* do those things, we face a future of disease, scarcity, and discomfort . . . at best.

Those of us who are not directly personally affected by the changes environmental dislocations will bring about can take some philosophical comfort from reflecting that all these things are going to be happening in a good cause. That isn't likely to cheer a newly unemployed person up, but there's a bright side here, too. Although many jobs will disappear, many new ones will be created and more often than not the new jobs will be better than the old.

Does the local automobile factory close down because no one's buying new cars right now? Too bad; but the fact that people don't want to drive cars very much any more doesn't mean they're willing to quit traveling entirely. They'll be customers for the trains, perhaps the magnetic levitation trains[29] we talked about earlier. Somebody is going to have to build those maglev trains, as well as the light street rail systems and the monorails and the new fuel-stingy[30] aircraft. If the car company's managers deserve their opulent salaries, they probably will have diversified in those directions before the car market dries up entirely. After all, they did

---

26. a person who is always trying to do good actions. Used in a derogatory way to describe an obsession with these actions   27. a type of owl (a large, nocturnal bird) which is considered rare and in danger of extinction   28. ground up, softened wood used to make paper   29. a very fast train which uses a magnetic effect to make the train rise above the ground to avoid friction and allows the trains to go faster   30. cheap (normally about a person); derogatory

so very well once before when, under the stresses of World War II, they switched over to a completely new product line of tanks and Army trucks and bombers as easily and successfully as they had made cars before. The major manufacturers who convert, in time will flourish. The ones who don't, won't.

Then there are all those homes to retrofit[31] and the new ones to build. There's all that national infrastructure—the decaying water and sewage systems, the rusted and worn bridges, tunnels and public buildings—which need to be rebuilt before they collapse entirely from their present decades of neglect. If lumbering[32] slows down to a crawl,[33] there are whole huge new industries to create in the Pacific Northwest, like fish farming in the mouths of the great rivers, or building and tending power-generating windmill farms, or even "agriforestry" to provide food from clear-cut lands. There is a great need, which will surely become a greater one as our population ages, for health workers of every kind, from paramedics to RNs or even MDs.

Some of the myriad new jobs will not attract the skilled worker, but we have all those unskilled workers who are now cut out of the job market entirely. For them there will be service jobs, some traditional, like working in fast-food stores, and some relatively new, like sorting trash for recycling. The social value of creating jobs of this sort is immense; it can convert welfare clients into productive wage-earners. But probably most of the new jobs will actually be better ones than the old, at least in the sense that they are less damaging to the health and the spirit than mining coal or working on a heavy-industry assembly line.

So there will be plenty of new jobs.

We should face the fact, though, that such consolations will be of little comfort to the man or woman who is put out of work in the prime of life, since he or she will have no guarantee of getting one of those better jobs—if any job at all. The only certainty for these unemployed is that their painfully acquired working skills and experience will never again be wanted.

The other fact we must face is that, sadly, there is very little chance that any of us will see any real benefit from all our environmental efforts right away.

It is impossible for us to make things instantly better, no matter what we do. We can't. The best we can achieve is to prevent them from getting unspeakably worse. The damage to the ozone layer won't go away; in fact, it will increase, at least for a time, no matter how hard we work to limit it. Nor will the global warming stop, nor will our destroyed soil and water return at once.

Even so simple and local a thing as cleaning up a body of water won't produce immediate results that we can see. If you somehow manage to make your nearest lake sparkly clean, it won't stay that way. It will soon be contaminated again by airborne pollution unless a great many other people, living hundreds or thousands of miles away, also act.

Indeed, in the case of some very highly polluted rivers, the first effects[34] of a cleanup may make them look worse than ever before. As the cleaner waters begin to dissolve out the accumulated sediments of generations at the bottom of the riverbed, lumps and clumps of filthy pollution are likely to break free and float away on the surface.

---

31. to fix traditional houses so that they will accommodate new energy and fuel-saving devices   32. cutting down trees (timber) to be prepared as building material   33. barely moving   34. one thing affecting another, which affects another, etc. ripple = small wave

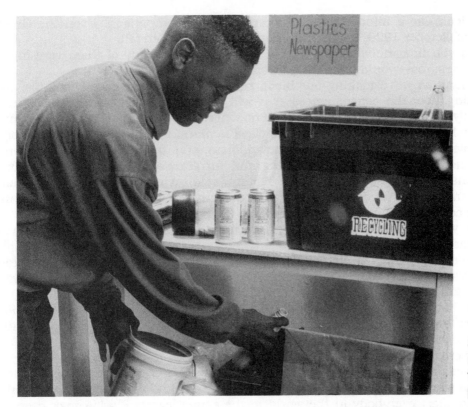

Separating and recycling garbage is the law in many places today.

And the final, in some ways the scariest, consequence of environmental action we must face is the ripple effect from the inevitable economic changes.

Let's take a deep breath, brace ourselves[35] and do that now.

Let's suppose that tomorrow the American government decides to put the necessary environmental measures into effect at once. Congress passes the necessary bills, and the President signs them into law.

Let's say that in that first legislative bundle are such relatively moderate, preliminary measures as a total ban on all CFCs, a fifty-cent-per-gallon tax on gasoline to cut consumption, a stiff requirement that the cars of the near future average 50 miles per gallon, a three-cent tax on every kilowatt-hour of electricity produced by the burning of fossil fuel, and even a cutback on military excesses by abandoning a dozen new weapons systems, phasing out many bombers, missiles, tanks and warships, reducing troop levels, and closing many military bases.

For starters, can you imagine what that kind of simultaneous bad news about autos, oil companies, public utilities, and defense manufacturers—the bluest of blue chips[36]—will do to the stock market? The October 1987 one-day drop of more than 500 points in the Dow-Jones averages [37] (which meant that one-fifth of the dollar value of every American stock investment disappeared in a single day)

---

35. get ready for danger or a shock; hold oneself steady   36. highly valued and priced stocks   37. an average of a selected number of good quality stocks

would look like a minor "technical correction" by comparison. Even the Great Crash of October 1929[38] might pale alongside that sudden fall.

Can you imagine what the loss of all those jobs—many of them very high-paying jobs, too—would do to the national unemployment figures?

As long as we're making our blood run cold with worst-case scenarios, try imagining, too, the consequences that will inevitably follow as some of these suddenly unemployed homeowners can no longer meet their mortgage[39] payments and are foreclosed;[40] as upper-middle-class families, accustomed to having considerable disposable incomes[41] but now jobless, stop buying new cars, TV sets, VCRs, household appliances, clothing and furniture—cut back on travel and vacations—begin to sell off their own accumulated savings, in the form of stocks, bonds and mutual funds, so that they can meet their living expenses . . . and thus further contribute to the plunging market?

Can you imagine a Congress voting for, and a President signing, laws that will do all that to the economy?

And even if we can stretch our imaginations that far, so that we can persuade ourselves that the United States would be willing to take the first dose[42] of this unpleasant medicine, what about the rest of the world?

For that may be the hardest part of all. If it seems that it will be difficult for America to change, consider what those changes mean for most of the other 140-odd[43] countries in the world.

The environmental problem is not an equal-opportunity threat.

For example, the effects of global warmup—even severe warmup accompanied with the whole panoply of ills like high sea-level rise and violent weather—aren't going to affect everybody in the world to the same degree. Florida may have to worry about how high the ocean tides will rise. Switzerland has no such fear. If the American midwest suffers crop losses from a radical climate change, the Sahel,[44] for instance, may actually find that in the changing precipitation[45] patterns their own climate has improved.

In that event, what should we expect? Can we ask the Sahelians to join with us in preventing what will actually for them be a blessing? And if we do ask, will they agree? Will they, for instance, display enough charity to overlook the fact that we, not they, are the ones who have actually created the problem?

To make a difficult problem even more complicated, it is unfortunately true that some parts of the human race may find themselves better off with a limited amount of global warming. It is also true that, as in the case of the Sahel, a good many of those areas are presently impoverished and indeed desperate in the face of the living conditions they now endure. How do we persuade those people to cooperate? It is a good deal to ask of any nation that it turn down a possible improvement in its own miserable lot for the sake of keeping our comparatively fortunate one from getting worse.

Even for Third World countries which would not benefit from the climate changes, we can't realistically expect them to stay undeveloped simply because it suits our convenience.

---

38. the stock market crash of 1929   39. a loan for property   40. take away property for lack of payment of a mortgage or taxes   41. income available to spend on things that are not necessities   42. a specific quantity, usually of a medicine; an amount of something unpleasant   43. more or less 140   44. semi-arid region of Africa, south of the Sahara, which suffered a devastating drought   45. any form of rain or snow

Some moralists might raise that as a question in ethics: Do we Americans have any right to ask an African, Asian, or Latin American peasant to foreswear any hope of ever owning a car or a dishwasher, or of flying in a jet plane? But as a practical matter, whether moral considerations would let us do that or not, we won't have the privilege of making that decision.

Whether or not we ask them to abstain, few Third World people are going to be willing to abandon their hopes of making their own lives better for the prospect of some abstract future good—not while they can see every day, on their little black-and-white village television sets, that the rest of us are enjoying copious quantities of these things already.

It is not merely peasants who will be less than overjoyed at the prospect of making economic sacrifices. Some highly industrialized societies are in similar straits, if not worse ones.

The most conspicuous of them are the nations of Eastern Europe. Miraculously and wholly unexpectedly, they threw off the state Communism that ruled them for nearly half a century. It wasn't entirely ideology that caused that astonishing revolution. The desire for free speech, free elections, and all the other freedoms certainly played a part. But most of all, the driving force was simply a hunger for a better life—for better food, more conveniences, more of all worldly goods—for, in short, the good life of material well-being that Communism had promised and so abjectly failed to provide.

We have already seen that the industries of the countries of the former Warsaw Pact[46] are notoriously the dirtiest and most destructive in the world, and the ones most in need of reform for all our sakes.

And yet, if it comes to a choice between either cleaning their industries up or, alternatively, producing more goods for the people of those countries—as it surely will at least in the short term—which way do you think they will decide? For that matter, which way would you decide?

What we have here, in effect, is one more example of the unhappy economic principle which Garrett Hardin calls "the tragedy of the commons."[47]

Hardin expresses it in an allegory, which goes like this: In a certain village twenty families live, and they share a common greensward[48] which can pasture their household milk cows. The commons is just big enough to support exactly twenty cows. As long as each family puts just one cow out to pasture there, there will be plenty of grass for all of them, and all will have milk.

That's a good steady-state arrangement, as long as it stays that way.

If, however, one family puts two cows there, none of the cows will get quite enough to eat. The difference won't be large. None of the animals will starve, but their straitened diet means that each one of them will produce a little less milk each day. The total volume of milk the village's cows produce altogether will be pretty much the same, but it will be divided by twenty-one instead of by twenty.

What's the effect of this change?

It's an immoral one: selfishness triumphs. The selfish family that has put an extra cow on the common now has nearly twice as much milk as it had before . . . but each of the other families has to get along with a little less.

So, seeing this, enlightened self-interest causes each of the other families to put in a second cow as well. . .

---

46. former Soviet-bloc countries that had signed a mutual-protection agreement. **47.** a piece of land used by an entire community 48. green grass area

And the ultimate effect is that now there are forty cows on a pasture that can't support more than twenty. It isn't just a matter of lowered milk yields now. After a while the whole herd starves to death.

Each family, you see, has acted rationally according to its own best understanding of what will serve its interests. The tragedy that results is that the effect of all this "rational" individual behavior has collectively ruined them all.

In just the same way, a cooperative strategy for dealing with the assaults on our global environment will promote the general good. . . but it may be to the advantage of some nations and some individuals to act contrary to it.

That's the cheating problem in a nutshell.

Country X will well understand that it, along with all the rest of the world, is threatened by increasing carbon dioxide emissions . . . but its leaders may reason that if everybody *else* does the no doubt difficult and expensive things necessary to deal with the problem, the relatively small damage that will be done to the environment by the Xians won't make any real difference. Therefore X can coast along in the good, old-fashioned, high-polluting way—and be able to outcompete the rest of the world in the price of their export manufactures while they do it, since they won't have to pay the bill for the sacrifices.

How can we deal with that?

We can start by trying to persuade every country in the world to sign appropriate treaties, of course. But then what do we do if some countries cheat, or refuse to sign in the first place? Do we declare war on them?

The longer we look at the problems, the harder they seem. The only thing that spurs us on to try to solve them is that we don't have a choice: the costs of not solving the problems are even higher.

 ## Comprehension and Discussion

A. *Circle the correct answer. If the answer is false, tell why.*

1. The writers say that unless we change our profligate ways, large-scale change is inevitable.

    True   False

2. Good company managers will know how to change to other products when the products they make are less in demand.

    True   False

3. The writers admit that if we make changes in our life-style to help the environment, some people will be hurt and some of them will never recover.

    True   False

4. Although it isn't possible to make environmental conditions better very soon, by working to clean up the world and by making changes in how we live, there will be improvement.

    True   False

B. *Answer the following questions as completely as possible.*

1. Briefly explain how actions that are good for the environment could have negative effects and how these negative effects can be turned into positive ones. Explain the general idea first, and then give examples to prove the ideas.

2. Explain, in your own words, how the environmental problem is not an "equal-opportunity threat" and what consequences this inequality has.

3. What different reasons are given that would make it difficult to ask Third World countries to cooperate in plans to help stop global warming? Give as many as possible.

4. How does the "tragedy of the commons" relate to environmental pollution?

5. The writers state that we should try to persuade every country in the world to sign treaties to protect the environment. Then they ask, "what do we do if some countries cheat, or refuse to sign in the first place?" What is your opinion? What should or can be done in this case? What can be done to insure that all countries follow international agreements concerning the environment?

6. A number of ethical issues are brought up in this reading. Does a country have the right to pass legislation that may put people out of work for the sake of an effect on the environment that may be conjectural? Do rich countries have the right to expect poor countries to sacrifice when the poor countries might actually benefit from climate changes? Or do rich countries have the right to ask poor countries to give up technologies which helped make the rich countries rich in the first place? What is your opinion on these questions or any others you can think of relating to this topic?

Word Forms

Working with a partner, complete the following chart with the different forms of the words. Use your knowledge of other words and their different forms to help you. Do not be afraid to guess. A dash means there is no form.

Noun	Verb	Adjective	Adverb
—	—		abjectly
allegory	—		
	—	conspicuous	
	contaminate	—	—
	—	copious	
	diversify	—	—
1. ...	—	notorious	
2. ...	—	—	—
	—	profligate	

Vocabulary Practice

Complete the sentences below with the correct words from the following lists. You may have to use different word forms and tenses. Do not use a word more than once.

Sentences 1 - 5	Sentences 6 - 10
abjectly	coast
pale	allegory
myriad	copious
foreswear	drain
contaminate	panoply
profligate	spur
flourish	notorious
straits	yield
diversify	phase out
infrastructure	conspicuous

1. One of the problems with ecological issues is that when a country uses materials or methods that pollute the environment, the _____ does not just stay in that country. Pollution does not respect borders.

2. Even many of the developed countries are in very serious economic (a.) _____ these days. The (b.) _____ social problems of the cities require a great deal of money to overcome. In addition, the long-neglected (c.) _____ has to be repaired or replaced before it is too late.

3. However, the economic problems of the developed countries (a.) _____ by comparison with those of many developing nations. Many people in Third World countries are living in (b.) _____ poverty. Is it fair for developed societies which, by comparison, are (c.) _____ to ask poorer ones to sacrifice?

4. Poor countries contend that it is the (a.) _____ of the rich countries that has caused most of the environmental problems. Consequently, the rich have no right to ask the poor to (b.) _____ the use of the same technology which the rich used to become rich.

5. The poor countries say that if we want them to cut down on the use of fossil fuel and to _____ the types of fuel they use, we should help them financially.

6. During the Cold War, (a.) _____ amounts of money were spent for a (b.) _____ of weapons. Opponents of this spending felt that too much money was being (c.) _____ away from the serious social problems of the country.

7. Some people feel it is necessary for world peace to maintain these weapons. Others feel that it is time to _____ many of the weapons and to use the savings for social or environmental problems.

8. It is well-known that the United States is the most (a.) _____ consumer of energy in the world. Americans are (b.) _____ for their love of large cars, low-priced gasoline, central heating, and air-conditioning.

9. Environmentalists feel that some action must be taken now, that if we just (a.) _____, the earth may run out of time. They contend that although the investment may be expensive, the (b.) _____ will be worth the expense.

10. Governments do not often make or change policy based on the type of (a.) _____ presented by Asimov and Pohl. Unfortunately, it usually takes a major disaster to (b.) _____ governments on to action.

Focus on Form: Future Perfect Tense

If the car company's managers deserve their opulent salaries, they probably *will have diversified* (future perfect) in those directions before the car market dries up entirely. (They will diversify *some time before* the drying up of the car market.)

vs.

Some of the new myriad jobs *will not attract* (simple future) the skilled worker. (The new jobs will not attract the worker *when they happen.*)

The future perfect:

- is formed with *will* + *have* + the Past Participle *(-ed)*
- is formed in the passive with *will* + *have* + *been* + the Past Participle
- is formed in the continuous with *will* + *have* + *been* + Present Participle *(-ing)*
- is used to show an action that will be completed *before* another time or action in the future
- is replaced by the simple future with the verb *to be* + an adjective

(The sea level will very likely be *higher* by the year 2050.)

Grammar Practice

Complete the sentences with the correct form of the verb in parentheses. Decide between the simple future form or the future perfect. Be careful of the passive voice. In some sentences, both tenses may be possible.

1. It is doubtful that there (be) _____ a 50 percent cut of emissions of carbon dioxide by the middle of the next century.

2. Irving Mintzer, of the World Resources Institute, predicts that the world population (stabilize) _____ at about eight billion in the year 2075.

3. Mintzer also predicts that the industrialized countries (stop) _____ using CFCs by 2020.

4. Conventional wisdom says that consumers (pay) _____ high taxes for carbon-rich fuels in the next century.

5. Whether we take drastic measures or not, we can be almost sure that the earth (be) _____ warmer by the year 2050.

6. Unfortunately, by the time scientists know more about the size and timing of global warming, it (become) _____ more difficult to handle.

7. When the year 2075 arrives, coal (replace) _____ to a great extent by natural gas and by solar, nuclear, and renewable fuels.

8. By 2010, nuclear plants in Sweden (phase out) _____ completely.

9. We can only hope that the global warming (have, neg.) _____ devastating effects on the environment when the United Nations finally decides to take strong action.

10. In the late 1980s, the share of carbon emissions of poor countries was only about 15 percent while that of the rich countries was approximately 85 percent. By the year 2020, the share of poor countries (be) _____ significantly greater.

11. Between now and the year 2020, it is possible that the population of the poor countries (almost, double) _____, whereas the population of the rich counties (increase) _____ by about 15 percent.

12. Assuming that we continue to use oil as an energy source to the same degree that we use it now, it is possible that by 2050 the world's oil reserves (deplete) _____.

13. One of the difficulties of convincing people to change their habits is that the major effects of our actions today (take, neg.) _____ place for many years to come.

14. Although the world population is growing, the percent of growth per year has been slowing down. It is estimated that by the year 2030, the average annual population growth of the world (decrease) _____ for approximately 60 years. The average annual population growth of the world was just under 2 percent in 1970. In 2030 it (be) _____ less that 1%.

Grammar Practice

Write five sentences predicting what you think will have happened by (that is, before and up to) the year 2050. Your predictions may be about the population of your country or of the world, about the environment, employment, health problems, scientific, technological or medical advances, etc., or they may be personal.

1. . . .

2. . . .

3. . . .

4. . . .

5. . . .

Class Project

Work on one or more of these projects individually or in groups of two to three students. Then present your findings to the class.

1. Hold an international conference on global warming. Act as representatives of different countries, either from your own country or from any other country you choose. A good cross-section of countries, both developed and developing, should be represented. (The following countries should definitely have representation—the United States, China, Brazil.) How do you think your chosen country would react, for example, to the following proposals of the organizing committee:

    a. cutting down the use of carbon-rich fuels, particularly coal
    b. setting a specific target of maximum CO_2 emissions
    c. stopping or at least limiting deforestation
    d. levying higher taxes on energy, including gasoline, to cut down on use
    e. lowering the speed limit of cars
    f. stabilizing population growth through birth control
    g. putting a moratorium on the building of all nuclear power stations
    h. setting fuel efficiency standards for all new cars and energy efficiency levels for all electrical appliances
    i. imposing an economic boycott on countries that fail to meet these requirements or that are found "cheating"
    j. offering subsidies from developed countries to developing countries as an incentive to undertake environmentally responsible measures

    These proposals may be modified or eliminated. New proposals may be added. Countries of similar interests may group together to try to put pressure on other countries. Compromises may have to be made, but a treaty must be signed. (If you want to be more certain as to how your country might respond, go to the library and look up what happened at the Montreal Protocol in 1987, the 1992 U.N. Conference on Environment and Development in Brazil, or any other national or international meeting on the environment.

2. Recently, many books and articles have been written about what changes average people can make in their daily lives to help the environment. What can one do to be "environmentally responsible?" Find articles or books on this subject, and make a presentation to the class on what can be done on a daily basis to help our planet.

3. Find out what is being done in your community, city, or state to help the environment. For example, are there special regulations concerning the separation and disposal of garbage? Are there recycling centers? If there are, try to visit one. What else is being done in your community that could be termed "environmentally responsible?"

4. What is done in your country regarding garbage disposal, energy conservation, environmental consciousness raising, or anything else that is done to help the environment? Do you think that these efforts are more or less progressive than what you have seen or read about in the United States? How does pollution in your country or city compare to what you have seen in the United States? Why?

Discussion and Writing

Discuss the following topics, first in pairs or small groups and then with the teacher and the entire class. After your discussion, pick one (or more) of the topics and write an essay about it.

1. What steps should governments take to implement actions that will help the environment and slow down global warming? Be realistic in your recommendations; take into account economics, employment, and politics.

2. Do poor countries have an obligation to take measures to help slow down global warming even if it seems they will not be adversely affected by it? Should rich countries do anything to give poor countries an incentive to take these measures?

3. Two of the reasons given for not making drastic changes in the production of different types of machinery to make them more energy efficient, such as developing battery-driven automobiles on a large scale, are that it would be too expensive and it would have far-reaching effects on the economy and on employment. Defend or oppose this position.

4. Asimov and Pohl admit that "it may be to the advantage of some nations and some individuals to act contrary to" a cooperative strategy for dealing with problems in the environment. What can international organizations do to encourage countries to follow international environmental guidelines? What can be done if some countries cheat or refuse to cooperate?

5. Summarize the problem of global warming. What are its causes? What is being done and what else can be done about it? What do you think will happen in the future?

6. Discuss the issue of developed countries with a decreasing rate of population growth but a very high rate of energy use per capita vs. developing

countries with an increasing rate of population growth but a low rate of energy use. What is the responsibility of each in protecting the environment?

Word List

Below is a list of the new words, and their different forms, presented in this chapter.

Noun	Verb	Adjective	Adverb
		abject	abjectly
allegory		allegorical	allegorically
alteration	alter		
	coast		
conjecture	conjecture	conjectural	
conspicuousness		conspicuous	conspicuously
contamination	contaminate		
copiousness		copious	copiously
		crucial	crucially
diversification	diversify		
drain	drain		
embarkation	embark		
enhancement	enhance		
	flourish		
	foreswear		
ineptness		inept	ineptly
infrastructure			
intimidation	intimidate		
intrigue	intrigue		
		myriad	
notoriousness		notorious	notoriously
notoriety			
	offset		
	pale		
panoply			
	phase out		
profligacy		profligate	profligately
spur	spur		
straits			
	swamp		
	tackle		
	(un)tangle		
viability		viable	
yield	yield		

Part II Review

Grammar

Circle the best answer for each of the following sentences. Use only the information given in each sentence.

1. A friend of his recommended _____ in this school.

   a. him to study
   b. he studied
   c. that he study
   d. he studies

2. Q: Did you have a good trip here?
   A: If I _____, I wouldn't be so tired now.

   a. had had
   b. did
   c. had
   d. would

3. No sooner _____ the phone rang.

   a. did I close the door when
   b. I closed the door than
   c. had I closed the door when
   d. had I closed the door than

4. Her advisor arranged _____ the course for a grade of Pass/Fail.

   a. her to take
   b. for her to take
   c. that she takes
   d. she take

5. _____ information was given to the passengers, and they were angry at being kept uninformed.

   a. A little
   b. A few
   c. Little
   d. Few

6. The _____ people use fossil fuels, the better it is for the environment.

   a. fewer
   b. less
   c. few
   d. little

7. It is obvious _____ for a long time before they took the test.

   a. for them to study
   b. that they study
   c. they study
   d. that they studied

8. No matter what we do now, it is apparent that the population of the earth _____ considerably larger by the middle of the next century.

   a. will have been
   b. will be
   c. be
   d. is

9. In none of the travel books _____ a reference to this monument.

   a. I read did I find
   b. did I read I find
   c. did I read did I find
   d. I read I found

10. They _____ if the weather had been better.

    a. might stay
    b. might have been stayed
    c. might had stayed
    d. might have stayed

11. A _____ money was spent on the project than had been planned.

    a. great many more
    b. quite a bit
    c. great deal more
    d. lot of

12. Q: Did you have a car when you first came here?
    A: No. I wish I _____. I would have seen a lot more.

    a. did
    b. had had
    c. had
    d. would have

13. _____ their older sisters and mothers, who often had children late, many young women today say they would like to raise their children first and then go to work.

    a. Whereas
    b. In contrast
    c. Despite
    d. Unlike

14. Regardless of _____ Russian for years, she was unable to speak it.

    a. she studied
    b. her studying
    c. her having studied
    d. that she studied

15. His doctor said it was essential _____ to take the medicine regularly.

    a. that he not forget
    b. that he don't forget
    c. that he didn't forget
    d. not forgetting

16. Q: Do you have tickets to that concert?
    A: No. I wish I _____. It sounds like it's going to be great.

    a. had
    b. had had
    c. would have
    d. did

17. Unfortunately, she wasn't accepted to the school she wanted to go to. If she _____, she would be much happier now.

    a. were
    b. had
    c. had been
    d. was

18. When I was young, I always wished that I _____ a younger brother or sister.

    a. had had
    b. had
    c. have had
    d. would have had

19. They were able to give him _____ money but not enough to live on, so he had to work while he studied.

    a. a little
    b. a few
    c. little
    d. few

20. Korean families are similar to Japanese families in regard to _____.

    a. they are both traditional
    b. the importance of tradition
    c. the former is traditional and the latter is also
    d. their similarities

21. The student government made a proposal that a student _____ to choose whether to take a course for a letter grade or for Pass/Fail.

    a. allow
    b. allows
    c. be allowed
    d. is allowed

22. If you had done what you were supposed to do, we _____ in the situation we're in.

    a. wouldn't have been
    b. wouldn't be
    c. weren't
    d. hadn't been

23. I wish you (A.) _____ me you were going. If you (B.) _____, I (C.) _____ with you.

    (A.) a. told
          b. would tell
          c. had told
          d. had been told
    (B.) a. had
          b. would
          c. did
          d. were
    (C.) a. would go
          b. had gone
          c. would have gone
          d. will go

24. She finished the race despite _____ the oldest person ever to run in the marathon.

    a. that she was
    b. she being
    c. she was
    d. her being

25. A: She seems like such an intelligent person.
    B: I don't know. She wouldn't have done what she did if she _____ so intelligent.

    a. were
    b. was
    c. had been
    d. would have been

26. By the time you get here, I think he _____ all of the work.

    a. will finish
    b. has finished
    c. will have finished
    d. will be finishing

27. _____ people signed the petition, but not enough to stop the building from being torn down.

    a. Few
    b. Little
    c. A few
    d. A little

28. If they _____ a contract at the beginning, they might not be involved in this court battle.

    a. signed
    b. would have signed
    c. had signed
    d. would sign

29. Not until _____ the article _____ that he had won the contest.

    a. did I read . . . did I realize
    b. I read . . . I realized
    c. did I read . . . I realized
    d. I read . . . did I realize

30. I wish they _____ that noise. It's driving me crazy.

    a. had stopped
    b. stopped
    c. 'll stop
    d. 'd stop

31. _____ must be done to find alternative sources of energy.

    a. A great many more researches
    b. A great deal more research
    c. Quite a bit more researches
    d. Quite a few research

32. _____ a college education is usually free in many European countries, it can be quite expensive in the United States.

    a. Regardless of the fact that
    b. Unlike
    c. Whereas
    d. Conversely

33. The _____ we have about global warming, the _____ we can convince people of the need to do something.

    a. less evidence . . . less effectively
    b. fewer evidences . . . less effectively
    c. less evidence . . . less effective
    d. fewer evidences . . . less effective

34. Q: Are you going to visit your parents during the next vacation?
    A: I wish I _____, but I have too much work to do here.

    a. would be
    b. would
    c. were
    d. was

35. By the time he _____ his studies, he _____ here for five years.

    a. will finish . . . will have lived
    b. will finish . . . will have lived/will have been living
    c. finishes . . . will have lived/will have been living
    d. finishes . . . will have lived

Vocabulary

Circle the word which best completes the sentence.

1. The _____ response of the people to the proposed nuclear plant forced the politicians to change the location.

    a. contagious
    b. detestable
    c. vitriolic
    d. abject

2. The children _____ such a crazy story that their parents had to laugh even though they knew it was a lie.

    a. ventured
    b. concocted
    c. conjectured
    d. fostered

3. You have to be careful about how much you believe of his stories. He has a/an _____ to exaggerate.

    a. propensity
    b. hyperbole
    c. notoriety
    d. extolment

4. The people lived in such _____ misery that it was difficult to keep from crying when we saw them.

    a. hyperbolic
    b. myriad
    c. abject
    d. aftermath

5. He was so _____ by the news that he was unable to respond.

    a. traumatized
    b. taken for granted
    c. eroded
    d. grappled

6. When the police raided the gang's meeting place, they found a _____ of weapons, enough to wage a small war.

    a. profligacy
    b. plague
    c. proscription
    d. panoply

7. She had such a/an _____ way of speaking that her voice became famous everywhere.

    a. profligate
    b. intrinsic
    c. idiosyncratic
    d. cumbersome

8. All of the publicity about the trial _____ the basic issues.

    a. eroded
    b. plagued
    c. paled
    d. clouded

9. In the United States, many people _____ vitamins as a way to fight disease and to live longer.

    a. lure
    b. balk
    c. extol
    d. instill

10. Many illegal immigrants live on the _____ of society, afraid that they will be discovered and forced to return home.

    a. periphery
    b. aftermath
    c. restraint
    d. donation

11. Political campaigns are typically full of (A.) _____. It is only in the (B.) _____ of the election that we can see whether or not the politicians can live up to their exaggerated promises.

    (A.)   a.   misanthropy
          b.   regimen
          c.   ambivalence
          d.   hyperbole
    (B.)   a.   aftermath
          b.   venture
          c.   rigor
          d.   diagnosis

12. The _____ of high moral values should be one of the major functions of a good family unit.

    a. prescription
    b. ubiquity
    c. instillment
    d. copiousness

13. The judge was in a/an _____ as to how to decide who should receive custody of the child. Neither parent seemed to be a model of a good father or a good mother.

    a. aftermath
    b. conjecture
    c. trepidation
    d. quandary

14. Most scientists today _____ to the belief that something should be done about the amount of carbon emissions in the air.

    a. empathize
    b. subscribe
    c. ostracize
    d. flourish

15. Because of the increasing number of regulations against smoking, many smokers are starting to feel like _____.

    a. epithets
    b. cold turkeys
    c. plagues
    d. pariahs

16. The once-_____ Marlboro man is slowly disappearing from view in many countries around the world because of prohibitions against cigarette advertising.

    a. elusive
    b. precocious
    c. ubiquitous
    d. notorious

17. Some psychologists fear that test-tube children may be _____ if other children find out how they were conceived.

    a. begrudged
    b. intimidated
    c. ostracized
    d. restrained

18. Seeing their children as much as they would like is often a/an _____ goal for many working parents.

    a. disdainful
    b. elusive
    c. precarious
    d. ambivalent

19. In the past, society treated divorced women with great _____.

    a. disdain
    b. alarm
    c. notoriety
    d. viability

20. That smoking is harmful to one's health is no longer _____.

    a. viable
    b. conjecture
    c. hyperbole
    d. prerogative

21. The United States is _____ throughout the world for its great number of lawsuits.

    a. viable
    b. profligate
    c. notorious
    d. inept

22. Most nations agreed in theory with the proposal to cut down on pollution. However, some participants wondered about the _____ of such a proposal.

    a. vulnerability
    b. viability
    c. curtailment
    d. stance

23. The '50s and '60s were an era of _____ in regards to oil consumption. Fuel was used as if there were no end to it.

    a. diversification
    b. copiousness
    c. inroads
    d. profligacy

24. Many religions have not taken a _____ on whether surrogacy is acceptable or not.

    a. stance
    b. constituency
    c. reservation
    d. restraint

25. Smokers feel they are being _____ as anti-social when people who take private cars to work instead of public transportation may be doing more damage to the environment than they are.

    a. passed over
    b. put up with
    c. phased out
    d. singled out

26. The fact that the politician's announcement about new pro-environmental efforts _____ with the announcement that he was running for re-election made some people suspicious about his motives.

    a. curtailed
    b. stepped up
    c. coincided
    d. circumscribed

27. The _____ of funds for a water purification plant upset the environmentalists.

    a. implementation
    b. extraction
    c. venture
    d. curtailment

28. Granting scholarships to students from developing countries can be a way of _____ good will between countries.

    a. prescribing
    b. doting
    c. fostering
    d. glimpsing

29. Many environmentalists feel that the earth is in a _____ position and that if we do not do something to help it today, tomorrow may be too late.

    a. precarious
    b. precocious
    c. diverse
    d. profligate

30. Some of the situations in this book were so _____ that I could hardly believe they were true.

   a. devout
   b. prescriptive
   c. coincidental
   d. bizarre

Definition Game

The class is divided into four to five groups of three to four students each. Each group draws lots to decide who will be first, second, third, and fourth to play. Each group in turn picks a category and a number of points. The more points there are, the more difficult the word. When the first group has chosen a category and point value, the teacher gives the clue. Students have 15 seconds to discuss among themselves and give an answer. If they are right, they get the points, and it becomes the next group's turn. If they are wrong, the next group can try. If the second group gets the right answer, they get the points and another chance. The game continues until all the words have been given. The group with the most points wins.

Points	Smoking	Surrogacy	Pets	The Family	Global Warming
10					
20					
30					
40					
50					

Appendix A: Common Irregular Verbs

Base Form	Past Tense	Past Participle
arise	arose	arisen
awake	awoke	awoken
be	was/were	been
bear	bore	born
beat	beat	beaten
become	became	become
begin	began	begun
bend	bent	bent
bet	bet	bet
bid	bid	bid
bind	bound	bound
bite	bit	bitten
bleed	bled	bled
blow	blew	blown
break	broke	broken
bring	brought	brought
build	built	built
burst	burst	burst
buy	bought	bought
catch	caught	caught
choose	chose	chosen
come	came	come
cost	cost	cost
cut	cut	cut
deal	dealt	dealt
dig	dug	dug
dive	dove/dived	dived
do	did	done
draw	drew	drawn
dream	dreamed/dreamt	dreamed/dreamt
drink	drank	drunk
drive	drove	driven
eat	ate	eaten
fall	fell	fallen
feed	fed	fed
feel	felt	felt
fight	fought	fought
find	found	found
fit	fit	fit
flee	fled	fled
fling	flung	flung
fly	flew	flown
forbid	forbade/forbad	forbidden

Base Form	Past Tense	Past Participle
forget	forgot	forgotten
forgive	forgave	forgiven
freeze	froze	frozen
get	got	gotten
give	gave	given
go	went	gone
grow	grew	grown
hang (a person)	hanged	hanged
hang (a picture)	hung	hung
have	had	had
hear	heard	heard
hide	hid	hidden
hit	hit	hit
hold	held	held
hurt	hurt	hurt
keep	kept	kept
kneel	knelt/kneeled	knelt/kneeled
know	knew	known
lay	laid	laid
lead	led	led
leave	left	left
lend	lent	lent
let	let	let
lie (down)	lay	lain
light	lighted/lit	lighted/lit
lose	lost	lost
make	made	made
mean	meant	meant
meet	met	met
misspend	misspent	misspent
mistake	mistook	mistaken
misunderstand	misunderstood	misunderstood
offset	offset	offset
pay	paid	paid
prove	proved	proved/proven
put	put	put
quit	quit	quit
read	read	read
ride	rode	ridden
ring	rang	rung
rise	rose	risen
run	ran	run
say	said	said
see	saw	seen
seek	sought	sought
sell	sold	sold
send	sent	sent

Base Form	Past Tense	Past Participle
set	set	set
sew	sewed	sewed/sewn
shake	shook	shaken
shave	shaved	shaved/shaven
shine	shone	shone
shoot	shot	shot
show	showed	showed/shown
shrink	shrank	shrunk
shut	shut	shut
sing	sang	sung
sink	sank	sunk
sit	sat	sat
sleep	slept	slept
slide	slid	slid
speak	spoke	spoken
speed	sped	sped
spend	spent	spent
spin	spun	spun
split	split	split
spread	spread	spread
stand	stood	stood
steal	stole	stolen
stick	stuck	stuck
sting	stung	stung
stink	stank/stunk	stunk
strike	struck	struck/stricken
strive	strove	strove/striven
swear	swore	sworn
sweep	swept	swept
swell	swelled	swelled/swollen
swim	swam	swum
swing	swung	swung
take	took	taken
teach	taught	taught
tear	tore	torn
tell	told	told
think	thought	thought
throw	threw	thrown
understand	understood	understood
undertake	undertook	undertaken
uphold	upheld	upheld
upset	upset	upset
wake	woke/waked	woken/waked
wear	wore	worn
weep	wept	wept
win	won	won
wind	wound	wound
write	wrote	written

Appendix B: Answer Key

Chapter 1

Reading 1: "We, the People"
Vocabulary Practice (p. 2): 1. A. a., B. b.; 2. c.; 3. A. b., B. c.; 4. A. c., B. b.; 5. b.; 6. a.; 7. a.; 8. A. b.,B. b., C. c.; 9. A. b., B. c.

Comprehension and Discussion (p. 6): A. 1. T; 2. F (They had become cheap before the 1880's.); 3. T; 4. T; 5. F (Ellis Island and the Statue of Liberty are only on the graph to mark a time frame. All other events noted on the graph affected immigration to some degree.); 6. F. (Only in the beginning were most of the people "speaking the same language, professing the same religion, attached to the same principles of government, very similar in their manners and customs.") **B.** *Answers will vary.*

Vocabulary Building (p. 7): Adj. *-ent, -ant*; Noun *-ence, -ance:* important, dependent, observant, ignorant, pertinent, intelligent, significant, relevant, impudent, indigent, abstinent, resilient, penitent, dominant, etc.; Adj. + *-ness* = noun; happy, sad, heavy, light, dark, rude, polite, industrious, lazy, loud, kind, fierce, gentle, fit, tender, willing, drunken, soft, hard, thick, thin, careless, spacious, hopeless, weightless, etc.; Verb + *-ment* = noun; punish, amaze, abolish, pay, confine, place, retire, govern, induce, embarrass, refine, entitle, commit, manage, arrange, equip, assort, amuse, measure, achieve, judge, admonish, appease, commence, assign, impair, treat, abandon, resent, enlarge, etc.

Vocabulary Practice (p. 8): 1. fled; 2. turmoil; 3. sought; 4. haven; 5. unprecedented; 6. roughly; 7. sparse; 8. absorb; 9. upheavals; 10. stemmed (from); 11. opulence; 12. diminished; 13. overwhelmed; 14. pernicious; 15. apt to; 16. heritage

Focus on Form (p. 9): 1. c; 2. a; 3. b.

Grammar Practice (p. 10) *Possible sentences:* 1. Ellis Island opened in 1892. 2. The Irish Potato Famine lasted about 4 years. 3. Throughout the 19th century, many different social and political events influenced immigration patterns to the United States. 4. At various times in the early part of this century, more people left than entered the United States.

Reading 2: "The Hunt for New Americans"
Comprehension and Discussion (p. 13): A. 1. F (Family reunification will also be allowed.); 2. F (Immigrants have a negligible effect on unemployment. They take jobs, but they also make jobs.); 3. F. (There is no national identity card. The new law may bring about a national worker identity card to prevent discrimination against foreign-looking job seekers.) **B., C.** *Answers will vary.*

Grammar Practice (p. 15): 1. have warned; 2. replaced, opened; 3. came, have replaced; 4. have been criticized, has been cut; 5. stemmed; 6. were; 7. rose; 8. have had; 9. was accused, was acquitted, has filed; 10. have changed, has had

Grammar Practice (p. 17): A. 1. In contrast; 2. In contrast; 3. On the contrary; 4. On the contrary; 5. On the contrary; 6. In contrast; 7. In contrast. **B.** *Answers will vary.*

Reading 3: "Newcomers Alter Society, Politics of the Big Apple"
Vocabulary Practice (p. 18): 1. a. continuous, meaningless sound; 1. b. widespread; everywhere; 2. humble; unimportant; 3. bring back to life; 4. fall behind; 5. total involvement; 6. a. conflict; 6. b. push gently; 6. c. force out; 7. a. make a sudden attack; 7. b. something that causes anger; 8. hidden motivation; 9. hold back

Vocabulary Building (p. 23): Verb *-ize;* Noun *-ization;* Verbs ending in *-ize* can become nouns by adding *-ization:* industrialize, capitalize, formalize, civilize, materialize, organize, fertilize, fossilize, colonize, authorize, liberalize, legalize, naturalize, martyrize, centralize, etc.

Verb + *-(s)ion* = noun: confuse, diffuse, disperse, fuse, tense, invert, divert, convert, avert, pervert, invade, evade, deride, explode, conclude, exclude, preclude, decide, expand, extend, comprehend, apprehend, etc.

Vocabulary Practice (p. 23): 1. a. friction; b. assault; c. displacement; d. undercurrent; e. revitalization; f. provocative; g. pervade 2. a. hindrance; b. menial; c. immersed; d. babble; e. lag; f. to nudge.

Grammar Practice (p. 25): 1. was discovered; 2. had traveled; 3. started; 4. encountered; 5. played; 6. were prohibited; 7. were excluded; 8. were hired; 9. was completed; 10. had built; 11. lost; 12. became; 13. had opened; 14. faced; 15. were turned; 16. had been used; 17. were allowed; 18. was done; 19. expanded; 20. contracted; 21. became; 22. were blamed; 23. had grown; 24. passed; 25. forbad (forbade); 26. was repealed.

Grammar Practice (p. 26): 1. has been; 2. left; 3. tended (have tended); 4. caused; 5. started; 6. had immigrated; 7. was; 8. had gone; 9. began; 10. have been reflected; 11. brought; 12. meant; 13. had left; 14. returned; 15. have estimated; 16. entered; 17. left; 18. entered; 19. had made;

20. has accepted (has been accepting); 21. have sought (have been seeking); 22. have fled (have been fleeing); 23. had come; 24. has emerged; 25. have accepted (have been accepting); 26. has contributed (has been contributing); 27. has been undermined.

Chapter 2

Reading 1: "Classrooms of Babel"

Vocabulary Practice (p. 30): 1. c; 2. b; 3. a; 4. c; 5. a; 6. c; 7. a; 8. a; 9. b

Comprehension and Discussion (p. 34): A. 1. F (The high dropout rate of Hispanic students is an argument used by opponents of bilingual programs to show that the programs do not work.); 2. F. (The Supreme Court ruled that immigrant children had the right to special help, but bilingual programs are not financially feasible if there are fewer than 20 students who speak the same language in the same grade.); 3. T; 4. F (Although the newcomer schools work very well, they do not reach enough children. The norm is much less optimistic.); 5. T; **B.** *Answers will vary.*

Vocabulary Building (p. 35): Adj. *-ent -ant;* Noun *-ency -ancy:* proficient, efficient, deficient, sufficient, fluent, lenient, expedient, prudent, permanent, consistent, decent, solvent, complacent, flagrant, truant, vagrant, malignant, dormant, militant, flippant, mordant, verdant, etc.; Adj. *-ble;* Noun *-bility:* feasible, able, viable, capable, liable, responsible, dependable, attainable, culpable, visible, compatible, accountable, comparable, believable, amiable, impeccable, inflammable, agreeable, respectable, excitable, fallible, etc.; Noun *-ism;* Adj. *-istic:* euphemism, communism, capitalism, socialism, fascism, tourism, fatalism, antagonism, realism, impressionism, egoism, behaviorism, hedonism, idealism, naturalism, etc.

Vocabulary Practice (p. 35): 1. proficient; 2. Advocates, to handle; 3. feasibility; 4. be immunized; 5. be enriched; 6. euphemistic; 7. poses; 8. nurture.

Reading 2: "Asians Question Admissions"

Vocabulary Practice (p. 36): 1. causing to admire; 2. overwhelm in number; flood; 3. have great affection for; 4. rapid increase or rise; 5. close inspection, examination; 6. solve, find a solution, understand a problem; 7. obeying a demand or regulation; 8a. gather; come together in groups; 8b. reject; 9a. make consistent, make opposing ideas agree; 9b. unclear; 10. unwilling, hesitant

Comprehension and Discussion (p. 41): A. 1. T; 2. T; 3.

T; 4. F (The percentage of Asians admitted of all Asian applicants is lower than that of whites.); **B.** *Answers will vary.*

Vocabulary Building (p. 43): Verb + *-ance* = noun: comply, ally, apply, rely, defy, attend, adhere, utter, repent, resist, clear, assist, appear, accept, allow, disturb, endure, inherit, perform, repent, resist, vary, resemble, etc.; *(-ence):* depend, resurge, interfere, exist, infer, prefer, defer, etc.; Noun + *-ize* = verb: scrutiny, subsidy, colony, apology, elegy, fantasy, sympathy, empathy, jeopardy, harmony, deputy, agony, monopoly, philosophy, burglary, hospital, capital, scandal, idol, moral, woman, satire, symbol, propaganda, winter, fertile, civil, popular, central, solemn, equal, familiar, formal, natural, secular, special, tranquil, national, mobile, social, brutal, industrial, miniature, standard, etc.

Vocabulary Practice (p. 43): 1. a.reluctant; b. are turned down; c. figuring out; 2. a. deluge; b. impress; c. scrutinize; d. complying; e. cherished; f. upsurge; 3. a. reconciled; b. murky; c. to cluster.

Grammar Practice (p. 45): 1. That the rising rate ... systems is apparent. It is apparent that the rising rate... systems. 2. No one knows for sure how we should teach...classroom. 3. Whether (or not) affirmative action can undo ... is the question being debated. The question being debated is whether (or not) affirmative action can undo past discrimination. 4. That many immigrants put ... in education is not surprising. It is not surprising that many immigrants put ... in education. 5. Students are naturally worried about whether (or not) the school of their choice will accept them. 6. I don't understand why American schools are so interested in extracurricular activities. 7. I wonder if (whether (or not)) American universities put a quota on... accept. 8. I have no idea how long it takes to find out ... university.

Grammar Practice (p. 45): 1. a. What many Asian Americans wonder; 1. b. That a person's admission to college may depend on club activities; 2. how hard it is for us sometimes.; 3a. the fact that a TOEFL score of 600 is required.; 3b. just what an ice cube might be.; 4. whether students can learn academic subjects if... English.; 5. that something must be done about our schools.; 6. what he wanted to hear.

Grammar Practice (p. 46): *Possible sentences:* 1. *Noun Clause as Subject:* a. Why Americans tend to go directly into the job market with only a B.A. interests me.; b. Whether foreign students are taking the place of Americans in graduate schools is debatable.; 2. *Noun Clause as Object of Verb:* a. I resent that this bill was passed.; b. I'd like to know why many foreign students do not receive financial aid.; 3. *Noun Clause as Object of Preposition:* a. I'm worried about why some Americans have fears about foreign graduates.; b. I'd like to know more about the fact that Americans are motivated by different goals. 4. *Noun Clause as Subject Complement:* a. What interests me is why so many foreign students come to the U.S. to study engineering. b. The most interesting aspect of this situation is that less than 3% of the total college population of the U.S. is foreign. 5. *Noun Clause as Adjective Complement:* a. I am curious why so few Americans do doctoral work in engineering.; b. I think it's interesting that foreign students can bring prestige to American universities.

Reading 3: "Foreign Students Under Fire"

Comprehension and Discussion (p. 50): A. 1. T; 2. F (All state residents would pay the same tuition.); 3. T; 4. T.; **B.** *Answers will vary.*

Vocabulary Building (p. 51): B. 1. unable; 2. infertile; 3. impossible; 4. unemployed; 5. inappropriate; 6. immoral; 7. unsanitary; 8. unofficial; 9. imprudent; 10. unprincipled; 11. untrustworthy; 12. illicit; 13. unreliable; 14. inconceivable; 15. incomprehensible; 16. undetermined; 17. indeterminate; 18. undeniable; 19. indefinable; 20. indecisive; 21. undecided; 22. unlucky; 23. unforeseen; 24. illegible; 25. unquestionable; 26. inexcusable; 27. inexplicable; 28. unlawful; 29. imperceptible; 30. unpremeditated; 31. unmanly; 32. unmovable; **C.** *Answers will vary.*

Focus on Form (p. 53): Do you have any idea why some Americans resent foreign students? Can you tell me if the admissions officer is in?

Grammar Practice (p. 54): *Answers will vary.*

Chapter 3

Reading 1: "Busybodies: New Puritans"

Vocabulary Practice (p. 58): 1. b; 2. b; 3. a; 4. c; 5. a; 6. c; 7. a; 8. c; 9. b; 10. c; 11. b

Comprehension and Discussion (p. 64): A. 1. T; 2. T; 3. T; 4. F ("Busybodyness" is as American as "cherry pie." It began with the Puritans and has been a recurring theme in U.S. history.); 5. T. **B.** *Answers will vary.*

Vocabulary Practice (p. 65): 1. a. undaunted; b. secular; c. arbitrarily; d. barred; e. refrain; f. apprehended; g. penalized; 2. a. disparate; b. concede; c. intrusion; d. endorsing.

Focus on Form (p. 66): A. 3; **B.** 1; **C.** 4; **D.** 2.

Grammar Practice (p. 68): 1. might (may) have been,

might (may) have suspected, might (may) have been seen; 2. must (should) have known; 3. must have been; 4. should have; 5. could have agreed; should have only considered; 6. must have been surprised and thrilled, might (may) not have, might (may) have decided; 7. couldn't (mustn't) have been; 8. must (could) not have had; 9. shouldn't have done, shouldn't have handcuffed and arrested, could (should) have given, given, could (should) have been doing; 10. must have hated, must have felt, might (may) have been trying (have tried).

Grammar Practice (p. 70): 1. had to; 2. had to let; 3. must have been; 4. had to fight; 5. must have been; 6. had to pay, give; 7. must have complained.

Reading 2: "Loving America"

Vocabulary Practice (p. 72): 1. great in size; 2. born with (a quality); 3. almost completely; 4. anger at an offense; 5. giving a feeling of strength, making one feel good; 6. insult; 7. unavoidable; 8. unreachable; 9. cannot be untied or separated; 10. agree or decide to do; 11. loss of one's dreams; 12. come together from different points, intersect; 13. confusion; 14.a. limitation, restriction; 14.b. free; not stopped or hindered; 15. contradictory statement or idea

Comprehension and Discussion (p. 78): A. 1. T; 2. F (Americans are loyal to the institutions themselves.); 3. F (People love one's parents simply because they are one's parents; Americans love America for what it does, not for what it is.); 4. F (America sees itself as the shaper of its own destiny.); 5. T; 6. F (Money was seen as a sign of divine grace.); 7. T. **B.** *Answers will vary.*

Vocabulary Practice (p. 80): 1. inextricably; 2. vast; 3. paradoxical; 4. invigorating; 5. virtually; 6. undertake; 7. constraints; 8. resented; 9. hampered; 10. disillusioned; 11. attain; 12. inevitable; 13. innately; 14. a. affront; b. baffling; 15. converge.

Vocabulary Practice (p. 82): 1. outdo (outshine); 2. outselling; 3. outnumbers; 4. outbid; 5. outrun; 6. outsmarts (outfoxes, outwits); 7. outweighed; 8. outweighs; 9. outwear (outstay); 10. outwork; 11. outplay; 12. outlive; 13. outshines (outdoes).

Grammar Practice (p. 83): A. 1. There was nobody else around. He had the motive, the means, and the opportunity.; 2. Why not? He had the motive.; 3. He felt he had no other choice. His children were starving. He doesn't regret it.; 4. It was a stupid thing to do. Now he'll have to spend years in jail.; 5. He was there. He had the opportunity. But we know he didn't do it.; 6. He wasn't even near the scene of the crime, and he can prove it.; **B.** 1. must have suffered; 2. might (may) not have; 3. could have all been killed; 4. must (could) not have been; 5. could (should) have stopped; might (may) have been; 6. might (may) have been telling (have told); might (may) have been; 7. couldn't have accepted; 8. should have been going (have gone); 9. could (should) have sued; 10. must have thought. *(Students' answers will vary.)*

Chapter 4

Reading 1: "The Custody Case That Went Up in Smoke"
Comprehension and Discussion (p. 93): A. 1. F (A higher judge can overturn the ban.); 2. T; 3. F (Custody does not matter. She cannot smoke in front of her son until he is eighteen or the ban is overturned.); **B.** *Answers will vary.*
Reading 2: "In Child Deaths, a Test for Christian Science"
Vocabulary Practice (p. 94): *Sentences 1–6:* 1. causing great anxiety or pain; 2. a belief, usually of a religion; 3.a. oppose; meet an attack with another attack; 3.b. take over another's rights; 4. complete; not lessened in any way; 5. a. free from; allow not to have to do something causing great anxiety or pain; 5. b. by the nature of a person or thing; 6. produce; *Sentences 7–14:* 7. avoid by going around; 8. something that holds back, stops, or blocks; 9. secondary; with inferior rank; 10. express a belief; 11.a. say or affirm something to be true; 11.b. ability to achieve results; 12. forgiving; merciful; not strict; 13. believe something to be the result of; 14. go or turn to when help is needed
Comprehension and Discussion (p. 99): A. 1. F. (It was the latest of a number of successful prosecutions of Christian Scientists. It is significant because it happened in Boston, which is where the religion was founded.); 2. F. (Ms. Swan is the founder of a private organization called CHILD—Children's Healthcare Is a Legal Duty.); **B.** *Answers will vary.*
Vocabulary Practice (p. 101): 1. a. infringing on; b. tenets; 2. a. counters; b. exempt; 3. a. have agonized; b. unmitigated; 4. a. inherent; b. generate; 5. a. hold; b. efficacious; c. attest; d. attribute; 6. subservient; 7. leniency; 8. circumvent; 9. impede; 10. resort
Grammar Practice (p. 102): 2. that went off in the prosecutor's head; 3. that followed . . . whose children died agonizing deaths after spiritual healing failed.; 4. medicine considers congenital, incurable, or terminal.; 5. on whom the tenets of this church are based; 6. where Christian Science was founded; 7. when prosecutions of Christian Science parents for involuntary manslaughter

or child endangerment have been on the increase.
Grammar Practice (p. 103): 1. that, who; 2. that, which; 3. that, whom, Ø; 4. that, which, Ø; 5. whose; 6. whom, whom ... on, that ... on,   ... on; 7. which, which ... for, that ... for,   ... for.
Grammar Practice (p. 104): 1. whose, that/which; 2. that/which/Ø; 3. whom/that/Ø; 4. in which/where; 5. that/which, that/which, that/who; 6. that/which/Ø, that/which, that/which; 7. whom; 8. that/who, that/which
Reading 3: "Can Choosing Form of Care Become Neglect?"
Vocabulary Practice (p. 105): 1. accusation; 2. evidence; 3. criticize; 4. belittle; 5. arrogant; 6. keep; own; 7.a. take away; ignore; 7.b. prevent
Comprehension and Discussion (p. 108): A. 1. F (Ms. Cheng's doctors have permitted her to continue to give her daughter Chinese medicine and to be treated by a homeopathic practitioner.) 2. T; 3. F (The court proceedings were closed to the public because it was juvenile court.); 4. F (At the time of the article, the case was in federal court to decide if it is a federal matter.); **B.** *Answers will vary.*
Vocabulary Practice (p. 110): 1. rebuked; 2. testimony; 3. disparagement; 4. a. allege; b. overridden; c. preclude; d. harbor; 5. cavalier
Vocabulary Building (p. 110): 1. overjoyed; 2. overate, overslept; 3. overdue; 4. overcharged; 5. overtime; 6. overlook; 7. overthrow; 8. overdrawn; 9. overlap; 10. oversight; 11. overcame.
Vocabulary Building (p. 111): *Answers will vary.*
Grammar Practice (p. 112): 2. Services, *which has temporary custody of Shirley Cheng,* is being criticized . . .; 3. husband, *whom she met in China.*; 4. operation, *which the doctors describe as necessary,* would release . . .; 5. Ms. Cheng, *whose daughter was born in the U.S.,* was born . . .; 6. Dr. Zemel, *to whom Ms. Cheng went for medical advice,* declined . . .; 7. Chinese medicine, *about which little is known in the United States,* has . . .
Grammar Practice (p. 112): 1. Throughout the centuries, the Amish have held tightly to a biblical command which/that states that we should not conform to the world.; 2. In the 1800s, the Amish, who were being persecuted for their religious beliefs, went to Pennsylvania, where they found religious freedom.; 3. The Amish, for whom there are only two types of people, call all the non-Amish "English."; 4. The Amish, many of whom live in Pennsylvania, are also called Pennsylvania Dutch.; 5. The name, which the "English" gave them, was a mistake.; 6. They were originally from the

German part of Switzerland and spoke German, which in the German language is "deutsch," which was misunderstood as Dutch.; 7. When a number of cases of polio broke out in Pennsylvania, the Amish, whose religion prohibits the use of modern medicine, would not let their children take the polio vaccine.; 8. The problem that/which/Ø the state government had was to get. . . .; 9. Finally the Amish, who do not like to make problems for their "English" neighbors, agreed to take the vaccine.; 10. The Amish, whose values are totally unlike those of most Americans, are gentle people whom/that/Ø many admire for their simple lifestyle.

Grammar Practice (p. 113): 1. . . . daughter, whom . . .; 2. . . . statement that/which/Ø Mr. Athanson said . . .; 3. Ms. Cheng, who visits her daughter twice a day, said, "Shirley . . .; 4. . . .time when/in which the . . . Services, which. . . Cheng, has been . . .; 5. . . . sister, both of whom . . .; 6. . . . conviction that/which followed . . . Scientists whose . . .; 7. doctrine . . . (that/which/Ø . . .); 8. . . . couple whom/that/Ø everyone . . .; 9. Rita Swann, whose son . . . organization whose . . .; 10. The Twitchells, who have . . . parents whose tragedy . . .

Chapter 5

Reading 1: "Employers Becoming Court Targets in the Fight to Halt Drunken Driving"

Vocabulary Practice (p. 118) 1. b; 2. a; 3. b; 4. c; 5. b; 6. c; 7. b; 8. b.

Comprehension and Discussion (p. 123): A. 1. F (The plaintiff in the Florida case is a mother whose son was killed by a man who had been drinking for business purposes.); 2. T; 3. F (Three states have exempted social hosts. By extension of this exemption, corporations cannot be considered in the same way as those who sell drinks. In other words, if a person who gives away drinks at a party cannot be held liable, a corporation that gives away drinks should not be held liable either.); B. *Answers will vary.* 7. The article says Mrs. Greenbaum not only lost her son but also her best friend. There is no explanation of this. Was her son also her best friend or did someone else die in the accident?

Vocabulary Practice (p. 124): 1. reimbursement; 2. accountability; 3. unscathed; 4. overindulgence; 5. indelibly; 6. a. disassociate; b. held liable; c. cognizance.

Vocabulary Building (p. 125): Rule: adjective + *-en* = verb: wide, short, dark, light, bright, soft, hard, tough, rough, loose, quick, cheap, fat, moist, damp, deep, fresh, ripe, red, dead, flat, live (with *up*); **Nouns:** length,

strength, fright; **Adverb:** less

Grammar Practice (p. 126): 1. knowing, to serve, (to) sell, trying, to be held; 2. not being sold, to pay, to be served, to serve, to be, deciding, to sit, to drive, being told, to say, being involved, to risk being; 3. thinking, to overdrink, keeping, giving, filling, to have; 4. giving, not to drive, to learn, to appear, to revoke, to do, drinking, stopping, working, to learn.

Reading 2: "Now Barkeepers Join Drive for Safer Drinking"

Vocabulary Practice (p. 129): 1. b; 2. c; 3. a; 4. (A.) b, (B.) a; 5. c; 6. a; 7. c; 8. c; 9. (A.) b, (B.) a; 10. b; 11. a.

Comprehension and Discussion (p. 133): A. 1. F (They are being trained to spot clues that drinkers are getting drunk and to try to get them to stop drinking alcohol.); 2. F (It is not the only one of its kind. Other training programs have been produced by the National Restaurant Association and the National Licensed Beverage Association. It is successful because there is great public anger over drunk driving. Courts are awarding high damages against businesses that serve drunk patrons who later maim or kill someone, and insurance companies are offering discounts to businesses where three-fourths of the alcohol servers have passed the TIPS exams.) 3. F (They are in favor of the programs. This may be because they are genuinely worried about the effects of drunk driving. They may also be worried that some day they will be sued.) B. *Answers will vary.*

Vocabulary Practice (p. 134): 1. to proliferate; 2.a. rowdy; b. to confront; 3. depicted; 4. toast; 5. swollen; 6. a. obnoxious, b. caustic; 7. staggering; 8. to sustain; 9. stock; 10. incentive; 11. is maimed

Grammar Practice (p. 136): 1. didn't appreciate (1) having to tell him (2); 2. claimed (1) to be (2); 3. regrets (2) having drunk (1); 4. don't appreciate (2) having had (1); 5. seems (2) to have decided (1); 6. appear (2) to have been arrested (1); 7. claimed (2) to have been (1); 8. resented (2) not having been told (1); 9. regretted (1) having to tell (2).

Grammar Practice (p. 138): 1. to have drunk, to walk; 2. to think; 3. to pick; 4. drinking; 5. drinking; 6. to give, having served; 7. drinking; 8. to be; 9. to have lost; 10. to carry, to remember, to put.

Reading 3: "Loan Puts Widow, 91, in Jeopardy"

Vocabulary Practice (p. 139): 1. someone who lives through great suffering or who dies for a belief; 2. difficult situation or condition; 3. a. argue; assert; maintain; 3. b. extremely poor; 3. c. cause someone to judge prematurely or unfairly; 4. admit; 5. leave out; eliminate; 6. build up; amass; 7. triumph; overcome

Comprehension and Discussion (p. 141): A. 1. T; 2. F (The article does not mention any charges against Mr. Stuart.); 3. T.; **B.** *Answers will vary.*
Vocabulary Practice (p. 142): *Sentences will vary.*
Vocabulary Building (p. 142): 2. conclude; 3. preclude; 4. recluse; 5. include; 6. seclude. **B.** See *Word List* (p. 147).
Vocabulary Practice (p. 143): A. 1. seclusion; 2. preclude; 3. conclusive; 4. recluses (accent on first syllable); 5. inclusion, exclude
Grammar Practice (p. 143): 1. to hear; 2. drinking; 3. to avoid; 4. getting; 5. being held; 6. to be; 7. to worry/ worrying; 8. to pay; 9. being; 10. not having; 11. proving; 12. taking; 13. to hold; 14. letting; 15. to serve; 16. to have had; 17. to be; 18. to have; 19. to pay; 20. to provide; 21. serving; 22. not announcing; 23. serving; 24. to supply; 25. having; 26. to do; 27. to be held
Grammar Practice (p. 144): *Answers will vary.*

Part I Review

Grammar (p. 148): 1. c; 2. a; 3. c; 4. c; 5. b; 6. b; 7. b; 8. c; 9. (A) c, (B) a; 10. c; 11. c; 12. a; 13. c; 14. a; 15. c; 16. a; 17. b; 18. c; 19. c; 20. c; 21. (A) c, (B) c; 22. (A) a, (B) a; 23. c; 24. d; 25. (A) b, (B) d; 26. (A) b, (B) c; 27. b; 28. b; 29. c; 30. c; 31. c; 32. a; 33. b; 34. b; 35. d
Vocabulary (p. 153): 1. c; 2. d; 3. a; 4. d; 5. c; 6. b; 7. d; 8. b; 9. c; 10. c; 11. d; 12. b; 13. a; 14. c; 15. c; 16. a; 17. c; 18. d; 19. c; 20. c; 21. c; 22. d; 23. d; 24. b; 25. c; 26. d; 27. a; 28. b; 29. d; 30. a.
Definition Game (p. 158):
The teacher gives the clue and the part of speech for the category and the number of points the students choose. The answers are in parentheses after the parts of speech.

Points	Immigration	Education	Americans	Parents	Drunk Driving
10	a safe place (noun) (haven)	come together in groups (verb) (cluster)	very serious (adj.) (grave)	give evidence in court (verb) (testify)	drink to someone's health (verb) (toast)
20	wealth (noun) (opulence)	unclear (adj.) (murky)	unavoidable (adj.) (inevitable)	oppose an argument (verb) (counter)	not drunk (adj.) (sober)
30	lessening in importance or rank (noun) (diminishment)	examine carefully (verb) (scrutinize)	statement of support (noun) (endorsement)	arrogantly (adverb) (cavalierly)	crippled (in an accident) (adj.) (maimed)
40	confusion (noun) (turmoil)	sudden increase (noun) (upsurge)	cannot be separated or untied (adv.) (inextricably)	criticize formally (verb) (rebuke)	growing in great numbers (noun) (proliferation)
50	dangerous (adj.) (pernicious)	make two opposing ideas consistent (verb) (reconcile)	insult (noun) (affront)	not lessened in any way, complete (adj.) (unmitigated)	triumph, win a victory (verb) (prevail)

Chapter 6

Reading 1: "Why Smoking Bans Are Dangerous"
Vocabulary Practice (p. 161): 1. pass a law; 2. hate; 3. without change; constantly; 4. a. deliberately and constantly avoid; 4. b. not consider; disregard; 5. peculiarities; characteristics peculiar to a person; 6. a. position or attitude; 6. b. harmful; dangerous; 7. a. acting on a sudden inclination or urge; 7. b. outgoing; preferring to be with others instead of alone; 7. c. staying away from or denying oneself pleasurable things, such as alcohol, tobacco, or sex

Comprehension and Discussion (p. 163): A. 1. T; 2. F (He is also against them for personal reasons. He worries that one day the authorities may go after him and his bad habits.); 3. F (He says that some insurance companies offer lower rates to people who reduce their cholesterol levels. Studies show that in some corporations the pressure to eat right has become extreme.); 4. F (He says these scenarios are not farfetched.); B. *Answers will vary.*

Vocabulary Practice (p. 165): 1. a. impulsively; b. idiosyncratic; 2. stance; 3. noxious; 4. detestable; 5. be passed over; 6. abstinence; 7. enactment; 8. extroversion; 9. a. invariably; b. are (will be) shunned.

Focus on Form (p. 166): 1. b; 2. c; 3. d

Grammar Practice (p. 166): *Example:* The California Medical Association is proposing = main clause; that the state ban smoking in all public places = noun clause; 1. The CMA also suggests = main clause; that cigarette sales from machines be banned = noun clause; 2. It is important = main clause; that we not make bans against smoking = noun clause; 3. The tobacco industry has made the recommendation = main clause; that vending machines not be included in the ban = noun clause.

Grammar Practice (p. 168): 1. prohibit; 2. be allowed; 3. be given; 4. attend; 5. not enact, rely

Grammar Practice (p. 168): 1. The doctor insisted (demanded) that he cut down on foods that are high in cholesterol.; 2. He demanded (insisted) that Mr. Glassner get some exercise.; 3. The doctor recommended (suggested) that he try walking to work once in a while.; 4. He suggested (recommended) that Mr. Glassner eat more green vegetables . . .; 5. The doctor requested that he pay the nurse on his way out.; 6. The friend proposed that they jog together.; 7. Mr. Glassner preferred that the friend not tell anybody that they were doing it.; 8. "I move that a smoking room be established (set up) for those who want to smoke."

Reading 2: "Smoking Ads: A Matter of Life"

Vocabulary Practice (p. 170): 1. b; 2. a; 3. c; 4. a; 5. c; 6. b; 7. a; 8. b; 9. b; 10. a; 11. (A) a, (B) b.

Comprehension and Discussion (p. 173): 1. T; 2. F (She is against making cigarettes illegal for social and practical reasons. It would make smokers into criminals and farmers into bootleggers.); 3. F (The proposal to ban all forms of cigarette advertising has elicited a higher level of controversy.); 4. T.; B. *Answers will vary.*

Vocabulary Practice (p. 174): 1. was extolled, plague; 2. cold turkey; 3. back; 4. trepidation; 5. a. constituents; b. clout; 6. a. brainchild; b. hooked; 7. intrinsic; 8. contagious; 9. elicit.

Reading 3" "Asia: A New Front in the War on Smoking"

Vocabulary Practice (p. 175): 1. a. awkward; clumsy; heavy; 1. b. hard; harsh; unbending; 2. friendly relationship because of a common cause; 3. wear down because of constant, usually long-term contact with a force; 4. a. advance or invasion; 4. b. increase efforts or commitment; 5. reduce or cut down; 6. secret; not open; 7. a. happen at the same time (two or more events) without plan; 7. b. harsh; bitter; scathing; 8. tempt or attract with promise of pleasure or an award

Comprehension and Discussion (p. 178): *Answers will vary.*

Grammar Practice (p. 180): 1. put; 2. to post, be made, not to drink; 3. to advertise, not be allowed, is; 4. become, to change, not to smoke; 5. set, be used; 6. to take, prefer, not smoke; 7. not be allowed, not be shown, not associate; 8. are being targeted (are targeted), stop, not be placed, receive.

Grammar Practice (p. 181): *Possible sentences:* 1. Many nonsmokers are demanding that separate areas be set up for smokers.; 2. Many smokers are only asking that they be left in peace. (...asking to be left in peace.); 3. The AMA feels it is essential that young people be educated about the dangers of smoking.; 4. Many consumer advocates feel it is clear that advertising for cigarettes tries to make smoking look glamorous and cool.; 5. Ellen Goodman, in her essay on cigarette ads, does not propose that we make cigarettes illegal.; 6. The U.S. government requires that a health warning be put on all tobacco products. (. . . requires a health warning to be put . . .); 7. Barry Glassner feels it is imperative that smokers' rights be defended. (. . . for smokers' rights to be defended.); 8. If people are smoking near you and the smoke is bothering you, you could request that they not smoke.; 9. Some nonsmokers who believe that smoking is a personal decision feel that we can advise that people not smoke (people not to smoke), and we can urge that they quit (them to quit), but it is important that people be allowed (for people to be allowed) to smoke if they want to.; 10. Regarding advertising for tobacco and alcohol, my recommendation is that it be limited to magazines which are bought mainly by adults.

Grammar Practice (p. 182): *Answers will vary.*

Chapter 7

Reading 1: "Whose Child Is It?"

Predicting Vocabulary (p. 186): *Possible vocabulary:* in vitro fertilization (IVF), to fertilize, petri dish, test-tube baby, sperm donor, to inseminate, artificial insemination, surrogacy, surrogate mother, traditional surrogacy, gestational surrogacy, uterus, sperm, eggs, ova, pregnant, pregnancy, to become pregnant, to bear or carry children, to conceive, embryo, fetus, fertile, infertile, sterile, genetic engineering, genes

Comprehension and Discussion (p. 188): *Answers will vary.*

Grammar Practice (p. 189): 1. If Ms. Calvert could have (were able to have) her own children, she wouldn't be in this strange situation today.; 2. Ms. Whitehead would (might) not have visitation rights to her daughter if she didn't have a genetic ink with her.; 3. The Calvert-Johnson case would (might) be less complicated if Ms. Johnson and the child she bore were the same race.; 4. It would (might, could) be easier to decide who the mother is in these cases if all the states had laws concerning surrogacy.; 5. If we knew the psychological problems children born to surrogate mothers might have, we could (would be able to) prepare the children.; 6. If a woman who is poor and unemployed had more options, she might not decide to carry another woman's baby.; 7. If the problems of new technology could be foreseen, it would be easier to avoid these complicated legal and ethical issues.

Reading 2: "A Custody Fight for an Egg"

Vocabulary Practice (p. 190): 1. place into; insert; 2. fall apart; 3. hold back; control; deprive of freedom; 4. separate; 5. on the side; the area far from the center but within the boundary; 6. very unusual; completely unconventional; 7. a. taking out; removing (by force); 7. b. person who gives or contributes something; 8. result or period after a misfortune

Comprehension and Discussion (p. 194): *Answers will vary.*

Vocabulary Practice (p. 195): 1. peripherally; 2. split; 3. restraint; 4. a. disintegration; b. aftermath; 5. bizarre; 6. donating; 7. a. extracting; b. implanting.

Vocabulary Practice (p. 195): 1. b; 2. c; 3. b; 4. a; 5. c.

Vocabulary Practice (p. 196): *Possible sentences:* 1. This one's a doozy. 2. Joe always has to sweep up after his brother. 3. Come on! Give me a break! 4. No. It's up for grabs. 5. It's a sticky issue.

Grammar Practice (p. 197): 1. hadn't signed, would (might) have been; 2. wouldn't have signed, had known; 3. had been given, wouldn't have had; 4. could (would) have fought, hadn't accepted; 5. hadn't been given, would have appealed; 6. had had, would (might) have been; 7. would (might) not have made, hadn't

been; 8. wouldn't have agreed, had known.

Reading 3: "All in the Family"

Prereading Question (p. 198): 1. The twins were born to a woman who acted as surrogate for her daughter. The daughter's eggs were fertilized in vitro by her husband's sperm and then transplanted into the mother. Therefore, the woman who bore the twins is both mother and grandmother. The woman whose eggs they are could be thought of as both mother and sister. The twins could be thought of as both sister and brother and aunt and nephew to each other.

Vocabulary Practice (p. 198): 1. a. make up; invent; 1. b. to exaggerate; say in a way intending to shock or arouse interest; 1. c. generally accepted; it must be accepted as truth; 2. to say or express what might be criticized or considered foolish; 3. to destroy; 4. stimulating and very exciting; 5. lessen in importance; diminish; 6. a. practicality; dealing with events as they are; 6. b. deeply religious; 7. to make unclear or confusing

Comprehension and Discussion (p. 201): A. 1. F (The style of writing and the words used tend to give a very favorable impression of Ms. Schweitzer. See *Word Analysis*, p. 203); 2. F (Two years after they found out that Christa had been born without a uterus, she and Ms. Schweitzer were visiting a doctor at the Mayo Clinic. Ms. Schweitzer realized that she was young enough "to lend" her daughter her uterus.) 3. T; 4. T.; **B.** *Answers will vary.*

Vocabulary Practice (p. 202): 1. concoction; 2. admittedly; 3. sensational; 4. to pale; 5. pragmatically; 6. cloud; 7. devoutness; 8. devastation; 9, exhilaration; 10. venture

Vocabulary Building (p. 202): *Words in article:* reply, recall, exclaim, observe, imagine. *Other possible words:* admit, announce, answer, argue, assert, beg, claim, complain, confess, confide, confirm, contend, cry, declare, deny, explain, inform, inquire, insist, instruct, interject, note, order, plead, promise, reiterate, remark, report, respond, shout, state, suggest, swear, warn, whisper, wonder, etc.

Word Analysis (p. 203): cheerful; cozy, split-level house; photographs of smiling kids: grandchildren, nieces and nephews; has, well, got her mother in a family way; radiate a sense of calm; her voice as clear and as strong as a church bell; her mother's tummy; a stay-at-home mom; she says impishly; refreshing, down-to earth pragmatism; a devout Roman Catholic; etc.

Grammar Practice (p. 204): 1. wouldn't be, had; 2. wouldn't have agreed, were; 3. would have been, were;

4. wouldn't have picked, didn't have, were; 5. hadn't been set, would be; 6. had adopted, wouldn't have; 7. wouldn't have been/wouldn't be, had gotten; 8. had had, wouldn't have had; 9. weren't, wouldn't be

Grammar Practice (p. 205): 1. d. weren't = weren't poor women; 2. d. could = could carry children; 3. a. had = had had enough money to hire a good lawyer; 4. b. had been = had been laws for surrogacy in that state at that time; 5. d. had been = had been given custody; 6. c. could have = could have afforded a costly court battle

Grammar Practice (p. 206): 1. didn't; 2. weren't; 3. hadn't; 4. had; 5. didn't; 6. had been; 7. had; 8. hadn't been; 9. were; 10. did

Grammar Practice (p. 209): *Possible Sentences:* Ms. Seymour is not fertile. If she were, they wouldn't have gone to a surrogacy service. If they had known that Mr. Reams was also infertile, they wouldn't have decided to use a surrogate. If he hadn't been infertile, they could have had a child with a genetic link to one of them. If the surrogacy agency had known about the sperm donor, it would have cancelled the contract. If it had, Ms. Stotsky wouldn't have gone through with the surrogacy. Ms. Stotsky might not have asked for custody if either of the contract parents had been a biological parent. If one of them had been, the case wouldn't have been so complicated. If Ms. Stotsky had been the biological mother, she might have had a chance to get custody of Tessa. She might not have changed her mind if she weren't poor. The state of Ohio has a law which states that . . . If it didn't, Ms. Stotsky would have had a good case for custody. Since she was the biological mother, she might have gotten custody of Tessa. If Mr. Miner had asked for custody, the case would have been even more complicated. If he had, there might have been a possibility that he would receive custody. If the court had decided in favor of Ms. Seymour, Mr. Reams would be alive today. If he were, Tessa would at least have a home with one of them.

Chapter 8

Reading 1
Vocabulary Practice (p. 214): 1. showing too much fondness or care; 2. a person who uses strength or size to hurt weaker people or make them afraid; 3. a doctor or lawyer's clients or business; 4. a person one is responsible for; 5. a conversation in which only two people are involved; 6. overly active; 7. wearing glasses; 8. showing anger, usually by being silent and usually

without great cause; 9. one who ruins the fun of other people

Grammar Practice (p. 218): 1. Nowhere have I seen people treat pets as they do in New York.; 2. On no account would I spend thousands of dollars to keep a pet alive.; 3. Only in New York do people hire baby sitters for their pets.; 4. By no means could I let a dog keep me from traveling.; 5. Under no circumstances should people spend so much money on their pets when others are starving.; 6. Not only do New Yorkers talk to their pets, but they also call them on the telephone.; 7. Rarely are people so crazy about pets in my country.; 8. Not until I came to the United States did I realize that pets could be so important in people's lives.; 9. Never again will I be surprised by what I hear about New Yorkers.; 10. No sooner had I arrived in the United States than I saw a dog wearing a raincoat, a hat, and boots.

Reading 2: "Freud Should Have Tried Barking"
Vocabulary Practice (p. 219): 1. b; 2. (A.) a, (B.) c, (C.) a; 3. a; 4. c; 5. (A.) b, (B.) b; 6. c; 7. a; 8. c; 9. (A.) b, (B.) a, (C.) c; 10. a; 11. c; 12. b.

Comprehension and Discussion (p. 223): A. 1. T; 2. F (Studies show that children who have pets show greater empathy toward others than children without pets, but the exact reason for this is unknown. It could be the pets or it could be that parents who buy pets have beliefs or personalities that instill empathy in their children.); 3. F (The effect of animals on humans is still being studied. For many patients, any kind of change is helpful.) 4. T; **B.** *Answers will vary.*

Vocabulary Practice (p. 224): *Word List A:* 1. tolerate; 2. attribute to a cause or origin; 3. hatred of mankind; 4. severe; thorough; demanding; 5. marital (of a marriage); 6. exaggeration; 7. encourage to develop; 8. doubting; disbelieving; *Word List B:* 9. pull hard (slang); 10. equal; same age or rank; 11. understanding of another's feelings; 12. varied; diverse; 13. connection; tie; 14. implant in the mind or introduce by slow, persistent efforts; 15. struggle; fight; 16. become white or pale (usually because of shock or surprise); 17. inclination; tendency.

Vocabulary Practice (p. 225): 1. hyperbole; 2. a. conjugal; b. put up with; c. ascribe; 3. skepticism; 4. misanthropic (misanthropes); 5. a. foster b. rigors; 6. propensity; 7. peers; 8. eclectic; 9. blanched; 10. a. grappling; b. yanked; 11. a. bond; b. instill; c. empathic

Vocabulary Building (p. 226): 1. to give something as a cause of; 2. to contain or limit; restrict; draw a line around to attribute; 3. the act of forcing into military service; to draft; person who is drafted; 4. to tell about in detail; 5. to engrave; to write or print on wood, stone or paper; to sign (formal); 6. to give as a rule or a guide; to suggest or order as a medicine; 7. to prohibit; 8. to contract to receive and pay for a certain number of issues of a newspaper or periodical; to contribute money; to express approval; 9. to copy; transfer information from one system to another; record of one's grades

Vocabulary Practice (p. 227): 1. prescriptive, descriptive; 2. ascribed; 3. inscription; 4. transcript; 5. subscribe; 6. proscription; 7. conscription; 8. subscription; 9. prescribed; 10. circumscribes; 11. transcribed

Grammar Practice (p. 229): 1. do I feel; 2. do people let; 3. had he sat; 4. would I; 5. will he leave; 6. did I realize.

Reading 3: "High-Tech Medicine at High-Rise Costs Is Keeping Pets Fit"

Vocabulary Practice (p. 230): 1. system of therapy; 2. a. animals on a farm; 2. b. medical opinion about the nature of an illness; telling what is wrong; 3. mercy killing; 4. spending; 5. dilemma, state of uncertainty; 6. sudden, fanciful idea; 7. a. complain; 7. b. kill (animals); 8. medical opinion or prediction about the outcome or course of an illness; 9. strange people

Comprehension and Discussion (p. 234): *Answers will vary.*

Vocabulary Practice (p. 234): 1. livestock; 2. expenditure; 3. whim; 4. oddballs; 5. prognosis; 6. euthanasia; 7. balk at; 8. diagnose; 9. regimens; 10. quandary; 11. put to sleep.

Discussion (p. 235): *Answers will vary.*

Grammar Practice (p. 235): *Answers will vary.*

Grammar Practice (p. 237): 1. neither did; 2. so has; 3. neither have; 4. so will; 5. so can; 6. so would; 7. neither was; 8. neither could; 9. neither does; 10. so had

Chapter 9

Reading 1: "Shifting Suburbs"

Vocabulary Practice (p. 244): 1. b; 2. c; 3. c; 4. a; 5. b; 6. c; 7. b; 8. a; 9. b; 10. a; 11. c; 12. b; 13. c.

Comprehension and Discussion (p. 249): A. 1. F (According to demographers and social scientists, this will happen before the beginning of the new century.); 2. T; 3. F (Parental involvement has declined.); **B.** *Answers will vary.*

Vocabulary Practice (p. 251): 1. ostracism; 2. intactness; 3. pariahs; 4. befit; 5. ambivalence; 6. walk out; 7. precociousness; 8. a. alarmed; b. dysfunctional; 9.

ubiquitousness; 10. traumatic; 11. fend for; 12. reservation

Grammar Practice (p. 252): 1. c; 2. c; 3. a; 4. d; 5. a; 6. c; 7. d; 8. b.

Grammar Practice (p. 254): 1. hadn't left, would come, had never married, didn't have; 2. had spent, were able to go (could go); 3. had; 4. had had; 5. would get; 6. were able to help (could help); 7. were; 8. hadn't had, hadn't been left; 9. were; 10. hadn't matured

Grammar Practice (p. 258): *Answers will vary.*

Reading 2: "The Dreams of Youth"

Vocabulary Practice (p. 260): 1. alike, without distinctive qualities; 2. cause to increase in importance or level of controversy; 3. accept or expect without question; 4. reject, send away or out of one's thought; 5.a. an indication of excellence or quality; 5. b. revise, change, renovate; 6. a quick look; 7. fall quickly, dive; 8. done without preparation; 9. right or privilege of a person or a group; 10. avoid, escape understanding; 11. do or give unwillingly; envy someone else's enjoyment; 12. dangerously unstable or insecure; 13. provide anything another wants; 14. unprotected; open to injury, abuse; 15. a. a feeling of contempt or superiority for someone else; 15. b. an adjective or phrase used to describe a person, often, but not necessarily, an insult.

Comprehension and Discussion (p. 267): A. 1. F (The differences between men and women are better celebrated than repressed. Young women don't want to slip unnoticed into a man's world.); 2. T; 3. F (They saw their parents' marriages end in divorce. "Young daughters watched..."); 4. T.; **B.** *Answers will vary.*

Vocabulary Practice (p. 268): 1. plunged; 2. hallmark; 3. fueled; 4. vulnerability; 5. dismissed; 6. indistinguishable; 7. epithet; 8. revamp; 9. glimpse; 10. improvising; 11. prerogative; 12. cater; 13. precarious; 14. elusive; 15. a. disdainfully; b. begrudge; 16. take ... for granted.

Grammar Practice (p. 270): *Possible sentences:* 1. Unlike many European countries, where paid maternity leave for women is guaranteed by the government, in the United States it is not. The United States differs from many European countries in that paid maternity leave for women is not guaranteed by the U. S. government. Whereas many European countries guarantee paid maternity leave for women, the United States does not.; 2. The American family is similar to the German family in regard to size. Like the American family, the German family has become smaller in the past 50 years.; 3. The previous generation . . . life; however, younger . . . earlier. Unlike the previous generation of American women, who had children later in life, younger Ameri-

can women are having children earlier.; 4. Young
people in northern Europe resemble young Americans
in that both often leave home before they get married.
Young people in northern Europe often leave home
before they get married. Likewise, young Americans
often get their own apartments while they are still
single.

Grammar Practice (p. 271): *Answers will vary.*
Grammar Practice (p. 271): *Answers will vary.*
Grammar Practice (p. 272): 2. her having six children; 3.
his having been at the peak of his career; 4. Ms. Allen's
not having been elected; 5. her having a full-time job;
her full-time job; 6. his having threatened not to pay
child support; his threat not to pay child support
Grammar Practice (p. 273): 1. Despite this country's
having more . . .; 2. Despite the fact that he was raised
. . .; 3. In spite of her ambition . . .; 4. Even though he is
politically liberal . . .; 5. Despite her lack of interest in. . .
Grammar practice (p. 273): *Answers will vary.*

Chapter 10

Reading 1: "The Warming Globe"
Prereading Questions (p. 278): 5. *Possible vocabulary:*
Chlorofluorocarbons (CFCs), gases, carbon, carbon
dioxide, nitrous oxide, methane, pollution, ozone,
greenhouse effect, atmosphere, emissions, ultraviolet
rays, aerosols, propellants, plastic, refrigerants, deforestation, combustion, nuclear power, fossil fuels, conservation, coal, environmentalists, precipitation, drought
Vocabulary Practice (p. 278): 1. b; 2. a; 3. (A.) c., (B.) a; 4.
a; 5. b; 6. c; 7. a; 8. c; 9. c; 10. c; 11. c; 12. b; 13. c; 14. b; 15.
a
Comprehension and Discussion (p. 284): A. 1. T; 2. F
(In spite of the massive oil price rise and the spread of
nuclear power stations, carbon emissions still grew by
1.5% a year.); 3. T; 4. F (It is at its lowest level in real
terms since the Korean War.); **B.** *Answers will vary.*
Vocabulary Practice (p. 285): 1. embarked; 2. a.
swamped, b. altering; c. enhancing; 3. awkwardness; 4.
to tackle; 5. conjecture; 6. viability; 7. untangle; 8. a.
ineptness, b. offset; 9. curbs; 10. intimidation; 11.
intrigued; 12. wary; 13. crucial.
Vocabulary Building (p. 286): A. tingle—a sensation
similar to little needles, but not one that hurts; boggle—
overwhelm with wonder, surprise; shatter—break in
many pieces; curdle—spoil, go bad (usually said of
milk); wrack—punish, wreck, destroy; 1. revealing;
making one aware; 2. disgusting; 3. frightening, scary

(but not in an extreme way); 4. touching, moving,
emotional (in a nice way); 5. causing great admiration
or awe, exciting; 6. allowing to keep one's self-respect;
7. delicious looking or smelling, making one hungry; 8.
extremely loud; 9. causing great anxiety; 10. amazing,
causing one to be amazed or in wonderment; 11. very
frightening; 12. attractive, causing one to look at
something (not used for people); 13. very funny; 14.
very hard or difficult (about work); 15. tragic, causing
great disappointment or sadness, **B.** 1. nerve-wracking
(nerve-racking); 2. ear-shattering; 3. heartwarming; 4.
breathtaking; 5. stomach-turning; 6. eye-opening; 7.
mouth-watering; 8. face-saving; 9. bloodcurdling; 10.
heartbreaking; 11. eye-catching; 12. sidesplitting; 13.
mind-boggling; 14. backbreaking; 15. spine-tingling; **C.**
Possible sentences: 3. . . . story that warms your heart.; 4.
The Grand Canyon is such a beautiful sight that it takes
your breath away.; 5. . . .; they just turn my stomach.; 6.
That conversation really opened my eyes.; 8. Allowing
him to resign was a device (way) for him to save face.; 9.
. . . I heard this scream that curdled my blood.; 10. It
broke my heart to see the reaction . . .; 11. . . . . They
always catch your eye. 13. . . . It boggles the mind how
she does it all.; 14. . . ., but it's really work that breaks
your back.
Grammar Practice (p. 290): *Quantifiers may vary.* 1. far
fewer fossil fuels; 2. a great deal more coal; 3. many
more countries; 4. (a great) many more gases; 5. much
less interest; 6. a great deal more energy; 7. much less
gas; 8. much less energy, far fewer appliances and
machines; 9. much less nuclear power; 10. a great many
more people, far fewer natural resources; 11. much less
population growth; 12. far fewer chloroflourocarbons;
13. a great deal more research; 14. quite a bit more
pollution; 15. Many more possibilities
Grammar Practice (p. 291): 1. a little; 2. few; 3. a few; 4.
a little; 5. little; 6. little; 7. few; 8. a few; 9. few; 10. a few
Grammar Practice (p. 293): *Possible sentences:* 2. The less
(often) we buy new cars, the fewer cars manufacturers
need to make. (The fewer cars we buy, the fewer . . .); 3.
The lower the production of cars, the fewer people
manufacturers need to employ.; 4. The higher the rate of
unemployment, the higher the crime rate.; 5. The more
dangerous the streets, the more likely people will stay
home.; 6. The less people go out, the more businesses
will close.; 7. The less business restaurants and
nightspots do, the more quickly downtown areas will
become deserted.; 8. The fewer people neighborhoods
have, the less people want to go there, and the more
businesses will be affected.; 9. Consequently, the more

we drive our cars, the better the economy.

Grammar Practice (p. 294): *Answers will vary.*

Reading 2: "How Hard Will It Be?"

Vocabulary Practice (p. 295): 1. very wasteful; extravagant; 2. the process of exhausting; using up and taking away; 3. spread out investments or business activities; vary; 4. be successful; grow well; 5. basic installations for the functioning of a government, national or local; 6. a very large, indefinite number of; 7. made impure; polluted; 8. lessen in relative importance; 9. complete display; 10. promise to give up or not to do something; 11. abundant; large in number; 12. difficult position; 13. obvious; noticeable; 14. miserably; 15. widely and unfavorably known; 16. a superficial story to show or illustrate a deeper point; 17. amount produced; profit on an investment; 18. eliminate gradually, one step at a time; 19. move without any additional effort or acceleration; do the same as before; 20. stimulate; urge

Comprehension and Discussion (p. 302): A. 1. F (Large-scale change is inevitable because of our profligate ways. The only choice we have is in deciding which kinds of change will be best in the long run.); 2. F (Good company mangers will know before. They will have diversified before the market dries up.); 3. T; 4. F (Things won't get better. The best we can do is prevent them from getting much worse.). **B.** *Answers will vary.*

Vocabulary Practice (p. 304): 1. contamination; 2. a. straits, b. myriad, c. infrastructure; 3. a. pale, b. abject, c. flourishing; 4. a. profligacy, b. foreswear; 5. diversify; 6. a. copious, b. panoply, c. drained; 7. phase out; 8. a. conspicuous, b. notorious; 9. a. coast, b. yield; 10. a. allegory, b. spur.

Grammar Practice (p. 305): 1. will have been; 2. will stabilize; 3. will have stopped; 4. will pay; 5. will be; 6. will have become; 7. will have been replaced; 8. will have been phased out; 9. will not have had; 10. will be; 11. will have almost doubled, will have increased; 12. will have been depleted (will be depleted); 13. will not take; 14. will have been decreasing, will be.

Grammar Practice (p. 307): *Answers will vary.*

Part II Review

Grammar (p. 310): 1. c; 2. c; 3. d; 4. b; 5. c; 6. b; 7. d; 8. b; 9. a; 10. d; 11. c; 12. c; 13. d; 14. c; 15. a; 16. d; 17. c; 18. b; 19. a; 20. b; 21. c; 22. b; 23. (A) c, (B) a, (C) c; 24. d; 25. a; 26. c; 27. c; 28. c; 29. d; 30. d; 31. b; 32. c; 33. a; 34. c; 35. c.

Vocabulary (p. 315): 1. c; 2. b; 3. a; 4. c; 5. a; 6. d; 7. c; 8. d; 9. c; 10. a; 11. (A) d, (B) a; 12. c; 13. d; 14. b; 15. d; 16. c; 17. c; 18. b; 19. a; 20. b; 21. c; 22. b; 23. d; 24. a; 25. d; 26. c; 27. d; 28. c; 29. a; 30. d

Definition Game (p. 320):

The teacher gives the clue and the part of speech for the category and the number of points the students choose. The answers are in parentheses after the parts of speech.

Points	Smoking	Surrogacy	Pets	Women	Global Warming
10	very good idea (noun) (brainchild)	separate (verb) (split)	strange person (noun) (oddball)	frighten (verb) (alarm)	change (noun) (alteration)
20	hate (verb) (detest)	one who gives (noun) (donor)	one who ruins the fun of others (noun) (spoilsport)	fall quickly (verb) (plunge)	fear from a threat (verb) (intimidate)
30	influence (noun) (clout)	hold back, control (verb) (restrain)	understanding another's feelings (noun) (empathy)	mixed (adj.) (ambivalent)	obvious, noticeable (adj.) (conspicuous)
40	awkward, heavy (adj.) (cumbersome)	say what might be considered foolish (verb) (venture)	prohibit (verb) (proscribe)	revise, change (verb) (revamp)	abundant (adj.) (copious)
50	fear (noun) (trepidation)	excitement (noun) (exhilaration)	give as a cause or origin (verb) (ascribe)	right or privilege (noun) (prerogative)	a very large, indefinite number (adj.) (myriad)